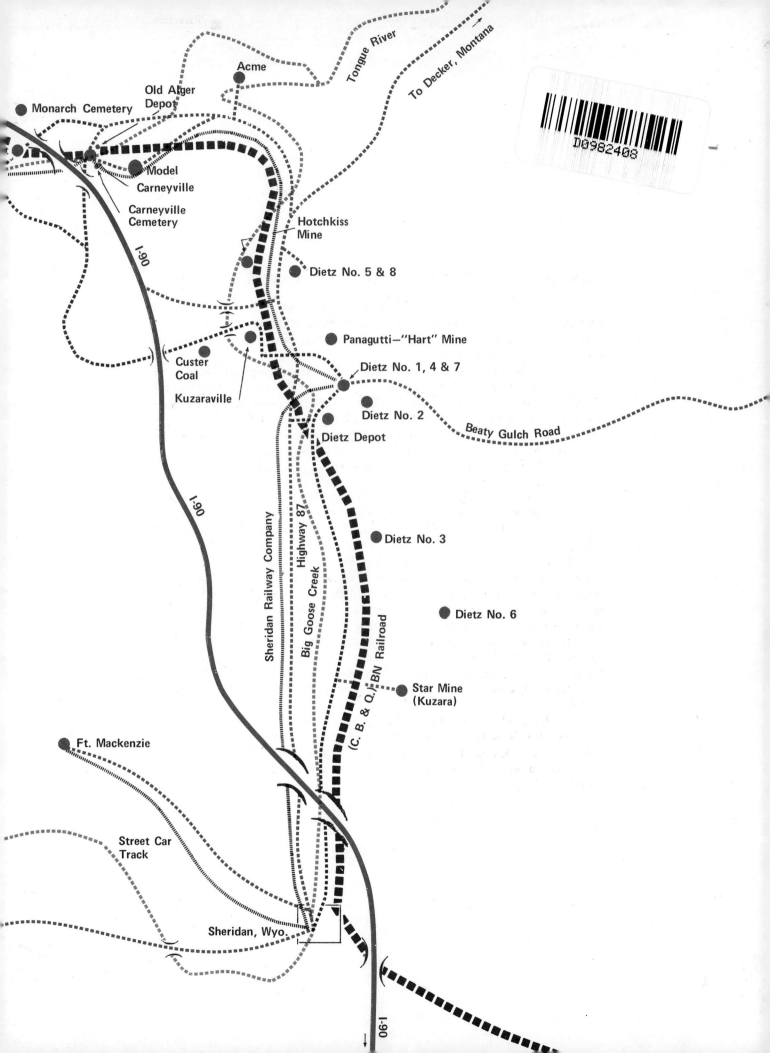

MAP OF THE COAL MINING AREA OF SHERIDAN, WYOMING

This map was drawn by the author. Using an official map of the Chicago, Burlington & Quincy (now Burlington Northern) railroad as a base, all of the mining camps, mines, etc. were then located as accurately as memory permits.

Thus, the map includes the locations of the Camps of Dietz (the main camp); Dietz No. 5 & 8 (which are one and the same camp); Acme; Model; Carneyville (later changed to Kleenburn); Monarch and Kooi. Also included are most of the smaller so-called "wagon mines"—those not shipping coal by rail. Not considered a camp but which did ship by rail was the Hotchkiss mine located between Dietz No. 8 and Acme.

The Sheridan Street Railway route appears in red while rivers are shown in green.

Although the map is not drawn strictly to scale, the proportionate distances do come quite near; for example, the distance from Sheridan to Dietz is about 4 miles, and to the most distant camp of Kooi, about 14 miles.

It will be interesting to note that for one reason or another, there were areas within some of the camps as follows: In Dietz No. 7, a row of white houses in which families of many of the supervisory personnel lived, was called "Piano Row." Another section of Dietz was called "Alfalfa Patch" while another section was referred to as "Hunky Town."

In Acme, there were three such sections. One was the "Circle" called so by virtue of the area being surrounded by a circular street; another, "Jap Town," originally occupied by a number of Japanese laborers; and the third, "Macaroni Flats," obviously an area of a number of Italian families.

In Monarch, there was a "Silk Stocking Row," again a section occupied by families of supervisory personnel; and across the river with access from Monarch by a swinging foot bridge, was "Crooked Town" containing a dance hall and only a few houses; however, a center of much social activity.

Black Diamonds of Sheridan

A Facet of Wyoming History

Stanley A. Kuzara
10-22-81

By Stanley A. Kuzara

"Old miners never die—they just gradually slacken up."
—*Kuzara*

Coal Miner's Memorial

By John Kuchera, sculptor, born in Carneyville, Wyoming. Statue dedicated June 24, 1973 to the memory of the coal miner and now on display at the Tourist Information Center, Sheridan, Wyoming.

John Kuchera, sculptor, with his welding torch putting finishing touches on Miners Memorial statue, 1973. *(Photo by Elsie Pratt)*

Another more recent memorial to the miner by the same sculptor, 1977.

Contents

Prelude

Several years ago, I was asked by Miss Dorothy Waisner, English teacher at our local Sheridan High School, to appear before her class and give a talk about the early life of our former local coal mine camps, knowing that I was an early resident of one of the camps.

Encouraged by the fine reception I received from those high school students, I willingly accepted subsequent requests for similar talks which later even included the projection of a number of photographs. At one of these, I was very pleasantly surprised when she arranged for a member of their photographic department to take a videotape which was projected at the next class while I sat back in a seat watching myself on the screen. Suddenly I realized that here was a documented, though very brief, history of the mines, and when I inquired if there was any way this tape could be preserved, I was told there was no such budget, but that if I could get the local historical society to purchase a blank tape, they would hold this one pending its receipt. It so happened that I was the current president of the local historical society and knew its financial position, so I personally ordered a tape and when it arrived, we then traded.

The students must have reported the talks to some of their parents for it was not long before I began receiving requests to talk before service and civic clubs, women's organizations and many other groups. It seemed that everywhere I appeared, the talks were enthusiastically received and it was not long before other groups began to request appearances, even in Buffalo, Wyoming and Gillette, Wyoming, with some asking for return engagements.

In these talks, I would tell how I was born of Polish parents immediately breaking the ice, so to speak, by telling how Polish was the first language I spoke, and jokingly how when I finally went to school and learned to read, my doubts were raised as to whether I was actually Polish. Being the sixth child of twelve children, I learned that every third child born in the world was Chinese! Or, the time my youngest brother,

Henry who was the eleventh child, was applying for a job and being questioned by the personnel clerk who finally asked if he, by chance was related to Walter Kuzara, my oldest brother. Henry scratched his head and said, "Well, just distant. You see, he was the first child and I was eleventh." These things did not actually occur, but with a few added "Pollock" jokes, it made good listening.

And so, as I look back in retrospect, I feel now that it really was a unique privilege to have been born in the coal mining camp of Dietz No. 5, Wyoming; and, naturally, I'm proud of the fact that my parents, although born in a foreign country and without any formal education, were able to provide me with the encouragement to continue my own education and to make whatever sacrifices necessary to see me through college.

Since it was my destiny to have been born in Dietz and to have had the experience of being reared in an environment which was so different from that of the city of that period and particularly so different from that of today, but yet so interesting, I feel that someone should record some of it while it may still be possible; to attempt to describe life as it existed—the fun, the frivolity, the pathos, the hardships, etc., insofar as my memory and research will permit.

The very welcome reception to my talks about the mines' history eventually activated my desire to make a sincere effort to accumulate further information and to collect more material; and although I found that it was now becoming somewhat difficult to unearth, I was able to accumulate a number of photographs and other material of a historical nature.

To begin with, I had no idea that I would ever attempt to take the time, nor did I think I had the ability as a writer to actually write a history book. As a result, I did fail to make proper notations of all those individuals who might have donated photographs—some given to me outright and some of which I made copies.

For this, I humbly apologize and must beg their forgiveness for not giving them proper credit.

As time went on, however, and after some forty or fifty appearances, I began to realize that sometime I might attempt to write just such a history. With this objective now becoming more firmly implanted, I proceeded, even more seriously and in fact, vigorously, to gather material, to interview some of the old miners, what few remain, and research whatever material I could find.

Therefore, although much of the following may appear to be autobiographical, and in fact, it will include many of my personal experiences, it will also include stories which have been told to me, as well as information taken from the Sheridan newspapers, research in periodicals, manuscripts, records, etc.

There can be no guarantee that all of the information herein is absolutely accurate in every detail, since much of the material is taken from memory which, quite naturally, has been dimmed somewhat by the passage of so many years.

With the possible exception of newspaper articles covering current events as they occurred, it appears that no known effort has ever been made to write a history of the Sheridan coal mines or camps. And now, after all these years, and with time having taken its toll of those who had worked in those mines, the resources for such material have also likewise disappeared.

Much credit, therefore, must be given to those remaining few who have so generously contributed of their experiences and recollections, given or loaned pictures, photographs, memorabilia and, not to overlook encouragement.

Many incidents which even though they might have been related in the newspapers of that day, would not bear repeating due to the possible embarrassment to the descendents of those involved. Naturally, as in any society, there were violations of the law, and of course, there were fights, and even some killings. During prohibition, especially those who had grown up on their beer, wine and other forms of liquor, were simply not to be denied. The manufacture of alcoholic "vodka" or "gorzalka" was rampant resulting in many raids by the authorities.

There was the story, for example, of the father, who at the insistence of a suitor, "sold" his quite attractive gypsy-looking daughter to one of the miners who was much older than she. After paying the father the agreed $400.00, she was given in marriage. Of course, she was not in love with him, and when she subsequently asked for a divorce, no way was he going to allow it unless he was reimbursed his $400.00. This, the father refused to do, and soon afterwards when the couple were together, an argument ensued followed by a shooting in which the husband was killed. In the subsequent trial, the young wife pleading self-defense, was acquitted.

It is with these reservations that this history is written with the hope that it will serve, not only as a documentation of a part of this area's past (which otherwise may never be told and eventually completely forgotten), but with the hope that the material contained may provide some information about life at the mines, as well as knowledge about an industry which was so vital to the economy of the area. Hopefully, some may even find some enjoyment and pleasure in reading this review.

Chapter 1

The Author

Born of Polish immigrants, Stanley (Christened "Stanislaw") A. Kuzara was born on October 15, 1906 in the coal mining camp of Dietz No. 5 (this camp was later re-named Dietz No. 8 after the Dietz No. 5 mine had closed down and a new mine opened up a few years later). He was the sixth child of twelve children of George and Sophia Kuzara—seven boys and five girls. His father at that time was employed in the mine and they were living in a converted barn located across the slough from the present "Country Nite Club" which was formerly a camp grocery store and post office.

When he was about a year old, his parents bought the "John Hecht Place" located about midway between the Dietz No. 7 and the Dietz No. 5 camps; however, in moving into the new location, due to a possible misunderstanding, the former owners had not yet vacated the premises. Although it was a cold Fall, the family set up a tent on the property which they occupied pending occupancy of the dwelling. It was while in this tent that Stanley's mother had him in a high chair placed near the coal range to keep him warm, when one of the other small boys began to climb on the high chair causing it to overbalance. The child fell on top of the hot range, severely burning his right cheek which resulted in a scar on that cheek remaining with him to this day.

After attending the first grade in the Dietz No. 1 camp, his parents moved to Roundup, Montana where his father purchased the Three Star Saloon in the Roundup (No. 3 mining camp). There, he attended the second grade. After selling their business a year later, the family moved to Windham, Montana where he attended the third, the fourth (two years in the fourth grade when the teacher refused to pass him because of arithmetic) and the fifth grades. Again, the family moved. This time they returned to Dietz where he continued the rest of his grade school education.

Realizing that failure in school meant work-

ing in the mine, he enrolled in Sheridan High School where he studied very hard, and by his Junior year was appointed Managing Editor of the high school paper, the "Ocksheperida." This was a signal achievement, particularly because, up to this time students from the mines (what few there were) were considered "from across the tracks." The following year, he was offered the editorship of either the paper or the senior annual year book, and chose the latter. That same year, he was elected to the National Honor Society and served as its vice-president. Also, during his Senior year, he won the javelin event at the Wyoming state high school track and field meet. Upon graduation, he was awarded a four-year scholarship to the University of Wyoming.

There, he enrolled in a course preparatory to a law degree, and after completing three years in pre-law and one year in the Law College, he received his A. B. Degree with a major in Social Science and History, with Minors in English, Law and Spanish.

On our way to the University of Wyoming in September 1925 (arrived in Laramie on third day.) L to R: Stan Kuzara, Clarence Marshall, Richard Ralph.

While in college, he was a member of the Independent Club, a social fraternity which was petitioning for a charter of Sigma Chi, and during those four years, he worked diligently toward that end.

In each of his four years in the university, he earned his athletic letter throwing the javelin (he still has a white gold Elgin open-faced watch which he was awarded as winner of that event at the Colorado Relays in the Spring of 1929, and in which some twelve universities participated).

In 1927, his Sophomore year, he was elected to Iron Skull, an honorary Sophomore society (today it is a Junior Honorary); and was editor of the athletic section of the University year-book his Junior Year.

With his scholarship paying his tuition, income from various jobs and some assistance from his parents, he completed three years of college; however, for his fourth year, he was forced to borrow and did receive a loan from the Whitney Foundation of Sheridan.

Following his graduation and with a Liberal Arts degree, but very conscious of his obligation, rather than borrowing more money to continue towards a law degree, he decided to work and proceeded directly to Detroit, Michigan where he had two brothers employed. Jobs were scarce and practically nothing available to the inexperienced, but with a little deception about his experience, he finally secured employment as a clerk in the service department of the Wm. F. V. Neumann & Sons, a Pierce-Arrow sales and service agency. A few months later, the stock market crashed; however, he continued in this employment until the Fall of 1930 when, through his position, he opportunely met some folks driving a new Pierce-Arrow to Oregon who wished someone to assist in the driving. This was his chance to return to Wyoming to attend the inaugural ceremonies of his fraternity which was finally granted a charter of Sigma Chi. Actually, he left on leave without pay for this trip West; however, due to the depressed conditions in Detroit, he never returned, but instead, after driving to Oregon, he returned to the University, attended the fraternity ceremonies, then re-enrolled in courses in the College of Education which he continued throughout the following summer. That Fall, he taught in a rural school at Boulder, Wyoming taking over the upper elementary grades as well as teaching English, Spanish, General Science and Geometry to the Sophomore class (there were no pupils for a Freshman class). For his services he received $100 per month, except for the last month of the school year, when the district ran out of funds and that month, he taught the high school

students for $5.00 per pupil (three were able to raise the money—two did not).

On his return to Sheridan, he stopped briefly at the University of Wyoming where he met his future wife, Miss Pauline Caywood, a student who was also from Sheridan.

Returning to Sheridan, he was appointed Deputy County Superintendent of Schools at $75.00 per month by Marie Smith, recently elected County Superintendent. He held this position for the year 1933 when he was asked to assist in the County Treasurer's office. He resigned his former position but after accepting the latter position, it was discovered that he was politically registered in the opposite party. The pressure then became so great on the Treasurer that she was forced to release him after only a few months.

The Fall of 1934, he ran for the office of county treasurer. This was quite a departure from tradition as that office had been occupied by women for many, many years; however, after defeating his lady opponent in the primaries, he was subsequently soundly defeated in the general election by a woman.

The famous "depression of the 30's" was at its height, jobs were exceedingly scarce, and chain letters were taking the country by storm. After working at various part-time jobs which included some substitute work in teaching, and in spite of economic conditions, he and Miss Caywood (on some money made in chain letters) were secretly married in Golden, Colorado on June 8, 1935.

Unemployed, no announcement was made of the marriage; however, that fall, in desperation, he accepted employment from his brother, Andrew, at the Star Mine (Andrew had taken over the ownership from his father). At any rate, it was a job and it did pay a salary—the announcement of the marriage soon followed.

Working at the mine was short-lived, however, as he was selected for the position of District Director of the National Youth Administration through the efforts of Mr. Jack Gage, State Superintendent of Public Instruction as well as recommendations of Mr. R. A. "Dick" Keenan, a legislator from Sheridan County (the same Mr. Keenan who was president of the Hotchkiss Coal Company described in another chapter—also the first mayor of the town of Kemmerer, Wyoming where, incidentally, J. C. Penny had his first store).

This position began on January 1, 1936 and

the territory covered the five Northeastern counties of Wyoming. In 1941, he was promoted to Area Director for the northern half of the state with headquarters in Casper. It was then that he and his family which included his wife and two children—Janet, born in 1937 and Richard, born in 1941, moved to Casper. The National Youth Administration was one of the several government programs offering unemployed youth an opportunity to earn and gain work-experience on a part-time basis; however, with the advent of World War II, the program was phased out in 1942.

Mr. Kuzara then took a temporary job in the office of Peter Keiwit & Sons who were constructing the Casper Air Base facility. That fall, however, he resigned to accept employment as Assistant Field Director for the American Red Cross Military & Welfare service, and after a short training period in Washington, D. C. and Fort Sheridan, Illinois, was assigned to an office at the Roswell, New Mexico Air Base. In the Spring of 1943, he was transferred to Fort Warren, Wyoming at Cheyenne. When a vacancy occurred in the veterans division of Red Cross, because of his legal training, he was transferred to that department representing veterans in their claims for compensation against the Veterans Administration with offices at the Cheyenne Regional office. A few months later, he was transferred to administer the Denver office as Field Director.

After two years, he resigned to become Director of the Veterans Information & Referral Center in Colorado Springs, Colorado. This position he held until 1948 when the objectives of such an office had been accomplished and most of the veterans of World War II had returned and adjusted themselves to their respective niches in civilian life. Here, their third child, Robert, was born on July 29, 1946.

In searching for something to do, he became attracted to owning his own business and it so happened that at that particular time, a new root beer drink was being introduced in the area—Dad's Old Fashioned Root Beer—which seemed to receive instant reception by the consuming public. Therefore, after some investigation including a trip to the franchise owner in Chicago, he accepted the challenge by investing in a distributorship for Pueblo County, Colorado; however, after a year of almost inhuman labor and exceedingly long hours, he sold out his equipment and returned to Sheridan, Wyoming

where he immediately purchased his fourth home, a large home which was built in 1902, and although well built, needed some remodeling. With very little outside help, he worked on this house for one year.

Finally, the time came when he must find employment. Reasoning that he might do well in real estate after successfully having bought and sold homes, he fortunately found an opening in association with Mr. Homer Loucks, a real estate broker who, by the way, was the son of the founder of the city of Sheridan. Thus, in the Fall of 1950, he took the Wyoming real estate salesman's examination. Having passed, he became officially associated with the Homer Loucks Agency in January of 1951. After two years, he took his broker's examination which he also passed, but remained with Mr. Loucks for another two years before striking out for himself.

Therefore, in 1954, he opened his own office in his garage. This building was a good-sized building for a single garage. Built of solid concrete, it was located at his residence only four blocks from down town. Also, it was built next to the sidewalk facing the side street—a very good location for such an office. Here, he experienced some degree of success, and being his own boss, found time to participate in community activities.

From 1953 to 1955, he served on the board of the Community Chest and in 1956 served as its president. He became active in his Elks Lodge which he had initially joined in 1937, serving on various committees, offices and eventually became its Exalted Ruler for the year, 1958-59.

As Chairman of its cemetery committee for a number of years, Mr. Kuzara organized the Elks Permanent Cemetery Fund for the perpetual care and improvement of its cemetery project resulting in a fund of over $100,000.00. For his dedication, the Lodge awarded him a coveted Honorary Life Membership in 1961.

In his professional activities, as a Realtor and Insuror, he served as President of the Sheridan County Insurors from 1960 to 1966, and President of the Sheridan County Board of Realtors in 1957, 1959, 1960 and 1962; and after serving in various offices of the State association, was elected and served as State President during the year 1963, and it was in the following year that he was elected to Omega Tau Rho, an honorary real estate society.

In 1969, after twice having been selected

Sheridan County Realtor of the Year, he was chosen Wyoming Realtor of the Year.

He was President of Wymo Oil, Inc., an oil producing company with wells in Cut Bank, Montana, and so served from 1955 until the company's assets were sold to the Philips Petroleum Company in 1969. In 1967, he was included in Marquis's "Whos Who in Commerce & Industry, 15th Edition."

In 1960, as an avocation, he organized the International Association of Turtles, Inc., of Sheridan, Wyoming, a non-profit, tax-exempt fun and charitable organization. Acting as its President and "Imperial Turtle" from its inception until the end of 1973 when, retaining the presidency, he turned over the title of "Imperial Turtle" and the operation to his nephew, James Kuzara. This silly organization, without dues, and beginning with only a 25¢ membership fee, by 1977 had built a membership of over a million and a half and had contributed over a third of a million dollars to various charitable organizations in the United States and Canada.

In 1969, he served as President of the Sheridan County Historical Society, and that same year, his name was included in Marquis' "Who's Who in the West," 12th Edition, and in 1971 in the American Biographical Institute's "Personalities of the West and Mid-West."

Again, in 1976, he was in the 15th Edition of "Who's Who" in the West and Midwest, also "Who's Who in Finance and Industry."

Mr. Kuzara just completed several years of service on the Sheridan Planning Commission until his resignation in 1976.

He is a member of Big Horn Mountain Lodge No. 43, A. F. & A. M., a 32° member of the Scottish Rite and a member of Kalif Shrine, and in 1971, was an official representative of the latter at the Imperial Session in Miami Beach.

In 1969, he was given an Honorary membership on the Board of Directors of the North American Indian Foundation and in 1974 of the All American Indian Days.

In 1972, he was selected Outstanding Citizen of Wyoming by the Wyoming State Elks Association; and in 1973, elected President of the Sheridan-Johnson County Pioneer Association. That same year, he was designated Honorary Chairman of the Board of Trustees of the Cedars Home for Children of Lincoln, Nebraska, and also, Honorary Colonel Aide-de-Camp of the Alabama State Militia, appointed by Governor George Wallace.

In the Fall of 1974, Mr. Kuzara was elected Regional Vice-President of the National Ass'n of Realtors at its annual convention in Las Vegas, and was installed to that office in San Antonio in February, 1975. As Regional Vice-President, he served as liaison to the states of Colorado, New Mexico, Utah and Wyoming.

Also, during the year 1975-76, he was District Deputy Grand Exalted Ruler for Wyoming North supervising some nine Lodges of the B.P.O. Elks. In these latter two capacities, both he and Mrs. Kuzara traveled extensively attending Realtor Conventions in the states under his jurisdiction as well as Elks Lodges of northern Wyoming.

Currently, Mr. Kuzara is serving on the Elks Grand Lodge Committee on Credentials and in July, 1977 will assist at the annual convention in New Orleans, La.

His latest appointment came last summer as a member of the Advisory Council of the European Heritage Project of the University of Wyoming in conjunction with the Wyoming State Historical Society to revise the history of Wyoming to include in it some of the many contributions in the development of Wyoming made by European immigrants settling in that state.

STANLEY A. KUZARA

Chapter 2

Kuzara Family

The Kuzara Family, 1932—all 14 of us. Standing l to r: Helen, Joe, Anna, Stanley, Walter, Andrew, Rose, Mike, John, Mary. Seated: Henry, Father and Mother—George and Sophia, and Charlotte.

Inasmuch as the population of the mining camps of the Sheridan, Wyoming area was composed of so many foreign people, many of them of Polish origin, this chapter is written on the assumption that it might be of some interest to learn of the experiences, the development, the life and of the ultimate assimilation of just such a family.

I have chosen to write a brief history of my own, the Kuzara family, only because of my close association with it; and while I must admit I don't feel that it may be as typical as some; first, because, although most foreign families had several children, not many had twelve as did our family; also, while so many of that element seemed rather complacent and satisfied to simply work in the mines to be followed by their sons just as soon as they were old enough to do so, my father seemed to have somewhat higher aspirations. Generally he was in some sort of business of his own, and his work in the mines was usually only of a temporary nature.

George Kuzara was born in that part of Poland which was taken over by Austria in the famous partition of Poland, the area known as Siedliska, Poland, on June 11, 1876. He stated to us that his ancestory however originated in Metz, France, and that his father, although a moderately poor farmer, did hold a title of Justice of the Peace.

He had only two or three years of formal schooling and just what he did during his early years, I do not recall him telling other than that all of the members of the family (of which there were also twelve) had their work cut out for them, he taking care of the geese as a very small boy, having to herd them all day for there were no fences, and later graduating to the more complex and difficult duties of primitive rural life.

As was common in those days, he had heard of the wonderful opportunities in the "new world" and in 1892, at the age of 16, he came to this country, going probably directly to Pennsylvania where he obtained employment in a factory in the town of Hoytville which no longer exists. During this time, he began to learn to play the violin practicing until he became quite an accomplished fiddler of Polish song and dance tunes. For the rest of his life, he was constantly called on to play at weddings, christenings and other Polish festivals.

My Mother, Sophia Medrek (the first "e" has a small curlycue under it to give it an "n" sound causing the name to be pronounced "Mendrek"), was born also in Poland, not too far distant from my father's birthplace. She used to tell us that her ancestors originated in Sweden. She never attended school a single day in her life as her parents were very poor and at a very tender age was put to work tending the flock. She told of how later she cut and carried the wheat from the field to the barn where she helped thresh by beating the wheat to separate the kernels.

Little more is known about her childhood, but as a young girl of seventeen or eighteen, she came to this country all alone and unable to speak English. Although she did apparently have a sister living in Elmira, New York, for some

reason unknown, except that she had heard of factory work available in Pennsylvania, she ended up at Hoytville. It was there that my father and mother met each other and it was there that they were married on August 5, 1897. A year later, in August of 1898, my oldest brother, Walter, was born.

In the latter part of 1899 or very early in 1900, they moved to Chicago where John, the next child was born in January of 1900. After only a short year in Chicago, they migrated west to the comparatively young coal mining community of Dietz, Wyoming. As those mines were rapidly developing, he immediately went to work at the Dietz No. 2 mine where there were already a number of his countrymen employed.

By this time, the population of Dietz consisted of many nationalities, and while there was very little written about the "foreigners'" social life, there existed much activity in their enjoyment of their Polish customs.

It was while he worked in the Dietz No. 2 mine that he was quite seriously injured when he was accidentally squeezed between a coal car and the side of the mine, and while he recovered sufficiently to return to work, he did complain of residuals of this injury throughout the remainder of his life.

Andrew, the third son, was born in Dietz in 1901; and in 1903, brother Joe was born. It was also in the year of 1903 that he became an American citizen on December 4th. According to papers on file at the Sheridan County Clerk of Court's office, his witness was one "Stanizalow Kotcher" who later changed his name to "Steve Kutcher."

It was in 1904 that the folks moved to a small rock house near the mining camp of Dietz No. 5 when my father changed jobs. This camp was about a mile and a half north of the original Dietz camp, and the rock house was located just west of the C. B. & Q. railroad where some of the strewn rock is still in evidence. It was at this location that my oldest sister, Mary, was born on Jan. 1, 1904.

Converting a barn into a living unit, the family then moved into the main camp. This building was located just across the slough from the present Country Nite Club which at that time was the company store. (Both Dietz camps had sloughs, evidence of the former Big Goose Creek which meandered around, but which was diverted by the B. & M. railroad in 1892 to avoid building several bridges). It was in this converted barn that I was born in 1906. That same year, my father joined the Sheridan Eagles Lodge. I recall how proud he was of that membership and even persuaded many of his foreigner friends to join.

The following year, in 1907, my father bought the old "John Hecht Place" which was located about midway between the two Dietz Camps. This consisted of a dwelling, a saloon, a bakery, and a large barn and ice-house combination. Here, he finally was able to fulfill his desire to be in business for himself. (Previously, Mr. Hecht had been issued a liquor license and had operated a saloon there, also a John Heczko had a bakery on the place).

While in business for himself, he did enjoy a favorable patronage from the principally walking traffic between the two Dietz camps. In addition, on his approximately two acres of land located next to Big Goose Creek, plus some additional adjacent land he rented, he took a great deal of pride in raising a menagerie of animals including horses, cows, pigs, geese, China geese, chickens, Polish hens, Guinea pigs, Guinea hens, turkeys, peacocks, etc. In those horse and buggy days, he raised some very fine horses and owned some lovely carriages and sleighs.

We children, those old enough to attend school, were required to walk to the main Dietz camp, a distance of about a mile, usually along the railroad track which was hard and sometimes dangerous walking but certainly preferable to walking on the sometimes gumbo muddy road.

In 1908, Rose, the second oldest girl was born to be followed by Anna, the eighth child, in 1910.

Taken from the *Sheridan Post*, 4/2/09— "George Kuzara is running a second hand store along with his other business. He can furnish anything from a 10¢ washpan, to a whole set of furniture, even to garden tools."

We raised practically all our own livestock to provide meat for our family. We even had a slaughter house on the premises, containing, among other things, a hoist consisting of a huge wooden wheel, its axle being a round pole about eight inches in diameter, and extending from wall to wall. There was a rope around this axle to which was hooked the carcass. By turning the large wheel, one could easily pull up a heavy animal for skinning and cleaning.

One of the more nostalgic memories of mine was when my Uncle Joe who operated a butcher shop on the place, had just completed smoking some Polish sausages. As he brought them fresh out of the smoke-house, he must have read my mind, for he proceeded to cut off a generous portion—I even recall quite vividly how he cut it quite diagonally rather than straight across (which in those days was a common practice), and handed it to me. The flavor of that freshly-smoked Polish sausage even exceeded the aroma which preceeded it! This must have been in about 1911.

It was in the Spring of that same year when a very tragic accident took the life of my little cousin, George Kuzara, while he and I were playing together on the roadway near our place. My own recollections of this incident appear in another chapter; however, a detailed account appeared in the March 31, 1911 issue of the *Sheridan Enterprise* as follows:

Sheridan Enterprise, March 31, 1911

NEWS-NOTES OF LOCAL INTEREST

"The first automobile fatality chronicled in the history of either Sheridan county or the entire northern part of Wyoming, so far as known, occurred last evening near Dietz when George Kuzura,* the three-year-old son of Joe Kuzura, met instant death in being run over by a five passenger car owned and driven by C. H. Wilkins.

The accident occurred shortly after 5 o'clock and was about a mile north of Dietz, along the county highway. Six people were in the car at the time. Mr. Fetterly occupied a seat alongside of the driver, and in the rear seat were four people, Mr. and Mrs. J. R. Wade, Maj. T. K. Birkhaeuser and James Day. The party had left Monarch previously and were proceeding to Sheridan at a slow rate of speed. Crossing the Tongue River† bridge, a few hundred yards from the scene of the accident, they were proceeding south when they noticed two small boys dart across the road in front of them. They came from some point between a meat market and a bakery shop, about 300 feet in advance of the car and ran to the left hand side of the road, and stood there evidently waiting for the car to pass. When within about ten feet of the two boys one of the lads, George Kuzura, started to cross in front of the car and stopped for a second or two

* Name misspelled, should be "Kuzara"
†This should be "Big Goose," not "Tongue River"

on the left hand track of the road. Mr. Wilkins made a quick turn with his steering wheel, throwing the car to the right of the road, with the intention of passing of the two youngsters at least five or six feet away.

After a short pause, however, the lad again darted across to the right hand side of the road, and was caught by the left front wheel of the car.

One witness at the coroner's inquest proceeding this morning, stated that but for the quick action of the driver in turning the car to the right instead of proceeding straight ahead, that both the boys would have been struck instead of one. The action in turning the car to the right was made so quick that he thought the car itself would topple over.

Mr. Fetterly at once jumped from the automobile and ran back to where the prostrate form was lying in the road, the face bruised and bleeding from many bruises. Tenderly the limp form was lifted up in the arms of Mr. Fetterly and given over to the father, who had arrived by that time. The father in turn transferred it to the arms of the agonized mother and from her it was taken by Mr. Birkhaeuser and Mr. Wade and carried into the house, where it was undressed and examined.

Life was already extinct. Its eyes were almost bulging from its head and its face was lacerated and swollen almost beyond recognition.

Mr. Wilkins succeeding in stopping the car within twenty-five or thirty feet from the point of contact and then all the occupants hurried back to offer any possible assistance. Mrs. Wade was overcome by the spectacle and swooned away.

A buggy driven by D. E. Diltz was following the automobile about 150 yards distant and within a few minutes after its arrival Mrs. Wade regained consciousness and proceeded on the trip with him.

Meanwhile Mr. Wilkins had gone on to Dietz to secure the services of a physician and returned in a brief time. Upon examination, it was found that the first shock had been sufficient to cause death, the little fellow's neck and lower jaw being broken.

Speed of Ten Miles an Hour

From the evidence adduced at the coroner's inquest at the court house this morning it developed that the car was being driven at a speed between ten and twelve miles an hour. The car was stopped within twenty-five or thirty feet from the scene of the accident. The roads in that particular neighborhood were rough and uneven at this time of the year and it is doubtful if this thirty horse power car with such a heavy load could have picked up a higher speed. To corroborate this statement a wagon became stalled on the highway this morning only 100 feet north of where the accident occurred. It required the services of another team to pull it out of the deep ruts before it could proceed.

When it was found that the boy was past all medical or surgical aid the automobile party resumed its trip to Sheridan, and within two miles overtook the buggy. She again took a seat in the car and the party came on to Sheridan. Upon their arrival in this city, Dr. C. R. Halley, the county coroner, was at once notified and hastily summoning a jury, consisting of Messrs. Oliver H. Walsh, Grant MacLeod and A. R. Kreighbaum, proceeding to the scene of the tragedy and view the remains. They returned to Sheridan in the evening, and were present at the inquest proceedings at the court house this morning.

Mr. Wilkins, the driver and owner of the car, is at present master mechanic of the Wyoming Coal Mining company at Monarch, and has owned the car for the past four months. He has become familiar with its operation by driving it practically all of last year, and is now considered most proficient in its management. No blame or responsibility is attached to him or any occupant of the car because of the absence of any negligence on his part or of any of the car's occupants.

Boys Were Cousins

George Kuzura, the lad who was killed, was three years of age on the 8th of March. His companion at the time of the accident was his cousin, Stanley Kuzura, a youth of four and a half years.

Accidental Death

At 3 o'clock this afternoon the coroner's jury returned a verdict of accidental death, and therefore no blame is attached to the driver or any of the car's occupants for the loss of life."

* * * * * * *

Sheridan Enterprise, March 31, 1911

"The funeral services of little George Kuzura, the three year old boy who was killed by an automobile Friday evening, occurred yesterday afternoon and internment occurred at Mount Hope cemetery. Many friends and relatives followed the remains to the last resting place."

In 1912, my parents decided to visit their native Poland. In addition to taking Anna, only a baby then, they agreed to take one other member of the family, and to avoid any argument, determined that we should all draw straws. John was the lucky winner. As they were preparing to leave, the report was received that the Titanic had sunk, causing a delay in their departure date; however, they later did leave. After they returned, they reported having seen some of the debris of that ship.

Their stay in Poland was not as long as they had planned. For one reason, my mother did not feel too well while there, and another reason may have been that they might have been just a little disappointed in the changed conditions causing the old country to lack some of the luster as they remembered it.

The following year on January 8, 1913, Michael, the ninth child was born, and later that year, my father bought the "Three Star Saloon" in the No. 3 coal mine camp near Roundup, Montana, and during that summer, we moved there. Soon afterwards, my father returned to Dietz and assisted by Mr. Robert Thirlwell, herded his several horses all the way from Dietz to Roundup, a distance of about 200 miles.

While in Roundup, my brother, Walter, worked for the Roundup Record newspaper during the summer and after school, setting type. At the same time, I sold their papers on the streets. I recall that I was too bashful to ever call out the name of the paper. If it got dark, I would be afraid to walk to the No. 3 camp, actually adjacent to the town, and would have to wait for Walter who sometimes would not be through until late at night.

It was while we lived here that I learned to swim. On a dare once in the early Spring while the water was still quite high in the Musselshell river, I swam across the river for the first time not knowing that Walter, knowing that I had nothing more than "mud-crawled" before, followed immediately behind in case I could not make it.

It should be noted here that over the few preceeding years, some of the older members of the family were developing a growing resentment against liquor and the liquor business my father was in, and as the pressure continued to increase, he began to consider some other method of earning a livelihood.

Through some friends who had moved to a new coal mining camp of Leheigh, a few miles from Windham, Montana, he was told of the sudden and rapid growth of that camp as well as of the agricultural potential of the area. So, with his knowledge of several languages, he decided to locate at Windham which was a small village on the Northern Pacific railroad only about six miles from Leheigh and about eight miles from the county seat of Stanford, Montana.

With the thought of serving both communities, he bought some lots in Windham and after constructing a new building with living quarters in the rear, he opened a furniture store. At first, it seemed he was enjoying a good business, but after only about a year, the Great Northern railroad which owned the coal mines at Leheigh, decided to close down the mine. Although there continued some sort of coal operation for local consumption, this was quite a blow to the economy of the area. In addition, the farmers were experiencing hard times due to successive seasons of drought. In an attempt to compensate, he added groceries to his line until that became his principal business, but soon after, decided to go into partnership with a Charles Dunsmore. This turned out to be a sad mistake when it was discovered that his partner contributed practically nothing to the operation, and it was not long before the accounts receivable forced the closing of the store. He then went to work for a competitor, the d'Auterment Store, as a clerk, but the town was rapidly decaying.

During this time, two more children were born: Helen in 1915, and Henry in 1916, bringing the total now to eleven children. Only nine were at home, however, as both Walter and John were in France serving in the Army during World War I.

Fortunately, when the family moved from Dietz, my father retained his property there, renting it to the John Goryl family. So when he decided to leave Windham in 1918 and return to Dietz with our only assets being a Model T Ford

Windham Mercantile (Kuzara Grocery and Hardware Store), Windham, Montana, 1916. George Kuzara and son, John.

touring car and eleven children, be they assets or liabilities, we moved back to Dietz temporarily crowding in with our Aunt, Mrs. Mike Parot (my father's sister) pending the vacation of the property by the Goryls. So, here we were, back in the old "Hecht Place" for another new start.

Again, I enrolled in the Dietz school—this time in the 6th grade, in the old "high school" building which was still there in its old location. This school, as later described, was about a mile from where we lived and it was necessary for all of us to walk—usually along the railroad track, especially when the dirt road turned to a ribbbon of mud, and although very dangerous, fortunately none of us had any accidents.

Much against his will, my father returned to work in the Dietz No. 8 coal mine, but was assisted by brothers Andrew and Joe, the former working in the Carneyville mine and Joe at Acme, helping to supplement our income. Also, my father moved some small houses and cabins onto our property. These, he rented to miner bachelors and to some families, thereby further adding to our income.

Brothers Walter and John were serving in the army when our family moved to Dietz, but after returning home, left to make their living elsewhere. The following year, 1919, our youngest sister, Charlotte, was born, completing the family of 12 children.

After only about a year at the mine, he decided to go into business for himself, but he needed some capital. I happened to accompany him when he went to an old miner friend of his in Dietz No. 7 requesting a loan. It made quite an impression on me to observe this old miner who lived in a little tarpaper shack as he went around that one room picking out a $20 bill here from behind a loose board, another from under a certain board in the floor, one from behind a calendar, and so on until he had a total of $300.00 which he loaned to my father. There were no papers signed.

And so, after converting his Model T. Ford into a light delivery truck, and converting his old saloon building into a grocery store, with a few counters, show cases, etc., and with his knowledge of several languages and a lot of intestinal fortitude, he was in business!

At about this time, also, he remodeled what used to be a bakery years before and then a butcher shop into a more practical bakery unit. He re-built the oven using tile which we illegally salvaged from the nearby railroad ballast, installed mixing bins and after completing it, rented it to Mike Sikora, who, although a miner, was really a baker by trade, and a good one at that.

By now, my father had a small village often referred to as "Kuzaraville." It thrilled him tremendously anytime the Interurban conductor would call out the station, "KUZARAVILLE" or when he would occasionally receive a piece of mail at our Dietz postoffice addressed to him at "Kuzaraville, Wyoming."

The bakery business was bound to thrive with superb bakery products. Unfortunately, poor Mike Sikora could not resist offers of sociable drinks as he made his deliveries until he became quite alcoholic. Time after time, he would come home in a stupor until finally, it affected his mind. Frequently, he would be observed standing alone for hours mumbling to himself philosophical expressions and simply staring into space, apparently harmless, but frightening and irrational.

It was reported on more than one occasion that when he was unable to start his little old Ford after repeated cranking, he was seen down on his knees for a prayer, and believe it or not, another crank and the Ford would start. Eventually, however, his condition got to the point where he had to be committed to the State mental hospital.

In the operation of his grocery business, my father's plan was to keep from buying any more stock than necessary to fill whatever orders for groceries he had received the day before. And so, when he returned after the first day out taking orders, although somewhat disappointed, he was not discouraged when he received orders for only enough to fill one small grocery box.

The following morning, he went to the wholesale house in Sheridan and bought only enough of split cases to fill his orders. These, then, he delivered while taking orders for enough to fill two boxes. Gradually, his business increased to the point where, a year later, he bought an additional second hand Studebaker truck. As his business continued to increase, I found myself assisting during summer vacations operating one of the trucks while he delivered with the other. It was particularly during these years, that I became somewhat familiar with the other camps.

As many of the miners had chickens and cows, much of his deliveries consisted of 100-pound sacks of bran, corn, wheat and as much sugar as his quota would allow (this was during prohibition and many of the miners made their own moonshine, beer and wine). In the Fall, my father would take orders for grapes, and after getting a sufficient number of orders, would buy a carload for distribution.

My sister, Mary who had gone to school only through the sixth grade when she had to quit to help care for some of the smaller children, was his very capable store clerk, putting up orders, and tending the store without whose able assistance he certainly could not have been able to survive.

Occasionally, while making his deliveries, at the insistance of some of his customers, he would take a sociable drink, and sometimes another, and even sometimes still another only to come home to a very disapproving wife. But I never have seen the time when he could not or would not get up the next day at his regular time to face the work of the next day.

In the meanwhile, we continued to have our cows, chickens, pigs, etc., gather our own ice from the river, eating cutout portions of over-ripe fruit and vegetables, and in general, use every means of cutting corners.

By 1921, the Dietz No. 7 mine was already closed and the camp was now becoming vacant. That same year, the Model mine closed down, then in 1922, Kooi and Dietz No. 8 mines closed, followed by Kleenburn in 1924. The demise of the coal industry seemed inevitable with the advent of natural gas. Some of the inhabitants of the Camps were able to find employment in Sheridan while others moved away from the area. Still others were employed by the mines at Monarch, Acme and the Hotchkiss mine.

Naturally, as the economic picture was changing, so was my father's grocery business affected, as well as the bakery business of Mike Sikora.

Therefore, in about 1926, my father bought a small coal mine from one of his old Polish acquaintances, Steve Kutcher. (This was the same person who was my father's witness in 1903 when he received his naturalization papers). This mine was located about two miles north of Sheridan on land owned by the Tuttle sisters of somewhere in Texas to whom he paid a royalty on each ton of coal extracted.

Having previously worked in a coal mine, and not being satisfied with some of the methods used by his predecessor, he closed down the unit and started a new slope a few hundred yards north. My brother, Walter happened to be home between jobs about that time and assisted him. The crudest methods were used to begin with, consisting of a few rails of track leading into the excavation or slope and a single horse walking around a turn-table, winding a cable, the other end of which was hooked to a car pulling each load of dirt, a car at a time. Eventually, they reached the vein of coal which at first was sold unscreened and unweighed, but sold by the car. It was never the intent to ship any coal by rail even though the C. B. & Q. railroad was quite near, but instead, merely to sell to local trade as the customers came in with their pickup trucks, wagons, trailers and to those making a business of hauling for others.

Although there were several other so-called "wagon mines" in the area, his business flourished and he was constantly improving his methods with more modern machinery—developing his own steam with large steam boilers whose steam provided the necessary energy to operate a motor-generator thereby generating his own electricity. The cars of coal were pulled up the slope by a steam-operated hoist. His coal was screened into the various customary grades; viz, slack (discarded), pea, nut, egg and lump—each larger size commanding a slightly higher price.

After a short period of time, Walter, who had other commitments, left the mine to go East. Brother Andrew then took over as my father's assistant and right-hand man; and except for two or three attempts to divorce himself from the work of a "miner," would, each time, return to the Star mine. Thus, he remained working with my father and the mine throughout the remaining life of the operation.

So, during the famous depression of the 30's, my father was able to maintain a complement of employees—as many as 35 during the winter months, paying them wages slightly less than those paid to the men working in the so-called "railroad" mines. The latter would work spasmodically as the coal orders were received; in the summer months, sometimes as few as one day per week, but when they did work, they would usually work a full crew. In the "wagon mine" my father never did know when the trucks, etc. would come and to be prepared, usually did work a full crew. Many times, if the demand was not there, these men

"Kuzaraville" taken from across Big Goose Creek looking east—1923.

The Kuzara Family in 1958—Wives, husbands, children and grandchildren—some twenty-three missing; however, six or eight cousins pictured.

had nothing to do, but were nevertheless paid, as only occasionally were they sent home after once reporting for work.

During the 1930's, my father ran some cattle on the surface of the coal land, and also acquired some land of his own in the vicinity, in the area referred to as the Beatty Gulch area. The raising of cattle was actually his first love, but never could he afford to go into the cattle business, but now he had accumulated a herd of about 75 head. So as he was advancing in years, and Andrew having assisted him for all the years, in 1935 made an agreement to sell the operation to him.

Andrew then continued to operate the Star Mine as described in more detail in Chapter 15, until it was finally closed in 1942.

So, for those latter years, my father worked his cattle, branding calves, repairing fences, building reservoirs, riding horseback, and enjoying every minute.

Almost suddenly, however, in the Fall of 1950, he became ill and shortly after, in October, passed away at the age of 74.

Mother continued to live on the old place, while brother, Mike, wife Betty, and their family of nine children occupied one of the houses on the place.

Then in 1951, she sold "Kuzaraville" to him believing that with his large family, he was the logical one to have it. And so, that year, brother Joe moved the old house which had its origin at Kooi, Wyoming to 1329 Spaulding street in Sheridan and completely remodeled it into a new home. There, Mother enjoyed her gardening and flowers until 1963 when she, too, passed away at the age of 86 leaving 103 children, grandchildren, and great-grandchildren!

Chapter 3

Sheridan Railway Company

Sheridan Railway Company—City street car. Frank Colson, motorman (on steps); Joe Drier, conductor.

Sheridan Railway Company—Interurban, Joe Drier, conductor.

Sheridan Railway Company—Interurban. Getting shale at end of line at Monarch. (Man on left, standing on flat car, said to be Nick Julio).

Street car on unpaved Main Street in Sheridan.

In reviewing old issues of the Sheridan newspapers, frequent references were made to the energy potentials using coal or water power as a source of energy with visions of an electric railway system for this whole region.

Even after the construction of the B. & M. Railroad through Sheridan and its extension through the mining camps north of Sheridan, there existed a need for some method of more convenient travel between the camps and Sheridan; and in an attempt to meet some of this need, it has been told how two particularly enterprising business men of Sheridan, Mr. George Messick of the Messick Clothing Store and Mr. Harvey Fryberger of the Stevens-Fryberger Company, both owners of clothing stores, used to charter special cars on the Burlington railroad on paydays to bring in the miners to town to spend their money.

It was not until 1910, however, that a group of investors (some say Chicago, and some say New York) of which a Mr. Robert E. Emanual of Dayton, Ohio, was President, that work actually began on the construction of an electric railway system in the City of Sheridan. An early reference covering the beginning of this system was personally obtained from Mrs. Walter Harker, now deceased. She was the daughter of Mr. and Mrs. James McCoy, he being a former pit boss at the Dietz No. 4 mine, and when in the fall of 1911, she began to attend the first grade in Dietz and had been in school only a few weeks, she recalled she was forced to quit and re-enroll in the Sheridan schools when her father resigned his position at Dietz to become the first Master Mechanic for the Sheridan Railway company, working under a Mr. Perin, the Superintendent. (Mr. McCoy later became superintendent). According to the records in the Sheridan County Court House, researched and reported by Mr. Joe Drier who first went to work for the company as a track layer and then as conductor, the franchise for the operation was issued in the Spring of 1910. (More about this appears later in the form of excerpts from the *Sheridan Post*, the *Sheridan Enterprise* and the *Sheridan Journal* newspapers).

In 1911, the line was extended as an Interurban line as far as the mining camp of Monarch. It is told that Jerry Warner, a son of one of the owners of the Sheridan Inn, cut the ribbon at the dedication.

Except for the Coal Camp of Kooi, located about three miles beyond Monarch, the line then served and connected all the coal camps with regular transportation service to Sheridan with hourly trips throughout the day.

The street car which operated inside the City of Sheridan and to Fort Mackenzie was a smaller car than the interurban; the former had only one trolley pole on a swivel which was manually moved by a rope attached to the trolley by swinging it around from front to rear and vice versa. The larger interurban cars had two sets of trolley poles. As the car was headed in one direction, the rear trolley was raised to the trolley line and the front lowered to a horizontal position, and vice versa.

All units of the Sheridan Railway Company were powered by "Direct Current" electricity as opposed to "Alternate Current" as is generally used.

There was a direct current electric generator located at the Sheridan County Electric power plant at Acme, Wyoming which was turned by an alternating current motor. This electricity was connected to the trolley line near Acme. It is said that there was an additional converter (alternating current motor turning a direct current generator) located at the Sheridan County Electric Company substation in Sheridan on Broadway Street.

Direct Current electricity was also used to power the motors in the mines with each mine generating its own in its individual power house.

Albert "Pot" Goodmay who operated and drove motors in the mines for a period of some 25 years, states that the reason for using direct current was because it was less dangerous in case of contact in that it would tend to repel while the alternating current tends to attract in the event of contact; and also, because it takes only two wires to carry the heavy voltage rather than the three wires required by alternating current, and just generally easier to work with.

All of the cars were housed in the street car "barn" located on the corner of West Alger and Dow streets in a building formerly built and occupied as an indoor swimming pool. The interurban route extended from Burkitt Street on Main, north to the Mines. The street car route, in addition to the route to Fort Mackenzie from Main street along Alger avenue and along Lewis street past the high school and fair grounds, it extended along Main Street, around the Sheridan Inn, east on Fifth street, south one block on Broadway then west on Fourth street, up Main street, east on Burkitt, up Coffeen avenue, then up Sumner, east on Montana avenue, on Illinois to Coffeen avenue, and on that street back to Main.

An earlier reference was made stating that the interurban went as far as the Holly Sugar plant during the sugar beet season. Not only did it haul passengers to that location, but also pulled cars loaded with sugar beets from growers north of Sheridan. It was not too unusual to see a street car hitch on to a wagon which might have become mired and stuck in the deep mud along Sheridan's Main Street before there was any paving in the north part of town.

One of my earliest recollections of the street car, was when I accompanied my parents to Fort Mackenzie in about 1912. We took the inter-urban to Sheridan then transferred to the street car. Upon arriving at the end of the line at the Fort, all passengers got out and assisted the motorman and conductor turn the car around on a turn table, heading it back toward Sheridan.

Not only did the interurban haul passengers, it also served as a vital link between the Mines and Sheridan hauling payrolls, milk, furniture and all sorts of freight. On certain holidays and various celebrations, the cars would be so loaded with passengers that they might be hanging on the sides and even riding on top of the car.

My first "real contact" with the interurban was when I was actually hit by one of the cars and knocked into a ditch at Dietz. I was in the first grade coming from school and while two girls were playfully chasing me, I ran along the shoulder of the interurban track which followed right down the middle of the street. I had just approached a sharp corner near the Company store when the car came along.

By way of explanation, the wheels of a car are normally positioned a number of feet from each end under the car so that when it goes around a corner, the end of the car protrudes some distance beyond the rails. In this instance, as the car rounded the corner, the rear end sort of slapped me down into a slightly muddy ditch. I was uninjured but inwardly a little glad it happened when the girls came up and began to clean off the mud with their handkerchiefs.

From the year 1921 through the Spring of 1925, while I attended Sheridan High School, there were quite a number of Mine students using the inter-urban as a means of transportation to and from school. It was during this period that I was (very illegally) permitted to operate some switches at Dietz.

At the point where the inter-urban crossed the C. B. & Q. railroad in Dietz, there was a "frog" or "de-railer" on the inter-urban track which would cause the car to derail if the car did not come to a stop and certain procedures followed. To insure that there be no collision with a train, there was located near this crossing a small locked building containing six huge switch handles extending up from under the

floor for about four feet, and by using a combination of pushing some and pulling others, certain semaphores up and down the C. B. & Q. railroad track were raised to alert any possible oncoming trains. After this was accomplished, the conductor would remove the derailer and the car would then cross the tracks. After the car would pass, this procedure was then reversed and the car would continue on its way. To my knowledge, I was the only one ever allowed to perform this operation, but always, of course, under strict supervision.

Then, just beyond the Camp of Dietz on the northern edge, it was necessary for the car to go onto a side track to await the car coming from the opposite direction. Again, the car would stop while the conductor would turn a switch directing the car to this siding. To do this, it was necessary to manually shift the trolley pole from one line to the other. Here again, I was permitted to perform this operation usually done by the conductor by reaching out the rear window to pull the rope holding the trolley pole, but to make it more interesting and since I was not restrained, I would crawl through the rear window and while sitting on the rear headlight, and while the car was in motion I would shift the trolley. In this, I had developed quite an expertise to be able to make this shift in one motion. If the line did not nestle in the groove of the trolley wheel, there would follow a great many sparks. To be allowed to perform both of these operations gave me some pride and a great feeling of accomplishment.

The only regular stops, or stations, were those listed on the Schedule of Fares except in town where the car would stop at the end of any block upon being given the signal by a passenger who would press a button, buzzing the conductor who in turn would pull a cord signalling the motorman—one such ring for a stop; two rings, to proceed; three rings for reverse (two rings while travelling meant to speed up).

As an accommodation, the car would make some stops for the convenience of passengers at unscheduled places. One of these was at the Kuzara place situated about half-way between the two Dietz camps, and it gave my father a real sense of pride if the conductor in announcing the stop, would yell out "Kuzaraville."

It was told that on one return trip to Sheridan, on the final run of the day, the motorman was not too alert when a bull which had broken through the fence was on the tracks near the Wrench Ranch. The car struck the bull killing him on the spot. To avoid discovery or blame for the accident, both the motorman and the conductor who were alone on the car, there being no passengers to witness the incident, somehow were able to drag the animal to the highway adjacent to the interurban right-of-way at that point, and after depositing it, and erasing all evidence, they proceeded on their way to town. As nearly as they were to learn later, it was assumed that the prize animal was killed by a passing motorist.

Some of those employed by the Sheridan Railway company included: Mr. Frank Colson, motorman (still living in the state of Washington and from whom I received a Christmas card this last Christmas of 1976); Mr. Howard McKinley, conductor; Mr. Frank Speakerworth, motorman; Mr. Tracy Allen; Mr. Ralph Bady; Mr. Tom Lytle; Mr. Richard Donavan, motorman, Ed Ferguson, conductor; Harry Beck, motorman; Tom Broderick, conductor; Tom Newman, conductor; and Mr. Joe Drier who was employed probably longer than any of the others from the inception of the company to its very end. Mr. James McCoy who worked at the shop and in the office also had a very long tenure with the company.

It was during this period, 1921-1925, that the activity at the mines was beginning to dwindle, and by the latter part of 1925, the interurban ceased to operate and in 1926, the whole system was closed, thus terminating another facet in the history of Sheridan and the Mines.

The information contained in these previous pages is taken largely from my memory; however I find many facts and figures in my research which greatly adds to what I have written so far, as will be noted by press releases contained in the Sheridan newspapers as follows:

1/3/10—"Sheridan Electric Railway Assured—Development Company is Incorporated To Finance and Construct Traction System—H. R. Kay Made President"—Incorporators—H. R. Kay, D. D. Warner, Frank Murray, Ralph Denio and F. Blume—Capital Stock, $100,000."

1/6/10—"RAILWAY STOCK ENTIRELY SUBSCRIBED—$10,000 quickly raised—Promoter, E. F. Wheaton leaves for east to raise $40,000 among capitalists there." Local investors include: H. R. Kay, D. D. Warner, Frank Murray, Fred H. Blume, Ralph Denio, Henry A. Coffeen,

Chas. Murray, Wyo. Mutual Investment Co., J. D. Powers, S. B. Crandall, Austin Dry Goods, Hunter Loan, C. B. Holmes, Geo. Brown, Jack Hune, James Burns, A. D. Flores, Dr. M. A. Newell, E. C. Williams, Fred Schroeder, Malcolm Moncrieffe, Bloom Shoe & Clothing, New York Store, Peret & Luce, Ferguson & Pearson, Jacob Wren, A. W. Wilder, Jouvenat Hardware, H. H. Parson, P. Cusick, Peter Demple and Anonymous."

Also, on January 8, 1910, there appeared an article in the *Sheridan Enterprise* as follows: "ANOTHER RAILWAY LINE PLANNED HERE—RANCHESTER MAN INFORMS CHAMBER OF HIS PROJECT—HAS BEEN WORKING ON PROMOTION OF ROAD TO MINING TOWNS AND TO DAYTON—EASTERN MAN IS INTERESTED" "That other promoters of electric railroads besides E. F. Wheaton, the Cleveland traction man, have recognized in this county a promising field for the building of interurban lines, was made known at the Chamber of Commerce meeting last night by the reading of a letter from V. C. Shickley, secretary of the Riverside Coal company, of Ranchester. The letter was written to C. R. Massey and referred by him to the Chamber.

Mr. Shickley in his letter says that he and others are particularly interested in the construction of a line from Sheridan, via Dietz, Carney, Monarch, Acme, Kooi, Riverside and Ranchester, to Dayton, and to that end have been working for some time. He declares that the men he has been working with do not believe in publicity as a factor in the promotion of projects of this kind and have therefore been working quietly.

He says, however, that the project has been laid before men of practical experience with encouraging results, and mentions William R. Sullivan, of Dayton, O., Electric Street Railway company, as one of these men. He says that had not Mr. Sullivan been engaged in the construction of two other lines, he would have been here before now to look over the field."

4/15/10—"THE IMPORTANT FEATURE IS LINE TO COAL CAMPS—Say Street Car Builders at Open Meeting of the City Council—Confidence Expressed by Citizens—

Estimated Cost, $500,000

Total estimated trackage, fifteen miles.

Three miles of trackage to be built first year.

The proposed route would supply a travel medium for 18,000 people.

Building operations to start when entire proposed line has been secured.

A clear right of way must be given through the city streets of Sheridan.

Line must go through to the coal camps else the proposition would fail.

A bond of $5,000 to be voluntarily placed by builders when franchise is granted to show their good faith.

The builders of the projected car line are Messrs. Albert Emanuel and William R. Sullivan of Dayton, Ohio.

Proposed route via Fort Mackenzie to Kooi coal camps, a distance of twelve miles and not over three miles in city of Sheridan.

City must not impose a license or occupation tax, but that all property holdings would be subject to city and county taxation as any other corporation.

The meeting of the citizens to further discuss the street car proposition last evening was held at the city hall and presided over by Mayor J. J. O'Marr. The hall was well filled with interested citizens.

City Attorney Carl L. Sackett again read the proposed ordinance granting to the builders a franchise for a city traction and electric proposition. Mr. Sackett stated as yet the matter had assumed no definite form but was only in the shape of a rough preliminary draft subject to discussion and alteration if necessary.

Inasmuch as the builders would have to generate an immense amount of electric current for the street car motive power they contended it should also be their privilege to sell to outsiders electricity for lighting and motive purposes. Twelve cents per kilowatt would be the maximum charge for motive power and the minimum rate for business and residence houses would be $2 and $1.50 respectively.

State Treasurer Edward Gillette took exception to the section giving the builders a right to construct a line on any or all thoroughfares of the city and thought a blanket franchise would serve the purpose better. As the section read the builders could keep any other traction company out of the city. They would have preference to hauling sugar beets through the city by rail should a factory be erected or would prevent a line being built from Sheridan to any of the mountain resorts. However, Mr. Emanuel replied that there was a wide difference of opinion as to the route to be taken. At this time he was

unable to specify the streets, but suggested a proposed line and that if rails were not laid within a specified time they would forfeit their right to that particular street.

After the franchise had been given, Mr. Emanuel stated that the most important issue would be to secure a right of way to the coal camps, and if they could secure an amicable adjustment of any damages sustained by going through farms and fields they would be ready to go ahead with building operations two weeks after securing franchise. As a railroad corporation they could institute condemnation proceedings against any who were obstinate but so far as known those along the proposed route are favorable.

A period of ninety days is provided for the builders to file their acceptance to the franchise after its issuance by the council and another ninety days would be necessary for the grantees to commence building operations. If the franchise were given now and the provisions complied with, it would be September 1, before steel would have to be laid. This section might conflict with the plans of the city administration in regard to paving as it is their intentions to start laying the creosoted blocks by July 1, and it would only mean a tearing up of the streets three months later, to lay the street rails.

J. D. Thorn, cashier of the Sheridan Banking company, stated that these builders had his confidence after looking over their references. "They do not offer any bonds for sale," he said, "and they are asking no donations. They want a right of way and they will furnish the money and do the rest. From the fact that they offer a guaranty bond it shows good faith and we ought to welcome them and take this opportunity."

Herbert Coffeen states that he was heartily in favor of this ground floor proposition. He thought it wise to offer liberal inducements but at the same time "to guard against any possible error that would tie us up and prevent another line from coming into the city."

4/16/10—"STREET RAILWAY FRANCHISE IS PASSED BY CITY COUNCIL—At the special meeting of the city council last night, which was attended by all the councilmen in the city, and the mayor, the ordinance granting Messrs, Albert Emanuel and William Sullivan, of Dayton Ohio, the right to construct and maintain a street railway in the city of Sheridan was considered.

The ordinance was passed by a unanimous

vote, and has been signed by the mayor, and will become effective immediately after its publication in the *Daily Enterprise* Monday.

But few changes were made in the original draft of the ordinance, and as passed, it is eminently satisfactory to both the city and the street railway builders."

6/29/10—"STREET CAR MEN MAKE GOOD BOND—William R. Sullivan, the street car builder from Dayton, Ohio, arrived in Sheridan this afternoon on passenger train No. 41. He will accept the street car franchise as promulgated some time ago and file his voluntary bond of $5,000 as an evidence of good faith and that the work will be carried out according to ordinance.

Albert Emanuel and William R. Sullivan met with the city council several weeks ago and an exhaustive study was given to the street car building plan for Sheridan and Sheridan County. They made a proposition to build a street car and interurban line from Sheridan to Kooi, an approximate distance of fourteen miles. They would route their line via Fort Mackenzie and would take in all the coal mining camps north of Sheridan. They further agreed to have at least three miles of the traction line completed within the first year.

The eastern car builders asked no subscription from local capitalists and they asked nothing from the city and county other than a free right of way over the municipal and county thoroughfares. Their proposal to furnish a bond of $5,000 was entirely voluntary on their part and was made to show their good intentions.

They were originally given sixty days from April 15th in which to either accept or reject the franchise by the city council. This time expired on June 15th, but the city council a few days previously to this time had passed a resolution extending this time to July 1. As the matter now stands the street car builders will be given ninety days from June 15th in which to start active operations."

7/7/10—"STREET CARS ARE NOW A CERTAINTY"—The two city improvements will be worked in conjunction with each other—to employ over 200 men—William R. Sullivan posted $5,000 bond and city decided to pave.

7/11/10—"WORK ON THE CAR LINE IS BEGUN THIS MORNING—The Builders Arrived in the City Yesterday Afternoon and No Time Lost in Getting to Work—Albert Emanuel and M. J.

Shaffer of Dayton, O., arrived in Sheridan yesterday afternoon and today the activity in the Sheridan street car proposition is very pronounced.

It is understood some six or eight Sheridan men are interested in this gigantic proposition and their names will go down for several shares in this initial enterprise.

Articles of incorporation are now being prepared for the formation of the Sheridan Street Railway and Traction company and will be filed in due course of time with the county clerk and secretary of state.

Steel Shipment

Today it was expected the first shipment of steel rails would be shipped from Chicago and it is understood will equal four hundred tons.

W. J. McLaughlin, of the Big Horn Timber Company, is also in the city on business connected with this company, and it is understood the contract for furnishing all ties and other timbers has been let with his company.

Everything in connection with the Sheridan street car system is progressing most favorable and as the time advanced for the active operations the outside builders and local men interested are becoming more and more enthusiastic and they claim this great venture will not be a disappointment to them or the public."

10/12/10—"DISTRIBUTION OF THE RAILS FOR THE STREET CAR SYSTEM—The Sheridan street railway agitation has received a great stimulus within the last 48 hours by the active hauling of steel rails along several streets of Sheridan. Monday, these rails were laid along Coffeen avenue as far as Illinois street and thence south on that street to Nebraska street. Today rails have been laid on Nebraska street west to Main. These are the same rails which were unloaded near the Burlington depot several weeks ago.

All tools are in Sheridan for constructing the track system. In all probability the same excavation machinery used by Contractor James Kennedy on the street paving will be used for excavation of streets outside the paving district for laying of rails and ties.

This afternoon an official inspection trip was taken over the city with the object of selecting the proposed route of the street car system The track is sure to be laid where the rails have so far been deposited.

Rails were also being laid today along Lewis street on Nielsen Heights. This street will perhaps mark the course to be pursued enroute to Ft. Mackenzie.

The steel rails to be used on the Sheridan streets weigh 70 pounds to the running yard and are about five inches high. The wooden ties to be used will be purchased from the Burlington railroad and are preserved with a zinc chloride preparation at the local tie treating plant. The excavation of streets outside the paving district will have to be made to a depth of almost a foot from the surface so as to allow the top of the rail to be on the same level.

It is estimated that at least two blocks can be laid a day after the active operations are commenced. At this rate, by the first of the new year about four miles of Sheridan's streets will thus be laid, with the street car tracks pending favorable weather conditions. Nine street cars will be ordered for December delivery in Sheridan, which will be used until the spring season opens up.

Ernest Boehme will be superintendent in charge of all construction work in Sheridan. He has only recently come to Sheridan from Kansas, where he completed a street railway for the same builders as are interested in the Sheridan project.

Albert Emanuel of Dayton, O., who is actively interested in the success and welfare of the Sheridan traction system, is also on the ground, and is one of the parties selecting the proposed car route this afternoon.''

10/13/10—''THE PLUNGE SOLD TO STREET CAR CO.—Will Be Used as a Car Barn by the Tramway People—PRICE SAID TO BE $15,000.—The Building Will Be Remodeled to Suit the Purpose to Which It Will Be Put.—A deal was consumated in Sheridan's business circles yesterday afternoon whereby the Sheridan Street Car & Electric Co. takes over the auditorium or plunge, located on Marion street on the west side of Big Goose creek, and formerly the property of E. C. Williams. The same will be used as a car barn by the tramway people, and for such purposes it will at once be remodeled. A new floor will be laid in lieu of the cement one now in place. The front partitions will be torn out to conform to the plans of the Boehme Construction Co., now in charge of all active operations for the incorporated street car company. The stipulated price which was paid for this commodious brick building is not definitely stated, but it is understood to aggregate near $15,000.

Ernest Boehme made a trip to Carneyville today on business connected with his construction company. He has been acting in conjunction with Albert Emanuel and local capitalists of Sheridan in the matter of selecting a suitable route for the street car tracks in Sheridan. The first laying of steel will occur on Coffeen Avenue, Illinois and Nebraska streets and by the time it is estimated the paving work will have advanced sufficiently to start laying the steel on Main street in conjunction with them.

The route selected to Ft. Mackenzie will be via Lewis street to the high school building and thence out to the fair grounds. From there it will turn on to Ft. Mackenzie. Instead of following the county road to Dietz a direct line will be pursued from Ft. Mackenzie.

Albert Emanuel of Dayton, O., who has been in Sheridan for the past few days, is well satisfied with the local outlook. He deemed his presence no longer required in this vicinity and departed for his home yesterday afternoon, accompanied by his wife.''

10/17/10—''THE PROBLEM OF POWER FOR STREET CAR SYSTEM—One of the Propositions Under Consideration May Involve Purchase of the Present Electric Plant.

The problem upon which Ernest Boehme, the street car man, is working at the present is the power question. Several propositions are up for consideration at this time. One of them is in taking over the Sheridan Electric Light & Power Co. and using the new plant at Dietz for furnishing the electric power, and the other is in purchasing the plant at Carneyville. Should either of these propositions fall through it will then be up to the local street car company to build a plant of its own, which undoubtedly would be built adjacent to one of the coal camps north of Sheridan, where fuel would be more accessible than to Sheridan.

Street car ties were laid along Main street this morning, and within two days the work of laying the rails will be commenced. The Kennedy street grader will do all the excavation for the Boehme Construction Co., and the work will progress southward on Main as far as Burkitt. From there they will work along Coffeen avenue to Illinois street, thence south to Nebraska and west on that street to Main. It will be necessary to excavate Main street 15 inches from the surface for the ties and rails, while the paving people will go only nine inches below the surface. The ties will not be laid upon concrete, but the necessary bed of concrete for the block pavement will be laid over their surface.

The work of laying steel will progress as fast as the streets are excavated and it is estimated that two blocks a day will be laid, all depending on favorable weather conditions."

10/24/20—"PAVING WILL CONTINUE CAR LINE FOLLOW SUIT—Motion For a New Trial of the Injunction Case Was Withdrawn Late Saturday Afternoon—So intense had become public sentiment against Dr. F. A. Hodson in his paving injunction proceedings against the City of Sheridan et al, that a general riot was narrowly averted late Saturday afternoon by the withdrawal of his motion for a new trial in the district court of Sheridan County.

Early in the day a committee of business men consulted with both the plaintiff and his counsel, Attorney J. L. Stotts, and insisted that further proceedings be immediately stopped. William Kennedy, son of Contractor Jas. Kennedy of Fargo, N. D., had received a telegram from his father ordering all operations to cease entirely. Obeying this summons to the letter, the street grader was taken from Main street, and in another day or so would have been shipped from Sheridan. So long as the injunction proceedings were on the court docket the bonds of the contractor could not be sold on Eastern markets.

Some time after *The Daily Enterprise* had gone to press, Attorney Stotts proceeded to the court house and withdrew his motion for a new trial, thus settling for all time the paving case which has been the subject of so much discussion for the past year.

Today the street grader is again on the job and is plying between Fifth and Third streets.

The street car people would likewise have received a most serious setback and it is a conjecture whether they would have pursued the work of laying rails for the street car system. They had contracted with the Kennedy people to do all necessary excavation.

Work on both the street car line and paving will now be pushed as rapidly as possible. Five additional dump carts were to be used this afternoon to aid in carrying the surface dirt away. As soon as the necessary excavation is

made a gang of men will be placed on the streets laying the ties and rails, and will be followed later by the concrete crew of the paving people.

Dr. Hodson is still being censured a great deal for his attitude against the city and it is said but for his legal injunction proceedings against the city the work would be well under way at the present time several blocks already completed. Business men and the public in general had grown tired of so much agitation to prevent Sheridan from having paved streets and they were acting almost to a man in demanding the cessation of all further proceedings. It is said the principal agitators behind Dr. Hodson are known to be men who would not have to pay one cent for the paving of Sheridan's streets and a great many people today are wondering why Dr. Hodson allowed these people to place him upon the pedestal of public opinion."

10/28/10—"STREET CAR STRIKE REMAINS UNCHANGED—Attitude of Laboring Men May Have Bearing on Continuance of the Work—

The strike of the street car laborers on Coffeen avenue remains the same this morning. It is doubtful now whether a gang of Greek laborers will be imported to continue the work of laying the rails on the side streets this fall or whether the construction company will abandon its plans in this regard until next spring. Ernest Boehme, in charge of the street car construction work, states that the rails will be laid on Main Street, however, on Main street in advance of the paving people. It is understood that the teamsters employed on the construction work on Coffeen avenue yesterday were content to work at $2.25 per day, but they were forced to discontinue work along with the remaining laborers, who struck for a 30-cent increase in wages."

3/3/11—"STREET RAILWAY ROUTE—City and Interurban Lines Announced—Route to Mines Not Determined.

Announcement is made by Ernest Boehme of the Boehme Construction company, which will have charge of constructing the new trolley line, that the route as already decided upon is as follows:

Beginning at the Inn, Fifth street to Main, south on Main to Burkitt, to Coffeen, to Illinois, to Montana, to Sumner, back along Sumner to Coffeen.

Beginning at the corner of Alger and Main, west on Alger to Lewis, along Lewis through

Nielsen Heights, to the fair grounds, to Fort Mackenzie.

Mr. Boehme states that these routes are all that have been decided upon up to the present time. The route to the mines has not been determined, and additional lines within the city limits are not contemplated at present."

4/7/11—Car line is building—2 score men on job—32 wagons on Illinois street and Montana avenue. J. W. Philips, Foreman under Superintendent Boehme.

4/11/11—"MAIN STREET NOW RESEMBLES PLOWED FIELD—RAILS LAID ON FIFTH"

4/25/11—THE HOOP IS FINISHED—"INDIAN AS FOREMAN"—"J. W. Phillips, foreman, five-eighths Cherokee—"but this does not prevent him from being an efficient foreman."

5/12/11—"Must Build Double Track" City council requiring street railway to build double track. Company petitioned to build only one track down town. Much protest against the company petition.

5/16/11—Rains delay work on railroad—work resumed today—Paving crew now 150 strong. Installation of trolley lines shifted from Main street to Nielson Heights.

5/26/11—"Cars running by July 1st—Lay Rails Up Hill."

6/23/11—"By this evening the street car company will have finished the switches at Alger Avenue and Main street crossing."

6/23/11—"Boehme Smiles When Asked When Cars Will Run" Poles up on Coffeen and Illinois. Slow work on streets—Pavers Procrastinate."

6/30/11—"Paving Gang Has Doubled—Trolley Company Stringing Wires and Rushing Work in Good Shape—Operate by August 1st."

7/21/11—"Build Across Wrench Ranch—Trolley to Follow Straight Through Line North to Dietz—New Bridges Over Mill Race and Goose Creek." Contract for Grading the Line From the Halfway House to the Dietz Camp has been awarded to E. C. Bowman."

8/8/11—"Boehme Hero of the Hour—Street Railway to be Placed in Operation Tomorrow—Cars Arrive Today."

8/11/11—"SHERIDAN JOYRIDES—TROLLEY CARS RUNNING AND EVERYBODY HAPPY—PROMISES KEPT—First Car Leaves Barn at 8:30 A. M. Wednesday—Whedon Pays First Nickel—Scatter Flowers."

"Like a child with a new toy, Sheridan turned out en-masse, Wednesday, to see her first street car. Having (_____?), listened and cheered, she climbed aboard, paid her fare and joy-rode to her heart's content. Up the line, down the line, around the loop and back again she rode. She had found something new and made the most of it.

All day long, from morning until night, the cars were filled, in some instances almost to their full capacity of a hundred people. People gladly paid just for the novelty of the ride—"to see how it worked." It was a big day for everybody, including the trolley company.

The three new cars arrived on No. 45. Tuesday afternoon, and were placed on the track Tuesday night. It meant an all-night job for Supt. Boehme and his corps of assistants, but the promise had been made that the first car would leave the barn on Alger avenue at 8:30, Wednesday morning. It did not leave the barn, the barn, the starting point being changed to Alger and Main, but it left on schedule time, which was the principal object.

After being unloaded from the flatcars which brought them in, the trolley cars were hauled to the corner of Fifth and Broadway by horses and there placed on the rails for the first time. Assisting Supt. Boehme in getting the cars ready for service—putting on lamps, fare boxes, bell cord and other apparatus—in addition to a large crew of workmen, were a number of financiers, capitalists, city officials and others prominent in the activities of the city and interested in its welfare.

Many remained until 3:30 a. m. when the first car was brought up-town and around the loop on its maiden trip, the occupants cheering and yelling like boys. Then back to the barn it went, while the weary passengers repaired to their respective home, satisfied with their night's work. Supt. Boehme was one of the last to leave, arriving home at 6 a.m., according to his own admission at least.

During the early evening a large crowd gathered in the vicinity of the depot and the Inn and watched the operations of unloading and equipping the cars. Bright and early the next morning another crowd was gathered and cheered as the car passed by.

The first car to go out in regular service at the time appointed was filled with stockholders of the company, city officials, newspaper representatives and other invited guests. In the cars following, the general public rode. At Brundage street, on the return trip, the pathfinder car discharged its load and Supt. Boehme herded a number of the passengers over to the Elks' Club, where they officially celebrated the opening of the line.

City Treasurer Whedon enjoys the distinction of paying the street railway company its first nickel. As the fare boxes were being unpacked, preparatory to being placed on the cars, he dropped a coin in the slot and rang it up. The Post representative and others followed. After the cars had been placed in service an avalanche of nickels flowed into the company's coffers all day. One of the cars registered nearly a thousand fares.

A pretty incident occurred at Coffeen and Illinois, when the official car made the trip over the line, when Mr. and Mrs. Neri Wood, who live near the corner scattered sweet peas along the track in the path of the car and presented Supt. Boehme, who rode on the front platform with a huge bouquet of fragrant flowers. Another bouquet was presented upon his return downtown.

Fort Line

While the fort line is now practically ready for service, on account of the fact that the cars in use are not furnished with double-end equipment a loop or turn-switch will have to be built at the fort before cars can be operated over it. Supt. Boehme made a trip to the end of the line, yesterday and again this morning, to look over the ground, and will have the work done within a day or two. Cars will probably be running over the line by the middle of next week.

No Schedule Yet

No regular schedule of operation will be established until the fort line is finished. Car crews on the city line have been requested to report their average running time from day to day to Supt. Boehme. It is believed that the running schedule on the city line will be fixed at about fifteen or twenty minutes, and on the fort line at about thirty minutes for the round trip.

10/24/11—"Interurban Cars Arrive—Line to Dietz to be Finished Within a Few Days—Two cars—On Side Track Near Half Way House" "Will seat 72 passengers." Speed up to 40 MPH—27 tons each."

11/24/11—"Interurban Service—First Car Over Sheridan-Dietz Line Leaves City Tomorrow Morning" 25¢ round trip fare.

12/1/11—"Camp objects to High Fare" "Trouble over fare between Sheridan and Dietz—reduction asked (25¢ each way).

12/5/11—"Rush Interurban—Cars Running to New Acme by First of Year, Under Favorable Conditions. Cuts North of Dietz." Two big cuts south and north of Dietz No. 5.—From Dietz the new line will parallel the Burlington for a distance of about 3 miles to a point half a mile or more below Dietz No. 5, then cuts across the hills to Monarch via New Acme and Carneyville."

8/5/11—"CARS TO FORT TOMORROW NIGHT—Fare Ten Cents One Way upon transfer to Fort line."

2/6/12—"Interurban Opened to Carneyville—Passengers will be transferred from one car to another at Dietz—Services to start tomorrow." Until proper arrangements are made for signalling C. B. & Q. as car crosses railroad—passengers to be transferred from car on one side of C. B. & Q. to another car on the other side. Service to Monarch probably next week.

Fares:

To Dietz, single fare 20 cents; Round trip, 35 cents

To Dietz No. 5, single fare 25 cents; Round trip, 45 cents

To New Acme, single fare 30 cents; Round trip, 55 cents

To Carneyville, single fare 40 cents; Round trip, 70 cents

2/19/12—FUNERAL OF CHILD HELD AT MONARCH—DeForrest Linn Dies at Monarch—Street Car Employed in Bringing Funeral Party to Sheridan.

—"A special car, bearing the casket and funeral cortege, left Monarch at 1 o'clock, and was met at the Great Western hotel. From there the funeral proceeded by carriages to Mount Hope cemetery, where interment was made."

2/20/12—"SEMAPHORES SOON TO BE IN ORDER—The Mechanical-Locking Signal Plant Soon to be in Operation at Dietz Crossing.

Some time during the latter part of the week the mechanical interlocking signal plant at the Dietz crossing will be put into operation, although it will take several days longer to complete all the details. For the past three weeks three experience signal men, one carpenter and three laborers, have been at work under the direction of F. W. Patterson, foreman in charge. When completed, it will be practically impossible for a car to be run down by a train. The cost of installing the plant will be about $4,000.

M. J. Fox, general supervisor of signals, arrived Sunday night from Lincoln and spent yesterday at Dietz inspecting the work. It was through his courtesy that an Enterprise man was given an understanding of the plant. A derail on the traction line on each side of the Burlington crossing makes it impossible to effect a crossing without first coming to a standstill and setting the proper signals on the main line. These signals are controlled by a system of interlocking levers, six in number, but which must be operated in numerical order. Lever No. 1 when thrown forward sets a derail in the rear of the car and makes it impossible for the car to either go forward or backward. Lever No. 2 locks lever No. 1 and at the same time sets a distance or caution signal on the main line at a distance of three thousand feet from the traction crossing on the left hand side. Lever No. 3 locks lever No. 3 and sets the distance signal three thousand feet on the right hand side of the traction crossing. Lever No. 4 locks lever No. 3 and sets one home or stop signal five hundred feet from the traction crossing. Lever No. 5 locked lever No. 4 sets the home signal on the other side of the traction crossing and sets in motion a time lock which controls lever No. 6. The time lock gives sufficient time for a train that has passed the distance signal before it was set, time to pass the traction crossing before the car can be released. As soon as the time lock which realigns the derail in front of the car and allows the car to proceed across the track. Here another derail is encountered which makes it necessary for the operator to bring all the signals back to normal position before the car can proceed.

The distance signals are controlled by electric motors, the power of which is generated from forty-eight primary batteries which are enclosed in a concrete well near the crossing.

The home signals and derails are controlled by connected pipes which are set in anti-friction rollers, which in turn are each mounted on a concrete base.

As a whole the system when complete will furnish a simple method of protection from which the human equation is practically eliminated. And no matter how careless an operator or the station wanted to be it would be impossible to effect a crossing until all the necessary precaution had been taken.

5/18/12—"COAL MINING CAMPS WANT CAR STATIONS IN"—"Say They Have to Stand Out in the Rain to Wait for Cars—Platform At Monarch."

6/5/12—"School Boy Struck By a Street Car—And David Kahn Voices Vigorous Protest Against Keeping Children off Grounds. "Little Albert Hit on Coffeen near Coffeen school. Teachers not allowing children to play on school grounds—David Kahn protests teachers' actions."

8/30/12—"Interurban Will Handle the Crowds—Burlington Unable to Furnish Extra Equipment for Labor Day Celebration." Round Trip Fare Reduced and Arrangements Made to Carry Everyone. Celebration To Be Held in New Acme."

8/31/12—"Jones New Manager of Street Railway—Present Auditor to Succeed Ernest Boehme who goes to Dayton, Ohio. David Jones, present auditor of the Sheridan Railway and Light Company will succeed Ernest Boehme as superintendent of the street car interurban system on October 1st—"

9/12/12—"THINKS THERE SHOULD BE INTER'N STATION. Sheridan Resident Believes Patrons of the Lines Would Appreciate Shelter." "Conditions along the interurban line are not what they might be," remarked a Sheridan resident yesterday. "There is no sign of a station at any of the places where the patrons of the line take their cars and the inconvenience resulting is great. The other night I was at New Acme with my wife and baby, calling on friends there.

When we saw it was time for the car to arrive we went out to the track. The car was half an hour late and it was raining. The night was pitch dark and my wife was greatly frightened. The baby's health was endangered by the exposure. I could not help wondering what a woman would do there if she were alone.

"I understand the same condition is found at every point along the line, Dietz, Carneyville and Monarch. Sheridan is little better off. If it were not for the shelter of friendly drug stores and occasional saloons the patrons of the car lines would have no place at all to go.

"In the east where the interurban lines exist a car line rents some conveniently located store room and installs a ticket office, baggage room and all the usual accessories for a car line. Patrons can find shelter and comfort here while waiting for their cars to arrive.

"It would cost very little indeed for the company to build small houses at each town for shelter and light and heat them directly from the current provided for the cars. They would soon pay for themselves in the increased satisfaction of their customers."

10/24/12—"INTERURBAN CARS IN HEAD ON CRASH. Freight Car Loaded With Shale Runs Into a Regular Car—Former was Running Extra.

Running an interurban car without the right of way caused a head end collision yesterday afternoon north of Sheridan in the neighborhood of the Wrench Ranch. An Interurban car was transporting a load of shale for the macadamizing of Fourth street and was running without the right of way trying to get into Sheridan. Superintendent D. W. Jones was personally in charge of the car. The regular interurban car was late and running to make up the time. Jones was trying to reach the city limits before the regular car could get off the city line. The two met on a curve near the Wrench ranch. Both cars were damaged but no one was injured."

12/7/12—"A group from the mines request reduced fares and threaten a boycott of Sheridan business and the interurban. Committee consisted of L. A. McCluskey, A. V. Elliott of Monarch; Joe Somers and W. L. Kness of New Acme; Robert Hotchkiss and Joe Schaal of Dietz and E. M. Bateman and Ben Snooks of Carneyville.

12/9/12—"Car Boycott is up to the Financiers—Local Street Car Officials Send Demands of the Camps to Easterners—They will Decide—Miners and the Local Officials Both Make Concessions But Cannot Agree."

12/12/12—"One Way Rate on Interurban Agreed upon. Meeting of Miners, Sheridan Business Men and Street Railway Men Last Night. Vote on Round Trip. Mining Camps Will Settle the Last Named Matter This Evening by Referendum."

12/16/12—"To Build Station on Interurban—Manager Jones Says the Road Has Them Under Construction."

12/18/12—Miners requesting Burlington cars in lieu of interurban which they boycotted after failing to reach an agreement.

1/2/13—"Street Railway Puts In New Rates. Makes Effective Lower Fares Promised in Attempt to Settle the Boycott."

Round trip fares: Monarch, 60 cents; Carneyville, 55 cents; New Acme, 45 cents; Dietz, 30 cents. Single fares: Monarch 30 cents; Carneyville, 30 cents; New Acme, 25 cents; Dietz, 15 cents. A splurg of passengers prevailed for the next several days as boycott ended.

1/14/13—"Freight, Express Service Added to Interurban. Leave packages with conductor or at office "one door south of Great Western Hotel.""

11/4/13—"Establishes High Record. Interurban Carries Nearly Fifteen Hundred in One Day. Saturday's Passenger Traffic Unusually Large—Equipment of Company Adequate to Demands."

1/2/14—"GOOD CAR TRAFFIC." "Sheridan Street Railway Carried Many Passengers."

"Unusually good business was done by the Sheridan Railway company on the Interurban line Wednesday, nearly as many passengers being carried between Sheridan and the coal camps as on the record day of the fall. Hundreds of miners were in to do their New Years's shopping and in the evening many visitors from the city attended the dedication of the new Miners' hall between Carneyville and Monarch, where speeches, refreshments and dancing comprised a program which kept the crowd amused until far after the dawn of the New Year.

Not only was Wednesday the last day of the old year, but it was payday at the mines as well, and between $40,000 and $50,000 in cash was paid out to the men for work performed during the first half of December. On account of the warm weather prevailing over much of the Sheridan territory, relatively a small amount of coal was mined during those two weeks and the payroll was correspondingly low. It will be larger for the two weeks just ended, as business has increased at all the mines."

1/17/16—"SPECIAL CAR SERVICE FOR HIGH SCHOOL STUDENTS.

Since the adoption of the single session plan in the high school, the street car company has been running the 8 o'clock fort car around the loop in order to accommodate the high school pupils. The car leaves the corner of Montana and Illinois street at about 7:55 and the Western hotel at 8:05, reaching the high school before school is called at 8:30 o'clock. The people in the south part of the city appreciate this car service and many pupils are riding to school in the morning."

2/28/19—Demands to reduce interurban rates. Company files answer that rates to Monarch should be increased.

6/1/19—"STREET CAR MAGNATE ON INSPECTION TRIP.

Albert Emanuel of New York, president of the Sheridan Railway company, is expected to arrive in Sheridan next Tuesday, coming on a trip of general inspection and to look into the matter of paving of Main street, where the paving between the tracks has been damaged by the jolting of constantly passing cars. Mr. Emanuel is just out of a hospital after two month's sickness.

David Jones, superintendent for the company here, reports that all the material is now on hand to begin this work with the exception of one car of angle bars, which has been lost in shipment from Erie, Pa., and so far has not been located thru the tracers sent out, and if there is any delay in getting to the work immediately it will be because of the lost material which is quite essential in rushing the work to completion."

10/24/19—"STREET CARS HAULING BEETS DURING NIGHT"

"Owing to a great scarcity of cars, the Burlington is putting all the cars possible from the Sugar company now that they may be used for the transportation of coal, which makes the situation quite a serious one. This has put the proposition up to the street railway company which is hauling the beets out of its district north of Sheridan. This hauling is being done at nights and will result in getting all the crop from that district to the Sugar company."

2/18/20—"7 CENT STREET CAR FARE URGED BEFORE UTILITY COMMISSION—Local Street Car Company Lost $35,000 Last Year Manager Tells Board."

"Manager D. W. Jones reports to public utilities commission and asks for increase or removal of city lines. Raise of 26 percent to motormen January 1 increased company's cost. Believed raise will be granted."

3/16/20—"Man Goes to His Death in Front of Car—Mike Zourich Killed By Interurban Car at No. 2 Station—Pit Cleaner at Roundhouse Fails to Hear Whistle And Is Run Down."

7/23/20—STREET CARS IN NEW DRESS. Standard Color of Red Being Adopted—New Emergency Truck Installed By Company.

The cars of the Sheridan Street Railway company are undergoing a new dress and when the job is completed they will all take on one standard color, the same as that now borne by the large interurban cars—red. Only one other city in the state has a street railway system and that is at Cheyenne, where the cars ply between Ft. Russell, and make no endeavor to touch the residence section like in Sheridan. With its tracks extending west to the fair grounds, north to Monarch, and south to the sugar house, Sheridan is supplied with about 18 miles of trackage, and that the service is appreciated is shown by the good business with is now being done.

Superintendent Dave Jones announces that the company has just purchased a new emergency truck which is provided with a tower for use in mishaps which may occur at any time. It is of the International truck type."

12/ /20—"FUNERAL SERVICES FOR TOMMY LYTLE. Funeral services for the late Thomas Lytle, who came to his death Sunday through an accidental fall at the city car barns, will be held Thursday afternoon at 2 o'clock at the Methodist Episcopal church conducted by Rev. E. K. Morrow. Interment will be made at Mount Hope.

The accident which caused the death of Mr. Lytle is still wrapped in mystery. He was found Sunday afternoon by a fellow employe, Charles McCoy, in an unconscious condition, at the bottom of the repair pit at the car barn. It is presumed that he tripped and fell into the pit striking on his head, as his skull was fractured. He never regained consciousness, dying twelve hours later.

Mr. Lytle was 41 years old. He had been an employe of the street car company for the last six years. He is survived by his wife, his father, J. J. Lytle of Carneyville; three sisters, Mrs. John Fairkof of Crowley, Wyo.; Mrs. D. Wilson of Casper, and Mrs. Walter Wright of Gebo; two brothers, Claude of Gebo and J. J. Jr. of Acme.''

3/16/21—"M. McKinley of Sheridan who was conductor on the interurban railway for a number of years, resigned his position one day last week, as he expects to visit the coast. He is succeeded by Joe Driear who has been conductor on the night run. Mr. McKinley has always been faithful in the performance of his duties and will be missed by a number of his friends. Joe Driear is a valuable addition to the day run as he is quite an optimist, but he will be sadly missed by the boys who frequent the evening cars and who will miss his pleasant smile. Mr. Jones is to be complimented in picking such a nice crew of conductors and motormen. The traveling public in general appreciate every courtesy shown them no matter what nationality they may be and the present crew is most satisfactory.''

Schedule of Passenger, Freight and Express Rates

EFFECTIVE MARCH 15, 1920

INTERURBAN DIVISION

Single Fares

From	To	Rate	Tax	Total
Sheridan	No. 2	7c		7c
	No. 3	15c		15c
	No. 4	20c		20c
	Dietz	20c		20c
	Dietz No. 8	25c		25c
	New Acme	30c		30c
	Model	35c		35c
	Carneyville	35c		35c
	Monarch	35c		35c

ROUND TRIP FARES

From	To			
Sheridan	Dietz	35c		35c
	Dietz No. 8	40c		40c
	New Acme	50c	4c	54c
	Model	60c	5c	65c
	Carneyville	60c	5c	65c
	Monarch	65c	5c	70c

MILEAGE BOOKS

100 Mile Book	$3.00	24c	$3.24
300 Mile Book	7.50	60c	8.10

Mileage will be collected on the following basis:

Sheridan to Dietz	5 Miles
Sheridan to Dietz No. 8	6 Miles
Sheridan to New Acme	8 Miles
Sheridan to Model	9 Miles
Sheridan to Carneyville	10 Miles
Sheridan to Monarch	11 Miles
Dietz to Dietz No. 8	2 Miles
Dietz No. 8 to New Acme	2 Miles
Acme to Model	2 Miles
Model to Carneyville	2 Miles
Carneyville to Monarch	2 Miles

No Ride Less Than 2 Miles

SCHOOL CHILDREN'S RATES

Good on School Days Only.

From	To		Round Trips
Dietz	Sheridan	20c	20c
Dietz No. 8	"	25c	25c
New Acme	"	30c	30c
Model	"	35c	35c
Carneyville	"	35c	35c
Monarch	"	40c	40c

Excursion rates for parties of 25 or more at one time to one point by special arrangement as follows:

From	To		
Sheridan	Dietz	25c	25c
	Dietz No. 8	35c	35c
	New Acme	35c	35c
	Model	45c	4c	49c
	Carneyville	45c	4c	49c
	Monarch	50c	4c	54c

Children under six years of age free when accompanied by parents or guardian. Children between six and twelve half of regular single trip fares.

CITY DIVISION

All City Fares	7c
Children 6 to 12 years old	5c
Tickets Sold, 4 for	25c

FREIGHT AND EXPRESS RATES
EFFECTIVE MARCH 15, 1920

Wyoming Public Utilities Order No. 143.

INTERURBAN DIVISION
Express on Regular Cars

CLASS NO. 1
GENERAL MERCHANDISE

1	to	20 pounds	15c	1c	16c
20	to	35 "	20c	1c	21c
35	to	50 "	25c	2c	27c
50	to	65 "	30c	2c	32c
65	to	80 "	35c	2c	37c
80	to	100 "	40c	2c	42c

40c per 100 pounds thereafter with above scale for fractions of 100 pounds

CLASS NO. 2
Furniture, Stoves, Carpets, Trunks, Glassware and light bulky merchandise

1	to	20 pounds	25c	2c	27c
20	to	35 "	30c	2c	32c
35	to	50 "	35c	2c	37c
50	to	65 "	40c	2c	42c
65	to	80 "	45c	3c	48c
80	to	100 "	50	3c	53c

50c per 100 pounds thereafter with above scale for fractions of 100 pounds

CLASS NO. 3
Milk in Cans. Tickets Sold as Follows:

5 gallon can	20c	1c	21c
8 gallon can	25c	2c	27c
10 gallon can	30c	2c	32c

Tickets provide for free returns of empty cans to shipping point

CLASS NO. 4
Ice Cream in Freezers or Packers

3 gallon packer	25c	2c	27c
5 gallon packer	40c	2c	42c
10 gallon packer	60c	3c	63c

Tickets include free return of packers to shipping point

All shipments must be accompanied by bill of lading showing exact weight of shipment.

All packages to be marked plainly with destination and consignee. All shipments are accepted subject to being met at destination by consignee. Unless orders are given at time of shipment, for return of goods when not met by consignee, shipments will be left on platform at destination.

FREIGHT RATES

All freight on flat cars 10c per 100 pounds Minimum car load rate $10.00.   Tax 3 per cent

Stanley A. Kuzara
21 S. Jefferson
Sheridan, Wyoming

Sheridan Railway Co.

SHERIDAN, WYOMING

—

Schedule of Passenger, Freight and Express Rates

IN EFFECT ON AND AFTER
MARCH 15, 1920

—

AS PER WYOMING PUBLIC SERVICE
COMMISSION ORDER 143

—

"Service With Safety"

6/14/21—"STREET CAR SITUATION IS UNCHANGED, OFFICIALS SAY. No Apparent Intent to Seek to Give Up Service in Sheridan Has Been Noted, Is Report.

No change was in evidence today in the situation that resulted yesterday when the City Council declined upon petition of voters to grant the Sheridan Railway Company permission to abandon its service on that part of its line which goes through seven blocks of Sumner street and two blocks of Montana street.

Directors of the organization are formulating plans for action, but have not named a definite time for meeting when plans will be announced. Superintendent Dave Jones said. However, it was stated authoritatively this afternoon that the meeting will be held within the next few days.

As the situation stands today the car company is ready to petition the Public Service Commission for permission to vacate its tracks on the two streets named. This was the decision announced yesterday by Superintendent Jones and which he said this afternoon remained unchanged.

There is no apparent intention to ask to abandon the street car service in Sheridan, as far as could be learned today, after careful investigation.

Disinterested parties, appreciating the fact that the street car company is entitled to relief, have suggested that amicable service could be given patrons of the car company if one of its two cars were abandoned and only one car run over the line, make the loop on Sumner street as it now does. It would be possible for the car to give at least 25-minute service, it is claimed.

Whether there is any disposition on the part of the tramway company to work out such a schedule has not been determined."

4/25/22—"Mr. and Mrs. James Catterall with the formers brother Charles of Monarch were Sheridan callers Saturday.

Miss Lila Wade of Monarch attended morning services at the Christian church in Sheridan Sunday.

As there is no 7 o'clock interurban, the McKinley bus line leaves Sheridan every morning at 6 o'clock, reaches Monarch at 6:50 and at 7 starts back to Sheridan by way of all mining villages. At Monarch the stopping place is in front of the store, likewise at Dietz No. 8, and Kleenburn. Its schedule is every two hours, same as formerly the interurban."

12/5/22—"MINER DODGES LOAD OF COAL, DIES UNDER TROLLEY'S WHEELS.

John Sikora, 54, was instantly killed about 4:30 o'clock yesterday at the Monarch mine, when in dodging a carload of coal on the mine track he stepped in front of a trolley car of the Sheridan Railway company on the track adjacent and was run over. The man was known to have been hard of hearing and his death was declared by mine officials to have been entirely accidental.

He sustained a fractured skull. An inquest will be held at 2 o'clock this afternoon at the Reed mortuary, which has charge of the body. No funeral arrangements have been made. Ed Ferguson was conductor of the car which ran over him and Harry Beck was motorman.

Sikora had been in this country about 15 years and had worked at the Monarch mine of the Sheridan-Wyoming Coal company for that time. He leaves a widow and two children in Austria, his native country, and a half-brother, John Bury, also of Monarch, is the only relative he has in this country."

6/8/23—"SHERIDAN RAILWAY ADOPTS 15-MINUTE STREET SCHEDULE." "Superintendent Dave Jones of the Sheridan Street Railway company, announced Thursday that beginning Friday, the cars operating between the Sheridan Inn and the corner of Montana avenue and Illinois street will leave each point on the quarter-hour instead of on the half-hour, as in the past. This will give double the number of

trips, and the last car will leave each point at 10:15 p.m. instead of 9:30 p.m.

The mine cars will leave on the even hours as heretofore during the morning, but during the afternoon and evening they will leave on the odd hours.

There will be no change in the service of cars operating between town and the United States Veterans hospital at Fort Mackenzie.

The cars will operate over the same lines as in the past."

9/11/23—"START JUNKING OF TRAM TRACK. Bus Franchise Petition Being Heard as Railway Tears Up Line. Announcement that junking of the city tracks of the Sheridan Street Railway company, had been authorized by the Public Service Commission was made at the regular meeting of the city council Monday morning. Hearing for the franchise to the Sheridan Motor Bus company before the State public service commission is on in Cheyenne.

The point of beginning the work is at the intersection of Main and Burkitt streets and workmen started operations east from this point Monday morning. A date for the discontinuance of Main street service from Alger street has not been set, it was announced. Service will be maintained on Main street south of Alger Avenue as long as the tracks are intact, E. C. Gwillim, city engineer, stated.

M. W. Woodard of the Warren Construction company announced that as the street car track is removed and the storm sewer laid, workmen on those jobs will be followed by the paving squad. A considerable quantity of material is now on the ground ready to begin Main street paving, he said. Main street will be given the preference over other paving districts.

The bond and contract of the Warren Construction company was approved by both parties.

The protest of property owners against the paving of Thurmond street from Burkitt to Brundage was referred back to the city clerk for determinating the legality of the signatures.—"

9/12/23—"The work of tearing up the street car tracks on Main street is progressing at the rate of one block each day. Tuesday, the first day of the work, both the rails and the concrete pavement between the rails was taken up from the east property line of Main street at Burkitt to the intersection of Works street."

10/7/23—"Two large automobile busses intended for use on Sheridan streets and manufactured by the White automobile company, were reported as being tied up at Casper by the washout at Cole creek, by Mr. Tarrant Saturday. It is understood they will be offered to the Sheridan Railway and Light company, which has applied to the city for a charter to run busses on the streets. D. W. Jones, manager of the Street Railway company, went to Denver and eastern cities a few weeks ago to look at various makes of automobile trucks and get estimates on the cost of enough cars to fill the transportation needs of Sheridan."

10/9/23—"Two competing motor bus lines may operate in Sheridan, it was disclosed at the city council meeting when ordinances granting permission to the Sheridan Bus company and R. C. Tarrant were introduced."

10/11/23—"First Bus Line Started in City. Tarrant Concern Starts Operation of Motor Carriers on Streets."

10/31/23—"Single Interurban Car Track is Completed. Interurban cars, marooned from the car barns on Alger avenue for nearly ten weeks owing to the removal of the double line of tracks on Main street between Alger avenue and Little Goose bridge, were ready to be run into the barns Wednesday with the completion of the single track on Main street. Laying of the track, which completed the circuit to be used hereafter by the Sheridan Railroad & Light Company, was finished at an opportune moment, for the cars were badly in need of overhauling. Other cars from the barns are to be pressed into service at once while the cars previously in use are being overhauled.

Cars have stood each night at the Little Goose bridge while the track was torn up. Vandals have looted them repeatedly to steal electric light globes from them, it is said.

Interurban cars to the mining camps are to be loaded with freight at the corner of the Alger avenue and Main street when the regular service is restored."

11/11/23—"Ten Minute Bus Route Planned—Two Lines Put in Operation From Sheridan Inn to Montana Avenue—2 Buses—To use Main Street after paving—Tarrant Bus line—Also east and west on Loucks."

3/24/24—"Mackenzie Car Service Inadequate, Charge of Commandant at Hospital—Fort Had Only 10 Days of Service in Winter, Soper Tells Clubmen"—"D. W. Jones, General manager of the Railway and Light company, has informed the Commercial Club that the directors of the trolley company will meet soon to take action, it was announced."

3/31/24—"Fort Bus Line Adequate, Club Men Told Here—Mackenzie Commandant Thanks Business Men" for quick action—"

9/2/24—"Tom Broderick, 34 former street car conductor commits suicide"—was employed at Fort Mackenzie nursing staff and had just returned from vacation in Calif."

10/21/24—"LAST REMNANT OF STREET CAR SYSTEM IS GONE." "The last reminder of the days when Sheridan boasted of a street car system began to vanish Tuesday as the city started cutting down the tall iron posts along Main street that once supported the trolley wires.

The city has entered into an agreement whereby it becomes the owner of the posts if it takes them down, it was announced at the city hall.

The posts were being cut with an acetylene torch, and the holes in the sidewalk will be filled with concrete."

9/2/25—"Sheridan Street Car Hearing Will Start At Cheyenne, Sept. 3." "Cheyenne, Wyo., Sept. 2—The hearing of the application of the Sheridan Street Railway Company for a certificate of public convenience and necessity authorizing abandonment of interurban service which is to be conducted by the Wyoming public service commission, will open here Thursday morning.

Some protests have been received against the granting of certificates, it is understood, two of the protests coming from the United Mine Workers of America and from the Holly Sugar company."

4/28/26—"State's Last Electric Line Doomed—Plans For Bus Line to Mines Are Completed And Service Will Start Saturday Morning—Survey Shows Great Amount of Money Lost on Project Since First Railway Was Established."

Last trip to be made Apr. 30. Line in city closed in 1924—represented investment of about $360,000. 30-40 percent of investment by local people and remainder of Dayton, Ohio. Albert Manuel of Dayton, Ohio, President. Company burdened by heavy paving assessment."

4/22/26—"BUS LINE GRANTED PERMISSION TO RUN TO MINING CAMPS HERE. Sheridan Street Railways Granted Authority To Abandon Car Lines Because of Great Loss. Cheyenne, April 22—(AP)—The Wyoming public service commission today granted a permit to Robert W. Gart, owner of the Sheridan City Motor Bus lines, to operate an interurban bus service between Sheridan and surrounding coal camps west of the city. At the same time the commission issued permission to the Sheridan Street Railway company to abandon its Sheridan Coal camp lines. The bus line will be 12 mile long.

A permit to operate an electric light and power plant at Thermopolis also was granted the Monument Hill Electric company—

The Sheridan Street Railway company sought to abandon its interurban lines because its operations, according to the commission's reports, showed a deficit of approximately $177,000 in its 1925 financial statement. In 1924 the trolley company abandoned its lines in the city and its service between Sheridan and Fort Mackenzie, the bus company then commencing its transportation operations. When the company petitioned to abandon its interurban service, protests were filed by two local unions of the United Mine Workers of America and the central labor union of Sheridan, but the protests were withdrawn when it was proposed to supplant the street railway with a motor bus service. The service will run between Sheridan and Dietz, Acme and Monarch, the latter all coal camps."

6/6/26—"City Buys Two Bridges of Sheridan Street Railway—One across Big Goose at Dietz and one across same creek at the Hotchkiss Mine—each 60 feet.

SO ENDETH THE SHERIDAN TROLLEY!!

4/14/32—"Tom Newman Dies In State. Former Conductor On Street Car Line Dead in Thermopolis.

1/2/39—"Car Rails Removed From Streets Here—Work toward improving the streets of Sheridan was under way this week as Art Swickard, city street and water commissioner started a crew of men tearing out the ancient and long unused street car rails on North Main, Alger, Lewis, Coffeen and Sumner using WPA and city crews."

Sheridan Press, May 20, 1957 "Sheridan's Street Railroad Hauled Just About Everything In Its Heyday."

"Sheridan's electrically operated street railway was born in 1911, and during its time hauled everything from people to sugar beets. According to Tracy Allen, former employee of the line, the line operated an interurban, city, Ft. Mackenzie, and a freight haul service.

Interurban service involved Sheridan to Monarch. The whole system was built in 1911, and the interurban system had rolling stock consisting of 10 cars, eight passenger cars, and two freight cars. It ran from the Great Western hotel to Monarch an hour each way. A round trip took two hours, and nine trips were made each day.

The men worked 10 hours one day and eight the next for an average of nine hours per day. They were paid 54 cents per hour, and this included Sundays and holidays. Interurban charge was five cents to the city limits and 40 cents to Monarch, which made about three and one-third cents per mile. Mileage books were sold at two and one-half cents per mile.

On the city line, two cars operated from the Sheridan Inn to Montana Avenue. There was a double track on Main street and the cars passed every 15 minutes, one each way. Cars on that run worked 18 hours per day, and the fare was five cents straight.

The Fort Line started at Alger and Main street, went west to the fairgrounds and then north to Ft. Mackenzie. The trip took 30 minutes each way, and the fare was 10 cents. It was possible to buy 11 tickets for a dollar.

The freight haul included coal, sand and gravel, red shale, and sugar beets. The line handled all the sand and gravel that went into three miles of paving laid one year in Sheridan by the Warren Construction Company. When Main was paved to fourth street with red shale the line handled that too.

Beets were loaded into cars from a dump at the fairgrounds and were taken to the mill on a spur from Montana and Illinois streets.

A big sugar beet dump was located at the Wrench Ranch then were loaded on Burlington cars there, but the electric railway pulled the cars from the ranch to the Fort spur where the cars were transferred to the Burlington for transportation to the sugar mill.

According to Allen the city line and Fort

line were discontinued in 1922, and the interurban line was closed 31 years ago this month.
The freight haul went out with the interurban.

Emanuel and Sullivan of New York headed
the operation, but a number of local people held
stock in the company. D. W. Jones was general
manager and is now auditor for the same company in New York.

Thirteen motormen and conductors were
employed on the line. Allen started with the
company in 1913 or 1914 and quit in 1923.

Allen attributed the coming of the automobile to the demise of the electric line. Cable
used to operate the line came down in 1926.
Two of the posts are still in use, however, at the
Bank of Commerce. These are the posts used to
hang the large banners.

Last year during paving on Main street workmen dug up old ties once part of the line, and
four ties still remain on one of the streets to the
hospital.

"NO CHARGE FOR RIDING ON TOP OF
CAR" by Patty Ogan, Sheridan, Wyoming. *Star
Tribune*, Casper, Wyo., March 31, 1974.

"SHERIDAN—In 1909, the Sheridan Railroad and Light Company was granted a franchise
to operate a street car in Sheridan and to run the
cars to the coal mines.

Joe Drier was in on it from the very beginning. This is his story: "I went to work laying
track for the interurban in 1910. By the end of
the year I broke in as conductor. Before the
company went out of business, I worked my
way up from employ No. 28 to No. 3.

The interurban track started at the depot on
Main Street and ran 12 miles to Monarch. There
were seven mines between Sheridan and the end
of the line. They were Dietz No. 7, Dietz No. 8,
Hotchkiss, New Acme, Model, Car(n)eyville, and
Monarch. (The Kooi Mine and a few others were
beyond Monarch, so those miners came that far
to ride into town).

A car left every hour for the mines, from six
a.m. till midnight. The trip took an hour out and
an hour back.

I remember on pay days we ran three cars to
the mines because the people really came to
town on pay day!

Why, on one car I collected 165 fares, and
that didn't count those riding on the top. There
was no charge for riding the top of the car.

Two cars ran around the city every 15
minutes. They left the depot on Main Street,
looped through the southern part of town down

to Montana Avenue, and back to Main. The
route then went down Main to 5th Street,
around the Sheridan Inn and the Railroad depot,
then back to the depot. It took about a half-
hour for the full trip.

During the sugar beet campaign, there was a
special car which ran from Montana on out to
the sugar factory. We took one shift out and
brought the other shift in.

There were also two fort cars, one running
every hour from six till midnight. At that time,
the fort wasn't a hospital. Oh, there was the
ordinary infirmary, but Fort Mackenzie was an
army post with some of the old regular army
stationed there.

There was one other special interurban. It
ran morning and night, taking kids to and from
school in town. Then, there were more people
living in the mining towns than were in Sheridan.

To ride in town cost five cents, and you got
on or off wherever you wanted . . . the fare was
the same. Fare to the fort was 25 cents.

Children under six rode free, 6-12 for one-
half price. Dogs and baby buggies rode for 10
cents each. Dogs rode in the baggage compart-
ment or on the passenger's lap, if the other
passengers had no objections.

Round trip tickets to the mines ranged from
35-65 cents. In 1918 rates were increased from
3-5 cents, with increased coal and timber prices
given as the reason for the increases.

There were 28 employes, including track-
men, motormen, and conductors. We all got 25
cents an hour and worked a straight nine hour
shift. No lunch hours or coffee breaks then.

We belonged to a union, the Amalgamated
Association of Street and Electric Railway Employes of America. In 1913, through union
negotiations, we were granted a five cent an
hour raise.

In 1915 I had what the newspaper called a
'narrow escape from serious injury.' The car was
on Fourth Street and lightning struck the trolley
wire, followed the wire down to the control
box, and blew it out.

I remember feeling a numbness and seeing
fire all around me, but I wasn't injured.

I have another old newspaper clipping that
tells about an incident involving my brother, Ed
Drier. He was working for the interurban too.
His car was coming down North Main when a
team of horses, hitched to a milk wagon, ran
down the center of the track directly toward the

car. Ed put the car in reverse and the driver caught his team and pulled it over just before they collided. There were milk bottles and cans all over!

The street cars would occasionally jump the tracks. Then we had an iron tool we called a frog, similar to a jack, and we would jack the car up and back onto the track. Passengers got jostled up a bit, but I don't remember any of them ever being hurt.

We had other little problems. On one occasion, the cars were held up for a while because a horse got its shoe caught in the track. A blacksmith had to come free the shoe and the horse before the car could continue.

On Oct. 20, (That is right, isn't it, Mother?) 1919, I married Raymonde Z. Zoutte. She was born and raised in France. Her father had come here to mine coal.

In that same year, Dietz No. 7 shut down, putting 200 men out of work. The reason given was "an over supply of coal at the present time."

Up to this time, the mines had been individually owned. In 1926, Peabody coal purchased the mines and brought in large cutting machines. These machines would go in and cut a whole load of coal at a time.

Many men were laid off and there weren't enough passengers to support the line. People were beginning to get automobiles.

On June 25, 1926, the Acme Rotary Plant ran 11½ hours and closed down. On July 2, 1926, the Sheridan Rotary Plant ran for the last time, marking the end of the Sheridan Railroad and Light Co. It ran for 4½ hours, producing 200 k.w. I had Mel Knapp get those dates and figures and I figured some day, I might want to know that information.

I've kept all these old pictures, tickets, schedules, and newspaper clippings. Yes, this is a story I've been wanting to tell for a long time." Joe Drier was born in Boulder, Colorado, and moved to Sheridan in 1903. He worked as a sheep shearer before working for the railroad.

Following the closing of the railroad, Drier took up the carpenter trade. He worked for the government at Fort Mackenzie as head carpenter for 31 years.

In 1959, he retired and went into cabinet work on his own. His home is filled with handmade furniture. He will soon be 82."

Sheridan Street Car—After some fifty years, it was discovered that there remained a very dilapidated former Sheridan street car sitting in a field near town. As a Bi-centennial project, a group of mighty dedicated people including Jerry Buckley, Louis Poulus and Joe Drier, one of the original conductors undertook the ambitious project to reconstruct the old car. After an almost superhuman effort, this car is the result and now is on display in Sheridan as a reminder of the old days.

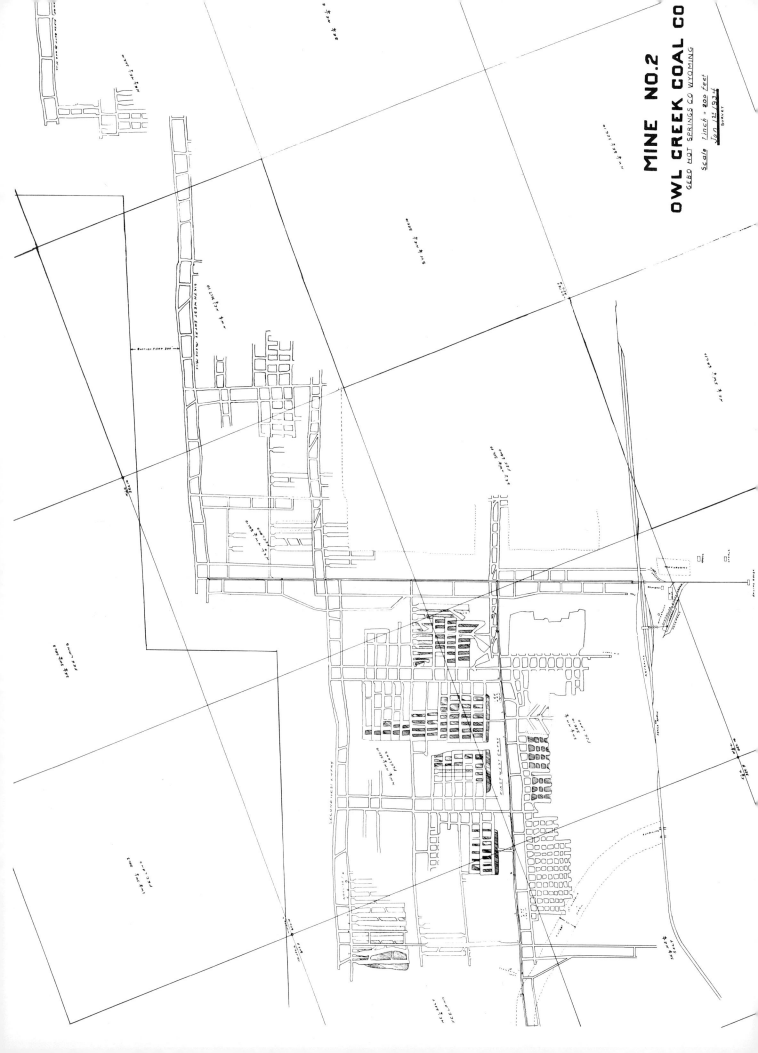

MINE NO.2
OWL CREEK COAL CO
GEBO HOT SPRINGS CO WYOMING

Scale 1 inch = 200 feet

Jan 12/1934
Survey

Chapter 4

The Mine

The underground mine was either an incline slope from the outside to the vein of coal or a shaft straight down from the surface to the coal. From that point, the pattern of the main entries and side entries would resemble a tree with its main trunk and branches, except that parallel to the main entry, there would be another one called the "butt" entry, the main object being for return circulation of air, and if the main entry should cave in, as sometimes would or could happen, this could serve as an alternate escape route. A third escape route usually was also available up the air shaft by ladder.

From the main entry, the side entries would branch out both left and right. From an entry heading north, for example, the first branch heading west would be called "First West"; the first entry extending east, of course, would be called "First East," and so on. The point at which a side entry would turn off the main entry, would be called a "parting." A "Room" was at the end of one of the branches and consisted of a larger area where the "diggers" or "loaders" recovered the coal, and the front wall of coal was the "Face."

Primitively, the diggers, working in their respective rooms would pick into the face at floor level, removing the coal in bits as far as the handle of the pick would permit, from right to left, undercutting a strip the width of the face. They would then, breast high, using a drill about two inches in diameter and about six feet long, drill six holes into the face, each some distance apart. In each hole, separately, a metal rod about one-fourth inch in diameter and about seven feet long would be inserted. This rod was called a "needle." Black powder, rolled in usually newspaper about the size of a stick of dynamite, would then be inserted in the very rear end of the hole, then by using some of the coal dust resulting from the drilling, and by mixing this with the correct amount of water, this mixture was firmly packed in to form a firm base for the explosive. The needle would then be removed leaving a very narrow passageway extending back to the location of the powder charge. The digger would then place a "Squib" in the hole left by the removed needle, light the squib, and run for the nearest parting. The squib, an early form of jet propulsion, would then sizzle, and in the manner of a jet, would propel itself to the rear of the hole thereby igniting the powder charge resulting in an explosion loosening the coal. The operation was repeated in each of the drilled holes, and as this was usually the last operation of the day, all of the loose coal lying on the floor was ready for loading the following day.

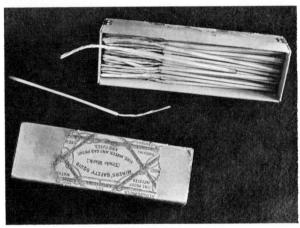

Some squibs.

As the coal was loaded into a mine car, the car was then pulled by a horse or mule by a "Driver" to a parting from which point, it was pulled by an electric motor which picked up cars along the way, forming a train by the time it reached the tipple. In some mines, the slope was so gradual that the motor would pull the cars of coal to the tipple, while in some mines, the slopes were too steep for the motor and the cars were pulled up the slope by a cable pulled by a hoist. In those mines having a shaft, the cars were raised individually in a cage.

As improvements were made, the tedious, back-breaking task of undercutting the face of

THE AUTHOR DEMONSRATING THE EVOLUTION OF THE COAL MINER'S LAMP AND CAP.

The candle

The oil lamp

The carbide

The electric and hard hat

At first, the only light the miners had to work by consisted of simply a candle or candles fitted into a holder which contained a pointed pick and which was designed to stick into a timber or whatever, but also contained a hook for hanging to the face of the miner's soft cap which had a metal face designed to accommodate the candle (or lamp). It is doubtful if this type of light was ever used in the Dietz mine as by this time, there was introduced the oil burning lamp containing a wick which fit also on the face of the miner's cap. While this was an improvement over the candle, it still gave off very little light. A further improvement was made when the carbide lamp came into being. It too was designed to fit on the miner's soft cap. With water acting in a controlled manner on carbide at the base of the lamp, acetylene gas was generated and upon being lighted by a spark created with a corrugated wheel rubbing on flint, the flame coming out of a burner with a reflector behind it providing a great deal more light than previous lamps. Later and finally the electric light was developed using a battery carried on one's back. The introduction of this coincided with required use of the "hard hat," and of course, was a vast improvement over any previous type of light.

Miner's hand drills (into the drilled hole was placed the black powder for shooting down coal).

"Dooley" drill were introduced. About 1928 saw the introduction of the "Joy" automatic loader. This machine practically eliminated the human loader, mechanically loading the coal into the cars.

the coal with a pick, was later replaced by a "cutting machine." This machine, usually powered by electricity and operated by one man would undercut the coal about six feet deep and about three feet wide. The machine would then be pulled out and reset for another cut adjacent to the previous cut, until the width of the face was completely undercut. This in and out process was called "sump and re-sump." A later improvement in the cutting machine eliminated the sump and resump, and would cut across the face with only one insertion.

About 1926, an improvement was made in the drilling of the shot holes, by using a electronically powered drill. As the cutting machine operator went from room to room undercutting the coal, he was followed by the hole driller. Each of these men was usually paid by the room completed. It was about 1926 also when the electrically powered cutting machine and

A typical miner's lunch bucket (in two sections—the bottom for water or coffee and the top for the lunch); an old fashioned original miner's light (a candle); the later oil burner; and the next generation, the carbide lamp. (The latest, the battery-operated electric light and the required hard hat not shown).

Miner's Safety Lamp—Used by the Fireboss who preceded the miners to detect the presence of gas with the use of this lamp.

	SHERIDAN WYOMING COAL COMPANY 42 Mine - Acme Wyo.							

List of horses used in mine. (This book contains the names, cost and disposition of all horses in each of the six mines owned by the Sheridan, Wyoming Coal Company in 1920-1921. One page shown here.)

As the mining of coal became more sophisticated with the introduction of improved machines, so the operation of the machines became more complex. By the 1940's the shooting down of coal by the use of the powder shot was replaced by "Cardox" and "Airdox."

A resume of the underground mining of coal in the 1940's is related in some detail by Tom Legerski who, while working at the Monarch, Wyoming mine, completed a course in the use of both the "Cardox" and "Airdox," and after graduating, became a licensed "shot firer." He describes the operation as follows:

TOM LEGERSKI'S DESCRIPTION OF IMPROVED METHODS OF SHOOTING COAL

"Each crew consisted of the following:
One foreman
One cutmachine operator and two helpers
One drill operator and one helper
One Cardox carrier
One shotfirer
One top trimmer
One sprinkler
One electrician or mechanic
One loading machine operator and one helper

One loading point operator
Two motormen and two brakemen (called Nippers)
Two shuttle cars, one operator for each car.
If the ceiling needed support, it took two or three additional men to do that work, these men were called timbermen.
If additional track needed to be laid, it took up to four men to do that job. These were called tracklayers.
Now I will begin with the time the shift begins:
The miners waited at the bath house for a train which was called the mantrip. This mantrip transported the miners to their destination and back to the bathhouse.
Before the whistle blew, each crew gathered in to their mantrip and waited for the whistle to

blow, after which the mantrip proceeded with its load of workers. Some of the crews travelled as far as four miles to their destination. There was a mantrip for each crew and consisted for four cars, and travelled about five miles per hour. Each man was paid from the time the whistle blew to the time he returned to the bathhouse.

Each crew had its own function and operated as follows:

First of all, the cutmachine crew moved into their location to undercut the coal. This machine was powered by electricity of 440 volts. It had a nine foot cutter bar containing a series of high grade steel bits.

After the cutting machine men completed their job, they moved the machine to another location. The drillers then moved in and drilled the required holes. This machine was also powered by electricity and gave the appearance of a cannon on four tires. The holes having been drilled, the Cardox carrier came in carrying on his shoulders the necessary amount of Cardox shells to shoot the coal in that location.

The shotfirer then came in, wired the Cardox shells, installed them into each hole, tied the wires together and connected it to a cable long enough to extend around a corner. After attaching the cable to a magneto, he would twist the handle and the shots were fired. As each location had both a lower row and an upper row of holes, it was customary to fire the lower row first. It took from ten to fifteen Cardox shells for each location. A "location" could be a room, entry or a crosscut.

A Cardox shell was a tube made of a high grade of steel. It was about four feet long, weighed 38 pounds and the diameter was about the size of a beer can. It contained a certain type of gas which was highly explosive and was ignited by a heater inside the tube. To ignite the heater, it took a very small current of electricity generated by a magneto. The shell itself had an area about six inches long on the edge of the shell. This area had a number of holes about one-half inches in diameter through which the explosive was emitted. The holes were at an angle for the more efficient shooting of the coal.

After the Cardox shells were fired, they were referred to as "empties" and were gathered up and returned to the cardox shop outside of the mine for refilling. They were transported in and out of the mine in a special car lined with rubber and were refilled and reused a number of times.

Later, the company elected to use another system in which to replace the Cardox shells. This system was called "Airdox."

The Airdox system was a tube made of high grade steel, was about nine feet long, weighed about 50 lbs., and was the same in diameter as the Cardox.

Air compressors were installed in the mine, which were capable of compressing 10,000 lbs. of pressure for each tube that was used in the mine. The air was supplied from the compressor room to a certain distance from the active place through a triple-strength ¾ inch steel pipe with copper gaskets in every joint. From the pipe to the active place, a triple-strength copper tubing was used. When the copper tubing became brittle, it had to be replaced.

Within a certain distance from where the shots were fired, the shotfirer had a valve which he opened to inject the 10,000 lbs. of air pressure in to the Airdox tube. After the tube was full, there was a relief valve on the same valve unit which was used to fill the tube, and when the relief valve opened, a plunger in the tube released the 10,000 lbs. of air pressure through small holes at the end of the tube and caused the coal to be shot out. There was no smoke from the Airdox. This system eliminated the Cardox carrier.

After the shotfirer completed his job in a location, another man came in. He was the "Trimmer." He had a coal pick and brought down all the loose coal off the top and sides making it safe for the other men following.

The trimmer was then followed by a "Sprinkler" carrying a water hose who could usually use a considerable quantity of water to sprinkle down the dust.

Then came the loading machine and loaded the coal into shuttle cars which were run by a large battery and which weighed 1,000 lbs., and were changed at lunch time and put on a charger in the battery station in the mine. The shuttle car was operated by one man hauling the coal from the loading machine to a machine called the loading point. The loading point conveyed the coal from the shuttle car to the mine cars which then hauled the coal to the outside tipple. There were sixteen cars in a unit and each car held about 4 tons of coal.

If a crew loaded 300 cars of coal a day, they were considered doing a good job.

The underground coal mining was hard work, the coal miners respected each other and maintained safety to the best of their ability and enjoyed the work underground.

Below is a sketch of a Cardox and an Airdox shell:

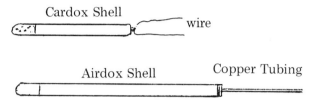

Cardox Shell

wire

Airdox Shell   Copper Tubing

Note: One Airdox shell could be used a number of times before going to the shop. The Airdox also eliminated the cardox shop."

* * * * *

Some of the positions in the mine included the "Trapper." This group generally consisted of the very young workers, sometimes as young as fourteen years of age. They were paid a much lower wage, usually about one-third the usual hourly rate. Their functions were to keep the horses from running into each other, as the horses did not have headlights, and the only light came from the driver's lamp some distance behind the horses, and their visions naturally somewhat limited. In addition to directing traffic, they also cleaned the track of debris. (If this function was taken over by anyone of a higher classification in the absence of a trapper as sometimes happened, that person was paid the wage of his position). During this period, the trapper was becoming acquainted with the mine.

A Trapper would usually "graduate" to the position of a "Nipper" and act as a conductor for a Motorman. It was the nipper who had so-called charge of a train of coal, flagging and giving directions to the motorman. A sort of "traffic director."

The "Motorman" was the operator of the heavy electric motors which functioned as the engine to maneuver the cars of coal and haul the trains of cars to the outside, switching the cars as required.

The "Digger" referred to earlier, customarily worked with a "partner." Frequently, such partners remained with each other for years. It was not too unusual for partners to be father and son combinations. The diggers were paid by the weight of the coal they produced and loaded. Inasmuch as the coal had to be removed as the entry was being extended, and also when "cross cuts" and "slants" were being made, the men

employed to perform this were generally paid by the yard of coal (distance).

The "Drivers" responsibility was to supply the diggers with empty cars and to remove the filled cars from the rooms and take them to the parting to be picked up by the motors. These cars were pulled by horses or mules operating beyond reach of the motors.

The "Barn Boss" was in charge of all the horses and mules. (Sometimes, especially in earlier days, all horses and mules were kept inside the mine throughout their lives, but later, due to certain laws passed, it was required that they be brought out periodically). All mines, however, did have regular barns inside the mine.

A "Water Monkey's" job was to water down the dust in the mine. Dust was a great hazard for not only was it injurious to a miner's health but it was highly volatile when allowed to accumulate in the air. In order to reduce the danger of explosions, constant attention was given to watering down the dust in the mine. Many years later, numerous miners received disability benefits through their Union organization for so-called "black lung," a residual lung condition resulting from years of breathing coal dust, and many widows of those miners continue to receive benefit checks.

The "Fire boss"—it was his responsibility to check the air and fire safety in the mine. Each week, the fireboss would check all the entries and the face with an anomometer to determine the cubic feet of air and make proper adjustments as required. The correct amount of fresh air, of course it goes without saying, was absolutely necessary for the health and safety of the workers. The fresh air was forced into the mine by huge fans usually set somewhere above the center of the area, and within the mine itself with the current being controlled by a series of doors and canvases. The fire boss also preceded the miners each morning carrying with him a "safety lamp." This lamp was specially designed to burn a particular fuel, probably a naphtha, burning with a small blue flame and contained in a small chamber in the lamp. This chamber was punctuated with some 1729 to the square inch exceedingly minute apertures so fine that the flame would not ignite any gas which might be present. Any change of color of the flame to a yellow or if the flame developed a "cap," it would indicate a presence of gas and if the flame had a tendency to go out, it would indicate a presence of black damp or a lack of oxygen, and preventative measures were immediately taken to correct the deficiency before the miners were allowed to enter.

Gas was a dangerous element in any mine and the cause of many fires and explosions, while black damp was dangerous to the miners in that, without any scent or other indication, it was fatal to anyone in the area, asphyxiating them without warning.

The "Pit Boss" was in complete charge of all operations within a mine.

Outside the mine, there were many and varied duties such as mechanics, blacksmiths, engineers, electricians, office staff, etc. Other than the office staff which came under the supervision of the General Superintendent and Office Manager, all operations came under the jurisdiction of the "Outside Boss or Foreman" who also had charge of the tipple operation.

The workers usually did not know from one day to the next if the following day was to be a work day or an idle day as it was customary for the company to wait until it had sufficient orders to work a complete complement of men. Naturally, in the winter months, the mines worked quite steadily each day; however, in the summer months when the demand for fuel was lacking, the mines sometimes worked as few as one day a week. Each mine had a whistle (except at the Dietz No. 8 mine which had a siren). These would sound each day at 6:00 a.m.; 7:00 a.m., 7:30 a.m.; 12:00 noon; 12:30 p.m.; 4:00 p.m. and 6:00 p.m. It was not until the 4:30 and 6:00 whistles blew that the miners were informed whether the mine would work the following day—two whistles meant that they report for work while one whistle meant no work. Of course the women were just as interested as the men—whether she had to prepare his lunch or not.

An important facet of the mining operation were the functions of the horses or mules within the mine whose duties were described elsewhere. One small observation is described by my brother, Joe, whose duty it was to "break in" horses in one of the mines. He tells how the horses had a tendency to walk on the rail thinking it to be a path, and it was not too unusual for them at first to raise their heads in a normal manner, but in doing so, would eventually come in contact with the 440 volt direct current electric trolley line which would instantly "flatten" them to the ground. They soon learned to beware of the trolley line.

Chapter 5

Reminiscences

One of the first things I can remember as a child was my mother's custom of having each of us, individually or in groups, kneel at her knee and say our nightly prayers. These were said in Polish which was the first language I spoke. I remember also our usually weekly baths in a small tin tub, then standing behind our kitchen range for warmth until getting dressed.

I particularly remember that tragic accident which occurred in the spring of 1911 when my little cousin, George, the son of Uncle Joe, was killed by an auto near our place, and although this was also described in another chapter, my own recollections of the incident were that he and I were playing in the nearby roadway, and simply with the use of our hands, we were making, with the use also of some imagination and dirt, little houses from the dust accumulated on the roadway. Suddenly, I noticed an automobile racing down the road coming toward us. I instinctively jumped into the barrow pit and turned just in time to see the vehicle pass over little George's body. The horrid scene of seeing the blood gush from his eyes, nose and mouth left such an indelible impression on my mind as to remain with me to this day.

Uncle Joe, his father, just happened to come around the corner of one of the buildings, I believe it was the butcher shop, just after the accident, and seeing his son lying there, naturally become very distraught, but with the assistance of those in the car, they carried the limp little body to the pump near the main house where Uncle Joe fainted. After pumping some water on the child's face, they then carried him into the house and placed him on a bed. By that time, I was also in the room standing beside the bed when I heard what I thought was sort of a sigh. This was his last gasp.

After the body was prepared and placed in a coffin, I recall that they brought it back to our place where it remained in Uncle Joe's house until time for burial a few days later in Mount Hope cemetery in Sheridan. Although they have since changed the route to the cemetery, I remember the old route up Linden Avenue. The funeral procession proceeded in horse-drawn carriages along this route. A detailed account of this incident appeared in the *Sheridan Enterprise* on March 31, 1911.

During that summer, some of my brothers decided they wanted to visit a bachelor friend of the family, Bob Harlan, whose farm was down on Tongue River, and located immediately past the present lower Tongue River bridge, a distance of about six or eight miles from our home. By early afternoon, we had arrived at the farm but could not find Mr. Harlan who, we found out later, was working in the field. As it was past the lunch hour and several hours since we had eaten an early breakfast, we were all very hungry, so, as was quite customary in those days, we went into his outside cellar and helped ourselves to whatever food we could find. I chose a can of corn which one of my brothers opened for me—I ate the WHOLE THING! In my memory, other that the Polish sausage I mentioned earlier, this was one of my most delicious meals I had ever eaten, and to this day, corn is one of my favorite foods. Mr. Harlan, upon his return, offered to feed us, but found that we had already eaten.

In the fall of 1912, as I was to be six years of age that October, I enrolled in the first grade at Dietz. No doubt I was at a slight disadvantage, as the first language I learned was Polish and by that time had not yet become very familiar with the English language.

It was not surprising, therefore, to misunderstand the name of my first teacher whose name was Tschirgi, but which I pronounced "Sugary" and couldn't understand why anyone would be so named. Actually, the name was more familiar in Sheridan as a street was named after that pioneer family. Nevertheless, I believe I called her "Miss Sugery" that year.

To get to school, I had to walk the distance of approximately a mile to the lower grade school which was beyond the upper grade school and which, by the way, was called the high school (only because it had two stories).

This lower grade school was located near the interurban bridge at the point where it spanned Big Goose creek as it approached the Dietz camp. The "high school" which we would pass on the way was about two hundred yards nearer our home. This school, by the way, was located at the present north end of the viaduct which now passes over both the creek and the railroad simultaneously (a part of its yard is actually covered by the fill of the highway).

From the time we moved to the "Hecht Place" only about thirty years after the Custer battle, many bands of Indians would come by our place on their way to Sheridan in the late afternoon or evening, and wishing to arrive in Sheridan in the morning, they would frequently camp over night across the railroad tracks from our place. I was very much afraid of Indians. I recall one incident when the band had broken up and was heading for Sheridan, but one young buck who had already saddled on his horse, remained behind and looking down at me, kept saying "hello," repeating it until I replied, "Hello" after which he drove away much to my relief. I don't seem to recall just how, in my fear, I happened to be so close to the Indians. It seems to me that it was the first time I spoke the English "hello."

That Christmas, I recall that my parents gave us a beautiful new sled named "Black Beauty." It was painted a very shiny black and had a red stripe. It was a low sled only about 4 inches high and had hand holes in the sides.

I took the sled to the nearby river which then was quite covered with ice except farther down where there was a section not yet frozen due to a swifter current. I was really enjoying myself with this new sled, running on the ice then falling on the sled and sliding as far as I could. I kept repeating this until I decided to take an unusually longer and faster run for a real ride. I fell on the sled and had not slid far when suddenly I saw the end of the ice and the swift water beyond. Instinctively, I pushed the sled out from under me, and sliding on my stomach, came to a stop just at the edge of the ice, but the sled went on into the swift current. Of course, I was too afraid to tell what happened, and when the sled was later found missing, no one knew whatever happened to it (until years later).

In another chapter of this book, it is told how my father moved our family to Roundup, Montana in 1913 and the following year to Windham, Montana, and finally returning to Dietz in 1918.

Upon our return to Dietz, I entered the sixth grade—it was Dietz No. 7 by that time, and during this period, it was a booming little city with its same two school buildings previously described, a large hotel and a smaller one, a pool hall, barber shop, union hall, company store, two saloons, a Catholic church, a Protestant church, several Lodge societies and organizations, etc.

It seemed rather easy to adjust to the new situations, the school, and the church. Our family, being devout Catholics, I became involved in church work and began service as an altar boy under Father Theodore Schultz. Both the Catholic religion and the Polish nationality were quite predominant at Dietz. Father Schultz spoke Polish fluently and delivered many of his sermons in Polish. He not only condoned but actively participated in the many Polish customs being ever sympathetic to all their practices.

As in any religion, however, many did not attend church very regularly, but on special holy days, such as Easter, Christmas, etc., the church would be packed. It was on these occasions that Father Schultz would deliver his especially-prepared sermons, emotionally appealing to his congregation to more faithfully practice their religion. Many were the times when he had them wiping their eyes, particularly when he would direct his remarks to those who had left their families in the old country with the promise that they would send for them as soon as they could accumulate enough money for their transportation, but for many that time never did arrive. (This accounted for the large segment of the population being bachelors).

We altar boys always looked forward to church weddings and christenings. On those occasions, it was customary, following the old Polish custom, for us to quickly run around to the vestibule of the church immediately after the services and before the bridal couple and their train could leave the church, they were stopped by a silken rope extended across their path allowing each couple to pass only after they had made a contribution. Needless to say, in their mood of the moment, they were very generous—and, of course, we were very receptive.

During the next several days, at both weddings and christenings, there followed much drinking, feasting and dancing Polish polkas and waltzes to the music of a local musician or band. At these functions, instead of giving gifts as is the custom in this country, it was their practice to provide the newly-wedded couple with money. At the dinner table, their would be a large bowl to receive any contributions. These dinners, by the way, were not just a meal, but tables loaded with many kinds of food being constantly replenished as needed. Then, at weddings, there followed the traditional "broom dance" when the bridesmaids would individually round up each man to dance a few steps with the bride to be followed by a contribution for the couple for which he was rewarded with a cigar or a drink. After all men were thus rounded up, the bridesmaids would then round up the women guests until all had been given the opportunity to dance with the bride. Sometimes this fund would reach staggering amounts thereby giving the young couple a good start in their married life.

The Catholic church bell at Dietz contained, in my opinion, one of the most attractive, sonorous tones of any bell I had ever heard and which could be heard far up and down the valley. As an altar boy, when the sexton did not happen to be available, I would be asked to ring the bell which I was always happy to do. The weight of that bell was such that, after pulling on the rope a few times until the bell was in full swing, I would sometimes hold on to the rope only to be pulled into the air. A few times I rang the bell too hard causing the bell to overturn completely. In those cases, it was necessary to climb into the steeple and turn it back (In later years, I discovered that this bell was acquired by Mr. Fred Weltner who had the bell installed in front of his home in Hardin, Montana, and a few years ago, he allowed me to clap the bell which responded with the same old beautiful sound of many years ago).

Another of the old Polish church customs came at Christmas time when we altar boys and sometimes some of the girls from the choir would go from house to house of the Catholic families, and with chalk which had been blessed by the priest, would print K + M + B over the doorway as a blessing of the house, the initials representing the first letters of the names of the three wise men, Kasmir, Melchior and Balthaser. I would play the violin and the girls would sing

carols at each home. For this, we would be given money.

It was about this time, 1918, 1919 and 1920, that the mines were in full operation: Dietz No. 7, Dietz No. 8, the Hotchkiss Mine, Acme, Model Carneyville (later name changed to Kleenburn), Monarch and Kooi. Also operating were the Storm King mine and the Black Diamond, both located west of Sheridan on the Big Goose creek road.

Some of the nationalities represented as I recall were: Polish, Hungarians, Welsh, Scotch, English, Italians, Czechoslovakians, Bulgarians, Austrians, Germans, Serbians, Montenegrans, Irish, Slovaks, Japanese, French—in fact, from nearly every European country. It was not too unusual for some of the English-speaking people, particularly the younger ones, to learn to speak in Polish. Of these, for example were Albert Atkinson, the Joyce boys and others.

Many of the names of those foreign-born were really tongue-twisters. There were the names such as: Wisniewski, Urbaczka, Kawalowski, Pyszko, Cieluszak, Heczko, Malyjurek, Roswadowski, the Rev. Peter Szymanski (one of the later Catholic priests).

Some saw fit to change their names and some had their names changed on the payroll books of the mining companies by clerks, purposely in some cases and inadvertently in others; for example: Bobula to Barbula; Piekarczyk (meaning baker in Polish) to Baker; Sieczkowski to Siegoski; Mleczek (meaning milkman) however changed to Mentock; Matjehovitz to Matches, some to Mathews and some retaining the original name; Kriston to Kristy; Pototski to Potescar; Gorzalka (meaning whiskey in slang) was retained unchanged; Czarny (meaning black) to Cherni. Some changed their names officially at the time of their naturalization; for example, Koczur to Kutcher and Josef Podczerwienski changed to Mike Patz, etc. while another Stanley Patzcenwienski became also Patz.

Sometime during the 1920's I believe, I knew one of the younger miners, a rather gay blade who did not wish to be handicapped by the name "Lupiezowietz." So Mike Lupiezowietz applied to the District Court making formal request to have his name changed. The Judge was somewhat surprised when Mike indicated that he chose the name "Mike Murphy" which was granted. Of course, the reaction of ridicule from all who knew him was not only instantaneous but continued and was the subject of many jokes. It was about two years later, I believe, that Mike returned to the Judge requesting his original name which was readily granted. The final climax to the experience came when the local newspaper announced the incident with the headline, "Mike Murphy Is No More."

Each of the mining camps had its own band which appeared in many of the parades held in those days—BIG parades on the 4th of July, Labor Day, and special celebrations. They also played at the many Polish weddings and christenings. There were many fine musicians among them, some of whom were particularly talented. One of the first groups to organize was the local band—how else could they have their polkas?

Just as soon as there were sufficient players, a baseball team was organized. Each camp had its own team and there was real rivalry among the various camps as well as with teams from Sheridan and the surrounding area. Even with us younger boys, baseball was one of our principal activities; however, instead of competing teams, we used to play "work-up"; that is, one would begin at left field position and as a batter was "struck out" or was put out, players would gradually move up a position until finally he would arrive at the batter's box where he remained until he was put out. Thus, the younger boys became very adept in each position, and they became particularly good batters, resulting in some very good baseball teams.

Even in the wintertime, the men were able to keep involved in some physical activity, and frequently with a keg of beer nearby, the frozen river became the scene of a game called "Pravo," sometimes referred to as curling. In this game of competition, one would run to a foul line and slide a disk or quoit along the ice, as in bowling, to an objective spot or line, frequently glancing off another's quoit to gain advantage.

We younger boys also played on the frozen river in the wintertime. We used to play a game which we called "Shinny"—actually nothing different than the present day "hockey," but instead of owning any manufactured hockey stick and puck, we used to find a willow or some other tree which had a crook in it shaped like a hockey stick, and for a puck we used to use a bung from a barrel. Even in the summertime as we tramped around in the trees, we were on the lookout for a better "shinny stick."

Another game the men played on the ice was called "Bolina." This game was quite similar to Curling except that instead of using quoits, balls were used. A smaller target ball was rolled a distance, then the larger ball rolled, or lagged, to see how near one could get to the target ball. In all of these games, enthusiasm ran very high.

Other popular pasttimes consisted of various contests of strength—boxing wrestling, weightlifting, throwing horseshoes, etc. I recall one instance when my father bet one of the more husky miners, Joe Stucca, that he could not lift a certain water-soaked oak railroad tie about 20 feet long which had only recently been removed from under the rails and near which they happened to be standing. The bet was $5.00. Mr. Stucca not only lifted one end of the tie on his shoulder, but gradually worked to its center until he had it balanced, then walked off with it. It was estimated that the tie weighed about 800 pounds.

Instead of celebrating birthdays, it was the accepted custom to celebrate so-called "name days." In the Church calendar, practically every day celebrated a certain Saint, some male, some female. The names of these Saints were considered christian names and were the basis for most of the newly borns' names. And so it was that on St. Joseph day, for example, every 'Joe' in the camp set that day aside for celebrating his patron saint. Or it may be on St. Maria day that all Marys would celebrate. So by the time all the 'Joes' or 'Marys' or whatever got together to celebrate they would have quite a party!

The Union hall in practically each mining camp would usually also serve as an auditorium for functions of other organizations and also for school plays and programs. The Christmas parties or programs were always the time for real fun and pleasure. Frequently, the officials of the mine would distribute gifts to the children. Under certain circumstances, these gifts were quite elaborate.

In Dietz, there was an organization named the "Dietz Mutual Benefit Association." I have been unable to find anyone that could give me any information about it except that the letters "D. M. B. A." stood for its name. I am quite certain, however, that its purpose was to assess nominal dues to create a fund for the assistance of any family whose wage-earner died or met accidental death in the mine. Its emblem was a four-leaf clover.

Another society at Dietz was the "Slovenska Narodna Podporna Jednota," an insurance society, the dues of which were $4.50 per month, and to which some of the miners subscribed.

Such organizations for the benefit of the families of miners were no doubt the result of situations like that which occurred in about 1912 when one Charlie "Brick" Brazik was killed in the Dietz No. 4 mine when a squib "hang fired"; that is, after it had been lit, it did not activate the powder charge, and when he returned to investigate, the shot went off, killing him. It was told that his family consisting of a widow and three children, was allowed only $300.00 by the company as compensation.

Recreation for us younger people consisted of a great variety of activities. It was a sure sign of spring when most of the boys as if by instinct appeared with their hair cut right down to the scalp (one of the reasons for many was to rid themselves of lice), but it was something I remember I looked forward to for the simple pleasure of my head being bald. And before the snow was all gone, we were down on our knees playing marbles or "migs", the luckiest using "pure agates" for "taws" (the shooting marble), and using for keeps such marbles as glassies, rockies, chalkies, grannies, pewees, steelies, etc. Each of these marbles carried its own value. The "glassie" for instance might be worth five "grannies" and so on. The glassie was made of glass and contained a design in it. Mostly we played for "keeps"—when a marble was knocked out of the ring, it became the property of the shooter. I personally never accumulated any great supply, but by staying clear of some of the better players, was able to hold my own. The accuracy of the better players was really astounding when from several feet distance they could consistently pick off a player's shooting marble, thereby "killing" him or knock marbles from the ring.

With a river nearby, swimming was a common pastime even though our parents were almost always opposed due to an occasional drowning. None of us owned such a thing as a swim suit, so we always swam in the nude; except on rare occasions when we would swim with the girls, we would wear overalls while the girls wore dresses (which really became quite transparent after getting wet).

Then, of course, there were games such as "Pump, Pump, Pull-away," "Run Sheep, Run," "Kick the Can" "Roll the Hoop," shooting with beanie shooters and sling shots.

To go barefooted in the Spring was always anticipated (I think much to the relief of my parents who had to provide shoes for seven boys), and it wasn't too long before our feet became so calloused we could go almost anywhere. I shall never forget particularly, Stanley Parat, a cousin of mine who actually could step on cactus in the hills without too much concern.

Often we would play with carbide. It was the habit of the miners to clean out their carbide lamps of the residue of carbide. There always seemed to be a convenient post near the exit of the mine, and it was there that one miner after another would unscrew the base of his lamp, knock it against the post and deposit the residue. This process repeated by many of the miners at the same spot would inevitably result in quite a pile of spent carbide powder. However, as the men would empty their cans, we children would finger through the carbide dust, picking out all granules of unused carbide. Sometimes we would merely pile it, drop water on it and light it; other times, place a supply of carbide in a bottle and after watering it, quickly cap the bottle and get quite a charge out of the resulting explosion.

Another pastime was either carving our initials or using a carbide lamp, smoke our names or initials on about every post around. One of the most prolific of these was "A.J.M." (Andrew J. Mentock)—almost everywhere one went, he could find those initials carved.

And what tasted better than a sandwich from a miner's lunch bucket; how we loved it! It seems that the combination of having been in the mine for a day and the moisture from the coffee in the bottom of the bucket, gave the sandwich a flavor all its own. As smaller children, it was quite customary for us to make it a point to meet our father as he came out of the mine to get those sandwiches left in his bucket, and to insure that there would be some left, mothers would invariably prepare extra sandwiches for this purpose.

Oh, yes, we would frequently go tramping in the hills and gulleys to pick choke cherries, bull berries, plums, sarvis berries, currents; and in the right places right after a rain, mushrooms of several varieties, not to mention the time spent fishing in the nearby river. I recall that as a small child we owned a fishing net which the older brothers would stretch across the river while we waded down from a distance up the river, finally arriving at the net. As the net was pulled up, it would be literally loaded with various fish— trout, red horses, cat fish, croppies, white fish, suckers, bull heads and perch.

Sometimes, we would "borrow" a hand-car from the C. B. & Q. railroad (left on the prepared siding of the tracks by the maintenance crew) and after some of the older boys carried it to the interurban tracks whose bed was not level as were the railroad tracks, we would all push the hand-car up to the top of an incline just to experience the sensation of coasting down at quite a speed. It was a wonder that we survived as the handles of the hand-car would be pumping up and down of their own accord and if by chance anyone ever got in their way, he would certainly meet with some sort of disaster.

In the winter, in addition to sliding down hills on homemade sleds, bobsleds and toboggans, we did quite a lot of ice skating, sometimes on the sloughs but mostly on the river which was sometimes kept clean of snow by over flooding. Of course, skating on the river was sometimes very dangerous since the ice was either very thin where the water was naturally swift or was even non-existent, so we had to remain constantly on guard. We did have some narrow escapes.

In those days, the only skates available to us were to old fashioned clamp-on type, to the heel and to the sole of our shoes. As our shoes got wet, the leather became soft, and that is when the skates would pull off—sometimes pulling off a heel or separating the sole of the shoe from the shoe itself. What a problem for our parents who simply could not stop us from skating, but who then had to keep the shoes in repair.

There were seven boys in our family and all seven skated and all their shoes had to be repaired—all of this in addition to seven boys getting their hair cut when needed. How my parents ever kept up, I'll never figure out, but they did—(years later we were reminded more than once as to how clean our mother kept our family).

Inasmuch as we did live between Dietz No. 7 and Dietz No. 8, we naturally did not participate in activities in the camps as much as those living in the camps; however, in the summertime, we would sneak away, and during school, we would frequently fail to return home after school only to get the tongue lashing we deserved.

On Sundays, it was routine for our family to attend Mass at Dietz. In the early 1920's, it was just as routine for a bunch of us boys from Dietz, following church services, to walk or hitch-hike to Sheridan (usually walking all the way as there was little auto traffic in those days), and with a nickel, we would attend the show at the old Gem Theater (located at 160 North Main Street now occupied by the Lansine Paint Store). At first, it was a serial, "The Lion Man" in silent movies, each weekly episode ending with the hero or heroine about to be killed by being thrown over a cliff or tied to the rail placing us in deep suspense until the following week. Then came "Tarzan" played, I believe by Elmo Lincoln. This was also in serials lasting week after week.

If we happened to have more than a nickel in our pockets, we would either go to "Tony" Roden's candy store across the street (Tony used to own a similar store in Dietz) or to Louies (Louie, the Tamali Man) for a hamburger, and if we happened to have more than the ten-cents, we would often buy seconds. Sometimes, however, we would go to the Schreibies Bakery on North Main street enjoying those delicious pastries on the way home.

Near our school (the "high school") there was a marsh containing some tall weeds which would lose their leaves each fall, leaving nothing except a tall, straight stem about six or seven feet in length with roots only about six or eight inches long. These could easily be pulled out of the ground and in doing so, there was just enough dirt left on the root to balance the shaft. These, then, made almost perfect javelins. While I was in the seventh grade, we would often pull up a supply of these weeds, build a "fort," chose sides and throw them at each other. Although I once was hit on a lip, I don't recall any of us getting seriously injured. Throwing spears seemed to intrigue me, and I believe perhaps I did acquire some skill. A few years later in high school, I had occasion to throw my first real javelin when Sheridan High School first introduced the event. Obviously, the experience received in throwing those "weeds" in Dietz helped in my progress in the javelin event, resulting in winning first place in that event at the Wyoming State High School track and field meet in 1925, and eventually earning a letter in that event in each of four years in college as related in more detail in another chapter.

Naturally, some of us boys had to try our hands at smoking and as we occasionally found a cigarette "butt," we would hide somewhere and smoke it; however, once when "Butch" Tynsky was caught by his father who, when he searched the boy's pockets, found some tobacco, paper and matches, made him eat all of it to teach him never to be caught smoking again.

When I was about 10 years old, my brother, Joe, and I decided we would like to fish above the town of Dayton near the mountains, optimistically hoping to catch a lot of fish. We could take a train from Dietz and ride to Ranchester, a distance of about 12 or 13 miles, then walk to Dayton for another five or six miles. Well, we went to the Dietz depot to catch the 2:30 a.m. passenger, but it was not until about 5:30 a.m. before the train arrived. We boarded it and in a few minutes we were in Ranchester. From there, we walked to Dayton, then to a point on the Tongue River about two miles above Dayton even though we had already observed the very muddy spring water. Needless to say, we were unable to catch any fish, so decided to return to Dietz, a distance of about 18 miles. I believe the total distance walked that day was about 25 miles. Obviously I was one tired boy by the time we arrived back home.

Then again, when I was about 13 years old, I accompanied Mike Sikora, the baker on our place for a week of fishing in Tongue River canyon (and a good baker he was). This was while Mr. Sikora was still rational and before he got to drinking. We drove in his little old Ford runabout as far as we could up the canyon above Dayton where we parked the car, then we packed our bedding, food and other supplies for an additional distance of about a quarter of a mile to an old abandoned prospector's cabin. As the door was missing, that night being afraid of bear, I recall that for my sake, we kept a fire a few yards in front of the cabin and kept an all night vigil, changing shifts from time to time.

The following day, as I fished up the river, I noticed another abandoned log cabin only a couple hundred yards away. This one did have a door, so we decided to move. Between the two cabins, however, there was a very steep chasm which was no obstacle since the old lumber flume gave us easy access across although it was becoming somewhat rickety and unstable. So, we packed up our goods and after several trips we finished transferring our supplies by late mid-afternoon.

That night, we slept without any further fear of wild animals, but we were both suddenly awakened about 2:00 a.m. by a terrible thundering noise which did not really frighten us as it had been raining and it did sound like thunder. The following morning, however, we were frozen by the sight which met our eyes—THAT FLUME HAD CRASHED TO THE BOTTOM OF THE CANYON! (By the way, during that week I came face to face with my first wild bear, and although I quickly hid behind a large boulder, he made no pretense of going after me. That same week, I caught the largest trout in my life of fishing—that could be another short story).

Upon graduating from the 8th grade at Dietz in the Spring of 1921, it appears I was the only one planning to go to high school—the girls to be soon married or needed to assist at home caring for smaller children, and the boys immediately to work in the mines.

Immediately after completing the 8th grade, my father thought he would like to indenture me to learn a trade. There was a German baker by the name of John Heczko who for years had operated a bakery located between the Camps of Monarch and Kooi, and did actually bake such tasty bakery goods as I had ever eaten. He delivered his goods in a horse-drawn enclosed bakery delivery wagon such as was common in those days. At each stop, it was necessary that he get out of the wagon and go to the rear, open up the two doors and draw out a large pan of rolls, cakes, pies, bread, etc. from one of the many built-in shelves. Very little of his business was cash; instead, upon making his delivery, he would then take out his stub of a pencil and note the order on the facing of the door. On the basis of this record, he would collect on payday. It was not too unusual for some figures to become accidentally erased; also it was a very common practice for the kids to swipe some of his goods, for just as soon as he got in his wagon to drive to the next stop, his vision of the rear became obscured and the kids would suddenly jump from their hiding place and help themselves. Mr. Heczko, taking into account such inevitable losses, always baked extra supplies accordingly.

And so it was, that one day, after taking the interurban to Monarch and after walking the approximately two miles to his home and bakery, I reported for work as previously agreed to between my father and Mr. Heczko. I arrived there in the evening just in time to be told to clean the barn. Upon completion of that, I came into the bakery and Mr. Hezcko stated in his very German accent that it would be some time before supper, so in the meanwhile, I could weigh some dough. Upon suggesting that I should first wash my hands, he said, "Let me see your hands." So I extended them face up and with one glance, remarked, "Oh, they're alright." So, I weighed dough!

After working for him for one full week cleaning the barn, weighing dough, hitching the horse and making deliveries (even on one occasion delivering to Kooi in his beat up Ford which he could not drive), I finally mustered up enough courage to ask how much I was being paid. He replied that if I worked real hard he would pay me $20 per month. I was thrilled and immediately suggested that I had already earned $5.00. He was quick to remind me that he had no intention of paying me while he was teaching me the trade. With my spirits completely broken, I waited for an opportune moment, and sneaking into my room, picked up my mackinaw and slipped through the back door. Just as I was going around the building, he accidentally saw me, and asked where I was going. As frightened as I was, I said, "I'm going home," and continued on my way as he threatened, "Just wait, I'm going to tell your father." As frightening as this sounded, I did not return; and after walking to Monarch, I caught the interurban and returned home. After explaining what occurred, I did not receive the lashing I really expected, for which of course, I was very thankful. Such was my first work experience!

Until sometime in the late 1920's, we had no modern conveniences at home, such as inside toilet or bath facilities, and so, as children, we used an outside toilet and took our baths in a round galvanized tub. Although I do not remember there ever being a bath house for the miners in the old Dietz No. 7 mine, the Dietz No. 8 mine did have such a facility. Each Saturday, it became our ritual to walk to Dietz for our usual weekly baths even though we were not legally entitled as our father was not employed by the Company. After the Dietz No. 8 mine closed, we then used to drive to Acme and later even to Monarch for our baths.

Our first electricity was in the late 1920's when my father installed a 32 volt direct current plant wherein a gasoline powered generator charged a series of batteries which would store electricity as do our present automobile batteries. This provided us with better lighting conditions, but the system did require a great deal of attention. Finally, in the early 1930's, we brought in the regular electricity at some considerable expense.

At about the time I was ready for the 8th grade, the Camp of Dietz No. 7 was beginning to dwindle and the former two-story school building was moved to the camp of Dietz No. 8. The 7th and 8th grades then occupied the building formerly occupied by the lower grades located near the interurban bridge on Big Goose Creek. Our teacher that one year was Leo Schultz, a brother of the Catholic priest. Inasmuch as he had only a high school education, he was hardly qualified for the job. Frequently we found ourselves correcting some of his errors.

Following my graduation from the 8th grade at Dietz, I enrolled in high school going to school usually with my father who made daily trips to Sheridan to buy groceries for his store and returning on the Interurban. There were also other students attending high school in Sheridan and they too rode the Interurban. I studied very hard as I was afraid that if I didn't, I might not be allowed to continue as my father could very well use me to help deliver groceries. I carried my lunch during the first year, but when I became somewhat embarrassed carrying it and being too bashful to eat in the high school cafeteria, I would usually go without any lunch except for those times when I would buy a 5¢ sack of peanuts. I never did get brave enough to eat in the cafeteria.

By the time I became a Junior, because of making fairly good grades in English, I was selected Managing Editor of the high school paper, the Ocksheperida. It was during this year that it became necessary to contact the Mills Printing Company down town about some matter regarding the paper. When I offered to go down town to talk to them, our faculty sponsor, Miss Van Boskirk suggested I call them on the phone. As I began to insist that I go there personally, she insisted that I call. Finally, in desperation, I revealed the fact that I had never used a phone and did not know how. Amazed, she accompanied me to the principal's office and leading me by the ear, said, "Gangway, folks, here's a young man who has never used a phone in his life." After instructing me how, I talked over a phone for the first time at the age of 17!

That same year, I was elected to the National Honor Society and during the elections for officers of that group, was elected its vice-president.

The following year, I was offered the choice of Editorship of the high school paper or the senior annual. I chose the latter. This book, previously bound in long form, I changed to more closely resemble the average book form. This did make it more difficult to budget on past year's costs. Upon receiving the printing estimate from the Mills Printing Co., in my innocence, I announced my intention to also get figures from Billings and Casper (previously, it was simply taken for granted that the printing would be performed locally). Before I was able to make contact with those other two printers, the Mills Company called stating they had reviewed their figures, reducing the amount about $150.00. We ended up with a profit of about $250.00. The *Sheridan Post-Enterprise* of March 13, 1927 had this to say about the issue: "Stanley Kuzara was the next editor, and Grace Blackledge, the associate editor. Miss Thompson had gone to Los Angeles to teach so Miss Bibby took her place and she and Miss Hull were the faculty sponsors. This Annual was about as perfect as one could wish for, but when advertisements came out for the 1926 edition they broadcasted that their annual would be the 'best yet' ."

With our profit, the class of 1925 commissioned Bill Gollings, the artist, who, after a great deal of research, painted "The Verendries" which painting was then presented to the school. This painting today hangs in the Sheridan Library.

I might explain that for years, the students from the mines and especially those of foreign extraction were considered "from across the tracks." We lived through it throughout our lives and simply became calloused to being referred to as those "Pollacks" or "Dagos," etc. So I felt a certain pride in the fact that I was able to be awarded the honors given me.

Although I did not come into contact with many of the residents in the various mining camps, it is known that there were those who did have some unusual and exceptional talents; for example, there was John Antonkiewitz who was a very accomplished violinist, playing only when the mood struck him and no amount of persuasion would get him to play unless he was in that mood, but when he did play, he could make that instrument literally talk.

Joe Wiesniewski, also a violinist of a sort and who taught me the fundamentals of violin (I later played the violin in the Sheridan High School orchestra) was primarily an inventor. He invented his "Seven Mile Boots"—two roller skates which fit over the rails of the railroad track. By placing one foot in front of the other, balancing one's self and propelling with a long balanced pole, one could glide down the rail, however it was discovered that it was too difficult to master. The idea did not take.

His next invention was an underwater pump, the paddles of which were rotated by the current of the river. As the paddles turned or rotated against the current, they would fold back and as they came around, the current would open them up, thereby operating the pump. After investing a goodly sum of money building one of the units at some factory back east, and after testing the unit in the river next to our place, he again took it to the factory for some refinements, but when he did not bring it back, when questioned, all he would say was that someone scuttled it when he was testing it back east. Never did hear anymore about it.

Then there was old Charlie Mazur, the "Polish Lawyer." He was not a lawyer but I'm certain he performed more legal counselling services than many practicing attorneys in Sheridan. He was, in fact, a very well-read individual. One of his main public functons was acting as an interpreter for the many Polish persons appearing in court for one reason or another.

I cannot resist the temptation of referring to our Polish sausage. As far as I can remember, it was the custom that our Easter breakfast include Polish sausage, hard boiled eggs, horse radish, home-baked bread and coffee. This traditional breakfast followed the abstinance of meat throughout the Lenten season. The first time I ever remember tasting Polish sausage—and I remember it well—was from my father's brother, Uncle Joe, the butcher on our place. I was only about 4 or 5 years of age when he had just finished taking some hot freshly-smoked Polish sausage out of the smokehouse, and, apparently reading my expression, proceeded to deftly cut diagonally a hunk of that sausage and handed it to me. The memory of that delicious flavor will forever remain with me!

Over the many subsequent years, it was always customary for my folks to supply us with a couple rings of sausage wherever we might be located. Before their passing I, too, learned their recipe and to this day, continue to make it. Usually, we make a little family party of it when Mary (two sisters, Mary Mentock and Helen Barello, get together, and after making the sausage, I then smoke it in the old smoke-house still on the old Kuzara place, now owned and occupied by Betty (Wadell) Kuzara, widow of brother, Mike who a few years ago was killed in an industrial accident at the Acme plant of Montana-Dakota Utilities where he worked.

It was rare indeed for anyone to get by without being called a nickname. Just how many of them ever got started, one simply does not know, although some of them did have some logic. Of those I remember, the following are a few: Andrew "Spider" Marosok (he was in fact a very fast runner with long legs); Anton "Briz" Marosok; Frank "Pinhead" Marosok (he, too, was quite slender); John "Bula" Mentock; Andrew "Splitz" Mentock; Andrew "Moose" Marosok, Jr.; Frank "Speed," George "Babs" and Charles "Merz" Matejowitz; Clair "Click" Moon; Walter "Goof" Mentock; Walter "Barber" Mentock; Albert "Pot" Goodmay; John "Red" and Stanley "Squeaky" Kristy; Stanley "Stash" Kuzara, etc.

And how about Leon "Leech" Siegoski (Sieczowski)? Once when a group of boys of Monarch were swimming at "third pier," Leon happened to have strayed into a muddy area in that part of Tongue River and came out with 22 blood suckers (leeches) fastened to various parts of his body—so many, in fact, that from then on, he has carried the nickname "leech," even to this day.

In further reference to swimming, after the Holly Sugar Company built a sugar factory in Sheridan, each fall during their campaign, their pulp waste was discarded in Little Goose Creek turning the water into a very murky gray completely polluting the creek as well as Big Goose Creek into which it flowed shortly down stream. From that point both creeks became so polluted as to kill all the fish down stream for many miles, preventing any further swimming and creating a stench which persisted until the end of the campaign and for some time afterwards. Even the raw sewage of the city of Sheridan was far less damaging as we were able to swim without any apparent ill effect, nor did it seem to seriously effect the fish population.

Much of our coal supply came from a rather unusual source. Up the river a few hundred yards and across on the other side, there was an outcropping of coal in an obscured gulley on Coal Company land. With the river frozen in the wintertime, there was provided a perfectly smooth highway to our house. By using the most primitive methods; that is, pick and shovel, we were able to load a sled made for this

purpose and without too much difficulty push this loaded sled down the ice to our home. Time after time, throughout the winter months we filled our coal bin—somewhat illegally perhaps—we thought we were being resourceful!

Also, each winter, we would stock up on our ice supply from the river. Usually, there would be a crew of us and whatever additional help we could get, generally it was the Banas's, our neighbors up the river; and when the ice was right, we would cut it in about two-foot strips for a couple hundred feet, then, after scoring cross-wise break the cakes in about four-foot lengths. At the age of 12, I used to run down these individual cakes of ice as they floated in the water leaving one just as it sank under the water, then, at full speed, quickly step on the next and so on down the entire length. This, of course, was a very dangerous thing to do, but it was just one of the many chances we youngsters used to take. We would fill our ice house then using coal slack for insulation, each winter's supply would then last us throughout the summer.

In the year 1923, the Dietz No. 8 mine also closed down; however, many of the houses and the school house remained, while those families remaining sent their children to that school and the men found work in the Acme or Monarch mines which were still operating.

It was about 1918, shortly after we returned to Dietz that someone was celebrating a wedding and my father had cleaned out the old saloon to be used as a dancing hall for this occasion. It was at this function that two girls, Ella Tkach and Rose Kumor persuaded me to dance the polka, and while I never did feel I ever was an accomplished dancer, the polka I could really dance. Over the following years with my wife also becoming a good polka dancer, we received many commendations—in 1975, during the Realtor Mid-winter Meeting of the National Realtor Association in San Antonio, they were celebrating their annual spring fiesta with, among other things, many bands playing on the famous River Walk. As we came out of the La Paloma Cafe, a band across the river was playing a polka. Of course, we could not resist the impulse to dance. As we danced, the crowd spread into an ever-increasing circle and when the playing stopped, we proudly responded to the general applause we received from both sides of the river.

And so, time marches on! For the next few years, as the family was growing older and some of the members getting married and going out on their own, it was not until the year of 1932 when the whole family—all fourteen of us—finally and for the very first (and last time)—were together. Previous to that, while brothers Walter and John were serving in WWI in France, Charlotte, the youngest, was born. Before Walter returned from France, brother John had already returned and left home. Following that, there was always one or more missing until this one time in 1932 and, of course, the first thing we did was to arrange for a photograph of the whole family.

In the early 1930's, following the stock crash, conditions were in a very depressing state. It was during this time that, in addition to the grocery store operating primarily for the family and those living in the houses on our place, and with coal customers, many of whom are unable to pay their bills, that my father, to supplement his income, began to hold regular Saturday night dances in our living room. He would, as usual, fiddle away his Polish polkas and waltzes. His neighbors and friends would come from various remaining camps to enjoy themselves. This went on week after week. Of course, there were refreshments served at these gatherings followed by a lot of hard cleaning the following Sunday morning, but it did help financially.

In describing our annual Christmas parties, for as long as I can remember, our family would gather at the table for Christmas Eve dinner, and as this occurred during the season of Advent (Christmas eve), no meat was served. Instead, the dinner usually consisted of borst, a few kinds of fish, mushrooms, braided bread, pirogy (dumplings containing cottage cheese, cabbage and some prunes), beans and sauerkraut, mashed potatoes, and various kinds of pies and desserts.

All of this was preceded by our father taking a sheet of "holy bread" (thin sheet of unleavened bread containing a spiritual design, about three by five inches, which had previously been blessed by the priest), and as he would go around the table, he would pause at each place while that person would break off three pieces after each of which he would deliver his wishes of health, happiness, etc., until all had thus been saluted. It was customary for the first table to consist of all the males and only after they had completed their dinner would the women then sit down to their meal. The smaller children were usually served at separate tables, except the infants who sat on their mothers' laps.

Thus, as the family grew and as they began to have children of their own, the crowd grew larger and larger. What fun we had! Eventually, as the second generation increased and the children grew, they began to entertain their own families. In 1950, my father passed away and several years later, when my mother passed away in 1964, she left 103 children, grandchildren and great grandchildren! (More since then).

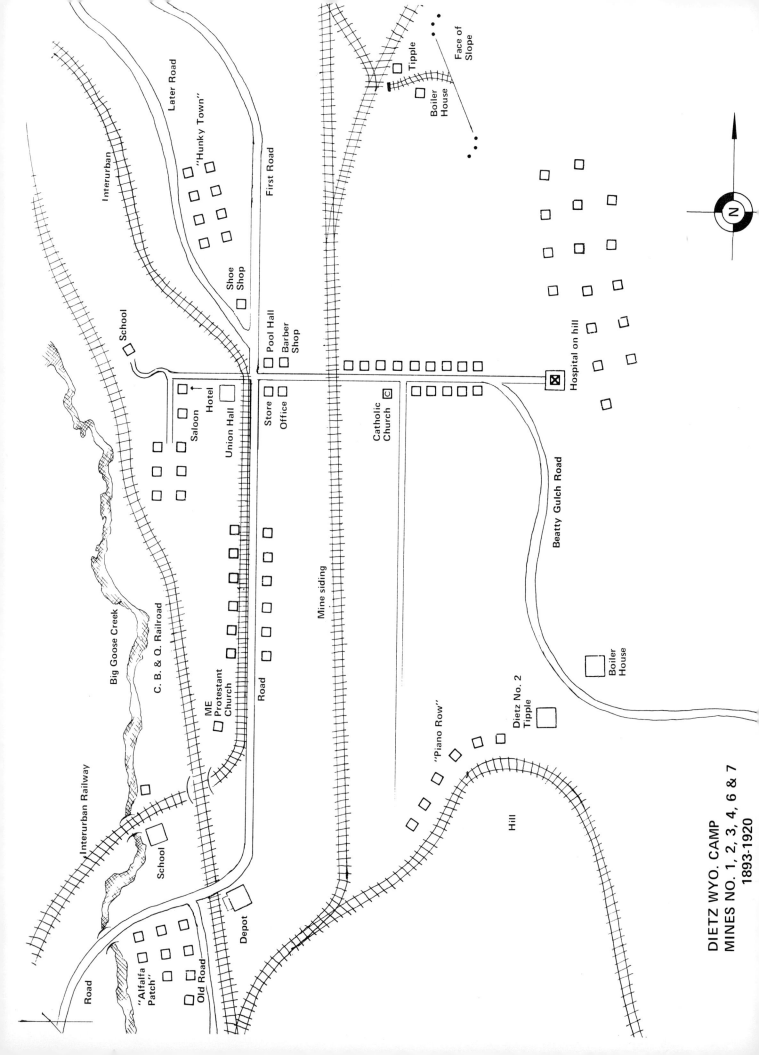

DIETZ WYO. CAMP
MINES NO. 1, 2, 3, 4, 6 & 7
1893-1920

Chapter 6

Dietz Camps Nos. 1, 2, 3, 4, 6 and 7

Almost a century has passed since commercial underground coal mining first appeared in the Sheridan, Wyoming area and the first coal mining camp developed about four miles north of Sheridan in the year of 1893; and almost a quarter century since the demise of the last underground mine when this type of mining was replaced by the more modern above-ground strip mining. Inevitably, time has also replaced most of the people who resided in the mining camps with a second and even, in some cases, a third generation, taking with them sources of information which will never be recalled.

To record a history of the mines, therefore, it was necessary to rely greatly on current news items appearing in the Sheridan papers; namely, the *Sheridan Post*, the *Sheridan Enterprise, The Sheridan Post-Enterprise*, the *Sheridan Journal* and the *Sheridan Press.* To these newspapers, I must give a great deal of credit, and especially am I indebted to Mr. Milton B. Chilcott, publisher of the Sheridan Press for his complete cooperation in allowing me access to those papers and permitting quotations from them.

In reviewing those papers, I am also deeply indebted to my wife, Polly, who so ably assisted in my research. Together, we scanned over 200,000 pages of newspapers. This, in itself, was a horrendous undertaking!

Much of the information following, therefore, will be sort of a "diary" of the events as they occurred and were currently reported in those papers.

And so, in reviewing the *Sheridan Post* of the year 1892, we find one of the earliest references to coal mining in the September 9th issue when the Trustees of the State Board of Mines, of which S. W. Downey was President and C. G. Coutant, the Secretary, were inviting memberships at $5.00 and also inviting specimens of minerals to be submitted.

Prior to that year, however, we know that coal was being mined in the southern part of the state along the Union Pacific railroad as early as 1868. Records also reveal that coal was being mined at Cambria, Wyoming near Newcastle several years prior to the opening of the mines near Sheridan.

While it is known that farmers were digging coal on their lands at an earlier date, the *Sheridan Post* of July 2, 1891 carried an advertisement of coal available in commercial quantity and offered to the public by Loucks and Becker's Furniture Store at $1.50 per ton delivered.

It might be interesting to note that during that same month of 1891, a powder house was shot at by a drunken Finlander in Rock Springs, exploding 1,500 kegs of black powder, the remains of which spread over 20 acres!

An April 28, 1892, A. T. Burgess advertised "deliver coal from the Becker mine on Big Goose at $3.50 per ton."

From the *Sheridan-Enterprise* dated May 28, 1892, an article states that the great coal mines at Cambria, near Newcastle, formerly operated by the Kilpatrick Brothers and Collins, "closed down due to a strike by the miners for higher wages."

On December 10, 1892, the *Sheridan Enterprise* ran an ad as follows: "I have recently opened up a coal mine 7½ miles north of Sheridan and one-half miles north of the well-known Moore and Peak bank. The quality is as good as can be obtained in the country. At the bank, $1.00 per ton; delivered in town, $3.50. Leave orders at the Post Office. Wm. Burgess."

Enterprise—2/18/93—"The famous Tongue River Coal will be delivered to any part of town by the Sheridan Transfer Co. at $2.50 per ton. Leave orders at old Sheridan State Bank building."

During that same month, the *Sheridan Post* tells of C. H. Grinnell and William Burgess, as owners of two coal mines between Sheridan and Tongue River and of them shipping a portion of their output to South Dakota and Western Nebraska. This article extolls the good features of the Sheridan coal.

On March 3, 1893, 160 acres, the N½NE, NENW and NESE quarters of Sec. 34, Township 57, Range 84 W. was sold by W. E. Palmer and wife to C. H. Grinnell, according to a recorded deed, and that month, "Articles of Incorporation (of the Sheridan Fuel Company) were filed on March 3, 1893 for the purpose of buying and leasing coal lands, and capitalized at $100,000.00 for 1,000 shares at $100 each. Place of business, Sheridan, Wyomngg. Trustees, C. H. Grinnell, J. R. Phelan, George T. Beck and Anson Higby," according to the *State Tribune*. (C. H. Grinnell was the grandfather of Mr. Harold Grinnell who is a retired carpenter living presently in Sheridan.)

It was quite obvious from information gathered, that Mr. Grinnell was the prime promoter and operator of the corporation when that same month, he traveled to Cambria to observe their coal mining layout and methods. Returning to Sheridan, he quickly set up a tipple about four miles north of Sheridan and opened up a slope mine to the first vein of coal. A mining camp quickly followed and was given the name of Higby, named after one of the original incorporators. Mr. Porter Kennedy, whose father became superintendent of the operation in 1898, states that Anson Higby was, he believes, the surveyor for the undertaking as well as one of the incorporators.

Also, in March of 1893, the first mine-related injury recorded, occurred at one of the smaller private "banks" on Tongue River when a William Niver fell from an overturned wagon on the side of a hill.

Horsepower, of course, was used exclusively at first. An ad in the *Sheridan Post* of April 20, 1893 revealed a horse strayed from the Sheridan Fuel Co's coal mine below Wrench Ranch "one blue horse.—Patrick Rooney for reward."

On June 8, 1893, (eight days after the first electricity in Sheridan was turned on at the Sheridan Inn on Saturday, June 1, 1893), the County Commissioners were petitioned for a county road extending from the Sheridan depot, along the west side of the railroad to Higby (thence down Tongue River).

Again, the records reveal that a German by the name of John Falkner was killed as a result of a cave-in at some mine used by neighbors located on public land on Tongue River.

By October of that same year, the Sheridan Fuel Company, whose reputation was gaining momentum, had contracted to furnish the Soldiers Home at Hot Springs, S. D. a winter's supply of coal.

Higby Mine Tipple (Later, Dietz No. 1. Dietz No. 4 and Dietz No. 7. Tipple improved from time to time.

On October 26, 1893, an article in the *Sheridan Post* described the Sheridan Fuel Company's product as "Black Diamonds" and its operations as quite extensive under the foremanship of A. P. Club. It consisted of two main entries and was located about five miles north of Sheridan. The vein of coal between 10 and 20 feet thick, and the mine itself being seven feet high. An analysis of the coal revealed .4368 fixed carbon; .243 moisture; .364 ash; .14025 volatile matter; water evaporation 1075 to the pound. There were reported to be 4 separate veins. H. C. Grinnell, Sec'y.-Manager; also, the Honorable Geo. T. Beck, R. J. Kilpatrick, Anson Higby and H. C. Alger (directors).

Dietz tipple, 1977.

The following month, the Sheridan Fuel Company began construction of a 22 ft. x 30 ft. commissary and a new boarding house 24 ft. x 50 ft. with an "L" extension 16 ft. x 32 ft.

By November, at a meeting of the Sheridan Fuel Company directors, it was reported that they were producing 18 cars or 450 tons of coal daily and tonnage increasing.

The following year, C. M. Dietz and H. F. Cady of Omaha came to Sheridan and visited the Sheridan Fuel Company mines, and while there seems to be no evidence that they became involved at that time, subsequently, it was revealed that Gould Dietz of Omaha became associated with the Company. By that fall, 30 cars of coal were shipped to Nebraska with 75 men working and the force being "increased as fast as good miners were obtained."

On March 38, 1895, there is a record of a mine explosion at Almy, Wyoming (on the Union Pacific Railroad) killing 60 miners. Contributions for the survivors were requested all over the state. (This was evidently the third such disaster in the last 14 years; the first occurring in 1881, the Rock Mountain Mine No. 2, killing 36 Chinese and 4 whites; and the second occurring in 1888, the U. P. Mine No. 4, killing 13).

By the middle of 1895, it was reported that about 8 mines were in operation in the vicinity of Sheridan with coal available from 75¢ to $1.00 per ton at the mine. In the Fall of that year, a Fred Wellman was killed and James Croghan seriously injured in a cave-in at the Wellman mine about 6 miles east of Big Horn, Wyoming.

In the Jan. 11, 1900 issue of the *Sheridan Post*, there appeared the following ad, "Beaver Creek Coal at $2.00 per ton delivered. Nelson Brothers." Also, this ad, "If you want nice hot pan cakes for breakfast, buy your coal of Fred McDonnough. Telephone Produce Exchange." And another ad, "Coal. $2.00 per ton—Sheridan Lumber, Phone 11."

By 1897, it appears that Mr. Gould Dietz of Omaha had become associated with the Sheridan Fuel Company acting as its treasurer, and apparently coming all the way from Omaha each pay day to pay off the miners.

Although I find nothing to reflect the exact date, the name of the thriving camp of Higby was changed to "Dietz," being so re-named after Mr. Dietz. This occurred probably in 1898, as

according to Porter Kennedy, the Kennedy family came to Higby in 1898 when Mr. Stewart Kennedy became superintendent of the mine. (I have a copy of the August 4, 1901 issue of the "Grange Judd Farmer" pamphlet, addressed to "John Hecht, Higby, Wyoming"), and issues of the Sheridan papers about this time referred to the camp interchangably "Higby" and "Dietz."

An article in the February 22, 1900 issue of the *Sheridan Post* relates, "The people of Higby demonstrated that they are of a generous disposition and willing to aid their fellow man. Mrs. A. Rennie, wife of James Rennie who had his arm amputated, has received generous contributions from the people of Higby." Also, in this same issue, reference is made to Stuart Kennedy* who accompanied Gould Dietz on a tour of Sheridan. Kennedy apparently became manager of the Sheridan Fuel Company in June of 1898. (Stewart Kennedy was the father of both Porter and Donald Kennedy of Sheridan, and the grandfather of Mr. Robert Kennedy who is currently the Potentate of the Kalif Shrine Temple in Sheridan).

In the 1901 issue of the *Sheridan Post*, an article appeared under the headline, "A BUSY LITTLE CITY." "Dietz, the Home of the Sheridan Fuel Company, as Seen By a Post Reporter." "A Number of Important Improvements Are to Be Made During the Summer." "No institution contributes so largely to the revenues and commercial interests of Sheridan County at the present time as the Sheridan Fuel Company which is located at the town of Dietz. The town was lately named in honor of the enterprising gentlemen that have brought the model coal camp into prominence and made of it an institution that in two years will be second to none west of the Missouri River.

A visit to the mines will reveal the fact that from 40 to 50 cars of coal are loaded and sent to points on the Burlington to give warmth at the fireside of thousands of residents who till the soil of the level plains and also furnish fuel for the many steam plants located in their midst. Dietz is indeed a busy little town that has all modern appurtenances; electric lights, a city water system, a club house, store, meat market, etc. The man behind the gun in this instance is Superintendent Kennedy who has complete charge of all things connected with the camp and the progress made since he undertook the

---

* More about Stewart Kennedy: p. 69, chap. 6; 128, chap. 10; 149, chap. 12; and 182, chap. 14.

supervision shows that the company selected the right man for the position. He took the reins when the few cars sent out created no comment, but a change was soon noticeable, more cars were needed, more railroad trackage was required and the building of comfortable cottages to a considerable number was a necessity. He investigated the coal beds underneath the camp and came to the conclusion that a better quality of coal was awaiting only the hand of man to bring it to the surface.

The assertion that the Dietz coal could be used successfully on locomotives was hailed with suspicion and doubt by the general public but Kennedy knew whereof he spoke and then he determined to sink a shaft to a lower vein, 180 feet below the surface, to test his theory; the company stood by him. About two months ago, the shaft reached the vein and a quantity was used to test the practicability of the scheme. The coal was found to be of a very superior quality and a test was at once made with the result that it not only gave good satisfaction to the engineers but was more economical. This gave the Sheridan Fuel Co. a chance to expand and being avowed expansionists they were not slow in taking advantage of the situation with their characteristic promptness and energy and today the new mine is opened. The foundations for the power house is to be built altogether of steel, 40 and 130 feet. Four immense boilers are being bedded by contractor John Johnson, which will furnish power to run the pumps, hoisting works, machine shops and also run the air compressors which will drive the latest devised power drills. A 20 feet fan, built entirely of steel has already been placed and so arranged that should one passage be closed by accident, the fan can be reversed and air forced through another opening.

A steel tipple is to be erected 82 feet high that will be arranged to load four cars at one time each with a different grade of coal. New tracks are to be laid immediately and arranged to facilitate the handling of the enormous output. The pumps will force the water which, by the way, is of a superior quality, to a reservoir which is situated on the top of an adjoining hill the height of which will afford a high pressure to the water after it is conveyed to the streets. A perfect water system will be put in operation and the surplus of water will be used for irrigating land what has heretofore been valueless for want of moisture. Anticipating the increase of population the company has let a contract which calls for 30 houses each to contain a cemented cellar, a garden patch and many other little conveniences that go to make up a miner's home. When the new order of things is completed we may see each house supplied with good water from the Main, and electric lights. The above does not include many minor changes that have and will take place in the bustling little city. All has been brought about by the intelligence and energy of Mr. Kennedy backed by influential and thorough going business men who are not afraid to invest their money in Wyoming coal lands and have shown their faith in the future by building a plant that in every particular is arranged for a duration of fifty years.

The 20 new engines recently purchased by the Burlington are provided with a special grate for the burning of Sheridan coal. That Dietz will make a great coal camp is assured. The two mines will be kept running to their fullest capacity and if the output is found to be insufficient the company will promptly open up new ones.

The miners think that a lucky star is over them while at work as Mr. Kennedy has a record of ten years as Mine Superintendent without a fatal accident. We will devote space in the future to another article in which the inner works and workers will be described, meanwhile the Post greets the newly named town and its promoters with best wishes for success in the great enterprise."

The above-described mine was known as the Dietz No. 2 Mine. Its location was just beyond the southeast edge of the Dietz Camp. While Dietz No. 1 Mine was a "slope" mine, the Dietz No. 2 Mine was a "shaft" mine going straight down into the ground and the coal brought up by an elevator usually called a "cage." It was to work in this mine that my father, George Kuzara, came to Dietz in the year 1901, and it was in this mine that he was quite seriously injured when he was accidentally squeezed between a mine car and the side of the mine, an injury from which he claimed he never completely recovered.

The evidence of this shaft can be seen today and consists of a round hole about 50 feet in diameter containing a body of water in the base and much evidence of people having since been using it as a dumping spot for their garbage and refuse.

As time went on, several articles about the Dietz mine and its activities appear in the Sheridan Enterprise:

1/12/01—Over 3,800,000 tons of coal produced in the mines of Wyoming. Of this amount 120,000 tons mined by Sheridan Fuel Co. at Higby with the Rock Springs Mine's leading, mining 479,200 tons.

1/23/01—"Last Saturday, payday at Higby and on Sunday, quite a few of the boys came to

foreman instructed to wait until he could check for gas with a safety lamp. Flames shot out of shaft, resulting in some serious burns to those nearby. Explosion halted work at the mine for the day as some of the woodwork was destroyed by the fire. This mine was known to contain quite a little gas."

3/30/01—"About 75 coal miners laid off at Higby mines as business slacked down and new machinery being installed."

Dietz about 1903, looking south. Row of white houses upper right called "Piano Row." Hospital on hill on extreme left. Upper left is tipple of Dietz No. 2 shaft mine.

Dietz today from same location—now a pasture for cattle.

Dietz No. 2 Shaft Mine and Power House.

town to celebrate which resulted in a number being arrested for drunkenness and disorderly conduct, among whom were Gust Weber, J. Currier. All jailed."

3/9/01—"Explosion" (probably Dietz No. 2) "took place Monday 7:00 a.m. 2 men entered shaft and caused by miners' open light although

4/13/01—"Carpenters arrived from Omaha to be employed at Dietz building 20 residences and 2 hotels which will be used by the miners."

4/20/01—"C. H. Grinnell has received contract to put in 4 more side tracks to the new coal mine shaft." (Dietz No. 2).

5/25/01—"State Coal Inspector Young came from Cheyenne this week to inspect the Dietz mines."

6/1/01—"The Dietz Camp described as a model camp with trees, grass and modern conveniences located about 4 miles north of Sheridan on the B & M railroad. Some 20 new residences have just been added. On the hill, immediately east of the town, there is being erected a commodius hospital for benefit of the miners."

On this tour, the representatives of the press and others were conducted through the mine and given a thorough description of the operation. "Inside the mine, the officials even served dinner to the guests, cooked and served by Mr. Price, after dinner, they toured the Company store, Mr. Hudson, popular in Sheridan, acting as guide. Under D. D. Warner, they were escorted to the tipple and given an explanation of the incline plane and the law of gravity with the operation completely described. The diggers of the coal, it was stated, were paid by the ton with about an average of 2 tons to a car with the average man loading about 4 per day, which at 40¢ per ton or slightly more than $3.00 per day—13 of these cars fill an average railroad car. About 30 such cars at this time of the year per day. However, in the winter when the demand is greater, more coal, of course, is produced, shipped as far east as Chicago. Recently, the B & M Railroad has placed in operation a number of new engines, specifically adapted to the consumption of the Dietz coal. The industry," the article went on to say, was "growing rapidly and contributed greatly to the economy of Sheridan. The camp is modern and has its own water system, and electric lights. Horses and mules are used to pull the mine cars to the entry. Upon entering the mine, after some 20 or 30 rods, you come to a spot where the track divides and an engine (motor) is used to pull the cars. John Wade was operating this motor. It was here that Mr. J. J. Lytle took over. At this point, the group got on a motor which took them a half mile or more at a distance of 70 or 80 feet under the top surface. The vein ranged from 10 to 14 feet in thickness. Pillars of coal are periodically left and wooden supports used to hold up the roof. Fire from spontaneous com-

bustion," it was stated, "was a dangerous enemy of the operation." This article also described the No. 2 shaft about a mile southeast of the present slope mine. "It had an 180 foot deep elevator or cage operated by a steam hoist. Three engines are used to operate the hoist and compressors operating the fan. The fan is a marvel of ingenuity and can be regulated to either inject air or suck it out. Carbon dioxide previously prevalent in the mine is dispelled by this fan. A large steel plated fire proof building is being built.

Digging coal in room, Dietz No. 2.

Electric Motor in Dietz No. 2 Mine (about 1904).

The facility is somewhat limited yet but is rapidly being completed to full operation within 30 days."

Visitors in Dietz No. 2 mine.

Early miners at Dietz No. 1. Emma Bylund's grandfather, Thomas B. Lee, father of Jack Lee, one of the bosses at Dietz, standing upper right. (Note old fashioned oil-burning lamps)

Another article appearing about this time, tells of a John Hecht being arrested for illegally selling liquor without a license, was arraigned and with the defense stating he was merely a carrier for others, and after hearing the testimony, Judge Blackburn discharged the victim. (It was John Hecht's property my father bought from him in 1907).

7/13/01—"Sheridan and Higby baseball teams to play on Sunday p.m. at the Higby diamond."

8/10/01—"Board of County Commissioners at its meeting last Thursday granted a liquor license to John Hecht to sell liquor in Dietz for a period of one year giving Dietz its first saloon."

10/26/01—"An ad appeared in the *Enterprise* calling for several dining girls to apply to Stewart Kennedy, Dietz, Wyoming."

11/23/01—"James Gilroy, an aged gentleman of Dietz, passed away of pneumonia and buried on Sunday at Mt. Hope Cemetery in Sheridan."

12/28/01—Letter to the Editor: "This Community really an active operation with about 400 miners and 200 outside and an important contributor to Sheridan's economy. Under the able supervision of Mr. Stewart Kennedy and Assn. Superintendent, Mr. Pearson and the store manager, Mr. Frank Dietz are the busiest men in Sheridan County."

1/11/02—Letter to the Editor: Correcting the name of the store manager to D. D. Warner, rather than "Pearson."

And in anther article: Told of a Charles (Brown?) a former Torres Rough Rider, taking sick and subsequently dying. A complaint was registered against the camp doctor for negligence in not answering the call for aid, asking for the doctor's discharge with a decision to be made by Mr. Kennedy. Evidently, a few days later Dr. Paul resigned and was temporarily replaced by a Sheridan doctor on an itinerant basis every other day.

"The store manager, Frank Dietz, left for Omaha to attend his father's funeral during which time, the store was under the able management of Jolly Jimmy Donovan." "Store crowded due to his personality."

1/18/02—"The School here a wonder with 116 enrolled scholars—average attendance, 80. Mr. Fulton, principal and Miss Nellie Smith his assistant crowded in one room 20 x 30."

1/25/02—"Two accidents this week—Mike Blitzki, a Pole, injured by falling pole and Andrew Johnson injured when he fell from the tipple breaking his leg."

2/15/02—"Jean Hinman and Tina Snooks married this week followed by a charivari. Yes, Dietz has a band. Dietz band provided the music at the Republican rally. while not comparable to Souza's aggregation."

3/31/02—"New offices of brown stone completed. Frank Deitz now left the store and replaced by Mr. Patterson who can talk in five different languages."

7/19/02—"Frank Kennedy, brother of Stewart Kennedy met with a nearly fatal accident between two coal cars in the mine while setting the brake, cutting his throat and breaking his jaw."

7/26/02—Kennedy advertising for a number of tons of hay for the horses at the mine, and 8/21/02, *Sheridan Post* ad for "2 horses strayed from Dietz. Any information. Liberal reward. Contact Robert Flockhart, Dietz, Wyoming."

9/11/02—"Fire burned new tipple which is the second time the tipple has been destroyed by fire caused by burning slack. The Dietz No. 2 shaft mine in the meanwhile now working 12 hours per day."

The following is an agreement, self-explained as follows:

"This Memorandum of Agreement made December 1st, 1902, between the Sheridan Coal Company, of Omaha (hereinafter called the Coal Company) and the Chicago, Burlington & Quincy Railroad Company (hereinafter called the Railway Company).

WITNESSETH, that inconsideration of the sum of Eight Thousand, Eight Hundred and Eighty-five Dollars and Sixteen Cents ($8,885.16) to be paid by the Railway Company to the Coal Company within Ten (10) days from the date of this Agreement, the Coal Company agrees to sell and deliver to the Railway Company, and the Railway Company agrees to receive and pay for, at the prices hereinafter set forth, a quantity of coal which shall not be less than 400 tons per day, nor more than Eight Hundred (800) per day, the actual quanitty delivered to be varied at the option of the Railway Company.

In further consideration of the prices named herein for the Coal, the Railway Company agrees to transport over its own lines to Dietz, Wyoming, all rails, mining machinery and repair parts for the same that may be required for the maintenance or extension of the Coal Company's mines at Dietz, Wyoming, at the following rates:

From Chicago and St. Louis $6.00 per ton.

From Mississippi River points and intermediate points East of the Missouri River $5.00 per ton.

From Omaha or Denver and intermediate points, $3.50 per ton.

Also to transport such oil, powder and tools used in the Coal Company's mines at one-half of the regular tariff rates, during the life of this agreement.

The delivery of the Coal shall be made on cars on the Railway Company's tracks at Dietz, Wyoming.

All Coal delivered under this agreement shall be prepared in the manner described below as may be directed by the Railway Company from time to time.

First, Screened Lump, which shall consist of all Coal that will pass over a standard screen having five (5) inch spaces between the bars.

Second, Egg Coal, which shall consist of all Coal that will pass through a screen having five (5) inch openings and over a screen having one (1) inch opening;

Third, Engine Coal, which shall consist of all coal that will pass through a screen having a five (5) inch opening;

Fourth, Mine Run Coal, which shall consist of the entire product of the Mine.

The weights and quality of the coal shall be subject to inspection by the Railway Company, and the Railway Company shall have the right to reject any coal which is not prepared in accordance with the foregoing specifications.

The daily shipments shall comply as nearly as possible with the Railway Company's orders, but the average of the daily shipment of each month shall be considered as the actual shipments for the purpose of this contract.

In consideration of the sale and delivery of the Coal, as aforesaid, and of the strict compliance by the Coal Company, with all the terms of this Agreement, the Railway Company agrees to pay to the Coal Company for each ton of coal so delivered, the following prices, viz:

—: STATEMENT SHOWING TONNAGE SHIPPED FROM NO. 2 SHAFT, FROM JANUARY 1ST TO 22ND, INCLUSIVE—MOST OF

IT INTENDED FOR RAILROAD USE.
—: : : : : : : : : : : :—

Tons Lump . . . . .3065 = 44%
Tons Nut . . . . .1400 = 20%
Tons Pea Nut . . . . .1212 = 19%
Tons Screenings . . . . .1170 = 17%
                                   6873 = 100%

Screenings and Pea Nut, 19% = 17% = 36%

Mine Run @ $1.00 = 100% of product.

Screened Coal without using Pea Nut or Screenings, 100% – 36% – 64%—$1.00 + 64% = $1.6525

Loading of **Mine Run** costs to me .03¢ per ton.

Loading of **Lump** costs to me same **amount** regardless of tonnage.

Mine Run tonnage or total 6853 x .03¢ = $205.59 + **Lump** tonnage or Total 3065 = .0676 per ton for **Lump**.

Lump—3065 tons at .067¢		
Nut—1400 tons at .06¢		
Pea Nut—1218 tons at .06¢	=	$379.98
Screen—1170 tons at .015¢		
Unloading and shoveling back slack at $4.25 per car	=	107.09
		$487.07

$487.07 + 6853 total tonnage =   .071¢ per ton
Cost of Loading Mixed =   .071¢ per ton
Cost of Loading Mine Run =   .03 ¢ per ton
Excess on **Screened** Coal   .041¢ per ton

Excess on **Screened** Coal should be 1.5625¢

Total, including difference $1.6035¢ per ton unloading and dumping

Slack

We should get, if no **Screenings** or **Pea Nut** used—$1.6035 per ton.
Mine Run at $1.00 = 100%
100% – 17% = 83%
$1.00 + 83% = $1.205
$1.205 – Excess of loading **Screened** Coal .041¢ = $1.246 per ton. We should get if **Pea Nut** used, and only **Screenings** thrown out, $1.246 per ton.

Dietz, Wyoming., January 24, 1902.
   (Ed. note: Above date probably should read "January 24th, 1903")

12/4/02—"Accident, Fay Cooley, 17 year old son of Frank Cooley was killed while working on the tipple. His father at one time was one of the editors of the *Sheridan Post.* Mrs. Cooley runs a private boarding house at Dietz. H. M. Pinkerton, preacher from Dayton performed the services and O. K. Smyth, funeral director. Burial in Mt. Hope Cemetery in Sheridan."

Then appeared a news article giving in some detail current observations of Dietz, as follows: "450 men employed, Camp population, 1,000, 112 railroad cars shipped out in one day.— 38,000 tons."

Horses live in the mine the year around, and here is the first evidence of the new compressed air drills replacing the old hand method. Detailed description of loading the cars in the mine, pulled by horses to the cage—drawn up cage by powerful engines to the top where car is automatically dumped onto shaker screens which separate the coal to four grades, lump, nut, peanut and slack and that shoots the coal into box cars where a loader throws the coal to the edge of the car—scale to weigh the cars— 1,200 tons per day being mines—7 veins of coal under the land—enough for ten generations—155 houses—rent at $18-$13 per month—new hospital recently built—miners earn about $100 per month—credit and coupon books available for purchases at Company store stocked with all kinds of goods—(author's note: books of coupons, perforated in different denominations would be issued at the request of the miner at payday—all pay in cash—in lieu of money—such books of $1.00 value costing $0.90 cents, the coupons redeemable only at the Company store)—Post Office located in store building where Postmaster Donavan handles the daily mail—two social and beneficiary lodges—Sunday School—Church—(author's note: from some information supplied by Ira Salveson of Sheridan, I was told that a Jonas Gabriel Strum built the stone store building and the Catholic Church at Dietz. Mr. Salveson states further that later on, this same man built a house for his father)—school with over 100 pupils—Principal, Beloit, and Dietz just purchased another 100 acres of land at $105 per acre.

4/2/03—(Dietz Items)—Dietz cornet band, gun club, etc. Ball team with game between Dietz No. 1 and No. 2. Clint Benedict and Anna Snook married. Mrs. Nick Scullen gave a dance in their honor.

4/23/03—Dietz miners strike accusing Superintendent Kennedy with refusing to recognize the union. 400 miners affected. Number of miners

Dietz, Wyoming—Upper left, Dietz No. 2 tipple complex; Upper right, Company store; To left, company office; Center, Dietz Camp; Lower left and right, Power Plant; Lower center, home of J. U. Gridley, Manager.

ordered to vacate the company houses. Superintendent says he closed the mines due to lack of orders of coal but it reported that he refused to meet with those no longer employed. Kennedy feels unions not needed. UMW of A ordered by James Morgan, President, to stay away from mine.

4/30/03—Strike declared off after agreement reached. Pres. C. M. Dietz of Omaha here.

In 1903 and 04, the interest in the coal fields around Sheridan was quite high when representatives from Cambria investigated the feasibility of establishing a mine near Sheridan city limits. A new company, the Horseshoe Company tried to buy the Dietz mines, but could not meet the price asked; and a party of railroad officials, A. J. Snider of Kansas City and G. W. Megeath of Omaha, came for a visit to the mines and returned East. Sup't. J. U. Gridley—building a new store—new Catholic Church being built—175 new pit cars ordered—Mr. Gridly complimented for his ability as Superintendent.

Also in the latter part of 1903 and the first part of 1904, the following items appear: Dietz, 50 more houses being built—population now estimated at 1,500—mines pushed to 10 hours per day—double shift—store building almost complete—Company being pushed with orders of 2,000 tons per day—Ben Dixon, died of typhoid fever and Father Sasse held services Sunday morning—Reid Murdock, Chas. Morey, Hazel and Gladys Smith in school at Sheridan—Mrs. Nick Scullens added a colored cook at her boarding house. Man killed at Dietz—P. J. Rooney struck by tramway car with fatal result last Tuesday when car jumped the track crushing his chest.

1/23/04—Special bond election for county court house with special polling judges, Frank Smith, James Birchby and John Hecht of Dietz named.

2/12/04—William Patterson, store keeper, in town last Saturday—walked to and from Dietz. States won't be boarding at the boarding house this time next year (thinking about marriage). Electric lights installed in Dietz houses.

Dietz Camp, looking northwest. Catholic church in center with steeple. Upper grade school, upper left, referred to as the "high school" as it had two stories.

View of the Town of Dietz, Wyo., Showing Loaded Dump-Cars and Tipple of Mine No. I.

Dietz No. 1 in 1903 looking west.

Dietz No. 1, same view as it looks today.

4/8/04—Don Stewart has contract for erection of a new school house at Dietz. Foundation being 24 x 40 and two stories high; and bids being also let for construction of houses under Sup't. Stout—erecting 15 six-room houses 1½ stories; and ladies of Dietz giving a hayseed party.

4/12/04—"Mr. Megeath, Sup't. of Dietz mines came up to Coal Creek Coal mines. Dietz to spend $100,000 and Mr. Megeath looking over latest machinery being used in other mines"— *Casper Tribune.*

5/15/04—B & M railroad building a nice new depot at Dietz. Work progressing rapidly on Mine No. 3. Coal reached after sinking a shaft and working three 8-hour shifts. And in July, the Dietz concert band appeared on the streets of Sheridan attired in brand new red uniforms— one of the best in the state.

Dietz No. 4 looking northwest, showing Protestant Church with steeple on extreme left. Catholic Church with steeple this side of mine tipple. Upper grade school at 1:00 o'clock from Protestant Church.

Dietz No. 4 same view as above as it is today.

Dietz Hotel—Left to right, Jack Stegelman, co-partner owner; Annie Jungers Stegelman, parents of Mrs. Joe Panetta; Mrs. Mary Dell Smith; Mrs. Horner; Jack Horner (two on right, unknown).

9/6/04—Fifty coal dealers of Nebraska and Omaha here in Dietz—entertained by the Sheridan Coal Company. Banquet to be given in the mine. Electric motors now used in No. 1 mine. New electric lights and power plant being installed. Electric cutting machines being installed in all of the mines. Post Office business increasing and Postmaster James Donovan has secured the services of Ethel Cooley as an assistant. Work progressing on the new hotel and Mr. Horner expects to have it in operation in about three weeks.

9/9/04—Details of the banquet in the mine, entertaining all of the visitors from Omaha and Nebraska. "As guests of Sup't. J. U. Gridley at a breakfast, later they all went to visit Mine No. 1, and were led into the mine in complete darkness. After traveling some distance, suddenly about 50 electric lights were turned on and just as suddenly everything became quite daylight, and there was a table completely covered with various kinds of food and five young ladies dressed in white pinned a bouquet on each of their lapels, and they were served turkey, chicken, ham, celery, hot coffee and other beverages. After many toasts were given, they were returned to the surface and treated to a baseball game by the Dietz team. In the evening, they were further entertained before train No. 42 took them homeward."

9/20/04—Chancellor Samuel Dickinson, Grand Knight of the Knights of Pythias arrived from Hanna this morning to start a new lodge at Dietz. Sheridan Lodge No. 9 assisted.

10/4/04—"H. Montagne died at the hospital Saturday p.m. at 4 o'clock. Montague had just been employed by the Sheridan Coal Co. and was engaged with a teamster moving goods. While the team was in motion, Montague fell from the wagon and two wheels of the wagon passed over him. The wagon was broad-tired and heavily loaded. He was taken to the hospital on Thursday when the accident happened, but died Saturday afternoon. He had worked only three hours for the company. Burial services were conducted and Rev. T. C. Williams officiated on Sunday. No relatives remained so he was buried by the Dietz Hospital Association."

12/9/04—Another accident occurred when Elliott Gettys had his eye seriously injured Saturday in the mine. "In the process of shooting down some coal, he lighted the squib and after waiting some time, he thought the squibs had gone out. He returned to the face when the blast went off. A large piece of coal struck him in the right eye. He was taken to the hospital where Dr. Lawrence and (Howell?) removed his eye. The M. E. Church was organized and a Junior League instituted which meets every Sunday p.m.

12/28/04—A new Lodge of Odd Fellows was instituted in Dietz last Saturday p.m. Several candidates were initiated.

12/7/04—"James Gilday," according to the Sheridan Enterprise, "who was injured in the mine, died Tuesday. Services took place at the Catholic Church in Dietz on Friday. Funeral was attended by the entire population. After services, a special train was chartered and brought the body to Sheridan. A funeral procession was formed at the depot headed by the Dietz band, playing a funeral dirge, followed by the casket and mourners and followed by the Miners Union of Dietz. The entire enrollment of the Order marched up Main Street fully six blocks long. Arriving at Mt. Hope Cemetery last rites were performed. James Gilday was one of the survi-

vors of the Hanna Coal Mine disaster and greatly admired by his comrades."

6/13/71—*Billings Gazette*—By Helen B. Fenton, Special to the *Gazette*. **"Cow-boy-Preacher."** **"Some powerful praying."**

"SHERIDAN, Mont.—Praying a powerful prayer, Charles Emery Fenton, a cowboy turned preacher, crawled out on the back of one of his horses.

He was praying for help to hang on to the knife in his hand and for help to cut the cow free. In the wagonbox afloat behind him in the swollen Big Horn River near Basin, Wyo., that spring of 1906 were his wife, Amanda, and his children Dora, 15; Ida, 11; Stanley, 9 and Ernest 7. The two boys were trying desperately to hang onto the crate of chickens they'd been told not to lose.

* * * * * *

Black-haired Charley Fenton had been raised on the powerful prayers of his mother asking the Lord to save them from wolves, starvation and Indians and to please bring her husband home safe.

Fenton's homes as a child had always been one of those pushing back the West's frontiers. The frontier was hard on both men and women, but Fenton's mother was hardier. She survived three husbands. Twice when she was widowed, a baby was on its way. In later years, with deep emotion, Charley Fenton often recalled those days telling how his mother and her other children would be left alone for weeks while his father, a Methodist preacher, was away.

Their home was often a log cabin with just a buffalo robe hung over the door opening and a mud and stick fireplace for warmth and cooking.

Many times, he'd recall, the wolves would stick their noses under the robe and his mother would grab burning fagots from the fire and rush at them trying to burn their noses. The wolves would draw back, slink out of her reach and howl.

The father died in 1876 when Charley was 8. A new baby was born a few months later . . .

Now, in 1906, Charley, who, too, had become a preacher, was ordered by the Methodist Church Conference to a new charge. As the crow flies, it was less than 90 miles from Basin in the Big Horn Valley to Dietz, near Ranchester in Wyoming's Tongue River Valley. But—in between lay the rugged Big Horn Mountains and a

8,950-foot high pass that was closed in the winter.

PREACHER FENTON, always quick to respond to a challenge, (his family called him "reckless") loaded into a wagon all his worldly goods, his wife, children, patchwork quilts, cooking utensils, dishes, his many books and Bible, logging chains, saw, ax and a crate of chickens. He tied the family cow to the back of the wagon.

He was the first to attempt to ford the Big Horn river after the spring runoff that year and people gathered on the bank near Basin to watch.

One of Fenton's horses was a "troublemaker," but the preacher hollered and whipped the team into the water. The cow, on a long rope, swam around in front of the horses and they were being pushed down-stream, their legs tangled in the rope . . .

In her late 70's, one of Fenton's daughters recalled between sobs, "We prayed! Oh, how we prayed!" . . .

*   *   *   *   *   *

Seven-year-old Ernest, who was to become Judge E. E. Fenton of Billings, shrieked as the crate of chickens slipped from his brother Stanley's grasp and floated away.

Meanwhile, Fenton had managed to cut the cow free and a cowboy from the far bank swam his horse into the river and helped pull the wagon the rest of the way out.

DEVOUT, red-haired Mrs. Fenton raised her face toward Heaven. "Praise the Lord!"

The preacher and his family found the going up the Big Horn Mountains rougher than they'd figured. They did not reach the meadows of the high pass until a Saturday night.

Food was short, but the preacher's wife would not break the Sabbath by cooking or doing other work. She interpreted the Bible literally. Preacher Fenton, not being quite so religious, looked at his hungry children and asked the Lord to put a few pine hens where he could shoot them. The Lord obliged and the youngsters were fed . . .

Years later the Fenton sons and daughters recalled how good those hens tasted, cooked over a campfire by their father.

But the mother had refused to eat, and the rest of the Sabbath was kept holy while the family and horses rested.

GOING DOWN the far side of the Big Horns,

Fenton had to put on log chains to keep the back wheels of the wagon from spinning. For the steepest places he chopped down pine trees and fastened them behind the wagon as a drag to keep it from pushing into the slipping, sliding horses.

It was after more than a week of travel that the weary hungry preacher and his family pulled into the yard of the parsonage at his new charge in Dietz. People bustled around and brought hot food to welcome them.

In those days, clothing for preachers' families came out of missionary barrels sent at Christmas time. The Fentons wore the garb whether it fit or not. And preachers received around $75 for a whole year, but people shared their food with the Fentons. And for that Preacher Fenton baptised, married, scolded, worried, praised, helped, pleaded, buried and prayed for his congregations in Southeastern Montana and Northern Wyoming.

HE SANG, played his portable organ, sermonized and shed tears for them. He shared his people's triumphs and their downfalls, his love of the Lord, his courage, his joy of life, his jokes and his hearty laughter until the day he died in 1939.

I know. Because he was my father-in-law.

His grave is in Bridger.

His children and most of his grandchildren and great-grand-children live in Montana. One son, Stanley, died in 1959 and was buried in Sheridan, Montana.

The other son, who became Judge E. E. Fenton of Billings, died in 1969 and his grave is in Billings."

4/2/07—*Sheridan Post.* "Big passenger auto which makes regular trips twice a day between Sheridan and Dietz was on its first trip after some repairs. While travelling down Main Street, frightened the Addleman & Settle dray teams which was standing near the George L. Smith Drug Co. store causing a runaway to Alger Avenue before Mr. Addleman could regain control. No damage."

5/17/07—Dietz. "School board meeting bids for a new school considered but not acted upon. Teachers elected. Prof. Henry Robison, Principal, and salary raised from $80 to $90 per month, and Miss Myrtle Marble, 5th, 6th and 7th grades, from $60 to $65 per month; Miss Ida Miller, 3rd and 4th grades, raised from $50 to

$60 and Miss Anna Jeffers, 1st and 2nd grades, from $60 to $65."

"Mr. Richard Keenan just returned from a trip to San Francisco where he visited friends." (Mr. Keenan operated one of the saloons in Dietz).

6/15/07—Dance held in Dietz under the auspices of the Star of Bethlehem Lodge. Meeting of petitioners for an auxiliary of the Rebecca Lodge Odd Fellows, and arrangements made for its institution. Officers chosen were: Past Grand Grand, Mrs. May Owens; Vice Grand, Mary Russell; Sec. Miss Ida Miller; Treas. Mrs. James Sampson.

6/18/07—"Man Killed in Dietz No. 5" (this no doubt should have been No. 4). "Jabes Sykes shot in Keenan saloon by Chas. Davis Sunday morning. Coroners jury ruled Davis killed Sykes without provocation. Davis arrested."

Page 148, "INVESTIGATIONS OF THE COAL FIELDS OF WYOMING" by the United States Geological Survey in 1907. Government Printing Office, 1909. Department of the Interior.

"DEVELOPMENT"

"Coal mining in the Sheridan District, except for local domestic fuel, is restricted to the coal beds of the Tongue River group on Goose Creek and Tongue River. The thriving mining communities of Dietz, Carneyville, Monarch and Kooi are an index to the rapid growth of the coal-mining industry. The following information in regard to the development of the field is obtained from an article by Stewart Kennedy (*Mines and Minerals, vol. 27, 1907, pp. 294-297) and from field work in 1907.

As early as 1880 coal of workable thickness was known and mined for domestic use by ranchmen at the present location of Dietz. From this time on to 1893, when the first commercial mining began, coal from several prospects on what are now known as the Dietz coal beds Nos. 1 and 2 was mined and hauled to Sheridan. A drift was run on the Dietz No. 1 coal near the east side of Sec. 34, T. 57 N., R. 84 W., in the winter of 1892-93 and the first shipment of coal was made in the following May. Operations continued until 1899, the coal being mined by pick and hoisted by mule power. A modern steam plant was erected in 1899 for the development of Mine No. 1 and the output was greatly

* See page 182

increased. A shaft was put down in 1900 in sec. 35, T. 57 N., R. 84 W., to the Dietz No. 2 coal bed and the development of mine No. 2 began with the erection of a complete hoisting plant and shops. Later a large electric plant was built and machine mining and electric haulage were established in the Dietz mines. In 1903 a shaft was sunk on the Dietz No. 2 coal bed in sec. 3, T. 56 N., R. 84 W., and a modern hoisting plant established as mine No. 3. Also a slope was driven on coal bed No. 2 in Dietz and a drift on the same bed 1½ miles north of Dietz, with adequate equipments, as mines Nos. 4 and 5, respectively. These mines at and near Dietz, operated by the Sheridan Coal Company, employ at the present time about 800 men and support a population of about 2,000 persons.—"

5/1/08—*Enterprise*. In an article written by Mrs. D. H. Warner entitled, "The Sheridan Coal Fields," she describes the coal mining camps of Dietz No. 1 2, 4 and 5, as well as the camps of Monarch, Carneyville, Kooi and the coal mine of Riverside, and stated, "This great industry of Sheridan County is of more vital importance than most people of Sheridan think. When these great industries are idle, the business of the railroad and merchants to a great extent come to a standstill."—and has the following to say specifically about the Dietz Camps of 1, 2, 4 and 5, "Producing in normal times about 3,500 tons daily and employs about 1,000 men. It has a monthly payroll exceeding $50,000.

The population of Dietz is about 3,000 people, and consists almost entirely of miners and their families."

In order to conserve both writing time and reading time, future references to the local newspapers will generally be identified only by date as follows:

1/19/09—"The little son of George Kuzara who fell in the burning slack, is getting along nicely under the care of Dr. Dawson. Both arms, both legs and his stomach were badly burned. Dr. Dawson is also caring for the Baker's little girl, who fell into a tub of boiling water and was severely scalded."

1/19/09—"This morning, Joseph Skulniski, who runs the saloon at John Hecht's old place, a half mile northwest of Dietz, was before Judge C. P. Story, upon complaint of John Hechko, the baker at the same place. Skulniski pleaded guilty to having drawn a pistol on Hechko, in his

Dietz No. 4—Just some of the miners. Note they are wearing oil burning lamps on caps (before the carbide lamp).

bakery. He paid the fine imposed, $50 and costs."

Further, in the Dietz column, it was stated, "If Sheridan county has a law to protect the boys, why is it not enforced? There are many bright boys here, and unfortunately, too many of them are taken from school and sent into the mines as soon as they are old enough to meet the requirements of the law. When able to work they think they should have all the privileges of men, and as no one seems to care where they spend much time in places where the influences are not such as will develop manly characters. Proprietors of questionable places put up notices "No boys under 18 years old allowed," but any time, until 10 o'clock at night, there are more boys from 5 to 20 years of age than there are men to be seen."

1/29/09—"BURNS ANNIVERSARY—One Hundred and Fiftieth Anniversary of Birth of the Scottish Bard Celebrated With Much Enthusiasm."

"The Scotchmen of Dietz are never behind in anything relative to their native land or the country of their adoption, and on Monday evening they celebrated the anniversary of Bobbie Burns' birthday in most fitting manner. In fact, the Scots are not alone in paying tribute to the memory of Scotland's bard, for everywhere there are admirers of the man who wrote Tam O'Shanter and other great poems that won his immortality.

The songs of Burns were sung, his poems were read and recited, and the entire program was replete with interesting features. The exercises were opened with "There Was a Lad Was Born in Kyle,' sung by John Robinson, and then followed a speech by Mr. Walter Russell, and an address by Mr. Richard Hotchkiss on the life of Robert Burns; song by Joseph Brown of Dietz; song by William Hunter of Carneyville; song by Gaythorne Henderson of Sheridan; song by Chittie Brown of Dietz; song by Barbara Lee of Dietz; song by Joseph Allen of Dietz; song by James Moffat of Dietz; duet by Mrs. Agnes Hotchkiss and—".

2/12/09—"Mr. Rudolph and Mr. Redle are operating Mine No. 6 and Mr. Redle has moved his family up there."

3/12/09 (Post)—(Dietz). "Harry Kettering and Mr. Isa Sturgeon were visiting friends in Acme and Kooi Sunday.

Mrs. Agnes Mcdoul and Christene Gibbons were business visitors in Sheridan, Tuesday.

George Hotchkiss and quite a number of his friends took in the boxing contest in Sheridan Monday night.

Mr. and Mrs. George Bateman and family have moved to a larger house and lot where they will have more room to raise lots of turkeys for the coming Thanksgiving.

The children of Dietz gave a farewell party to the Miles children on Tuesday evening. Games were played and lunch was served at 10:30 o'clock. Each one bid goodbye to the Miles children and hoped they would come back and visit Dietz again.

Grandma Laurie is reported on the sick list this week.

Mrs. Walter Russell and son, William, were Sheridan visitors Wednesday.

Some of the old friends of Mrs. Anna Miles gave her a farewell party. Mrs. Miles departed this morning for her ranch. Those present were: Mrs. Taylor Stork, Mrs. James Lytle, Mrs. Agnes Hotchkiss, Mrs. C. Gibbons, Mrs. Mary Finnan, Mrs. Rose Byerly, Mrs. Anna Rogers and mother, Mrs. Churchill. The party was held in Mrs. Sam Sturgeon's home on account of Mrs. Sturgeon being crippled with rheumatism. Everybody had a pleasant time. Lunch was served at 11 o'clock and participants departed at a late hour wishing Mrs. Miles much luck and happiness on her farm.

Clarence Babcock from Billings, Mont., has been visiting old friends in Dietz.

The stork seems to have a partiality for the street known as "Piano Row." On Lincoln's birthday he visited the home of Samuel Garrett, leaving a baby girl who was christened Anna Iona at the Catholic church. On Saturday, March 6th, he visited the home of James Wier, our justice of the peace, and deposited a son, who is said to be the largest ever born in Dietz. On Wednesday morning, he skipped one house and dropped down at the door of Fred Jensen's home and presented them with a wee girlie.

Dr. Buckle of the University of Wyoming, visited our schools and delighted the children with stories of the west wind, the dipper and many others, interesting to the children. He lectured Wednesday night at the Methodist church, but on account of the rough night, after the blizzard, your correspondent was unable to attend, so cannot give an account of it.

A number of Dietz men both young and old, attended the boxing contest at the Kirby Opera house Monday evening. They report Alex Flockart a very promising boxer.

Mrs. Frank Smith is still very ill, bordering on nervous prostration.

Tom Smith took a surveyor up to survey his homestead between Ranchester and Dayton.

Mr. and Mrs. Hanson have returned home, after several months spent visiting their daughter and other friends at Ashton, Neb. Miss Alma is a student at Lincoln, Neb."

6/8/09—"R. A. Keenan allowed to move liquor license from Carneyville to Dietz."

1/27/10—"MR. SHELDON TAKES A LEASE ON DIETZ NO. 6.

Charles W. Sheldon closed a deal yesterday with J. J. Rennie, for the lease of the mine known as Dietz No. 6 and took possession this morning.

The mine is located north of the city near the railroad. As yet there are no tracking facilities, the output of the mine having been in the past sold exclusively for local consumption.

Mr. Sheldon contemplates several improvements, but will probably not at present make arrangements for shipping, but will devote his attention to increasing the local sales. If the demand seems to justify the outlay, the output of the mine will be materially increased and there is practically no limit to the capacity.

Mr. Sheldon has demonstrated his business ability during his several years residents in Sheridan, and there is no question but this venture will be handled with the vim and energy that, barring accidents, promises well for ultimate success."

2/9/10—A display ad in the *Sheridan Enterprise* appeared advertising "NO. 6 COAL—AS GOOD AS THE BEST" "Mine North of Town" "C. W. Sheldon, Lessee. Office Phone 192. Residence phone 303."

2/27/10—"MINER IS INJURED IN MINE NO. 2 AT DIETZ"—"Robert Hotchkiss, motor runner in Mine No. 2 at Dietz, was badly injured in a head-on collision yesterday. On his trip out of the mine with a long string of cars, two cars became detached and remained at the bottom of the shaft. On his return, not knowing the cars were there, Hotchkiss, with the big motor, crashed into them. The cars were splintered and Hotchkiss was caught in the wreck and his body

badly bruised. The fingers of his right hand were also crushed."

3/7/10—"PHTHIAN SISTERS STAGE SIDE SPLITTING PLAYET AT DIETZ—BIG CROWD ATTENDS." (Correspondence)—Dietz, Wyo., March 7—From the moment Miss Maggie Flockhart in her original makeup as Charity Longface bounced into the club rooms of the Young Ladies Single Blessedness Debating Society, accompanied by her parrot and other paraphernalia, the spectators at the Dietz amusement hall never had a chance to straighten out their faces until the little one act farce entitled "The Spinster's Convention" was ended.

The affair was a brilliant success, not only from a financial standpoint, the proceeds going to the local lodge of Pythian sisters, but the actresses and actors surprised their friends in the way they carried through their parts without a hitch of any kind. The play was staged in a very elaborate manner, considering the disadvantages of a small stage and Mrs. Chas. Lawrence and Mrs. Jas. McCoy deserve great credit for their parts as stage manager and leading lady.

Miss Gweneth Lytle in the character of Sophia Stuckup, a dazzling young maiden of only thirty-nine, got herself and her ear trumpet into all kinds of difficulties. Mrs. Jas. McCoy, as Josaphine Ann Green, presiding officer of the young ladies' debating society, handled the gavel with skill of a girl of twenty and the appearance of forty and elicited the usual voting sign, consisting of the word man on all grave occasions of state.

Miss Elva Spangle, as Belinda Blue Grass was very fetching as an agitator in favor of dress reform and Miss Zuma Spanogle, as Rebecca Sharp, replied to her telling arguments in favor of this style of dress in such a way as to convince the assembled society that women should ever remain as the "clinging vine," man the "sturdy oak." The secretary read a list of the eligible young men of Dietz which shows there might have been more truth than poetry in some phases of the little playlet.

Jas. Madison and Thos. Newman as Professor Makeover and his assistant, proved a real hit and succeeded in demonstrating to the once young maidens that he had a machine which would transform them to full grown American beauties, instead of mere buds and other equally delightful things.

Little Loraine took the hearts of the audience by storm as a little fairy, as did little Misses Doris Newman and Helen McCoy. Frank Smith sung a coon song and gave evidence of his old time ability.

Mrs. Fred H. Sturm sang a semi-classical piece which was very well received and Misses Ruby Samuelson and Ruth Brown sang: "If I Only Had a Sweetheart," which made a hit with the audience. The entertainment was closed with tableaus by Mrs. Sturm and little Misses Lawrence, Newman and McCoy."

4/1/10—"MINER AT DIETZ SUCCOMBS INJURIES" "Received Injuries Tuesday Morning on Duty at No. 4 Mine, When Throttle Valve Blew Out." "Al Lytle died this morning at 1:30 o'clock from injuries received Tuesday when the big eight inch steam line which carries the steam to the hoisting engine at mine No. 4 at Dietz blew out the throttle valve and severely scalded the engineer.—Deceased was a member of the Tripple Link Lodge, I.O.O.F., of Dietz, and of the United Mine Workers of America. He had been connected with the coal company for over nine years.—The Odd Fellows Lodge and the United Mine Workers will have charge of the funeral, a special funeral train probably leaving Dietz Sunday morning for Sheridan, where interment will take place in Mount Hope cemetery. The death of Al Lytle, following so closely as it does the sudden death of Thomas Andrews at No. 5 mine yesterday, has cast a gloom over the entire community, and work of every description is at a standstill."

6/20/10—"SUES COAL COMPANY FOR LOSS OF A LIMB"—The civil suit of Mike Banas of Monarch versus the Wyoming Coal Mining Company came on for hearing yesterday in the district court. R. P. Parker represented the plaintiff while Lonabaugh & Wenzell appeared for the defendant. The action was to recover damages in the sum of $15,000 alleged to have been received by the Plaintiff.

Mike Banas took the witness stand yesterday in his own behalf and was followed by Mike Byrtas, John Molyka and Chas. Bazare, also for the plaintiff.

Defendant's witnesses were Alex Lewick, Robert Gault, Jasper Morrow, Mr. Bruce, James Landon, D. Keefauver, W. M. Hall, Joe Klein, Henry Neitman and Tom Allen.—"

7/12/10—"GIRL IS DROWNED IN BIG GOOSE CREEK" "MAGGIE FLOCKART LOSES HER LIFE WHILE BATHING IN STREAM" "THE BODY IS RECOVERED." "Another Girl Narrowly Escapes Death in Attempt at Companion's Rescue" "Maggie Flockart, the 17-year-old daughter of Mrs. Robert Flockart of Dietz, was drowned this afternoon at 2 o'clock while bathing in Big Goose Creek, one-quarter of a mile below Dietz.

The girl had been in bathing with several of her playmates and among them was a Miss Allen, who was at first supposed to have met the same watery grave as Miss Flockart. She was rescued, however, at the last moment in a thrilling manner and is alive at the hour of going to press.

The body of Miss Flockart was finally taken from the water at 2:30 this afternoon as a corpse, it having been submerged for fully half an hour.

Mrs. Flockart, the bereaved mother of this young girl whose life has so suddenly been snuffed out, was left a widow only three months ago. The family is numbered amoung the oldest residents of Dietz and the whole community has offered their services."

1/27/11—For the Dietz Bobby Burns celebration, there were 12 Scotsmen from Sheridan in attendance—Waddie Russell and Mr. Hotchkiss of Dietz managed the event for local Caledonians, including Alex Petrie, James McLennan, Gay Henderson, William Payton, Edward Stead, Grant MacLeod and A. B. Wilson.

5/19/11—(Dietz News) "Dietz is still alive, although rather sleepy. Frank Fedle* and Bob Terry, grocers; the Union tea man, John Zucca and Robert Thurwell, and the pop and ice cream delivery all find it highly profitable to make frequent trips here. *(Ed. note: Redle)

6/8/11—(Dietz Doings)—"The new suits for the junior baseball team have arrived and were very quickly donned by the young champions, who have not lost a game this year. They are a credit to the camp and the boys feel more than able to keep up their present reputation and challenge any teams under eighteen in this neck of the woods.

The young boys and girls of the camp are getting their tin cans and noise instruments into shape ready to use them any day that the wedding bells which are daily expected to ring out.

The post office department have abandoned the Pearl, Montana post office which mail is carried from Dietz twice weekly, effective June 15th.

F. Samuelson left yesterday for a business trip to Roundup, Montana.

F. G. Townson has moved from Dietz having accepted a position at the Sheridan hospital.

Odd Fellows Lodge, Triple Link Lodge No. 39, I.O.O.F. will tomorrow Thursday night, initiate into this lodge in the state of Wyoming. The Sheridan degree team of the I.O.O.F. will be here to put on the work and thirteen new candidates will receive the initiatory degree."

7/21/11—"ACCIDENT AT DIETZ." "Two Miners Caught Beneath Falling Coal and Both Were Badly Injured. Mike Stradincke, the miner whose skull was fractured, Tuesday, in the mine at Dietz, and who is now in the state hospital, is in a critical condition and the attending physicians have grave fears as to the final outcome of his injuries. Anton Mandry, who was injured at the same time, is doing well, and his recovery in only a matter of time. Mandry's right arm was broken above the elbow, and his right leg broken near the hip joint.

Mandry and Stradincke were working in one of the rooms in the mine when a large mass of coal fell from the roof. There was no warning of the danger, and neither of the men had time to move before they were crushed to the floor by the falling coal.

C. W. Morgareidge went to Dietz with the ambulance and brought the injured men to the hospital—"

3/20/12—"Sheridan Held Responsible For the Dietz Sickness" "Sheridan Coal Company suing City of Sheridan and petitioning court for restraining order to prevent city from further dumping sewage into Big Goose and causing a typhoid epidemic at Dietz."

5/6/12—"Suit Against City May Be Compromised." "Representatives of Sheridan Coal company Make Proposals to the City Council." "Dietz Would Connect With City Water Line and Pay Half of the Cost of Construction." "Attorney James A. Burgess, plaintiffs' attorney suggested to City Council, 'be cheaper for Sheridan to assist in construction of proper water system than to build a sewage disposal plant.' " Mayor Kutcher informed Burgess that city is building a disposal system which could relieve problem."

8/2/12—"(Dietz News)—L. J. Cake, assistant superintendent at the mine is enjoying a visit from his mother of Denver, Colo.

Mr. and Mrs. James Newman, and son, James, returned home on Tuesday from Iowa, where they have been visiting relatives and friends.

Messrs A. M. Dawson, Walter Russell, Mr. Hopka, Johnny and Walter Russell took a speedy trip to the mountains in Dr. A. M. Dawson's automobile Tuesday and came home with 100 fish.

Lou Hill attended the dance Wednesday night.

Mr. and Mrs. Putney, Mrs. Elizabeth Nemo, Misses Ruth Brown, Nora McDowell, Charles Story and Archie Parkerson from Acme, attended the dance Wednesday night.

George Hotchkiss was visiting relatives and friends in Dietz Wednesday.

Misses Gertrude and Pearl Bell and Miss Maggie Hunter, who have been visiting Miss Christie Hotchkiss for a few days attended the dance.

Mrs. Ellen Hunter, from Carneyville and Mrs. Katherine Dick, attended the Pocohontas lodge on Tuesday night.

Mrs. Ninna Peterson and daughters Mrs. Ethel Jones and Miss Rose Peterson, attended the Pocohontas lodge on Tuesday night and returned home on Wednesday.

Miss Grace McIntyre from Billings, Montana, who has been visiting relatives and friends for a few weeks, returned home Wednesday.

Joe Show has been quite ill this week.

Elmer and Claude Peters have gone back east to spend a month with their mother and sisters.

Fannie Council No. 1 gave an entertainment here on Tuesday night after lodge was over to friends of Dietz and other camps. They gave a good programme. Miss Grace MacIntyre sang "If I Only Had a Home Sweet Home," and "Is It Very Far to Heaven," which were much enjoyed. Little Gene Hotchkiss recited "Little Busy Bee." When she was reciting you could have heard a pin fall. A duet by Miss Christie Hotchkiss and Mr. Clinton Benedict, "Let Me Call You Sweetheart," was sung with great success. Misses Ruth Brown, Maggie Hunter, Christie Hotchkiss and Clinton Benedict sang, "Ragtime Violin." Messrs. Clinton Benedict, Stewart McDowell, Alex Flockhart, Ora Watson, Thomas Lytle, sang "Oh! You Beautiful Doll," which brought them great applause. Misses Agnes Hotchkiss, Ellen Hunter, Agnes McDowell, Mary Russell,

Nina Peterson sang "Annie Laurie," accompanied by Miss Christie Hotchkiss on the organ. Marceluse Goodmay and our comical boy, "Shy," sang a beautiful solo. Mr. Stewart from Big Horn sang some beautiful Scotch songs and Mr. Leuny McDowell also sang a song. After the program was over the Pocohontas lodge served ice cream and cake and then all kinds of games were played.

Misses Nettie and Rachael Kettering, Mrs. Ira Kettering, Oga Sturgeon and Messrs. Harry Kettering, and Dora Nealy attended the dance Wednesday evening."

United Mine Workers of America, Dietz, Wyoming Local.

8/29/13—"Teachers Assigned for New School Year" "Minnie E. Jeffers, Prin., Annie Jeffers, Primary. 10/7/13—Attendance: 41 and 33.

11/4/13—"Alexander Cammock, brother-in-law of Samuel Dunn who died as a result of a mine accident in Acme, died at his home on Piano Row, Dietz, Sunday morning—death was the result of having been burned at the mine in some way.

6/9/14—(Dietz)—"Mr. and Mrs. Ed Mattox were Ulm visitors over the Fourth of July with Mr. and Mrs. J. Adams.

Mrs. Christena Chesney and children, Ada and Richard, are visiting Mrs. Chesney's mother, Mrs. Agnes Hotchkiss.

Mr. and Mrs. Robert Hotchkiss and children, Georgiana and Genevieve, were week-end guests of Mrs. Hotchkiss' mother, Mrs. Catherine Dick, of Sheridan.

Mr. and Mrs. Charles Lawrence and children, Lorene and Charles, were weekend guests of Mr. and Mrs. Patsy Samuelson, of Sheridan.

Dr. and Mrs. Schunk are enjoying a visit from the doctor's father and mother, brother and sister, from the east.

Mrs. Agnes McDowell and Leonard and Flossie, Mr. and Mrs. Alex Flockert, and Alvin Linzey were fishing on Big Goose last week.

Among the Dietz people who celebrated the Fourth in Sheridan were Messrs. and Mesdames L. J. Cake, Dewey, John Dremer, Woodbury, Will Eyion, James Lytle, Charles Cola, Sam Garrett and children, D. Garrett, George Adkins, Mrs. Walter Russell, Misses Marie Dewey, Violet Cammock, Josephine Brewer, Margaret Woodbury, Dora, Dorris and Blanch Lytle, Nellie Ross, and Messrs. Joe Cammock, John and Walter Russell."

5/4/16—"NEW MANAGER AT DIETZ AND ROUNDUP." "H. S. Hopka, who has been manager for the Sheridan Coal company in Dietz for a number of years, has become general manager for the company at Dietz and Roundup, Mont., with headquarters at the latter place. Mr. and Mrs. Hopka left Monday night for their new home. E. C. Mattox, who has been with the company for a number of years, has been appointed superintendent of the mines at Dietz.

The Sheridan Coal company has been operating the mines at Dietz for a number of years, and have shipped thousands of tons of coal annually.

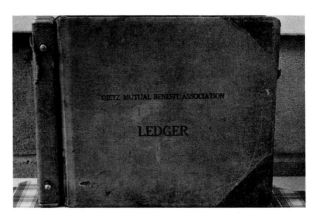

Dietz Mutual Benefit Association.

About a year ago they opened mine No. 7 on a new and deeper vein, and as a result they have been able to offer their patrons coal of a higher quality than ever before."

6/11/18—"NEW ROAD UP THE VALLEY." "Suburban Homes Donates the Land." "Will Follow the Track of the Interurban—Double Tracking the Burlington." (It will be recalled, the old county road to Dietz followed the west boundary of the Burlington).

3/4/19—"DIETZ CARRIES OFF HONORS IN CONTEST." "Monarch amusement hall was crowded with residents of Dietz, Monarch, New Acme and other surrounding town last evening when the eight-reel film "The Rosary" was shown.

After the picture was run, a singing contest was on the program, the contestants being the junior Catholic choir of Dietz (six members), and the junior Catholic choir of Monarch (six members), each composed of little girls averaging in age from ten to twelve years, Father Schultz of Dietz, master of ceremonies.

During the sixth and seventh reels, Mrs. Esther Virgin O'Neil, accompanied by Mrs. R. E. Crane of New Acme, sang Nevin's "The Rosary" and Gounod's "Ave Maria." The solos were chosen with care and Mrs. O'Neil was never in better voice than when she rendered the former selection, and her voice thrilled to every note of the song.

Upon termination of the program, Father Schultz gave a short talk, his theme being "The Mother of Christ." The priest has a strong personality and understands fully how to hold his audience.

Dietz, Wyoming, 6th and 7th grades, 1919?—Front Row, L to R, "Pinhead" Frank Marosok, Jean McManus, Tillie Kossar, Mary Baker, Rose Kuzara, Julia Mentock, Rachael McManus, Anna Mentock. Second row, John Kumor, "Bula" John Mentock, Andy Kosma, Louie Matzejovitz (Matches), Stanley Kuzara, Eddie Novicki, Richard Gibbons, Pete Kristy, Stanley Mentock, Mike Mentock. Third row, (standing) Louie Mentock, ?, Frank Kosma, Hannah Oliver, Ethel McCloud (teacher), Mary McManus, ?, ?, Eva Clouse, Joe Kumor. Donated by Woodrow McManus

Mrs. O'Neil, Mrs. Crane and Mrs. Craig, the last named of Acme, were the judges in the contest, and decided in favor of the Dietz choir. Both contestants, however, did good work."

4/8/19—"Activities At the Mines Show a Marked Decline." "Dietz Mine No. 7 Shut Down Last Saturday Evening (4/5/19), "with the result that about 200 men have been thrown out of work"—"six operating mines of this district working only about 2½ days a week."

4/11/19—"DIETZ NO. 7 MINE CLOSED; NOT NO. 8." "It was erroneously reported several days ago that the Dietz No. 8 mine had been closed. The mine which was closed was Dietz No. 7.

The management announced today that many of the miners who had been thrown out of employment with the closing of Dietz No. 7 mine were being transferred to Dietz No. 8."

1/10/20—"HOUSE BURNS AT MINE CAMP." "Dwelling owned by Chas. H. Cole and occupied by Harry Kettering, W. E. Denton, Louis Opal and Joseph Opiel. One lost about $700 clothing."

6/24/20—"RECEPTION IS GIVEN MR. AND MRS. MATTOX." "Departing From Dietz His Friends Gather to Show Their Regard." "That E. C. Mattox has been a popular superintendent at Dietz was attested last night by the social demonstration given in his honor by the people of Dietz. About two hundred people were assembled at Union Hall to bid farewell to Mr. and Mrs. Mattox and to present them with substantial tokens of the affection and esteem in which they are held, a heavy Masonic ring being given to Mr. Mattox and a beautiful cameo to his wife.

A number of people from Sheridan and from other of the mine camps were present. It was not long before the music was started and the floor was filled with dancers. A one-step first, then a waltz—and then a good old fashioned "square dance," with everybody whirling dizzily.

At one end of the long hall a big table was literally covered with good things to eat—cake, fruit—and the Lord knows what else. That end of the room was the peculiar and particular domain of "Grandma" Hotchkiss who knows how to preside where there are good things to eat and drink if anybody does, and whose greatest pleasure seems to be in dispensing delectable comestibles.

Dietz No. 2 shaft hole as it looks today.

Over on a bench the guest of honor was found. Mr. Mattox is very modest, and would rather talk about anything else than himself or what he has done. He was much more interested in the outcome of the Thye-Eklund match than in what he had accomplished at Dietz.

He came to Dietz in 1903, just after the Sheridan Coal Company had taken over the property from the C. N. Dietz interests. Mr. Mattox went to work as a clerk in the office of the company. He worked up until he was in charge of the office. This position he held for several years. From 1912 to 1916 he was assistant manager of the mine, and it was during this period that he got his training from the man who was then manager, H. S. Hopka, who is now at Roundup, Montana, and who gave him valuable training that was of great assistance to him in later years.

In 1916 Mr. Mattox was put in charge of all the properties of the Sheridan Coal Company at Dietz, and he held that position up until the consolidation on December 31. From then until the present time, he has been superintendent for the Sheridan Wyoming Coal Company.

When he came here there were no other mines operating in the valley except Dietz. At that time two mines were being operated at Dietz and three more were developed. At one time five mines were in operation by this company. He estimates that there have been at least six million tons of coal taken out of the Dietz mines since he has been there.

Dietz Number 8 was opened up and developed under his direction, and while he modestly disclaimed largely his directing genius that made No. 8 one of the best and most up-to-date mines in the state.

Mr. and Mrs. Mattox expect to start immediately on a long motor trip. They have their car equipped for camping, and expect to go as far east and south as Memphis, where Mr. Mattox's parents are now living. Both say they have found life in Dietz interesting and full of experiences that they have been worthwhile, and are loath to leave. This is the first real vacation Mr. Mattox has had, however, in the nearly 18 years that he has been at Dietz, and he says that the things in which they are both most interested now is to get out and take a complete rest for about three months.

When asked what he could say about his success—one of those silly questions which a reporter always asks a successful man—he simply said, "All that I have done anybody could have done with a like amount of application. I have only ordinary ability. I just worked hard and—hit the ball. Ek—do you think Ek can keep away from that wrist lock this time?

The people of Dietz did themselves proud—and Mr. Mattox certainly leaves with a feeling of warmth, for the people with whom he has worked so long. The merry-making continued until a late hour—and those who were out from Sheridan cast longing eyes at that table as they were compelled to run for the early car."

7/19/21—"Two Story Frame School House has been moved from Dietz to Dietz No. 8, and is located on Broadway Street.

10/9/21—(CAMP BREEZES—By Mrs. May Kovacic) Monarch, Oct. 8.—"A new choir has been organized by Father Shultz for the St. Hedwing's Catholic church of Dietz, the following young ladies being chosen: Misses Leona Seftic, Anna Yarmer, Genie Loss and Albina Eccli of Acme; with Anna and Rosie Kuzara of Dietz suburb. Splendid music for the holidays is being anticipated by the above, as they are very diligent and faithful at their rehearsals.—"

4/12/23—"Children for the first communion classes in the St. Thomas Catholic church of Kleenburn and the St. Hedwing Catholic church of Dietz have been chosen, Father Theodore Schultz announces. Dietz children will receive first communion in the St. Hedwing church on May 13; the church being re-opened on that day for the first time in several months. Services will be conducted there every other Sunday from that day on. On May 20 first communion will be given in the St. Thomas church in Kleenburn. The Kooi choir will sing in both these services."

5/9/23—"The St. Hedwig church will be re-opened Saturday morning, May 12, when a nuptial mass will be said at the wedding of Anthony Juroszk and Annue Legierska by Father Schultz. The ceremony will be at 9:30 o'clock."

6/26/23—"Frank F. Ferguson, city building inspector, reports that five houses from old Dietz mining town have been moved into the Sheridan city limits to be used as homes. Others are being placed on foundations on North Main street outside the city limits."

7/19/23—"MRS. SALMON TO SING AT DIETZ MASS"—"Mrs. Salmon, mezzo soprano of New Orleans, who is the guest of Dr. and Mrs. M. F. Amiot at Fort Mackenzie, will sing Gounod's "Ave Maria" for the offertory at the 9:30 o'clock mass Sunday morning at the St. Hedwing Catholic church at Dietz. Mass will also be read at St. Paul's chapel at Kooi at 7:30 o'clock Sunday morning. Special music has been arranged by the Kooi choir, with Miss Katherine Jones at the organ."

11/20/23—"Founder of Dietz Honored in Omaha" "C. N. Dietz, one of the pioneer coal operators of Sheridan county and after whom the mining town of Dietz was named, is the man to whom was dedicated the presentation of "The Sextet from Lucia," broadcasted by the Woodmen of the World station, WOAW of Omaha, Monday night. The number was received by several Sheridan people, including Joseph E. Toland of 339 West Burkitt street.

A quarter of a century ago Mr. Dietz purchased the mine and the camp just north of Sheridan which at that time was called Higby. He opened up the mine on an extensive scale, and named both the town and the mine after himself.

Since his return to Omaha, he has been president of the Omaha public library, and one of the officers of the Omaha Cattle company."

7/20/24—"Farewell exercises for Father Theodore Schultz will be held at the Catholic church at Dietz, Sunday morning, beginning at 9 o'clock."

7/28/24—"K. of C. Will Give Smoker as Farewell to Father Schultz." "The Knights of Columbus will have a smoker Tuesday night at the old Eagles hall on Brooks street as a farewell for Father Theodore Schultz, Kleenburn rector who will leave soon for Pittsburgh, Pa.

A wrestling bout between Dave Moore and Slim Hume has been arranged and there will be two good boxing bouts, it was announced.

A presentation of a gift to Father Schultz will be made during the evening at the smoker, which will begin at 7:30 p.m."

8/1/24—Mine Town People to Bid Farewell to Schultz in Party"

Residents of the mining towns north of Sheridan will gather at 8 o'clock Saturday evening at the Dietz hall to bid farewell to Father Theodore Schultz, pastor of the Kleenburn Catholic church which was destroyed by fire recently, who will leave Monday for Montana before taking up his new work in Pittsburgh, Pa. Dancing will be a feature of the evening.

Father Schultz plans to visit friends in Billings, Townsend and Helena, in Montana, and later will travel with his brother, John Schultz, by automobile to Pittsburgh. The brother has been visiting him here for some time.

The beginning of the evening will be occupied by a business session to voice protest at the burning of the Kleenburn church."

8/28/25—"Bug" Plunges Into River; Loaded With Watermelon Cargo."—"Although a red Ford "bug" loaded with watermelons plunged upside down into Tongue River near the Monarch railroad station at midnight Thursday night, the three occupants of the machine escaped virtually unhurt. Victor Eckley of Acme is reported to be the owner of the machine.

The car came to rest with its wheel sticking out of the water. It is believed that the three occupants of the machine were thrown clear when the car overturned. The car was heading toward Sheridan when the accident happened, and the cause of the wreck is not known.

When the car was pulled from the water Friday, it was found that one wheel was smashed and that the car had suffered other damage."

* * * * * *

Over the years, after the mines had been worked out and the supports removed, many cave holes appeared, pock-marking the surface. Some of these were especially dangerous with only a small hole in the surface held together by grass and vegetation but a larger void underneath.

* * * * * *

On one occasion, it was reported that some women were picking berries in the area in one of the gullies when one of them thought she saw a hat tossed into the air. Her curiosity aroused, she reported it to the others and they went to investigate. Looking down into one of the cave holes, they spotted a man who while hunting, had fallen into the hole unable to climb out. The women immediately went for assistance and with the help of some men from the camp, were able to remove him, thereby saving his life.

INTERVIEW WITH CHARLES KARPI—FEBRUARY 1973

Came to Dietz—"Dietz No. 1" What year? "1906, October 2nd" From what country?— "Hungary—no, I just come alone. I come with a bunch of people—come at that time—comin this country like anytime. All of them Polish people—just about 1907 open that Kooi mine. Open three mine that time—Kooi mine, Acme and Riverside. You know, goin' up to Ash Creek over there and this one open up 1911 (present Acme)—what is Acme now. Higby before Dietz bought it. That was just like a country mine.

Well, I tell you, I work in Dietz in 1906. I started—and a fella—Hungarian fella work in Monarch just a new mine, from that face where sunshine morning comin up you know because I work over there—take me over there to help him work on the machine and I was work on the machine in Monarch, but 1906 in the winter was over there, but no houses in Monarch at all, 1906 and 1907—and I was suffered over through the winter cause no houses, you know—just a full board up the 1 x 12 boards on the sides all around and then dry out and there was holes like that on the sides and I said we was batchin three together—no houses Monarch only was what the hell his name was got these house—the company build (boarding house?) boarding house was—dining room was a tent and the little shack was kitchen—lilla wooden shack. Went to Monarch in '06 and I say now I never put another winter in Monarch in a tent and 1907, October I quit. I comin' down Dietz again work in Dietz and I tol' my partner don' comin after me before April next year 1908 and he comin over there, and he was strikin and Union was strikin 10 hours for 8 hours but the company he don't let us keep the meeting on the camp—we have to gon out to dry creek union Monarch and Kleenburn and they bought an acre of land of these and there and they got a house over there Jenkins, George Jenkins living in there—that was a union property over there. We have to go over there—keep our meeting over there and Frank Welch and Bob Gould—Frank Welch was Secretary and Bob Gould was union President and same time he pulled that road thru you know around Acme in 1908 and he Frank Welch was in a company working on a bridge and my partner was real big drinker was danger was bull headed, you know—he don't care" he said, "No."—the union he don't give us that much credit. We keep our meeting in the school house like before. We don't give no company credit—anybody go work on that that bridge cause used to—like when your father was living, you know, we gotta gone through Monarch over there around that hill below that bridge—that's the place we go to Monarch. 1908 build that nother road alongside that railroad—go around Acme and around there—that's the place. And aright we say, "By golly, the union men anybody keep out meeting over there—nobody won't work on the bridge—that bridge belong to county—County road—county highway what you used to go to your father's place—Bozeman Trail—that's what they call it—that's county road—highway, and after that they fire us because they put us in jail—the company and we was—Helsberg was our sheriff. He live over there by Decker around that way—he got a farm over there and next morning by God, I got a bicycle I run away. I left him un he went in a tent and my partner and I comin down Dietz wit my bicycle over der where the Armstrong mine was, you know, da road comin right on top of the hill der and I comin aroun' wit da bicycle and I on da front wheel and I hit one rock und just turn over on da bicycle, and it put near killed me. By gosh, I can't walk but I pull dat bicycle down to dat brush in de draw, you know, I was rest over der, I was hurt myself awful bad but I was young an I see dat miner and I see—front of de horse and I said over der—and I see him comin to Dietz—old Andy Barber—maybe you remember Herb Barber or something—Ida Barbee—his was old timer—oh, yeah, he was a coal miner—he was here—family

when I come here in 1906 aready—live in that shack over there what that railroad goin there—Dietz No. 7. And I was work over der long as you don close Dietz down everyone I finish No. 1—I finish No. 4—I finish No. 7—I finish No. 2—1911—your fodder workin No. 2" (When did they close down Dietz No. 2? "1911—yeah Dietz No.—Dietz No. 4 and Dietz No. 5 was runnin and No. 2 yet, you know, after 1911 and open up No. 7")

(When you first came to Dietz, did they have electric motors in the mine?)—"By gosh, I tell you I don't remember now—no motor—horses—horses was in der and then motor and punch machine workin No. 2 mine—and after Dietz No. 2 was finished dey put em in No. 4 mine—punch machine, you know, just punch the goal out—vot a pick" (The punch machine was run by electricity, wasn't it?) "Steam—Air—compress air—I run that to 1904. I think so, and a chain machine comin electric machine and motor comin in 1914, and I vent on a chain machine—I vork alla time on a machine—cuttin machine— alla time." (Did you ever load?) "Thas ver I git hurt on da big loader comin up ya know and dats ver I get hurt—I lost my hearing—in "36 in Monarch—'46—'46, in Monarch."

(Did you ever work in Dietz No. 5 or No. 8?) "Dietz No. 8 I vorkin—I finish 'em up dat too—I never workin No. 5. Never work No. 6 because was jist a little mine—never amount to much. No. 3 vas workin—a little bit on the railroad.

(Went to work in Monarch about what year?)—"1940—after they shut all the mine down. Acme was shut down and we have goin to Monarch and "46 after workin to '46 after was broke my leg and I lost my hearing, you know—coal comin in out of the side—you see when I went to the big loadin machine—went the big one come in, I vent in a front right straight, you know, and after that coal comin down, you know, on a side and I got a cable and I vent in so far after come back with the loadin machine and cut em to that pillar—the rib, you know, and when I gon through over there I loaded couple _____ and I pushed the coal a little bit and the loadin machine what we call the arm, you know, and I can't get away no how because I was right on the center operate the loadin machine, you know, was about 30 feet long, the loadin machine. I got to goin 15 feet this way and 15 feet this way but I don't know what."

(Were there any explosions or fires?)—

"Monarch was in 1907 was a litta mine open up shaft mine—Monarch was closeup, you know, they shut that mine down cause was lots of gas and No. 8 was blown up 1919. My wife, she run the boarding house, old Dietz you know 1919 and we was in the yard and Charlie Francis was electrician—was Swede—'Oh, I betcha that's Dietz No. 8 blown up.' and I say, 'Oh, vot you talkin' and ve vent up there and by gosh we see that fan was blowed out already and it killed two men there. Bob Gault and his partner and I vork with Jo Ruszecki that time—thas vos Saturday. The mine no vork and ve vork all time, the machine men vork one day after the mine vork, you know, that vay ve get little more, and ve won't go in the mine the same time. George Aiken vas the pit boss and ve all machine men goes out—cuttin machine men and he changed our nobody vork and just Bob Gault because his daughter gonna be married Monday and he donna gone in Monday comin out Monday and he vent over there and he get killed. And good thing me no goes in and I vas vorkin that territory all the powder keg, doors and everything was zig zag was yeah, and three men track layers workin there that day—track layers vorkin every day—Joe Goodman, Jack Schmaltz and Stanely Niemec, old Mentock father-in-law—three men vorkin on a straight—way over there and eat dinner, that time, dinner time and he switched the machine in da one room-neck and that's the place he blowed up—full of gas—and open light you know. That was that same day, yeah, the light touched the gas—Bob Gault light-open lite—five people in the mine. Two, Bob Gault and his partner, Jack Schmaltz, Joe Goodman and Stanley Niemec.

I vas vorkin Dietz 8 and fellow he wanted go home, that Bill Patvaros, brother, he vanted go home and he open up that mine over there, Big Goose say Bill brother better buy that place of him, Big Goose mine there. I left Dietz 8—I vent over there on Big Goose about one year. I vas copany in there and that Bill Patvaros spent out everything he can, you know, can't stand it and I sell out for him for twelve hundred dollars. We vas four of us, and after I see that I sell out, he sign check and the Goddam Citizen State vank vent broke. I never got anything. I came back to Dietz 8 again. You father, he was sick that time when I went over there—hurt in the mine—horse kicked him, I suppose or something. I know after that your father never go back to the mine. Yeah, your father vas pretty old timer I vos over

there. I believe old Barbee? came early. Monarch, I work over there—no houses over there—just tents. One vinter, I build a big fire ina tent, you know, by god, I burned the tent there, you know. Ve vent to the Montenegro—they lotsa Montenegro—ve stayed over der till morning."

(Explosion in Monarch?)—"Oh, thats vas a different place out between Kooi and Monarch right between there—what you call it—75—Monarch Coal Company. Hauled coal to tipple in Monarch by rail—(no tipple at 75)."

How many mines in Monarch?—"Stanley, I know there were one, two, three, four. Two mines open up in Monarch—No. 1 go right straight into hill at Monarch, shaft mine open up over there—the shaft mine closed and he went up to the 75 what they big explosion was. I never was work very many time in Monarch after that fire in 1908. I don't think I worked twice in Monarch since I goin back work 1940.

(Mary Goodman, with whom Charlie Karpi was boarding and rooming—both Austrians—and who was listening to the interview then interjected), "My real father and my mother got remarried, she married Joe Goodman, that was my step father, but he got killed in Monarch—what year?—was 1946" (didn't remember just how he got killed). "I couldn't tell. He vent to work in he come home from war and second day in the mine he got killed there. Wasn't that too bad. Real father also was killed. In Dietz No. 7"

Charlie continued, "That's was a funny thing, I tell you, cause I know her father pretty good—John Verhovnik I just stood over there—he was bradichman—you know, bradichman—he stopped the air, you know—put the door some place need the door—place canvas, regulate, and he that place, his partner fixed the door because over der canvas he don last very much because the car he run back and forth so much over there—turn him loose and I was over there—want hang the door and I say, 'Go on over der and change the air and I help his partner hang the door and my partner, Joe Ruseczki comin and he say, "Charlie come over here—we got a place cleaned up.' I was workin on a cuttin machine and I say, 'Oh right.' So I left him over there and I hear a trip come in fast—trip you know and poor bugger, her father, he got no time to run away and he hold on side of a rib and squeezed him and I was cut the place and I was comin out the room and Harry Catron say, 'Charlie, you know what the news? Lilly (little) John—we called him Lilly John,

Lilly John got killed. I said, 'No.' 'Yeah,' he say, 'that trip, you know caught him, he say, and I told Joe Ruseczki, and I say, 'Joe you want stay—go head stay, I want see him cause we was pretty good friends together, and, by gollies, you know, I see dat ambulance with a horse ambulance, couple white horse—he just comin in with him. I can catch him over der—take him in the hospital—that old hospital and I comin in evening I want see him but he no want no-body—only his wife and next day he died—squeezed him to death.

Typhoid fever on account of claim it vas da vater—of course company made reservoir top of da hill and no cover—dead cow—dead birds—everthing and we drink from der and after while make company make good reservoir and pump right by the river over der."

(Remarks re: status of Kuchera's) "But he got that Louie Cake farm your father used to have that ranch, just south of his place—the place that Mike Banas had—Mike Banas—that was the Louie Cake farm homestead—I don know—he was civil engineer—Dietz Coal Company and he work there for Dietz Coal company and Mike Banas jus rented it, I suppose" (This land or a part of it, my father purchased years later)

Following a reference to the Beatty Gulch road which was above the Dietzhills—"I know—kill himself there—committed suicide" (I didn't get the connection). Dry country yet and this time you know your father take order for Christmas time—Easter time, you know, and distribute em. And Copperfellow, I don't know, I believe, Christmas. Copperfellow comin from Cody—finish the Cody dam, that big job over there and he had plenty of money and Stick Serovish was together—that two fellow what he come from Cody and Stick he went out—your father bring, I believe, it was 25 case of beer on the wagon and (presumably this was many years ago when my father operated a saloon shortly after taking over the John Hecht place) yeah, he gotta saloon that time, yeah and dat fella he goin out and he said, 'George, he say, I wanta case a beer,' and stop he say, 'I don't give you out of this because gotta order.' 'Oh,' he say, 'Give me three,' 'I don't give you two, I don give you one, how I give you three?' 'Goddam it stop ruin everything in the head house over there, you go take order for another one. They bought everything—about 24-25 cases of beer—all load—take him load him up. You got order—you

got order-goin after nodder one—10 gallown whishkey them two fella order by golly. And over there was one bunch dancin, drinkin, every-body there. And there was a Catholic priest—that from the old country—Catholic priest, you know an I tol him, I was younger and I says, 'Stick, what for you don't quit that booze,—you Catholic' and he says, 'if the United States goin be dry country, I don't drinkin' and I laughed at if U.S. be dry—whole lot worst roast pig—.'" "Henry Novicki come here every year—some-times twice. He's nice fella."

Re: Citizenship. "Naturalized, 1927, 5th of May—I joined Eagles at same time I get citizen papers."

(Mary 'Goodman,' where were you born?) "Well, I tell ya, when I was born, that was Hungaria—was divided up—Yugoslovia—I was married over there."

(Karpi). "I vork in mine 1906-1946—I vas vork in Pennsylvania little bit that same year vat I comin right away here. Two fellows I know from Moorcroft and we was in Pittsburgh, Penn-sylvania—them two—and he ship them two men to Colorado—Primero, Colorado to the mine—Primero, Colorado and for nothing you know, the company gave the transportation free. Al-right he come to Alliance, Nebraska, but before he left over there he tol me Charlie if you goin be better over there like here, we goin let you know and you goin over there. I say a'right, but I don't know goin be true or not but they comin to Alliance, Nebraska, two men on the train, agent, you know, goin around the depot—gotta changing trains, one comin this way another goin to Colorado and asked, them two, where they goin, they say they goin to Colorado. Say, mine there—"ya, we work back in Pennsylvania in a mine." He say, "What for you not goin to Dietz?" He say that's a union—pay better, better workin' conditions like Colorado. "Well," I say, "I go but we gotta ship over there." "But you want to goin to Dietz, but they say, "we not to goin there." He say, "Come on." And he took us to restaurant, feed em up, he tol em two stayin here—he went to the depot—the train go to Colorado already—meet my uncle here—my uncle come to this country before I was work and Charlie Gazdik, he meet them and he told my uncle that two fella I miss here—my brother he got address mine and my uncle wrote me right away come on here and that's the way I comin up there, see I start work in coal mine in May in Pennsylvania Westmorland—Primo—in

1908 all blowed up—killed night shift—500 men work night shift—but 1,000 men worked day shift—took tipple out—everything. Killed whole shift. I saved money—after that I come in Wyoming and lots of them people over there and they said, "Wyoming." I say, "Yeah," but Wyoming the Indian kill the white men in bright day light.' And by gosh, I was scared bit cause everybody say how wild here. Well, my uncle send me 50 dollars and I got about 70 dollars my own—I saved over there and I say, 'By god, buy me a ticket—was 35 dollars buy me a ticket.' (How old are you, Charlie?) "Goin to be 86 next Tuesday," (1973). "An you know, I comin here anyway, I no get out—no get out if nobody wait me on a depot I buy a ticket goin back and that agent, Hungarian agent, buy a railroad ticket and he told me I be there Saturday night, one o'clock—Sunday morning 1 o'clock. Ah right, train it stop—cause I buy dollar watch, you know—I look on it alla time and I believe we was someplace—Newcastle, one o'clock. When I vant to take my two suit case, that porter, that nigger, he chase me back. A'right and he come on and set down and he pulled his watch and he said, "7 o'clock—Dietz." Was about 1 o'clock—he tol me and Joe Brown, you know, and by God, what the hell his name was, Jack Lee—he comin this country same time. Joe Brown, he was a pit boss in Dietz you know and he was in England to visit and by God, he take Jack Lee with him and Teddy Brown and Willie Brown and we comin up from Chicago and we comin here. When Joe Brown was a great talker—he like talkin and he come in to me and talk to me, I don say nothing and I don't know nothing and a'right he left to go sit down—sit down over there and leave go. We change train and he comin on same train like I comin in again and after he comin over to me and talk to me again. I gave him the same answers as before and after he went back to the bunch, Jack Lee and Teddy Brown and Willy Brown, he say, Joe Brown, he say like this (Charlie made a circular motion with his finger pointing at his temple)—you know, I know what you mean but I con't help it—and then Sunday morning about 7 o'clock we was in Sheridan right here on depot and I want to get out, you know, and that nigger he don't let me goin out because I goin to Dietz and that much its late the train I guess and a'right I set down, who come—Harry and my uncle and I never know my uncle, you know, but he said, "Charlie," he said "Brother-in-law, here is the boy" in Hungarian, you know. "Oh," I says, "Jesus Christ what that, I never hear since I left Pittsburgh and he come out there to me and he said, "You know me?" What you come about 5 year to this country like I did. I say, "You Charlie Gazdik." "By gosh, you know me—and here your uncle." And he talk with me and Joe Brown, he comin over there—you know, he seen him talk with me and he see how he can talk with me and he say—"Hungarian," he say. He told my Uncle—he told me—says "Steve, I don't go now—not a week yet, you goin in the morning, tomorrow morning to Jimmy Lytle, he give you a job and Stanley, that man I tell you I don't think I like anybody better like I like him. He went to Roundup, Superintendent, Roundup, you know, from Dietz. He comin down he want I comin here. Joe Brown, he was big boss whole mine—top—5 mine runnin but he was top over there and he went Superintendent Roundup from Dietz—coal mine in Roundup too, you know. By gosh, you know that's funny thing how people he don't understant nothing comin out the language. No language own language, Hungarian."

(Mary Goodman)—"No resemblance to German—you can go just from one village to nother village. From where we comin from, we got Jugoslavians, Slovanians—"

(Charlie)—"That part over there where she's born, that country, like Missour, about 4 or 5 that same—she born in Washvega (sp), state, you know. Later that Austria and Hungary together—Franz Josef was king. Wilson cut the country—was a'right before but now the Hungary cut the Hungary altogether. He give 8,000,000, Jugoslavia 8,000,000 Czekoslavakia, 8,000,000 Romania, and Hungary left 8,000,000. Was 32,000,000 Hungarian population, you know, and that's the way it started second World War. Only sidewalk 2 x 6's in front of New York store. And farmers comin in spring wagon, stuck on main street. After dat, puttin wooden block you know and 1923 that flood comin."

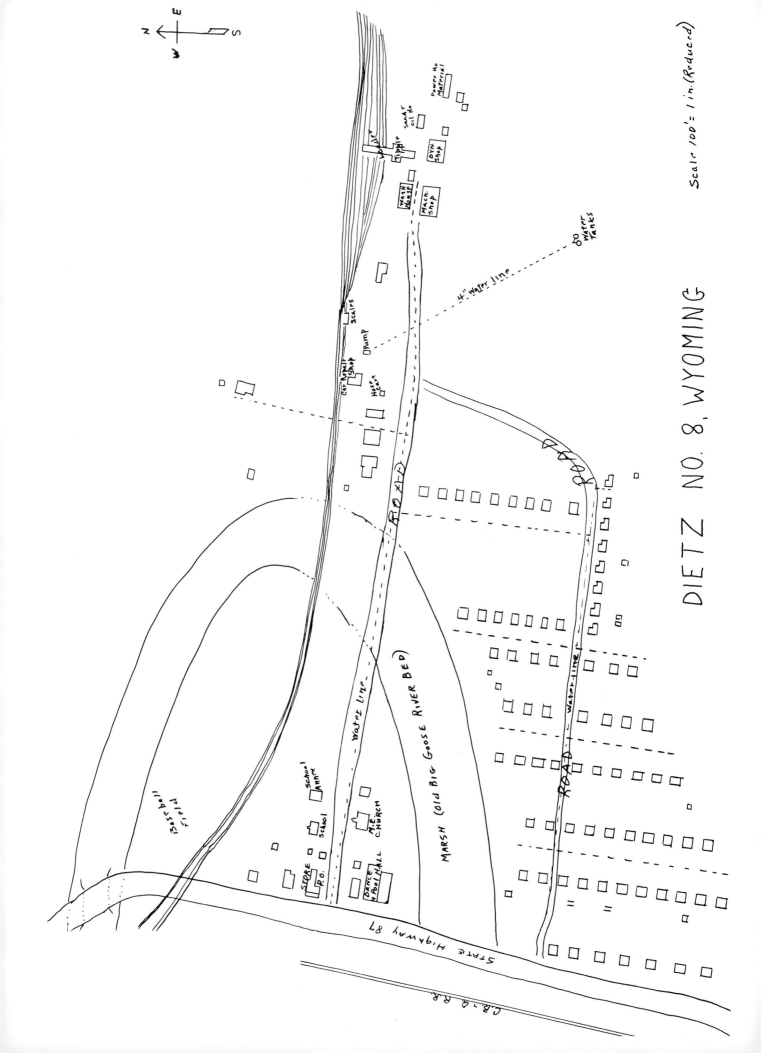

DIETZ NO. 8, WYOMING

Scale 100' = 1 in. (Reduced)

N
W — E
S

Power Ho
Material

Sand oil Ho

Y.D. Dry

Tipple

DYN
Shop

WASH
HOUSE

MACH.
Shop

80
Water
Tanks

4" Water line

ROAD

ROAD

ROAD   Water line

Scales

Pump

Car Repair
Shop

Hose
Cart

Baseball
Field

School
Annex

Store

School

P.O.

M.E.
CHURCH

DANCE
#Pool HALL

Water line

MARSH (Old BIG Goose RIVER BED)

State Highway 87

C.B.&Q. RR.

Chapter 7

Dietz Camps
Nos. 5 and 8

Dietz, Wyoming 1937

Same view as above as it looks today.

The Dietz No. 5 camp, one of the Dietz group of eventually eight mines, but one of the two Dietz camps, was located about one and one-half miles north of the main Dietz camp. It was immediately east of the C. B. & Q. railroad in the area of the former route of Big Goose creek before it was diverted by the railrroad leaving a circular slough within the camp location. (It was in a house near the bank of this slough that I was born). It is believed that this mine camp was established in about 1903. There seems to be very little available information or publicity about this mining camp which apparently closed its operation of the Dietz No. 5 mine in about 1910; however, a number of residents continued to live there while working at some of the other mines.

Articles from the Sheridan newspapers reveal some of the following:

3/29/07—ACCIDENT. William Ray killed in fall from car in Dietz Mine No. 5. Body brought to Sheridan by Geo. Levi Smith. Riding on mine car which jumped the track crushing him to death."

6/18/07—"Man Killed in Dietz No. 5." "Jacob Sykes shot in Keenan saloon in Dietz No. 5, by Chas. Davis Sunday morning. Coroners jury ruled Davis killed Sykes without provocation. Davis arrested."

3/2/09—"No. 5 school has closed because the children have all moved away; and Miss Lawrence will assist here in the High School building."

4/8/10—"Dietz No. 5 closed for the season and most of the families moved to Dietz."

4/12/10—"Mines 2 and 4 still working and "have their old time busy look."

In the year 1918, a new mine, the Dietz No. 8 mine opened up with a shaft 181 feet deep to a vein of coal 47 feet thick. This was followed by an immediate increase in the camp activity. This mine is the one referred to elsewhere as having a siren instead of the usual whistle. It was considered generally as a somewhat dangerous mine with an over-abundance of gas causing several accidents.

It was also shortly after this mine opened up that my father was employed by the labor union as a "checkweighman" whose function it was to check the company weighman to see that he was accurately weighing each loader's car of coal and giving him proper credit; in other words, to preclude any deception on the part of the company. I believe this employment was for a very short time as my father did not work in the mines very long before he went into business for himself.

Sheridan Post June 21, 1918

NEW COAL FOR Sheridan Consumers DEITZ NO. 8

47 FEET THICK

Dietz No. 8 Coal from the Sheridan Coal Company's new mine is now on the Sheridan market.

Dietz No. 8 Coal is a new Sheridan county product., coming from the largest and best vein in the Rocky Mountain district.

Dietz No. 8 Coal is free from impurities and low in ash content.

Dietz No. 8 Coal preparation is the very best, due to the last word in tripple and shaker screen construction.

Dietz No. 8 Coal has a Sheridan agency in the Rialto Block, with Mr. O. T. Solberg as manager, Phone 103.

We solicit your business and guarantee satisfaction and prompt service.

The Sheridan Coal Co.

Dietz No. 8 tipple and washhouse. (Looking east) tipple operated electrically. (No picture of Dietz No. 5 tipple available).

Dietz No. 8 tipple (looking west toward camp).

I recall one day, while I was attending school in Dietz No. 7, we suddenly heard a terrible explosion which we knew occurred in the Dietz No. 8 mine. We all instantly dropped our books and ran over the hills to the Dietz 8 camp. By the time we arrived, there was a throng of people surrounding the shaft. The conversations were being carried on in whispers as it was known there were a few men within the mine. Particularly frightened were the wives of some of the men who were known to be in the mine. Anxiety was especially tense each time the cage would come up. A more detailed report of this occurrence appears in the following item from a Sheridan newspaper:

6/4/19—"EXPLOSION AT DIETZ EIGHT COSTS LIVES OF TWO MEN" "Accident Occurs Just Before Noon—Seven Men in Mine But Five Escape." "CAUSE OF EXPLOSION IS UNKNOWN."

"Rumor of a Bomb Placed by Anarchists Is Not Substantiated—Investigation and Inquest to be Held Today."

"A tremendous explosion took place at the mine of the Sheridan Coal company known as Dietz No. 8 yesterday forenoon, the effect of which is said to have fairly shaken the hills and cost the lives of two men, Bob Gault and Frits Sucal. Fortunately seven men were in the mine at the time of the accident, and of these, three were so remote from the scene of the explosion that they scarcely felt its effects, while two who were nearer, while knocked down, escaped with only minor bruises.

While the explosion is generally attributed to gas, neither the mine officials nor the state inspector is prepared to make any definite statement as to the real cause. From the time of the explosion until 5:30 last evening when the bodies of the two victims were reached and brought to the surface all energies were directed to the work of rescue and no effort was made to investigate the cause of the accident.

Mine Inspector Hotchkiss, who was the leading spirit in the work of rescue and led the volunteers into the mine, found the entries filled with gas and fumes from the effects of which he suffered severely. Tonight he is at his home trying to recover from the poison and at six o'clock this morning will return to make investigations. All night men have been busy working the fans and clearing the mine of noxious fumes so that by morning it is hoped the mine can be safely entered and a deliberate examination made. At ten o'clock today an inquest will be held and the investigation to be made at that time may lead to the discovery of the cause of the catastrophe.

While the toll of lives was not large as compared with some of the mining horrors that have taken place in other sections, it was so unexpected that the residents of the little camp of Dietz 8 are stunned.

First Since 1911

In spite of the many men employed and the enormous extent of the mining industry in this section catastrophies in this field are practically unknown. This is the first explosion of any moment since 1911 and at that time there was no loss of life. Men have been hurt and killed occasionally by those accidents which are bound to occur in mines the same as on railroads, and the danger of explosion is scarcely known here.

2 MINERS ENTOMBED IN SHAFT AT DIETZ

An explosion of gas in Dietz No. 8 coal mine at 11:30 o'clock this morning entombed seven men, five of whom had been rescued at 3:00 o'clock this afternoon.

The two men who still are entombed are: Robert Gault and Fritz Sucol.

A large rescue crew is working to find the men.

All ambulances from Sheridan have gone to the mine but at 3:30 o'clock it was reported they were not needed.

Two of the five men who have been rescued were near the mouth of the mine and were able to escape unassisted. The remaining three were brought out of the mine early in the afternoon. They are not seriously injured.

It could not be ascertained if the mine is burning.

Only a small force has been working at Dietz No. 8 since early spring.

Thought It Perfectly Safe

Besides, the Dietz 8 is practically a new mine, equipped with the finest machinery money will buy and to a man unskilled in mining it looks to be one of the safest mines in the world. The immense thickness of the vein leaves a roof and floor of many feet in thickness when the entries are run so that a cave-in is almost impossible. The coal is clean and if there is a menace of any kind in the mine it is not apparent.

The entry to the mine is through a vertical shaft over 200 feet in depth. From the base of the shaft the main entry runs north. Some hundreds of feet from the shaft an entry puts off toward the west, known as the First West and this eventually bends to the south. It was in First West that the explosion occurred, but the exact point has not been determined.

The men who were killed were working on the face probably between the point of explosion and the air shaft, and it is said to be a fact that the force of a gas explosion always goes against the air. The men were no doubt very near to the point where the explosion occurred for their faces were badly burned and it is probable that they were instantly killed.

The horses were nearer the main entry and none was injured by the explosion although when the rescuers passed the barn in trying to reach the men they found one of the animals dead, it having jumped over the manger and choked to death.

Bob Gault, one of the dead men, is an old timer here and was known by many and respected by all. It is particularly pathetic that today was to have been the wedding day of his daughter and that only an unkind fate took him into the mine on the particular day when the accident happened. The other man was a miner not well known in the city but highly respected in his home camp.

The many bomb outrages that were perpetrated in the cities of the past on the day preceding the accident at Dietz have given rise to all kinds of rumors and in many quarters the belief is expressed that radical agitators are responsible for the explosion in the mine. It may be stated that no evidence of a bomb has been found but it must be admitted that no diligent search has yet been possible. At present these rumors cannot be disproved but the men best informed do not lay the blame to the reds.

Yesterday morning at 11:30 the first intimation of an explosion at the Dietz No. 8, came when the covering to the main air course, just back of the fan house was blown blazing into the air and scattered over considerable distance, giving information of a disturbance within the mine, where a small number of men were at work, but giving no intimation as to the extent of the damage done or the toll of life taken.

It was known that there were seven men in the mine at the time, and the relief force on the surface was calmly organized under the direction of Inside Foreman George Akin and Mining Engineer L. J. Cake of Roundup, who just happened to be visiting the mine, and information was sent to State Mine Inspector Bob Hotchkiss, who was at Sheridan.

Rescuers Enter Mine

The men were but a few minutes in fixing the fan covering and restarting the fan for a circulation of air, after which the first car was lowered, and Electrician Joe Foreman and Pumpman Joe Grzovich were found near the bottom of the shaft, where they had been knocked down by the concussion, but neither was injured to any extent.

The state mine inspector arrived shortly afterwards and an inspection showed that the force of the explosion had come from the south entry. He was accompanied into the mine by Geo. N. Akin, Bob Flockhart, Joe Kemmick and Dick Burke.

It was known that three men were working in the straight north main entry, Joe Goodman, Stanley Merritz and Jake Smultz. The heavy smoke and gas came from the south entry, making it impossible for them to move far in that direction, so the search was started for the men in the north entry, where there appeared to be much less smoke.

Did Not Realize Danger

The men were met coming out, not realizing the danger which had imperiled them. At 11:30 just as they were about to eat their lunch, they heard what they thought was a shot in the other end of the mine, but gave it no thought. Finishing their lunch they started in work again and shortly afterwards noticing the smell of smoke growing stronger, started to investigate. It was then that they met the relief party and were advised what had happened.

It was a slow process going to the heavy smoke and gas, necessitating bratticing as they went and at six o'clock in the evening very little headway had been made over the 1,000 feet necessary to cover.

Horses in Mine

The mine stables were located directly under the fan house where ten of the magnificent mine horses were tied, and while no report could be made on their condition, the rescuers could hear them neighing and kicking, indicating at that time that some of them were still alive, but little hopes were entertained that any living being in that end of the mine could survive.

Pathetic Circumstances

In the case of Bob Gault he had entered the mine that morning out of his regular turn in order that he might be off from work today, so he could attend the wedding of his daughter, Merna, who was to be married to Stewart Mc-Donnell, this afternoon. Mrs. Gault was at the mine soon after the accident occurred, and when a full realization came to her of the position of the entombed husband, she was overcome and taken to the home of a friend.

Fire Boss Burke was in that entry with them fifteen minutes before the explosion occurred and reports the air to have been in the best condition, and no one could offer any explanation of what might have caused the accident."

6/6/19—"CAUSE OF ACCIDENT NOT DEFINITELY DETERMINED." "With the report of the commission selected to investigate the cause of the explosion in the Dietz Mine No. 8, on last Tuesday, in their hands, the coroner's jury yesterday made a decision that the cause of the terrible accident, which resulted in the death of two men, Robert Gault, and Felice Sucali, was due to the accumulation of gas or the accidental discharge of a keg of powder located in the first west entry off the south side of the mine. The inquest started last Wednesday morning, but it was decided that an investigation was necessary before a verdict could be reached by the jury, and an investigation commission was accordingly named. Following is their report, upon which the verdict of the jury was based.

June 6, 1919

We, the undersigned committee appointed by Robert V. Hotchkiss, state mine inspector of District No. 2, to make an investigation of the underground workings of the Sheridan Coal Company's Mine No. 8, report:

The object of the investigation was to try and ascertain the cause of the explosion which took place on June 3.

We, the committee, believe that the explosion was due to an accumulation of gas or other accidental discharge of a keg of powder located in the first west entry off the south side. We find that the ventilation, on the date of our examination, June 5th, throughout the district where the explosion occurred was good. We found that all cross-cuts were driven according to the mining laws of Wyoming and all stoppings or overcasts were installed in a good workmanlike manner. On June 5th the committee found no evidence of gas in the west entry where gas was usually found. Yours very respectfully, (Signed) R. V. Hotchkiss, M. F. Peltier, Hugh McLeod, I. A. McQueen and Fred Bell."

Inside Dietz No. 8 Mine on motor. George Aiken, foreman on left. Other two, unknown.

George Aiken, fireboss in Dietz No. 8 mine. Man on right unknown.

Dietz No. 8 (with horse in mine). L to R: Dick Hughes (with hand on horse), Robert Flockhart, _____ Walker, unknown.

1/10/20—"Two Men Hurt By Powder Explosion"—at Dietz No. 8—Hon and Hugh Montgomery—Hon's clothing almost burned from body—Montgomery head struck track—premature powder shot."

7/19/21—"Two story frame school house has been moved from Dietz to Dietz No. 8—is located on Broadway street."

10/5/21—"The new dance hall at Dietz No. 8 is finally completed and has had its doors open to the public by having a free dance one night last week. Later in the season, photo motion plays will be shown there. The seating capacity accommodates several hundred persons, as the hall is quite comodious. The floor is in excellent shape for dancing, and Albert Wondra, self-appointed floor manager, sees that there are no wall flowers and finds dancing partners for all who wish to trip the light fantastic.

Miss Mary Kuzara of Dietz suburb was shopping at various Sheridan stores Thursday afternoon, returning home via interurban.

Mrs. George Kuzara of Dietz suburb, visited friends in Kleenburn Thursday."

It appears from some reports that the Dietz No. 8 mine was closed in the spring of 1921 but reopened in the Fall of 1922 after a general mine strike in the Spring of the latter year which created a shortage of the supply of coal, and it remained open until February of 1923.

Mike Basarich states that he obtained employment in Dietz No. 8 in 1923, but after working only 18 days, the mine again closed down.

11/12/22—"COAL MINING LIMITED AS DIETZ IS CLOSED." "Concentration of the production of between 125 and 150 carloads of coal is limited to four mines of the Sheridan-Wyoming Coal company, with the closing Friday of the Dietz 8 Mine, it was announced by Edward Bottomley, division superintendent. Acme, Monarch, Kleenburn and Kooi mines are still running, and the necessity of closing the Kooi mine, which on Friday appeared imminent, has been virtually removed, it was stated yesterday. Present developments in the weather give grounds for belief that the mines' activity will increase soon. At present they are running about four days a week."

12/20/22—"Fifteen miners with their families left Dietz yesterday on the noon train for Superior, near Rock Springs, Wyo. They had been thrown out of work when the Dietz mine closed down a few weeks ago, and the Peabody Coal company and the Union Pacific Coal company cooperated in sending them where work was to be found. Burlington officials reported the selling of 30 full-fare and 34 half-fare tickets to the miners and that several carloads of household goods were sent."

lowing program: Recitation, Master James Garrett; song, first and second grades; recitation, Miss Helen Clearwater; recitation, Leo Podgarnic; drill, first and second grades; recitation, Bernard Clearwater; song, "Holy Night," Ada Chesney, Sarah Joyce, Ruth Montgomery, Katie Matjovitch, Luella Coast, Sophia Nicholvitch, Helen Clearwater and Enid Marsh; dialogue, third grade; recitation, Miss Sophia Nicholvitch; song, Miss Roman's room; recitation, Willis Coast; drill, 10 boys of third grade; song, Ada Chesney and Sarah Joyce; dialogue "Marriage of Santa Claus," was played by the pupils of Mrs. Morris' room and a two-act play.

School kids Dietz No. 8 1922(?) (teacher's name unknown). Front row, Stanley Kristy, Gazel Koren, ?, Mike Kuzara, Leo Podgarnick, Donald Goodsen, Walter Mentock, Walter Marosok, John (Red) Kristy, Eddie Nowicki, Charles Matejovitz; Louie Panigutti, Evyln Gooden. Second row, Ada Chesney Williams, Molly Sims or Simms, Katie Matejovitz, Pina Panigutti, Kumor girl, Julie Kosma, Marty Etta Clouse, Anna Kuzara, Mary Mentock, McManus girl, ? Kumor girl, ? Joe Kumor. Third row: George Matejovitz (Bob), ?, ?, Frank Sims or Simms, Johnny Kumor, teacher, Ted Capps, ?, Stanley Mentock.

1/3/24—(Dietz No. 8)—"A large crowd attended the Christmas program that was given at the Wander's (Wondra) hall Friday for the children of this community. The teachers of the schools, Mrs. Moore, principal, Mrs. D. O. Smith of Sheridan and Miss Roman announced the fol-

Mrs. Ralph Peck, her mother, Mrs. E. Oliver, Miss Margaret Peck and Hannah Oliver, of Dietz No. 7 were over to the program Friday.

Mrs. Agnes Hotchkiss was Christmas shopping in Sheridan Saturday.

Andy Mekick has left for Illinois and Iowa

to spend a few months with relatives and friends.

Miss Hannah Oliver and Margaret Peck of Dietz No. 7 were in camp on Saturday calling for their mail.

Mrs. Gillespie of Sheridan was out on Sunday visiting with Grandmother Bateman.

Mrs. Alvert Hill, son and niece Emil spent Christmas with friends at Monarch.

The teachers of the M. E. church gave a very artistic Christmas program on Sunday morning, Dec. 23. The program follows: Song, "Onward Christian Soldiers"; prayer, by Mrs. Gillespie; devotional reading, "What Christ's Reign Means to the World"; offering; song, "Joy to the World"; introduction, La Verne Mock; greeting, Wilma Chesney; greeting, Jean Day; recitation, "First Christmas Gift," Marjorie Mohr; song, "Slumber Sweetly," Dorothy Weaver; recitation, "Under the Star," Sarah Joyce; recitation, "Hear the Glad Notes," Elmer Day; recitation, "Christmas Gifts," Wayne Mock; song, "Jolly Old Saint Nicholas," Albert Joyce, Christina Chesney, Jean Day, George Chesney, Francis Ranavier, Elsworth Bateman and Eilma Chesney; recitation, "Merry Christmas," Timothy Kawamoto; recitation, "Icicle Fate," Myrtle Cole; recitation, "The Wondrous Gift," Luella Coast; recitation, "Christmas Gifts, Jack Gage; recitation, "Christmas Bells," Francis Ranavier; song, "Silent Night," Gladys Clearwater, Ada Chesney, Morine Bateman, Luella Coast, Sarah Joyce Grace Kawamoto, Helen Clearwater and Sophia Nicholvitch . . ." etc.

Others appearing on the program, included: Wilho Alto, Merald Alto, George Matjovitch, Virginia Bondi, Rosie Bondi, Myrtle Cole, Elsworth Bateman, Grandma Bateman, Almon Moon and Dorothy Weaver.

"Mr. and Mrs. Wm. Hunter and Mr. and Mrs. Joe Holliday from Kleenburn were here on Sunday taking in the Sunday school program

Mrs. Arthur Bateman entertained Mrs. Gillespie of Sheridan Sunday.

Mr. and Mrs. R. F. Hotchkiss and family spent a few hours with their mother, Mrs. Agnes Hotchkiss, and sister Christina Chesney, on Sunday.

Mrs. Ed Meryhew of Kleenburn underwent a serious operation at the Sheridan Hospital Tuesday.

Mr. & Mrs. Boyd Gale and daughters Misses Leis and Barbara of Sheridan motored out here to call on Mrs. Christina Chesney and family on Sunday afternoon.

Mrs. Harry Scott was in from her ranch on Sunday visiting a few days with Mrs. Flockhart.

Grace and Timothy Kawamoto were over from Dietz No. 7 getting Christmas packages from the postoffice.

Paddy Scullen of Sheridan was calling on friends Sunday.

Mr. and Mrs. Joe Mentock, Mrs. George Baker and Miss Mary Baker of Fort Mackenzie, and Louie Mentock, Mr. and Mrs. Steve Wisstinsky and Mrs. Clemens Wisstinsky attended church service at Dietz No. 7 on Christmas morning.

The Morosock brothers attended church at Dietz No. 7 Christmas morning.

Richard Gibbons entertained for dinner Wednesday Louis Matjovitch.

Mr. and Mrs. Frank Day entertained for Sunday dinner her mother and father, Mr. and Mrs. William Hunter, and Mr. and Mrs. Joe Holliday of Kleenburn."

DIETZ SCHOOL
DISTRICT NO. 28
Sheridan Co., Wyoming
May 23, 1924

Mrs. McPherren,
Teacher

School Board
Walter Upton   Sam Garrett
Frank Smith

PUPILS

Kenneth Beck   Albert Joyce
Julia Matejovitz
Rosie Bondi   Helen Kuzara
John Kristy
Stanley Kristy   George Chesney
Martha Mikolvich
Bernard Clearwater Leo Podgornick
Ruth Montgomery
Frank Mentock   Josephine Mentock
Helen Clearwater
Sophie Mikolvich   Virginio Bondi
Sarah Joyce
Ada Chesney   Wilho Alto
Delmar Clearwater
Mike Kuzara   Merald Alto
Mary Mentock
Katie Matejovitz   Enid Marsh
Dorothy Weaver
Walter Mentock   Gazel Koren
Steve Czarny

*"Memory
like the ivy clings
to olden times
and ways
and things."*

THIS souvenir is presented to you with the best wishes of your teacher, believing that in the years to come it will serve as a pleasant reminder of our schoolday associations.

One of the two school houses at Dietz No. 7 (often jokingly referred to as the "high school" because it had two stories) later moved to Dietz No. 8 in 1921 and used as the school there. This picture was taken at the Dietz No. 8 location.

3/27/25—"MELON ROBBERIES PUT BOYS IN JAIL." "Robbing and destroying a water melon patch cost three boys five dollars and costs, and payment for the watermelons, when they were arraigned Wednesday afternoon before Justice D. G. Bruce.

Tony Morosock, Dick Gibbons and George Matches plead guilty to robbing the watermelon plot belonging to Mrs. Helen Mickalovitch at Dietz Tuesday night. Unable to raise the amount of their fines they were sentenced to jail to work out the fine at the rate of one dollar a day.

Pete Christy and Stanley Mentock who were arrested with the other boys, were discharged at the hearing before Justice Bruce. It is believed by officers who made the arrest, however, that still other boys are implicated in the robbery. Members of the local sheriff's office captured the offenders Wednesday morning when a warrant was sworn out by Mrs. Nickalovitch. Nearly the entire patch was destroyed, officers report."

6/16/25—"MARY GETS $500 FOR PLAYING "CUPID' THOUGH IT TAKES TIME TO COLLECT."

"Mary Belobrk's role as "Cupid" will net her $500, but the Dietz woman was forced to enter district court Tuesday to collect the expenses she piled up while making the match which resulted in the marriage of her sister with Joe Wian of Dietz, her former boarder.

Judge James H. Burgess decided that Mary was entitled to the expense money, plus interest, after hearing the love story unfolded in the case brought by Mary against Joe Wian, her brother-in-law. Mary was represented by John F. Raper, while Joe was represented by H. Glenn Kinsley.

The case had its inception way back in 1920, when Mary was preparing to take a trip back to her old home in Jugo-Slavia. According to the testimony, Joe Wian who was one of Mary's boarders, told Mary that if she found a nice girl over in the old country, to bring her back and he would pay all expenses. In fact, they even discussed the possibility of Mary's two sisters, it was said.

So Mary sailed, and discovered that one of her sisters was willing to come back and be Joe's bride. The sister had been married before, but her husband had been in the army and had not been heard from for seven years, it was related.

Mary and her sister then sailed back to the United States, but, according to the testimony, not before Joe Wian had signed an affidavit that he would support the sister. That was necessary in order to get a passport.

When they arrived at Ellis Island, Mary wired Joe to meet them at the train in Sheridan. The sister was released at once from Ellis Island and, with $100 Mary was said to have given her, started for Sheridan. On the other hand, some technicality held Mary at Elis Island for fifteen days.

In the meantime, Joe stopped work at the coal mines and came to Sheridan to meet the train. After waiting around ten or twelve days, he became disgusted and went back to Dietz. That was the day his prospective bride arrived.

Unknown and in a strange country, the sister was taken in by the Paul Nicklovich family, and they were the ones who introduced Joe and the sister.

Mary finally arrived, and, after fifteen days of courtship, Joe announced that he was satisfied and the marriage ceremony was arranged. Testimony was to the effect that Joe again at that time agreed to pay the expenses, which had mounted up to $328.

Joe is still happily married, but he has never paid Mary. So that's what the suit was about."

5/7/26—"DIETZ CHILDREN STAGE PROGRAM.—Music Week Is Observed at Mining Camp School.—The feature event of the Music week activities in Dietz No. 8 was held Wednesday evening at the Dietz hall. Mrs. Minnie Moore, chairman of arrangements for Music Week in Dietz arranged the program, assisted by Miss Mary Roman and Miss Edna Roman, teachers in the Dietz school.

A feature of the program was a descriptive song by "Grandma" Hotchkiss of Dietz. The program, most of which was presented by Dietz school children was: song, quarter, the primary department; song, Ada Chesney and Sara Joyce, Mrs. C. Williams, accompanist; violin duet, Enid Marsh and George Chesney; descriptive song, "Grandma" Hotchkiss; song, sextette; folk dance, primary grades; saxophone solo, Richard Gibbons, Mrs. C. Williams, accompanist; duet, Rose and Anna Kuzara; piano solo, Enid Marsh; vocal solo, Ben Joyce, Miss Mary Roman, accompanist; piano solo, Mrs. C. Williams; vocal duet, Helen Kuzara and Matha Miklovich; vocal duet, Rosie and Anna Kuzara; saxophone and piano, Richard Gibbons and Mrs. Williams; song, Dietz school Glee club; song of adieu, Sarah Joyce and Ada Chesney."

5/20/27—"Grandma" Hotchkiss Found Dead at Her Residence in Dietz."—"Grandma" Hotchkiss, well-known pioneer of northern Wyoming and a resident of Dietz for many years, passed away some time during last night, her death being discovered by her young grandson, who has been residing with her.

Mrs. Hotchkiss had been ill for several days and was being cared for by neighbors. One of these attended her until about midnight last night, and returned to her home when the aged woman fell asleep.

She is the mother of Dick, Tom and Bob Hotchkiss, founders and operators for many years of the Hotchkiss mine at Dietz. She had always taken a prominent part in the Bobby Burns celebration, and annual event at Dietz."

9/15/27—"Dietz Teacher Still Missing—Friends Say Teacher May Have Been Married."—"Edna Roman, 24, teacher at Dietz last five years.

9/21/27—"Missing School Teacher is Found Happily Married at Butte, Montana—Folks at Wheaton, Minn. Learn That Former Dietz Instructor, Miss Edan Roman, Is Now Mrs. Henry Ramey."

10/3/27—"WOMEN AND YOUTH GO AFTER MELONS BUT GET LARGE ELK." "Three young Dietz women and a boy went out after melons Sunday—and they brought home a five-point bull elk weighing 950 pounds.

It is not quite correct, though, to say that

they brought the elk home alone, because it took 10 persons to pull the animal down the mountain side.

Mrs. Bertha Mohr, Wilma Karpi, Georgia Mathews and young Stanley Mentock were up in the foothills after melons. At 1 o'clock they spied a band of five elk outlined on top of a distant hill. At 3 o'clock, young Mentock had shot the largest of the band and was bringing him home with the aid of several recruits.

Mentock, an 18-year-old youth who has done some fighting in the ring under the name "Kid Mentock," found the big bull lying in a gully. He shot him through the head.

"We'll go out after melons next Sunday," the women exclaimed."

9/11/29—"Fire At Dietz Camp Destroys Pool Hall and Dance Building. Loss of $12,000.00 Is Covered By Insurance—Cause of Flames Unknown as Blaze Starts Late at Night—Pool hall owned by Frank Wondra."

2/6/30—"No Trace Found of Lost Miner, Suicide Feared—Sup't. Does Not Think Man Leaped Into Shaft—No trace had been found by Thursday afternoon of John Pichonich 45, Dietz Miner missing since Sunday—Last seen walking toward 210 foot shaft filled with 45 feet of water."

8/20/30—Body of Miner Found in Water in Dietz Shaft—John Pichonic Had Been Missing For Many Days—Efforts to locate his body

Fourth or fifth grade—Dietz No. 8 Wyo. school, 1928. Left to right—back row: Angelina Kawulok, Theresa Kristy, Charlotte Kuzara, Frances Czarny, Miss Dorothy Bottomly (teacher), Eva Matches, Stella Kawulok. Middle row: Heretta Henderson, Nancy Woods, Christina Williams, Nellie Mae Stuka. Front row, Walter Mentock, Roman Marosok, Alfred Woods, Tony Pedgornik, Eddie Podgornik.

then were futile. Only after turning on the electric current once again in the old shaft and lowering a cage, which was done Thursday afternoon, were the searchers able to make progress. (A more detailed account of this incident and the recovery will be found in taped interview of Wade Ratcliff who aided in the recovery).

7/3/33—"Dietz Team Wins Two Ball Games— The mine team at Dietz won two games Sunday on their home grounds. They defeated Decker 11 to 4 and Crow Agency 8 to 3. Spider Marosok pitched the game against Crow Agency and B. Matches pitched against Decker. Other members of the Dietz team were Akie Atkinson, Bill Sopris, Walter Mentock, Les Moon, Bob Flockhart, Briz Marosok, Louis Matches and Frank Mentock."

Dietz No. 8 baseball team (sponsored by Hotchkiss Coal Co.). Top row: Joe Christy, Steve Czarny, Mike Mentock, Walter Mentock. Middle row: Andrew Marosok, Louie Matches, Tony Marosok, Lester Moon. Front row: Albert Goodmy, John Mentock, Frank Mentock, Bob Flockhart.

1/28/34—"Dance held at Dietz for benefit of Hockey team well attended. Dance given by Kibben Hardware to raise funds to send team to play the University of Wyoming.

4/21/35—"Albert Wondra of Dietz was granted a retail liquor license by the board of county commissioner at a special meeting Saturday.

11/18/35—"Lighted Baseball Field at Dietz is Assured By Dance."—"A lighted baseball field at Dietz was assured Saturday nite when a large crowd attended the benefit dance at the Dietz Hall." "We will have the field lighted in the Spring and ready for action when the season opens," J. Plott and Wade Ratcliff who spon-

sored the dance, declared today.—"We tried to give the people a good time and plenty to eat, and we were helped in making the dance a success by Mark Hayward and his orchestra." The field will be the first lighted diamond in this section."

1/7/36—"Mary Marosok Is Dead After Short Illness—Long Time Resident of Dietz Dies on Tuesday—Mrs. Mary Marosok, 60, died at the Sheridan County Memorial Hospital Tuesday after a short illness. She had been a resident of Dietz for the past 32 years.

Surviving are two daughters, Mrs. Andrew Brantz of Monarch and Mrs. Andrew Chieslar of Sheridan; five sons, Andrew, Frank, Antone and Raymond of Dietz and Walter of Sheridan; one brother, Joseph Mentock, and two sisters who reside in Rochester, N.Y.

She was preceded in death by her husband in 1932."

8/3/36—(Society column)—"Musical Evening— John Antonkovich was host to the members of the Americanization class at an evening musical last Wednesday at his home in Dietz (Kuzaraville)—During the evening. Selections were presented by Mr. Antonkovich, violinist; George Rubinow, accordionist and Joe Bocek, vocalist."

Sheridan Press, 11/16/37—"DIETZ ABANDONED AFTER BOOM GLORY.—The last of the Dietz coal camps is being abandoned by the Sheridan Wyoming Coal company. The Dietz No. 8 mine has been virtually deserted since the fall of 1922 when it was closed by its former owner, the Sheridan Coal Company. No coal has been taken from it since that time, but the town has remained to house the overflow population from the two other coal mines operated by the company, Acme and Monarch.

All of the houses of the little settlement will be moved out except the first the third rows which will remain to provide homes for the 75 people who will continue to make their homes there.

Neither the population of Dietz or the number of men employed by the coal company is being lessened by the project, which is really a plan to clean up the property and get rid of superfluous material and outmoded machinery, Robert J. Gandy, purchasing agent of Sheridan-Wyoming Coal company, said.

Thirty of the original 125 houses, many of which were moved there from the older Dietz

No. 7 when it was abandoned, will be left to house the workers of the Acme and Monarch

Sheridan Press, Tuesday, Nov. 16, 1937—"Work is underway at Dietz No. 8" toward abandoning the town and tearing down the tipple of the once famous Dietz No. 8 mine shaft. The picture shows workmen busy at work with acetylene torches tearing down the steel frame work of the tipple. This iron along with the other metal taken from the coal cars and machinery will be sold as scrap.

being drilled to furnish water for the two rows of houses that will constitute the town.

Tipple on the shaft mine which once soared 200 feet aloft is being cut down piece by piece by helmeted men who cling like flies to the steel beams and cut them down yards at a time with searing blowtorches. Workmen are expected to finish the cutting down of the tipple within the next few days.

Iron from the tipple and from the shaft cars and other mine machinery now useless is being scrapped and sold. The turbine that drew the cars up and down the shaft is still in good condition and will be sold.

ONLY SHAFT MINE—Most of the mining equipment and machinery was removed years ago after the owners had abandoned operations in the shaft mine for more economical operating of the two slope mines at Acme and Monarch. The Dietz No. 8 was the only mine in this vicinity to be worked through a vertical shaft, the others being worked by boring into hillsides where seams of coal are more conveniently mined.

This picture shows the front row of houses that will remain after the Sheridan-Wyoming Coal Company get through selling 85 of the 125 buildings. (The front row is the west row adjacent to the highway). This row and the third row will be the only remaining homes in Dietz. These houses are being kept to house the 75 people who will continue to live in Dietz. Front row, (from right to left), see only corner of house, John Platt, John Moon, Dorothy Marosok, Katie Marosok, Louis Matches, Martin Benegalia. Clyde Williams, Albert Goodmay, and across a slough, the company store and post office operated by Albert Wondra.

mines and their families. Of those remaining, 88 or 89 will be sold and removed. Only about 40 houses remain to be sold. Most of the houses are three and four-room dwellings, a few two-room.

Wondra's store and the school house will remain in Dietz. The watertank built to supply water to a large population will be abandoned with the completion of a new well which is now

The five years that the Dietz No. 1 operated saw the hey-day of the coal industry, when the markets of the warring world cried for fuel. Eastern coal went across the sea, middle-western coal to the coast, and the great mid-western market was left to the west to fill.

The great days of the Dietz No. 8 were during this time of the great scarcity and demand for coal. A shaft 215 feet deep was sunk in the great seam of coal that measured 47 feet and seven inches thick, modern and complete equipment was installed, a boom town hastily built, and the first shipment of coal made from this mine on December 1, 1917.

The large vein of coal at this mine measures almost twice in width those of the Acme and Monarch mines, which are around 38 feet wide.

The easier accessibility of the Acme and Monarch veins makes them more valuable because of the greater economy of operation.

In 1921 expensively equipped Dietz No. 8 produced 115,450½ tons of coal with an average of 172 men employed during the year. In 1922 however, only 45,000 tons were taken out of the mine, and 274 men employed. Intermittent strikes during the year accounts for the larger number of men employed during this year of production, company officials said.

CHEAPER COAL—In the fall of 1922, the Sheridan-Wyoming Coal company which purchased the three mines, Dietz, Acme and Monarch, found that more coal could be taken from the Acme and Monarch mines at lower cost with the Dietz mine not operating and the mine was closed at that time, probably never to reopen. A lower market also contributed to the closure at this time.

For several years, the company kept watchmen and pumpmen at the mine to keep water from flooding it against possibility of reopening. These precautions were abandoned, however, as the probability of its reopening became increasingly distant. Safeguards were taken away and the mine allowed to flood with water. At present the once-hollow underground tunnels through which coal was carried to the hungry markets of the world are filled with water and a gaseous mixture known as "fire-damp."

Today, the Sheridan-Wyoming Coal Company sees little chance of ever reopening the mine which is being held for reserve. The cost of pumping the water from the mine, securing new equipment and operating it would be much higher than that of using more shifts on the operating mines or even of drilling new slope mines in other veins, Gandy said.

Sheridan Press—"with the closing of the last of the eight mining towns to be named for C. N. Dietz of Omaha, Neb., at one time owner and promoter of many mines in this vicinity, a saga of mining days comes to an end. It is the story of high prices for the "Black gold" in the ground

and employment of many men to do what a few men and high-powered machinery do more efficiently today.

It is another chapter in the continual process of industrial revolution that is becoming so familiar. With the waning and final abandonment of the once booming and prosperous little mining centers there has come about a new order—one of efficiency brought about with less labor and more machinery—one of fewer miners and more abandoned mining towns."

First house sold from Dietz No. 8 camp to Stanley A. Kuzara. For quite some time, I waited in anticipation of the time when the houses at the Dietz No. 8 camp would be offered for sale, and when in the spring of 1937 I heard the rumor, I immediately drove out to the camp only to find that several of the coal company officials consisting of R. J. Gandy, Chris Shott, Jesse Kessinger and Wade Ratcliff were at that moment making inspections of the units. Approaching them, I inquired, "Are these houses for sale?" Their reply came in the form of a question, "Would you pay $200 for one?" Upon receiving an immediate "yes," I was told to take my pick. (I was later told that this quick sale prompted them to conclude the price was too cheap, and the remainder of the houses were priced at $250). The house I selected was one formerly occupied by the Harry Kettering family. I then went to the Monarch office of the coal company to make payment and in handing my check to Mrs. Nell Carmichael, I requested a Bill of Sale. Somewhat surprised, she stated they had no such forms, so I simply dictated one for her. In subsequently moving the house to Sheridan, it was necessary to cut it in two pieces to be able to move it along the narrow highway to town. The house is presently located at 538 Avon Street in Sheridan.

Dietz No. 8 tipple location as it looks today.

INTERVIEW WITH WADE RATCLIFF, 1973

Speaking of the McShane tie camp and flume—"But we did ride a boat." And in referring to an old story about one of the loggers killing a fellow worker "Well if he was, he was brought down in a boat—he can build a boat in a very short time."

When questioned about his mine experience, "The first winter I worked in the mine, I come and worked at Old Acme you know where Old Acme was? Johnny Cass come down and worked in there (Old Acme was located just this side of the old Riverside Mine), and then from there I went over to Kooi one winter. When asked who started Old Acme, "Craig, Archie Craig and then he come down and started New Acme. I knew him quite well—he was an awful nice fella"—"I worked there the winter of 1911 and then went back. I loaded coal. We got 20¢ a ton for loading it and they shot it. Johnny Cass and I worked there—they worked a half day at a time and shot down a half day at a time and you couldn't make nothing." How many tons? "Depends on how the trips come—you see you could load out 2, 4, 6 or 10—you could load out 10 ton a day, but if you couldn't get the car, you couldn't do it. I worked there 2 or 3 months then Charlie Conway and I went over the Kooi and worked—we loaded coal there and that was just about the same—such an outfit—I couldn't make nothing here. I left there and I came down here and they were puttin in the street car in out

there and I went to drivin team at old Dietz 8 for old man Neese and worked till that street car was finished—he was their contractor—he had a spot along there (a section of railroad bed). I think this was 1911. Worked in that till we finished there then I went to work in Monarch and I worked at Monarch for practically off and on—finished there that winter. I worked in the shop and blacksmith shop—my brother and I.

Next Spring, 1912, then I went to Riverton and worked over there—McLaughlin and I. He was one that was up here at the lumber camp and at Dubois, yeah, he wanted me to go up there so I went to haul ties that summer, then come down that river drive 8 miles above Dubois, and that was the call of a hundred and eight miles from Riverton there but twist and turn, it was a lot further and that river was the crookedest thing you saw Stanely—that was the Wind River. It come on down through there and through Thermopolis. Next Fall, came back to work at Monarch to do blacksmithing. Then after that, I worked on every thing at Monarch until 1920, then I went to Dietz 8—come to Dietz 8 to take care of the horses inside of the mine. Hauled em up and down on the cage. We had to bring em out onct a year—they passed a law that you had to bring em out onct a year for two weeks and then when the horses got on outside, we had to bring them out on a cloudy day. They just couldn't stay on the ground (they would run and jump in wild ecstacy). Brought em up onct a year and I rode the cage with them and had to bring em out for two weeks and them old horses, you know, as long as you ride that cage up and down, that was 181 feet and I was with em. They was alright but you know they was awful nervous—you try to put them on by themselves and you not go with them.

They were so tickled they couldn't stay on the ground for jumping.

At Monarch at one time we had about 68 head of horses there. But Dietz 8, we didn't have so many there—around 25 or 26. We had around 19 or 20 at once down in the mine down there. Carneyville was the only one that had mules. They (the horses) pulled the coal from the rooms to the main line—they had motors that picked them up and took them on to the shaft or the mouth—after they went into machine and they got these little gathering motors with cables on them and they got to using them and we got rid of the horses.

They was one bad explosion there that

happened just about a year before I went to Monarch and it blowed rails out of the mine—you know where the Heczko place was?—it blowed rails from there clear across the river. That was closed then and then they opened up a slope—not a one killed—they was ready to go in—the fire boss was in to inspect it and come back out to meet them and never went in—never hurt a man. He (the fireboss) made his rounds and I guess he thought there was something fishy that he couldn't quite understand, but he never thought there was anything like that and he come back out—met em on the outside there, and when they were down there, that thing blowed up—never crippled up a man in no way, shape or form—streak of luck."

Referring to the explosion at Dietz 8—"No, that happened just before I was there—was when Bob Gault and his partners got killed. Now there were several little explosions there, and there was a few little fires there, but there was never an explosion and Frank Day was in the first one there, right from where the barn were, was a little low place—kept a pump there and washed out the barn there inside the mine, and I had a door here, I cut the horses in fresher air see and it went on around but they had to have a certain amount of air, and when they'd come around here where the horses in here, it made a whirl-pool like water you see—help this slow air coming out—and it help down in there—it whirled and whirled quite a while to get out and that would only happen when the fan went out and the gas would accumulate—Dietz had a lot of gas—and then when they'd start the fan up, about 2 hours after that you didn't want to go in there and they learn that after 2 or 3 got killed. Bob Gault and his partner—Frank Day, got burnt and Frank Smith—you know Frank Smith didn't you—you know his boys—they used to live in Dietz—he was the tipple boss. Well anyhow Day was the first one and they used to run around and start the pump and he used to drive the motor around see and cause they run down into here, the trolley set it afire—sparks from the trolley—and so fire of course he jumped up and run—run back up into where the fresh air come in there and got out and up the manhole and walked out. He was burnt. I met him coming out and wondered what was wrong with that fellow. He had a coat on holding it over his head. He had blisters all over his head where he was burnt and when I got there I said, "What's the matter with you?"

"Oh," he said, "Explosion." Well, just the gas didn't explode. And he said, "I'm just all burnt to hell," he said. I said, "Heck, you're not burned at all—just a few blisters on your face here and you run into the rib and lost your mind—busted." And he thought he was burnt up. Yes, he really did and it was hurting him in that cold weather. Well, I seen he wasn't, but he was scared. His wife was going to have his youngest son and I seen I couldn't take him in that way—he was so scared. So I took him on down to the doctor's office and I says, "Frank, you're not hurt. Let me get a mirror and I'll show you." The doctor weren't there. I got a mirror and showed him and he came down there seen he wasn't so bad, but he thought he was really hurt. His hands and wrist was burnt. We got him cleaned up then went over and told his wife that he got scorched a little but, see. He come out of it. Then later on while he was off work, old man Smith—they had been changing, doing that work—so Smith went down in right along and the fan would do down somehow that juice would go off in the night and the next morning it started up and they'd go down in there too quick. Smith went down this time and he thinks, "Well I'll just not take the motor out. I'll just walk around." Took his flashlight and away he went and walks down there and he started up the arcs from the commutator set it afire again. Well, old man Smith he just fell down in the ditch down there and laid down there—he's a little English fella—"I'll never forget little old "cateye." He looked up and said, "Oh, that fire was sure red." I stayed down there, used to be a foot racer. I laughed and he said, "I'll tell you, I seen when it was hot enough where I could stay down there." He said, "You could a played carrot on my coat tail." He was an Irish man—he run up where he got some fresh air and I got out and from then on, they'd shut that fan down and then they'd go down there and just stay in there and with safety lights at a certain hour they'd cut that thing. It would take about three hours before it was safe. Said they'd went in there and they'd watch and watch and when two hours would come up and they didn't got nothing, so they'd just hung a safety light and they'd come back there and that blaze was goin up and when that blaze goes up you't better look out cause its gonna explode. You see, a safety light blaze is just like that, you got to lower that lamp down just real easy—keep from explosion—keep it down here and you see, the gas is high and get down and get out of there so they seen right there that there was something to it in about two hours or a little more."

In answer to a question about the color of flame in the safety light and if the color changed in the presence of gas, he replied, "Yeah, right, it got longer too. The more it comes, the longer that would keep stretching. If it stretched long enough then it would explode it."

Would gas in the mine catch fire from a safety light? "Right, see this safety light would go up here, get so hot and it has to be little holes in there for a little bit for it to burn."

"That was the time we was trapped in there after we was shut down" (referring to him climbing the ladder of the air shaft). "It had been closed down for the time being—remember after this Peabody bought 'em. They went to shutin down mines and so this one. Kooi was shut down and Dietz 8 was shut down, then Dietz 8 opened up after that. No, they was goin to open Dietz 8 but Kooi opened up a little while—then shut down again.

The air shaft, they wanted to keep it for emergency, for they was goin to open it again. They got piles of steel in there yet—heck they got oodles of it. When the shaft caved in later, we was still keepin the water out see, so this Sunday, this bunch of fellows went down there. Benny Joyce, Frank Day, Charlie Karpi, Charlie Gazdick, Joe Tysel, Louie Tysel and another big Hungarian, John, they called him. I don't know what his name was and myself. We went down and by George, we went down there and took a load of stuff up to go in there. Overhead heres where the air vent was the trap door, that's where we took that up through to get up in there to do this cribbing. Karpi was the guy with me. We come up and kinda shove that door up. I walked down that every morning. That was just for emergency door to go up and in there, to go into the air shaft—trap door to carry stuff. If you didn't, of course you would have to carry away around there, and I said, "Charlie, something wrong there—no air "cause before it would just blow your light out. I said, "I'm going climb up in here and see what's wrong." I went up there to the bottom of the fan—nothing—either this thing is plugged up or something or else that fan's down—one of the two. And this is right where the explosions always happen—right down in there—and of course I tell you they was scared and I was one of the youngest of the bunch so I knew it was dangerous—those steps

—but I figured we'd already been in here. This oughtn't to blow up now. And so I seen what's wrong and I come on down to the bottom and we couldn't get out, and Mr. Upton, he told us "Now I'm going up the canyon this Sunday" (he owned a summer cabin at the mouth of Tongue River Canyon). Couldn't get out because the air shaft had caved in where the stairs were and no one there to hoist it (the cage). Yeah, Mr. Upton let us down—he went up the canyon. He said, "Now I'll be back and hoist you up at quittin' time. So we was stuck there till 4 o'clock that evening. And so I think heck, I know that's a long climb just boards nailed on as steps, and 440 come down (electricity, I think he meant) and it was wet—tickle your hands to beat the band. I said, "I ain't goin to set here that long." I begin to put on an extra pair of gloves which didn't do me a bit of good because just as soon as they got wet that went through 'em just the same and they said, "What you goin to do?", and I said, "I'm goin to climb out here." They said, "Oh, no, you can't do that." I said, "Oh yes, I can. I can climb out of here." And so I started. They tried to keep me back and I said, "No." I was the only one that could run the hoist so been no use for them others and I was younger than them others too—several years. So I clum up there. I tell you 180 feet's a long ways when you just climb these little steps here—just a ladder was all it was—181 feet from this rail to that rail. And when I got up there then, this trap door was froze down—this was in February. And I said "Gee Whiz, am I goin to have to go back down and climb them X?/X? things again?" I had to go up them things over and over to get up there—them things were 8 inch rungs.

I had to reach over there—it was about 5 or 6 feet over there and boy I sure didn't want to have to go back down. I kept reachin over and finally I made it and I got hold of that and I jumped over there and then I clum up there where the cage come down, ran, got out of there and when I got out I hollered "goin to start the set up" and I'll bring you out" so I went in and talked to 'em over the phone—we had a phone—so they got in and we come out. The fan was running but they was plugged up and couldn't get up through there. It just as well been shut down. See, it caved in down there. That's what we was workin on. It just caved in one place there. See and cut off the air. (This was not the shaft he climbed. The shaft he climbed was the cage shaft). Where the cage come down. Oh yes, came up the cage shaft. That air shaft was closed down below there. Remember where that steel building was where the fan were. That's down below the mine—oh, a couple-three hundred feet. Now see, this air shaft, it had winding steps up and down, and the cave was down here and it just plugged the whole thing up..

(At some remarks about how the foreign people were sometimes looked down upon, and about the Bobby Burns celebrations, he continued, "Cooked a lot of food, danced the Highland Fling, the Scotch Fling, all this and lots of singin'. Had an awful lot of Scotsmen to put this thing on. Course, they had lots of other people to help them too. They all thought that Bobby Burns Day was a great day, you know.")

("The boarding house at Dietz No. 8) "Mrs. Groski run it. (My sister and husband, Helen and James Barello held their wedding reception in that boarding house when they were married). "I was there. Well years ago, you know, we used to get milk from you folks, and Helen and Charlotte used to bring it to us when they went to school.

Do you remember when that John Petchovnik (jumped) in that air shaft? He used to be in Dietz 7 and every time he got—now this is before I knew him and I never worked there—my brother worked there, and when he'd get drunk he'd say he was going to jump in that shaft at No. 5, you know, they shut that down. When he'd get drunk he said he was goin to jump in some of those cave holes and they had to watch him till he got sober, you know. And they had to watch him and this went on for years and years. He stayed with that Frank Voler, you know, and Frank got married and so John got on a big drunk, so he told. Frank went to work and he told his wife, "Watch him—old John said he was going to jump in that air shaft." We had the cages brought down—that mine shut down, and we had steel across there and them set on but you know that scamp crawled down and jumped in there. He xxxxxxxx them, and when he would go up there and one of the women would start watching him. (Asked where he jumped). Into the air shaft where the cages come up and down at the pit mouth there 181 feet down there. (Must have killed him—Laughter). I hope to tell you! You know Dietz No. 8— anyhow he just said that so they watched him and he went down toward the store and crossed the track and come

back where the baseball diamond is at on the other side and they seen him right up around the air shaft where the fan were and then he went where the cage was and that scamp went up there and jumped in between there and went down. When they got him out of there they was 85 feet of water in there (after the mine closed down), but see he had over a hundred feet—let's see, he had 94 feet to fall before he hit the water, see—he'd fall on one side and hit the other—knocked his shoe off, broke his shoulder——So, I'd been up there just a short time before where I was doing some blacksmith work fixin' some pipe and I was over at the barn there and the women come there and they said "Oh, John jumped down the air shaft." I said, "Oh no!" and they said "(Yes he did. We chased him right up there and he jumped in there." So I went up there and I'd look down there and that water would just trinkle, trinkle and the water was splashing so I said to the women, "He must be out here somewhere—he must be out among some of these pit cars around here. Look around." I wanted to get them away from there. I wanted to go back and look so I went back and looked and I said, "Well, he's in there, no doubt about it." So they couldn't get him out and couldn't get him out so they said, "Maybe he's not in there." I said, "Oh yes, I know he's there cause I looked in there too many times because I never seen that water splashing like that before." So they said, "Well, I'll tell ya—check the tanks a water up there—he might have jumped in there, but I know he's in that mine and I'll tell you which side of the cage he's on. He's on the south side too. The north side, cause I looked at both of them. So we waited for two weeks but it was so cold he couldn't come to the top. So the light company said when you run that cage the demand runs up so high and you have to pay that demand for the whole month—it be just the same as working right along, so, we'll furnish the electricity if you want to do that so we said "OK." So then they come over there and there were two cages laying over there and I had to start the thing, couple them together see. Well, I'd lift this one up so I could pull this steel so I could let it down, then I'd lift the other one up and let it down. Then I'd let this down till it'd touch the water and the other touch the top, so they were counterbalanced cause they were awfully hard to hold if I didn't have that dead brake but if the weight was both together they'd hold, so I done that. That's when Edward

Bottomly was here and L. S. Norman was the Mines State Fire boss—Mine Inspector. So I done that, they said, "Now I want you to run them—got to see run up and down and hit the water and run up and down for five or ten minutes and they said, "I believe surely, if there is anything (gas). I said, "OK." So I stood right out in front and they went in and let her down. They had a safety light and I said, "Go down slow so you can watch that blaze." I eased them down and eased them down, till they examined this side there, so I brought em up then. Got on this'n and went down slow—clear—you won't find him on this side here, so we got a bunch of men on there down they went. They had cables and grab hooks. Went down, fished and hooked on to him and just as soon as they hooked him the odor was so strong—just come up that rope—just made the men sick as dogs. Oh, they just vomit something awful. So as they got him up quite a little way, they lost him and he was so near floating, he just stood there and they fooled around and fooled around and they went back and fished and fished, but finally they found him and pulled him but boy, he was swelled big and they pulled him up through the cage and got him up and laid him off to the side and sent for a hearse to come and get him. But he was—broke, his shoe off, broke his shoulder. He was dead before he hit the water, banging from one side to the other. You know Frank Voler? They batched together for years and years and Frank married—Johnnie—what was those kids' name—Jack Smautz—you know the Smautz—well him and his wife separated and then Voler married her. Voler died here just a few years ago. She's living in town. Well, anyhow, they batched there for years and they had a batch of honey bees and evertime he got drunk, you know how they'd come, but when they'd swarm. Well, he'd put his head in there and they'd never sting him. He'd done that many a time, for I'd seen him.

(Once) Three boys huntin' and they went up there chasing rabbits you know, there and one run over there in an old mine cave hole) and one of the boys went (down) there and he just dive in and the other boy wondered what's on

and he went down and the other boy went home—he got scared. (The first two boys in going down had become asphyxiated by black damp) Black damp, boy that'll just knock—well you know when Frank Welch was runnin' the mine at Acme and those two Italians got killed there—one of them married that Mentock girl, John Mentock's youngest girl, Rosie—Corzan—John Corzan and another one (Santa Rossa). Well, his dad and another one. Well they got killed there. Well, they was workin' at this night and Frank Welch was in there and they knew they was Black Damp back in this and they wanted to get this stop lift and they had it up pretty high and they was a workin' and there was a cave come down and just throwd that xxxxxxx right there and down they went and old Welch was out here so he went back there and this one he was laying dead so he got him by the arm and drug him quite a ways and old Frank couldn't go no further. He died, the other Italian. (Corzan, originally named Coassin) (Old Frank Welch got sick for a long time) and his partner (Santa Rossa). I used to know them—Corzan's dad—I used to know Johnny well. His girl used to play ball with us. We used to call her Swede—big light complexioned—she played third, a good batter, too. Seen 'em at the gas station not too many years ago and Swede was with him so called her Swede. They're over in the Basin somewhere (in Gebo or Kirby)."

Just recently, in a conversation with Mr. Ratcliff, he told of how when he worked at the Monarch mine in about 1919 or 1920, he was assigned, as a guard and was required to go to Sheridan periodically to pick up the payroll for all the camps, some $157,540 dollars, all in greenbacks, gold and silver, bringing this payroll via the interurban. At the time, Joe Drier was the conductor on the interurban. He further relates that once, a person who knew of Mr. Ratcliff's assignment, suggested that he abscond with all that money and live a life of luxury instead of working for a living. I suppose some people would be tempted to do just that sort of thing, but knowing Mr. Ratcliff, I know that such was furthest from his mind.

Chapter 8

Hotchkiss 1918-1939

About a half mile north of the mining camp of Dietz No. 8 and located on the west side of the C. B. & Q. railroad, was the Hotchkiss coal mine, commonly known as the "Shoestring" mine. This was also a "slope" mine, the tipple being next to the railroad siding, while the mine itself located across Big Goose creek over which the tracks crossed by means of a bridge. This distance between the mine entrance and the tipple, was about two hundred yards.

Although there were a few miners living in the two or three houses which had been built near the mine, nearly all of the employees lived in the Dietz No. 8 camp—this mine never did have a so-called camp of its own.

The road leading to the mine followed a route leaving old highway 87 just beyond the hill north of Dietz No. 8, extending west proceeding under the interurban and the C. B. & Q. bridges where they crossed Big Goose creek, and those who got off the interurban at the Hotchkiss station, were required to cross the fences on both sides of the C. B. & Q.

Sheridan news media covering this operation, some of which are as follows:

11/15/19—"HOTCHKISS MINE INCREASES THE VALLEY OUTPUT." "Begins Operations with a Capacity of 100 Tons—Practical Miners are in Charge."

With the resumption of mining activities the Sheridan county field is to have another new mine which will materially increase the output of this district. Hotchkiss Brothers are the operators and they have everything in readiness to turn out the coal as soon as the labor troubles are settled.

The mine in question is located just west of Big Goose and about half a mile north of Dietz No. 8. It was recently purchased of Stout and Burns, who acquired the property and opened the mine about a year ago. During the summer operations were suspended, but were resumed during the fall and early winter. The Messrs.

Hotchkiss purchased the mine and took possession October 15 and have since been operating the mine and at the same time making a number of improvements.

At the present time the capacity of the mine is in the neighborhood of 100 tons per day, but it is fully equipped with electric hoists, coal cutters and other machinery so that if necessity arises, the output of the mine can be more than doubled.

The siding for the mine is on the east side of Big Goose and the coal is brought across the river to the tipple on a bridge. On this side of the creek are located the buildings which are being erected to house the employees. During the winter about 20 men will be employed.

Hotchkiss Brothers, the new owners, are practical mining men who know the business not only from the ground up, but from the "ground down." Their father, a Scotch miner, early took the boys into the mines and they have followed the business since boyhood. There are four of the boys and all are miners. Thomas and Richard are the operators at the new mine, Robert is state mine inspector—"

5/9/20—"NEW COAL COMPANY IS SURGING TO THE FRONT." "Recently Incorporated With a Capital Stock of $500,000—Will Soon Have a Capacity of 500 Tons Daily."

One of the recent coal companies to come into existence in Sheridan, and which has attracted considerable attention is the Hotchkiss Coal Company, which has recently been incorporated with a capital of $500,000, and which has been meeting with no little success in the local field and from outside points. While its tonnage is small at present, plans have been formulated and new equipment ordered to put it on a 500-ton daily output before the end of sixty days. It is a closed company all stock having been taken.

R. A. Keenan is president of the new company, with R. F. Hotchkiss, vice president and

The Hotchkiss Coal Mine—Showing entrance into hill across Big Goose Creek. Tipple is behind camera.

manager; R. E. McNally, secretary-treasurer, which three together with R. B. Minty form the directorate. The company has 486 acres of coal land, and the mine now being operated is on Goose Creek between Dietz No. 8 and Acme, working on a 16 foot vein, of which 12 feet is being taken, and which is supposed to be the No. 2 vein now being worked by the Sheridan Coal Company.

Blue prints have been received for the new tipple and the equipment has been ordered, all of which should be installed before the first of July and the company mining 500 tons daily. This machinery is of the most modern type for mining, and the mine will be fully equipped electrically both inside and out. Plans have also been formulated for the opening of the No. 3 vein about 70 feet below, which will be made through a new opening and brought to the same track. At present the output is 100 tons daily, insufficient to meet the demand which is being made.

It is the intentions of the Hotchkiss Coal Company as soon as the present workings are completed, to open another mine on its property adjoining the Monarch and Carney properties, and about half a mile west of Alger. This coal is on the Carney vein which is said to be the best in the district.

The president, Dick Keenan, is too well known to our readers to need any introduction. For many years he has been identified with the Sheridan Brewing Co., which was put out of business when prohibition became effective, but Dick is not the kind to be kept idle, and immediately set about for new exploits, which are to the credit of Sheridan, where he is the owner of considerable property, which includes the Keenan apartments, the finest apartment house in the state.

R. F. Hotchkiss, the vice-president and manager is a man well-known in the coal fields of Wyoming, and for over 12 years he was connected with the Kooi Coal Co., as superintendent, and as chief engineer and superintendent opened and developed those mines, every bit of which has redounded to his credit as a coal mining man.

The company is planning output for the coming year aside from that needed to fill the local demand, is contracted for, which includes one contract from the American Potash Company of Antiock, Neb., for 30,000 tons of coal passing thru a two and a half inch screen. This alone takes care of a class of coal which had been giving the company some worry, and since that was closed it has been necessary to refuse a contract with a Spokane firm for 10,000 tons more.

The prospects for the new company are the brightest and with plenty of capital it is planning on going right ahead and develop its properties as rapidly as possible. Today coal is selling in Sheridan for less than it was before the strike of the miners last fall, and is the only town probably in the coal districts of the country of which the same may be said."

12/13/21—"DICK KEENAN WILL BE AN ALIAS SANTA CLAUS TO FAMILIES WHO SUFFER FOR LACK OF COAL." "The spirit of Christmas is in the air.

Last evening R. A. (Dick) Keenan, president of the Hotchkiss Coal company advised the Post that this company had a carload of coal to give away to the needy in Sheridan, and that its distribution to the extent of thirty tons would be delivered free to the homes which may be designated to receive it. The Salvation Army will be called upon to designate the homes where it should be delivered, and the Post will be glad to have suggestions come from any of its readers where they know of meritorious cases.

The generosity of the Hotchkiss Coal company is going to be fully appreciated and as a result there are going to be a number of homes in Sheridan made more comfortable, and Mr. Keenan further advises the Post that this delivery will be made to those homes in plenty of time to properly heat the home for Christmas day, and also take care of the fire which will cook the Christmas dinner.

The Alias Santa Claus club is growing fast.

A line-up is being made of homes where a Santa Claus will be welcome, and as these homes are listed signers of the coupons will be advised of the homes.

One modest little lady, well known in Sheridan, who lives outside the city, and cannot be here on Christmas Day, mailed a check for $5 which she wanted to be expended in the manner possible to give the most pleasure to some child or children.

One Sheridan lady has asked that she be allowed to be Santa Claus for six girls on Christmas Day, indicating that they may be given some special entertainment.

The list is growing nicely and the names of the Alias Santa Claus will be published prior to Christmas Day, although there will be no publication of the names on whom Santa Claus calls."

4/28/22—"FIRST CASE UNDER THE NEW STATUTE"—"Hotchkiss Coal Company Institutes Proceedings to Force Right of Way From Mine to Railroad."

"Suit was instituted in the district court yesterday by which the Hotchkiss Coal company, seeks to secure a right-of-way from the Peabody Coal Company for a road over its property. The right of eminent domain in the past over private property for local uses has pertained more to ditches, canals, electric transmission lines, railroads, etc., but the last session of the legislature modified this so as to allow owners of coal mines to condemn a right-of-way between a mine and the railroad.

At the present time the Hotchkiss Coal company is preparing to build an extension track between the Burlington right-of-way and a new entry which is being opened for the purpose of mining government coal, under a lease which was granted this company under date of April 3, last.

This right-of-way will extend over the other property about 300 feet effecting about two acres of ground.

The Hotchkiss mine is located midway between the Dietz and Acme lines of the Peabody Company, and has been in operation for several years past. R. A. Keenan is president of the Hotchkiss company. Suit is brought at this time to determine the validity of the law, so that no estoppage of work may occur, by injunction proceedings, after it is once started."

3/12/23—"50-FOOT COAL VEIN OPENED IN HOTCHKISS MINE AND BIG DEVELOPMENT WORK PLANNED"—"Hot Kiss No. 2 Mine Is Opened For Development of New Deposit of High Grade Coal Here."

"Opening of a new fifty-foot vein in the Hotchkiss mine near Dietz was announced today by R. A. Keenan, president of the Hotchkiss Coal company. This coal, which will be placed on the market within a few days, has been tested and found to be of a very high grade.

A new tipple has been constructed and a steel and concrete bridge erected to span Big Goose and connect the new mine with transportation facilities.

One hundred men will be employed in the mine when it is developed on a large scale next fall by R. F. Hotchkiss, mine manager. Active development of the mine on a smaller scale is to begin at once, however, and will be continued without interruption.

The new mine is to be known as Hotchkiss No. 2.

The fifty foot vein of coal is an entirely new discovery, it is said. It is of tremendous depth and contains possibilities for great development for many years to come."

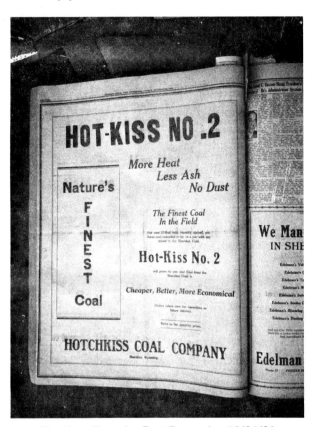

Sheridan, Wyoming Post Enterprise, 10/26/23.

11/17/24—"J. H. M'NAMEE TAKES POSITION WITH HOTCHKISS"—"Will Be New Sales Manager of Company, R. A. Keenan Announces."

"J. H. McNamee, for four years in charge of the traffic department of the Peabody Coal Company here, has been named general sales manager for the Hotchkiss Coal Company here, according to an announcement Monday morning by R. A. Keenan, president of the company.

Mr. McNamee, who is considered one of the best posted men in the state on the coal industry, will begin work immediately. The new Hotchkiss sales manager returned last week from Chicago, where he spent three weeks in the main office of the Peabody Coal company when the company cancelled operations in this district.

'I was offered a position in the Chicago office, and intended to stay there when I went back, but four years spent in Sheridan had given me a love for the west that couldn't be satisfied with the east, and I decided to come back,' McNamee said Monday.

Willard S. Doane, county clerk, is the new Hotchkiss Coal company auditor, succeeding the late J. P. Fleming."

12/2/24—"Auto Crash Victim Will Be Buried On Wednesday Morning"—

"Funeral services for Mrs. Paul Klus, who was drowned in the Big Goose Creek slough Saturday night as the result of an automobile accident on the Sheridan-Mine road, will be conducted at 10 o'clock Wednesday morning at the Catholic Church at Dietz, Father Peter Szymanski officiating—"

12/5/15—"HOTCHKISS COAL COMPANY MAKES WORLD'S RECORD—Miners' Output Tops All Figures, Is Claim Here."

"A world's record in coal production has been made by the Hotchkiss Coal Company of Sheridan during the three months from Sept. 1, to Dec. 1, 1925, it was announced Tuesday.

The record, which sets a new efficiency mark for coal mines, is verified by Martin Cahill, president of the United Mine Workers of District No. 2, it was said. The record follows:

An average total of 19.5 tons was taken out of the mine each day for every man working within the mine.

An average total of 10.4 tons was taken out of the mine each day for every man employed at the mine—whether working inside or outside.

An average total of 10.1 tons was taken out of the mine each day for every person connected with the coal company, from R. A. Keenan, president, down."

12/6/31—"Hotchkiss Miner Is Badly Injured"— Albert Kumor, 26, was recovering, etc. Kumor was caught between a moving car of coal and the wall of the mine—is one of the first to occur at that mine in some time.

1/24/34—"Hotchkiss Miner Badly Injured By Falling Coal—Frank Benegalia, 55 years old miner was in critical condition Wednesday"—as result of accident, suffering from broken pelvis, internal injuries and severe bruises. Benegalia's home is in Sheridan north of the elevator on North Main Street.

1/27/37—"State Senator Keenan Succumbs—

Well Known Local Citizen Claimed at 72—Flu Complications Fatal In Cheyenne Hospital.

—"located in Rock Springs in 1883 where he engaged in the coal mining business and liquor business. Was mayor of Kemmerer in 1898 and moved to Sheridan area in 1905 where he later became president of the Hotchkiss Coal Company for many years which was sold to the Sheridan Wyoming Coal Company. He was president of the Hotchkiss Coal Company at the time of this death.

The Hotchkiss Coal Mine continued to operate until about 1939" (shortly before then, I recall that my brother, Andrew who had assisted my father in the operation of the Star Coal Mine for many years, and a good friend of "Dick" Hotchkiss, worked for the Hotchkiss Coal Company for a short time).

Hotchkiss Coal Co. (Shoestring Mine) as it looks today.

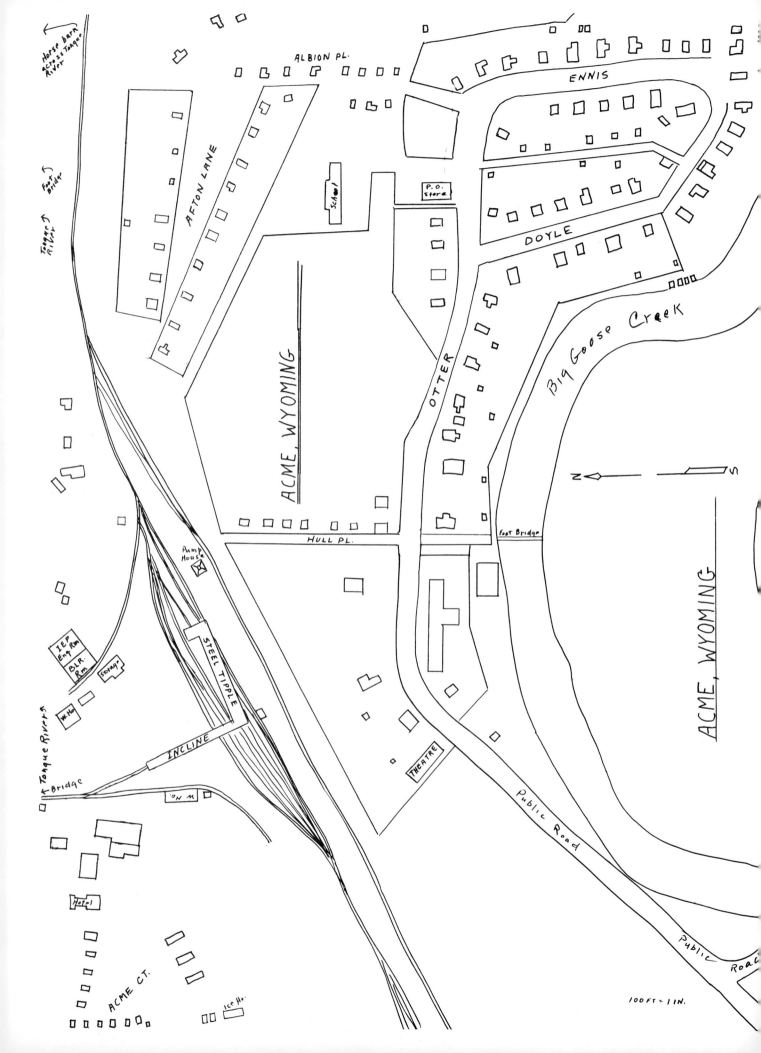

Chapter 9

Acme 1911-1940

The first reference in the news media regarding the Acme coal, appeared in an ad in one of the Sheridan papers, reading as follows: "Teddy has given up his trip to Africa—going to buy Acme coal. Foster, Phone 52."

The author has not talked with anyone lately who might have worked at this mine, and any recollections of that operation have certainly been dimmed by time. It is known that A. K. Craig opened up the mine in about 1909; however, the operation was not very large and employed only a few men. There was no mining camp as such, but contained only a few small miners' shacks. This mine, later referred to as "Old Acme" was located about a mile north and west of the Monarch mining camp at a point later erased by the gradings of the present U. S. Highway I-90.

Two years later, Mr. Craig acquired new land and established a mine in a new location as revealed in a news release of a Sheridan paper as follows:

9/29/11—"TIPPLE ALMOST COMPLETED." "Archie Craig of the Acme Coal Company states that the tipple at the company's new mine on Tongue River will be completed early next month, when the principal scene of operations will be transferred from the old to the new mine. Close to a hundred and fifty men are now employed at the new. With the completion of the new tipple the number at the new mine will be doubled and the force at the original workings reduced accordingly."

7/12/12—"Opening of the Acme Ball Park Was a Big Success." Initial opening of a new, handsome and commodious grandstand and baseball park of the new "Acme Alerts." Game between Sheridan Elks and Acme. Stand entirely filled. The game resulted in a 5 to 4 victory for the Elks.

9/5/12—"NEW ACME CAMP NEWEST COAL MINE." "Craig and Darnall Have Built Up Splendid Business in Short Time—Camp Is Ideally Located and Is Modern—Company Making Improvements." "By dint of much courage, perserverance and "stick-to-it-iveness," A. K. Craig and Ora Darnall have founded a mining camp in Sheridan county, flourishing and modern in every respect and rapidly coming to the front. This camp is at New Acme, the scene of the recent Labor Day festivities and visited on that occasion by thousands of people, who immediately became the guests of the operators and miners union No. 23" (old Acme was located just beyond Monarch camp but north of the C. B. & Q.)

Although Messrs. Craig and Darnall have been mining coal in Sheridan county for several years their output at old Acme was only mediocre until they opened up the New Acme mine, when they began to forge to the front. Their employes are loyal and are as anxious to see the camp leadinng the procession as the operators themselves.

The New Acme coal is mined from a 22 foot 6 inch vein of a very high grade character. The tunnel is now in 2,000 feet and has been placed to that distance without a single fatality or accident of a serious nature. One hundred and seventy-five miners are employed in the mine and during the summer season have been securing from three to four days work every week, netting them from $80 to $100 each. The capacity of the mine at the present time is 1,200 tons daily. Modern machinery has been installed and is now in perfect working condition. A steel and concrete tipple and screening plant has a capacity of 2,000 tons in eight hours of every working day and the operators hope to see the plant turning out its capacity before many more months. Coal from this colliery is shipped to distant as well as local points and the demand for Acme coal is becoming more pressing as its character is known.

Camp Conditions

The operators have been improving the camp

conditions for their employees with all the available profits from the coal. They believe that a miner is entitled to ideal conditions for his environments in home and out of doors and to this end they have been working. All the houses for employes have been built in a warm and substantial manner and are supplied with heat, water and light. The company will build a one-story brick public bathhouse designed especially for the benefits of the coal miners. It will have a capacity of 75 men an hour, and will be supplied both with bath tubs and shower baths. The central heating plant will be located here. To the west of the office building excavation will be started in a few days for a two-story brick amusement hall, 32 by 100 feet in dimensions. A billiard and pool hall, ice cream parlor, barber shop and reading room will be located in compartments on the first floor and the second floor will be used for dancing and lodge purposes with a small stage occupying one end of the hall.

The improvements already constructed on the grounds consist of a modern brick school building, a general store, meat market and fifty frame dwellings for employes. A fifty room frame hotel building, two stories in height has

been completed by the operators and were thrown open to the public Sunday for the first time. The park surrounded almost entirely by Big Goose Creek, affords a natural site for recreation purposes and the operators quick to perceive this advantage have erected permanent improvements there in the nature of a dancing pavilion and speakers and band stands. The Japanese laborers have a small settlement of their own and are more than content with their quarters." (One portion of the camp at the extreme upper end on the Tongue River side was nicknamed "Japtown" and was so called long after all the Japanese had left the area). (Another section was called "Macaroni Flats" due to the concentration of Italians in that area).

Ideal Location

The camp has an ideal location, with running water within a stone's throw from all the houses. The dirt and filth which ordinarily is an encumbrance and an eyesore to a mining camp is a minus quantity at New Acme and in its place gardens and lawns have been started.

Craig and Darnall commenced operations at New Acme on July 1, 1911 and already have one of the most thriving coal mining camps in

"Archie" A. K. Craig, founder of Acme, Wyoming camp and coal company.

Sheridan county. In addition to this camp they are still operating the old Acme camp, five miles distant, with a daily output of 1,000 tons. They started business there several years ago with a combined capital of $15,000 and at the outset were forced to spend $12,000 for their railroad to the mine. They have seen many ups and downs since then but by perseverance and work and a close application to business have gradually been working their way to the top.

The Sheridan County Electric Company has its big plant located on the New Acme grounds, deriving its water supply from Tongue River into which the Goose Creek flows only a few hundred yards away. From this location power is not only supplied to Sheridan and the Sheridan Railway Company but all the adjacent mining camps as well, with the one exception of Carneyville. Many visitors accepted the invitation of Manager Judson Bibb for inspecting this plant on Labor Day. The plant with its wonderful equipment and modern machinery, was a revelation to all and for the first time the people knew that Sheridan County can well boast of having one of the largest electrical plants in the entire northwest."

9/7/12—There appeared an ad in the local paper announcing a "Grand Masque Ball Given by the Acme Amusement Co. Thursday evening, Sept. 12th at The Acme Park Pavilion. Admission, $1.00."

1/10/13—"Dinners and Parties."—"New Acme— One of the most enjoyable social functions of the State Teachers' association meeting was the visit to New Acme. At 10:30 Friday morning the one hundred and fifty teachers left Sheridan in the large interurban cars. At New Acme they were cordially welcomed and piloted to the places of interest by Mr. Craig. After visiting the hotel, bath house, and the power plant, the party was taken into the mines by means of the coal cars, which had been thoughtfully cleaned and lined for the protection of holiday suits. After an interesting tour through the mine the party was collected in one of the large corridors. Then, when all were present, a canvas curtain was drawn aside, the orchestra began to play and the guests saw before them a long banquet hall, beautifully lighted, and two long tables loaded with good things to eat.

After an address by Dr. Long all did justice to the feast before them. Dr. C. A. Duniway, president of the state university, thanked the management of the mines in behalf of the teachers and led in three cheers for Mr. Craig, three for New Acme, and three for the miners.

Then, to add one more surprise, the teachers were treated with a pleasing program consisting of Scotch songs and an original "stunt." After this they regretfully turned their backs upon the scene of their good time and returned to Sheridan."

Acme, Wyoming looking west from top of hill, "Circle" in foreground, "Japtown" in upper distance, "Macaroni Flat" to right, not in picture.

Acme, Wyoming campsite almost from same spot as it looks today.

11/4/13—"TO INSTALL BOXCAR LOADER."
"Will Be Used at Acme Mine Tipple Shortly."

"The Acme Coal Company has purchased and will install immediately a new electric box-car loader at its mine tipple at New Acme. The loader will be run with a 112-horsepower motor, current being supplied from the Sheridan County Electric company's plant nearby. It is expected the loader will be in operation within three weeks.

The Acme Company has such a large force of men at work in its mines that it has been hard pressed to find quarters for them all. The dancing pavilion in the park has been pressed into service, divided into rooms, steam heated, and is

Acme, Wyoming "Japtown" in foreground near Tongue River. Union Hall, upper right building, large building in distance, Acme Hotel.

8/29/13—"Teachers Assigned for new School Year.—Helen Krajicek, Carolyn Thompson, Primary. Isabelle Alcorn, Dietz. 2 schools—attendance 31 and 21."

being used as a rooming house. It has been nicely furnished and affords an ideal home for the men."

11/4/13—"Samuel Dunn dies as a result of being

crushed in some way by mine cars at Acme."

11/11/13—"POST REPRESENTATIVES VISIT THE SHERIDAN COUNTY MINES." "ACME MINES FURNISH MUCH FOOD FOR THOUGHT—VISITED SATURDAY—Trip to the Heart of Sheridan County's Great Coal Producing District—Observations of the Trip."

"Coal from the Sheridan fields covers a territory reaching from the Cascades on the west to the Mississippi on the east and from Canada on the north to Colorado on the south. Furthermore, Sheridan coal comes into active competition with and holds its own against every coal mined in North America except in Nova Scotia, Alabama and Mexico.

marketing game. He feels that while much was gained by the recent decision of the interstate commerce commission, much remains to be done in securing rates for Sheridan coal. There is a vast market in North Dakota and north-eastern South Dakota which is not open to Sheridan coal. The supply there is brought from Pennsylvania and West Virginia by way of the Great Lakes, is handled several times and is naturally very high priced. Sheridan mines could easily compete if they would reach that market.

"An organized selling propaganda would increase the demand for Sheridan coal to 2,000,000 tons annually within five years," is another statement of Mr. Darnell's. The present output, limited by the amount that can be sold,

Acme tipple.

Those are but two of the interesting facts learned by the Post representative upon their second visit to a Sheridan county coal camp. The camp visited this time was New Acme, seven miles from Sheridan, and in the heart of the coal producing district. The truth of both statements was established by General Manager Ora Darnell, of the Acme Coal company, who opened his books for examination and traced the route of cars of coal from his mine to the ultimate consumer.

Mr. Darnell is a master of freight rate and transportation questions as well as of the coal

is something over 1,000,000 tons.

The New Acme

New Acme is, as its name implies, a new coal camp. Two years ago last July a crop of alfalfa was harvested and marketed from the land now occupied by the camp, the mine tipple and switching tracks. Everything at New Acme has been constructed since that time.

The second half of the camp's name is no more a misnomer than the first. The top, or highest point is Webster's definition of "Acme," and at New Acme the object of the company has

Acme tipple and bridge across Tongue River leading to mine entrance.

Mine office, Acme, Wyoming.

Acme Power Plant and bridge across Tongue River. MDU electric generating plant.

Acme boarding house.

been to reach the highest point in coal mining perfection and in living conditions for men. All machinery is of the latest and most improved make; buildings are neat and substantial grounds well kept and handsomely laid out.

Three hundred men are now on the payrolls of the Acme Coal Company, the large majority of them working at the New Acme mine. A few are employed at the Old Acme mine, the former scene of operations, and a relatively small amount of coal is being produced there, but headquarters and town are near the new mine.

The 300 men will draw in wages this month something in excess of $30,000 and are taking from the two mines between 2,000 and 2,400 tons of coal daily. Eighteen hundred to 2,000 tons of this output is from the new mine, the balance from the old. This coal is sorted and

loaded as fast as brought from the mine and is on the road to consumers within twelve hours from the time it reaches the surface.

Twenty-two Feet of Coal

Like the Monarch mine, the New Acme is the Monarch vein of coal and at this point the vein is of an average thickness of twenty-two feet of marketable coal. It is being mined in much the same way as at Monarch, being drawn from the mine by motors and transported to the tipple by the same means. The New Acme has the advantage of less distance between mine and tipple and of lower grades within the mine, the vein dipping less sharply there.

There are three main tunnels of the mine and from them are opened no less than 200 working chambers or rooms from which the coal

Scenes at Acme, Wyoming.

Acme swinging bridge leading to interurban station and "island."

Acme script. Script issued to miner run short before payday and redeemable at Company store. For each $1.10 charge against pay, $1.00 in script issued.

is taken. The main tunnels are electrically lighted and have tracks for the motors and cars with 65-pound rails throughout. The branch lines into the working chambers are temporary and lighter steel is used. There is a complete system of telephones in the mine with a phone at every point from which coal is being taken.

The coal is mined by means of "short-wall" machines, which undercut the coal at the bottom of the drift, penetrating about four or five feet at each cutting. Thus freed at the bottom, the coal is shot down with powder and loaded into the cars by hand. The cars are then dragged to the main line by horses and taken out by the motors. From eighteen to thirty cars, each carrying between two and three tons of coal comprise a "trip" or load for the motor. Four wall machines are used and are transported from chamber to chamber, keeping the miners supplied with loose coal at all times.

Underground Banquet Room

Unusual features of the New Acme mine are the underground stables for the horses and the underground banquet room. In the stable are kept all the horses employed in the mine, eighteen or twenty fine animals. Their feed is brought down day by day and the refuse taken out over the electric line. The horses are kept underground to avoid subjecting them to sudden changes of temperature and resulting colds and pneumonia, common causes of death among the animals. The banquet room in the mine has become famous throughout the state, having been the scene of some magnificent feasts, one of them during the state teachers' convention a year ago when the guests of Sheridan were entertained by music and good food far beneath the surface of the earth.

Drawn from the mine by the motors, the loaded coal cars are taken within a short distance of the tipple and released. Gravity takes the cars one by one onto the scales, where each is weighed. An endless cable then seizes the cars and takes them to the top of the tipple, where the coal is dumped into an immense hopper and the sorting begins.

This tipple is the latest word in structures of its kind. All the improvements so far devised are included and it has a capacity sufficient for all possible development of the mine. Thirty-four hundred tons of coal can pass over this tipple in eight hours and it is run to capacity.

Method of Screening

The first coal taken off is fancy lump. This coal, when it enters the car has been twice screened and is as clean as it can be made. It is here that the large electric box-car loader is being installed which will do away with much hand labor and greatly increase the capacity of the tipple. The coal which drops through the two screens over which the lump passes falls upon a conveyor which takes it to the re-screening tower, a structure of steel and concrete 92 feet in height. Here the coal enters a steel hopper twenty-four feet long and six feet in diameter, where it is again sorted.

The first coal to come out here is the slack. This falls into one of four bins, each of 100 tons capacity, from which cars are loaded. The next larger grade of coal is the pea; then the nut and lastly the egg. There is a separate bin for each grade. While the coal is handled with very little breakage, one screening is not considered sufficient even here. As the coal runs from the bins to the car at loading time, it again passes over a screen and the particles smaller than they should be for the particular grade fall out, going into a screw conveyor and elevator which carries them back to the rotary screen.

The cars for coal are handled on a switch which passes under the tipple and screening tower. The switching facilities are very complete. Above the tipple is room for eighty empties, low, room for eighty-five loads. Scales which are accepted by the road and by retailers, are installed above and below the tipples for weighing empties and loaded cars.

Automatic Feeding

The coal used by the Sheridan County Electric Company at its power plant is taken directly from the tipple here, transported to the plant by a miniature electric line and automatically fed to the furnaces. It generates all the power and light current used in Sheridan, the coal camps, the mines themselves and on the Sheridan Railway Company's lines. The plant is a magnificent one, requiring a separate article to describe.

Coal from the Monarch vein at New Acme is declared the nearest approach to natural gas mined in North America. By actual test under normal conditions the coal contains less than three per cent of ash. This was demonstrated by the city of Alliance when making tests before contracting its supply for this winter. The Acme company has hundreds of voluntary letters testifying to the selling and burning qualities of Acme coal.

While the actual operations of coal mining at New Acme are very interesting, they are less so than the town itself and the plans of its founders for making it a model coal camp. It has been the object from the first to provide the best possible working and living conditions for the men. That ideal has in a large part been realized already.

How Miners Are Housed

The permanent men of the camp and the men with families are housed in neat little cottages owned by the company. The extra men are provided for at an up-to-date boarding and rooming house and in temporary quarters made by converting the dancing pavilion into sleeping rooms. The men are given as much privacy as possible, their quarters are kept neat and clean, their food is exceptionally good and wholesome. Entering the rooming house, one would suppose himself in a first-class hotel. When he sat down to table he would know his supposition correct.

The plan of the town is unique. A civic center is the axis about which New Acme is being built. This is a large plaza surrounded by the hotel, the company offices, and other public buildings. Other structures to be built here are physician's quarters, a store building and an amusement and union hall.

The residence part will follow the same plan. Instead of straight streets and square corners, the town will be one of curves. The houses will be built around circles enclosing parks where grass and shrubs will abound. This plan is being worked out and already flower beds and trees surround the buildings. A small hot-house to provide plants is being erected now.

Crowning Features

The crowning feature of the camp is the public bath house erected by the company. Here are found scores of shower baths with hot and cold water accessible at all times. There are lockers for the men's clothing, each under lock and key, a barber shop and all conveniences. This building is heated by the central heating plant which will ultimately provide warmth for all the principal buildings of the town.

Amusement places have not been neglected. The public hall which will be built next year will contain billiard and pool tables, reading rooms, lodge hall and dancing floor. On the outside are tennis courts, croquet grounds and one of the best baseball diamonds in northern Wyoming. The school house, a neat brick building presided over by two teachers has ample playgrounds on all sides.

A gratifying feature of all this work for the comfort of the miners, a feature which contains the element of stupendous hope for the future, is the fact that the men appreciate what is being done and reciprocate to the best of their ability. The camp never lacks for men of the best class; the quarters and cottages are kept neat and clean; there is no refuse or trash in sight anywhere; it is in reality a model town. The men are contented and orderly. There is little or no drunkedness; there has never been a case of contagious disease in New Acme.

A number of Japanese are employed permanently at the mine as topmen and loaders. They have their own boarding house and keep pretty much to themselves. They have been found among the best and most efficient workmen obtainable.

A visit to New Acme is more than worthwhile, especially for Sheridan people. Mr. Darnell and Mr. Craig, owners of the mine, are more than hospitable and always glad to see visitors. It is their rule to treat all who come with the utmost courtesy and to spare no trouble nor expense in showing them all that is to be seen. In summer time, the New Acme park is a favorite resort. But a visit at this time of year is hardly less attractive, surely not less instructive.

The Acme Coal company owns 1,500 acres of land underlaid with two veins of coal. It is estimated that, taking out 5,000 tons per day, the coal will be exhausted in not less than 125 years. So you have plenty of time to visit the mine and see for yourself."

Display ad 5/12/14—"BENEFIT DANCE. NEW ACME PAVILION, FRIDAY, MAY 15TH" for the benefit of the striking miners in the Colorado district. Monarch 4-piece orchestra will furnish music. The last car will leave Acme for Monarch and Sheridan at 1 a.m."

7/12/14—"Acme"—"A. Ham was in Acme this week representing Armour's company. A social dance was given at Acme pavilion Wednesday evening by the B.P.O.E. R. E. Reckard was an Acme visitor this week representing Lindsay-Walker Food Co. Mrs. Fred White made a rushing trip to Sheridan Tuesday evening. Miss Helen Worth was a Dietz visitor Monday.

Mrs. H. Snively was shopping in Sheridan Wednesday.

Mrs. P. Putney was visiting in Sheridan a few days last week.

Mrs. W. Lobby was calling on Mrs. J. Renie Wednesday.

Mrs. J. Sampson left Monday to spend the week on the Landin ranch.

Erick Becker and orchestra spent Sunday picnicking on the Eaton ranch, and also furnished music for the occasion.

We have a new man in the band, his name being Becker.

Miss Helen Worth spent the week-end with her sister in Sheridan.

Mr. and Mrs. Worth went to Sheridan Saturday to attend the Chautauqua in the evening.

Mrs. J. J. Renie and daughter, Mrs. Cake, of Dietz, spent Thursday evening with Mr. and Mrs. J. A. Renie, of Acme.

Mrs. James was in Acme from the ranch visiting her daughter, Mrs. McLeod. Her little granddaughter accompanied her home.

Mr. and Mrs. H. Snively and family spent Sunday fishing on the ranch.

P. Putney returned home from Monatana Sunday where he had been visiting his sick sister. He left her some better.

Miss Cathrine Craig and Miss Samison entertained their high school friends Friday night with a dance and lunch at Acme.

A party headed by A. K. Craig left Saturday for an extended fishing trip in the mountains.

Mr. and Mrs. Snively motored to town Thursday evening and attended the show.

Mr. McLeod and Mr. Lewis were in Sheridan Friday on business.

Mrs. Eggart was in Acme Saturday with a load of produce and vegetables.

There will be a special train running from all the mines for the benefit of the miners on circus day, August 10th.

A new ball player arrived in Acme Saturday from New Haven, Conn.

The ball game Sunday between the Elks and Acme was a loss to Acme, the score being 7 to 5. Acme will catch up later. A large crowd attended the game from the neighboring camps and Sheridan."

Others mentioned in the Acme column as visiting in Sheridan, etc., included: Mrs. White, Mrs. C. Lewis, Mr. and Mrs. Benedick, Mrs. Terry, Mr. and Mrs. Clark McIntyre, J. J. Renie, Mr. and Mrs. E. Mattox and Mrs. J. McCain.

9/18/14—"Mike Nickovitch, the miner who was killed by a fall of coal Saturday afternoon, was buried Monday in Mount Hope cemetery."

4/23/18—"IMPROVEMENTS AT THE MINES." "ACME PROSPECTING IN AN UPPER VEIN." "Mine Owners Preparing to Meet Heavy Demand for Coal That Is Sure to Come."

"—At Acme the plans of the summer contemplate the opening of an upper vein of coal known as No. 3. This is 80 feet above No. 4 the vein that is now being worked and is a deposit fifteen feet thick. A contract for the prospect holes have already been let. The contractors are the Byerly Drilling company of Sheridan who have all their preparations completed and announce their intention of beginning work at the earliest moment the weather will permit.

It is not generally known perhaps that the Acme company already have what is really two complete mines. These mines are worked separately and are not connected in any way. As a matter of fact there is no place between the two workings where there is not a solid pillar of coal two hundred feet thick. To reach one mine from the other it is necessary to go outside. Should any unforeseen accident occur that would make it impossible to work one of the mines operations could go forward in the other.

What is known as the old mine, the one opened in 1911, has now a development that will permit 3,000 tons of coal to be mined every eight hours. The new mine, which is practically a twin of the old, has reached a stage of development that will permit the production of from

1,000 to 1,200 tons per day.

It is the intention of the owners to push the development work in the new mine until its production equals that of the old, which will mean that the company will have a capacity of 6,000 tons of coal every eight hours. Both these mines work vein No. 4, sometimes known as the Monarch vein, and even at the maximum rate of production mentioned, it is estimated that there is enough coal to last 100 years. The opening of the new mine in vein No. 3 will obviously add largely to the capacity of the mine.

At the Model mine a new steel tipple of latest construction has already been purchased and will be installed during the summer, and at other mines extensive improvements are being made or contemplated."

6/7/18—"ANOTHER VICTIM OF TONGUE RIVER. LITTLE THREE YEAR OLD BOY DROWNED. Body Has Not Been Recovered—Searching the River for Many Miles." A resume of this article reveals that little 3-year-old Stanley Patz, altho the son of Mr. and Mrs. Mike Patz, was making his home with Stanley Patz. The incident occurred at a point between Carneyville and Monarch two weeks previously.

Several children have been victims of drownings in this river. On May 16, 1917, Balvina Szewczyk, fell in the river at Acme, and it was not until nearly two months later, July 5, that her decomposed body was found on the John Logan ranch over a hundred miles below the place where she had fallen in.

2/25/19—"Mrs. Crane of Acme Gives Informal Tea.—Those who enjoyed the afternoon were: Mesdames H. Burns, J. E. Heaton, H. A. Churchill, James Brown, D. W. Jones, J. W. Wherry, E. R. Dinwiddie, Ethel MacFarlane and Whipple."

9/2/19—"LABOR DAY FITTINGLY CELEBRATED AT ACME"—"New Standard is Set by Which Future Celebrations Will be Judged"—"ELKS AND MONARCH WINNING TEAMS"—"Splendid Program of Athletic Sports—W. J. James, Orator of the Day Delivers a Splendid Address."

At this celebration, it was estimated that there were approximately 10,000 in attendance. Crowds jammed around the baseball park; grandstand and bleachers were a "mass of humanity"; also jammed were the dance hall, concessions and picnic areas. The first baseball game of a double-header, pitted Monarch Reds against the

Kooi which the former won, 9 to 4. The battery for Monarch was McLane and Berry; and for Kooi, Malyjurek and McCoy. (Upon reading the name McCoy, I this minute called Tom McCoy on the phone and was informed that he was the same McCoy who was the catcher on the Kooi team. Tom told of Jake Malyjurek's fast ball resulting in Tom's catching hand to be "black and blue to the elbow." (Tom McCoy is the father of Mrs. Glade (Eleanor) Kilpatrick and the grandfather of the author's son-in-law, Gerald G. Kilpatrick).

In the races which were conducted, winners were as follows:

Boy's race for boys under 6 years; Willie Cateral, first; Ira Whitten, second.

Girls under 12: Leona Seftick, first; Anna Mentock, second.

Boys under 14: Amil Mizera, first; Carey Allen, second.

Girls under 14: Mary Kuzara, first; Caroline Luke, second.

Boys under 16: Ross Allen, first; Carey Allen, second.

Girls under 16: Caroline Luke, first; Mary Kuzara, second.

Married Men: C. F. Thompson, first; F. L. Bolton, second.

Married ladies: Mrs. C. Spanogle, first; Mrs. Fred O'Conner, second.

Fat men: L. N. Hill, first; R. P. Fitch, second.

Fat ladies: Mrs. Katherine Herget, first; Mrs. Chris Rodovich, second.

Men: F. Allen, first; J. B. Bennett, second.

Free for all Ladies: Mary Kuzara, first; Caroline Luke, second.

Free for all men: Wilbur Wright, first; Charles Bateman, second.

Wheelborrow: F. Allen, first; J. B. Bennett, second.

Ladies three-legged: Mrs. C. Spanogle and Mrs. Fred O'Conner.

Fat men's three-legged: Joe Goodman and Philip Small, first; G. R. Murdock and Stanley Nemetz, second.

The Salvation Army, it was reported, collected several hundred dollars as a result of their solicitations from the crowd.

"The jam at the street cars when the rain began was so great that barely half could get on the 5 o'clock car and the rest waited until a later car arrived. Many in order to get a seat, took a car at Acme and rode to Monarch and back."

3/25/20—"Miner May Die of Injuries Sustained From Runaway Car. Joe Robin, age 40, a miner in the Acme mine was struck by a runaway car. Later, died of injuries."

2/24/21—Oscar Oshmer of Acme died as result of accident—went into room as shot was being fired.

6/2/21—"Mines Laborer Is Killed In Car Accident. Japanese at Acme Fatally Injured When Crushed Between Coal Cars." "T. Takahashie, deceased—no family survives."

1/24/24—"Miner, 19, Dies After Accident in Acme Shaft. Boy is Crushed Under Car, Expires From Internal Injuries at County Hospital." Fred Clearwater, a driver at Acme mine crushed beneath a "loaded trip car."

4/30/24—"Mine employee Dies As Result of Car Injuries. Arthur Bateman Falls Under Coal Train at Acme; Death Comes From Shock and Loss of Blood."

12/7/24—"ACME SCOUTS HOLD BASEBALL TITLE OF REGION. Handsome trophy awarded at Central Gym by Dr. I. P. Hayes of the Boy Scout Council. Team members were: P—Pete Loss; C—Stanley Shott and Stanley Mentock; 1b—Alec Barbula; 2b—Billy Wandra and Lester Moon; SS—Otto Varner; 3b—Joe Volney; LF—Ernest Cornett; CF—Rudolph Loss; RF—John Baker."

2/25/26—"Story on Acme Mine Appears in Coal Age. The story of the conversion of the Acme mine, a 3,000 ton operation, from a hand-loading operation to one completely mechanized even to its drilling, is told by Harry N. Taylor, of New York City, president of the Sheridan-Wyoming Coal company in a recent edition of the Coal Age, etc—."

12/4/26—"Wm. McLean, Acme Miner Injured By a Fall of Coal Tuesday—is a patient at the Sheridan County Memorial Hospital."

4/29/27—"The Acme Pool Hall Building owned by the Sheridan-Wyoming Coal company burned Wednesday night. The Acme fire department able to save the Acme Theatre—both owned by Andrew Cieslar."

4/29/28—"GROUND BROKEN TO REACH SEAM OF CARNEY COAL. Acme Will Not Become "Ghost City" Like Neighbors."—"The ground has been broken at Acme for a new slope down to what is known as the lower or Carney seams of coal, it was announced Saturday by Edward Bottomley, general superintendent of the Sheridan-Wyoming Coal company."

The new seam is 45 feet below the present vein but will be reached by a 12 per cent grade. "The Carney vein was formerly operated by the Carney Coal company at what is now known as Kleenburn."

7/3/28—"Acme Miner's Spine Fractured by Cave-in of Coal Late Today. Ed Larson, helper on loader hospitalized—partially paralyzed."

7/26/28—"Tony S. Pelesky of Sheridan hospitalized—injured internally while lifting while working as driller in Acme Mine."

9/9/28—"Acme Boy Drowns in Tongue River—Louis Erch Sinks Just Before Reaching Shore of Favorite Swimming Pool at Coal Camp."

12/16/28—"Clyde Williams of Dietz No. 8, employee of Acme Mine of Sheridan-Wyoming Coal Co., is recovering from severe injury received a few days ago while working in the mine. One rib was broken and his head was badly cut when he was caught between a car and the mine wall known as a 'rib'."

2/3/29—"Three men "Smoked" Badly at Acme Fire During Night." "Frank Welch, William Hair and Lee Manly effected by smoke as result of fire in the mine believed caused by spontaneous combustion."

8/27/29—"Acme Building Burns." "Loss in Blaze Estimated About $15,000—Mine Bath House is Destroyed by Flames." Efforts concentrated on saving hotel nearby. Edward Bottomley, General Superintendent, believes fire caused by mice knowing on matches of miner's lamp left not completely extinguished—building to be rebuilt.

4/23/20—Miss Lenora Green will teach in Acme.

6/29/30—"Miner Is Killed In Accident—Frank Olasek Succumbs To Injuries Here."—Elderly Man Caught as Sand Bank Falls"—was at work in blasting, according to Edward Bottomley, Superintendent.

3/16/31—"Injuries Prove Fatal to Miner In Acme Cavein—Death of Albert Woodhead Is First Due to Accident at Sheridan-Wyoming Coal Mines in Past Seven Years.—Charles Trembath also injured with severe cut on head.

6/26/31—"Miner Is Badly Injured at Acme—Stanley Kutcher Rushed to Hospital at Sheridan." Caught between wall of the Acme mine and a car which had jumped the track.

1/26/32—"Miner Is Injured In Acme Accident."—caught between the "ribs" of the Acme mine and a huge electric motor, Clair E. Moon of Dietz, age 25—apparently no fractures.

4/6/32—"Acme Miner Loses Toes in Accident—Joseph Braber, 44, Acme Miner lost two toes and had two others badly crushed when coal cutting maching accidentally dropped on his right foot.

3/9/32—"Cave-In At Acme Mine Hurts Two—Injured Miners Rushed to Hospital After Accident. George Hunter, 29, of Kleenburn and Frank Mathews of Dietz. Both received injuries to their legs while horse was killed outright. Being near coal car probably saved their lives when 65 tons of roof fell.

7/26/35—"Mine Accident Injuries Fatal—A. T. Covington, 62, Dies of Apparently Minor Hurts—Anderson T. Covington, 62 year old miner was crushed between two empty coal cars, died at the Sheridan County Memorial Hospital this morning.

8/25/35—"Paul Podzorski had three bones in his right foot fractured Friday when a horse stepped on the members while he was at work at the Acme mine.

12/18/35—"Mine Gas Fatal to Two Men—Lethal Fumes Overcome Pair—Welch left ill. "White Damp" Is Blamed for Acme Tragedy Underground—inquest to be held. Ricco Coassin, 42, Santo Rossa, 46, and Frank Welch, mine foreman, entered the mine about 5:30 Tuesday evening to wall up a room smouldering from spontaneous combustion and shortly after entering the room Coassin collapsed from presumed carbon monoxide poisoning. As the other two were dragging him out, Rossa also collapsed but Welch succeeded in dragging himself to the surface to report the incident. Dr. Louis C. Booth, mine physician testified Coassin died at the scene while Rossa died on the way to the hospital.

7/1/36—"Miner Injured As Coal Falls in Acme Shaft—Henry Caudron Is Taken to Hospital With Injured Side."

7/28/36—"Mayor A. K. Craig Dies Suddenly— Former Banker Suffers Heart Attack In Cabin— Man Prominent Here For Over 30 Years Claimed at Story—" Identified with the coal industry from the time, when, as a boy of 12, he worked as a breaker boy in the mines in various parts of the country, he continued his associations with the industry until 1920.

"Mr. Craig came to Wyoming in 1902 to become associated with the Sheridan Coal com-

pany, remaining with the concern until 1907 when he resigned to enter the coal business for himself.

He purchased the property now known as Acme, developing the mine into one of the largest in the extensive field just north. When one thinks of a coal mining camp, his thoughts picture row upon row of dingy miners' shacks. But such was not the case with Mr. Craig's camp. His was a camp of neat white houses, green

Coal Bowl Losers.
The Acme six man football team pictured below put up a fighting game before it went down to defeat at the hands of the Monarch club 33 to 12. Sunday afternoon on the Acme gridiron. Pictured below in their mine helmets, left to right, back row, Henry Stanko, Harold Griffith, Gruber, and Zowada. Front row, Wantulock, Dick Merryhew, and Plott.

Acme football team—12-12-38. Story on page 209.

lawns, flowers and shrubery around a series of circular graveled streets. And instead of the usual slack walking paths before the houses, Mr. Craig's camp had miles of wooden sidewalks. So it was that Acme became not only one of the largest coal camps, but one of the most pleasant and beautiful in which to live.

In 1920, Mr. Craig sold his interests to the Sheridan-Wyoming Coal Company, turning his interests to ranching and business activities, becoming president of the Sheridan Trust and Savings Bank which he sold to the Bank of Commerce in 1934."

11/8/37—"Charles Catteral Crushed At Mines—Charles Catteral, 33, employee of the Sheridan-Wyoming Coal Company at Acme, suffered serious injuries when he was crushed between a boading machine and a partly filled coal car in the mine Saturday morning. Catterall suffered a fractured pelvis—."

The Sheridan-Wyoming Coal Company continued to operate the Acme mine operation until 1940 when it closed down the operation, a demise which could be laid to the increasing popularity of natural gas as well as the continued increase in the cost of producing the coal.

This left only the Monarch mine in operation and while many of the workers of the Acme mine were transferred to the Monarch mine, some chose to live at Acme commuting to work. Some preferred living in Sheridan. Those who lost their jobs but wished to remain in the only type of work they knew; namely, coal mining, moved to coal fields in Utah and some to the Gebo, Wyoming coal camp.

The activity, at Acme, of course, now had dwindled. No longer were there the pavilion, the union hall or the theatre. Those who continued to live in the camp retained a certain civic pride in their homes, yards, gardens and in their camp. All this while, many of the houses were being sold and moved to nearby Sheridan while some were moved to neighboring farms and ranches.

James A. Barello, my brother-in-law (sister Helen's husband), it should be mentioned began working in the company store and postoffice after graduating from Sheridan High School in 1929. "Jim had a heart of gold, and in addition to his work in the store, he was in constant demand to perform favors from repairing a leaky faucet to repairing radios and later TV sets." He could never turn down such requests regardless how demanding. It was no wonder that he was frequently called the Mayor of Acme.

After many years, in 1943 when the then current postmaster and store manager, Mr. McIntyre, left the employ of the Tongue River Trading company, a subsidiary of the Sheridan-Wyoming Coal company, Jim took over as manager and postmaster.

Acme, it so happened, was not directly on the C.B. & Q. railroad line, but was located some several hundred yards away. Therefore, it was necessary for the postmaster to hang the outgoing mail on the "mail catcher and to pick up the bags of mail dropped by the passenger train as it went by. Later, the depot at Monarch, the Kleenburn station, was used as the depository for both incoming and outgoing mail pouches and were picked up at that point for the post office at Acme.

In 1953, the Sheridan-Wyoming Coal Company suddenly sold the complete camp of Acme to one of its bookkeepers, Mr. Gothard Bylund "lock, stock and barrel," all except the Montana-Dakota Power plant at that location. During Mr. Bylund's ownership, Jim and his wife, Helen bought the store business and continued to operate it until 1963 when Mr. Bylund sold the camp to a Merton Bond, following which shortly after, Jim retired and took over a rural mail route in the Banner community which he operated until his very untimely death in 1976.

In the spring of 1968, after about five years of owning and operating the camp, the Bonds decided that running a camp was more than they bargained for which caused Mrs. Bond to casually place an ad in a Chicago newspaper, "Town for Sale, Inquire Box 125, Acme, Wyo." That simple ad was picked up by an enterprising news reporter who then wrote a feature article. The reaction was immediate and the article hit the Associated Press and published throughout the whole country. Inquiries poured in flooding that little post office and within a few days over 300 were received.

In May of that same Spring, Mr. Bond sold the camp to Mr. and Mrs. Charles P. Evinger of Indiana who continued to own it until just this year, 1977, when the Big Horn Coal Company purchased it, but in the meantime, many of the units were removed or torn down and replaced by trailer homes thereby greatly relieving some of the housing shortage caused by the subsequent development of strip mining.

Then suddenly, the residents of that former mining camp were appalled when later that spring they received official notice to vacate as revealed by the following article appearing in the Billings, Montana *Gazette of May 15, 1977:*

"Mining company evicts 40 residents of Acme"—The approximately 40 residents of Acme, a tiny coal town which flourished in the 1930s, have received eviction notices from Peter Kiewit Sons' Mining Co.

Residents have been given until Sept. 1 to find new homes or parking spaces for their trailers, a company spokesman said Saturday.

Notices came as no surprise to Acme residents, who had been expecting as much since the PKS Co.—which owns the subsidiary Big Horn Coal Co.—purchased the town last January, according to a company spokesman.

The mining company announced plans to use the land for development of the Big Horn Mine. PKS plans to build a new bathhouse and other structures and to raze the remaining turn-of-the-century buildings.

Construction will begin this summer and is expected to be completed by late 1978.

The spokesman said that about a dozen families now living in Acme work for the mining company."

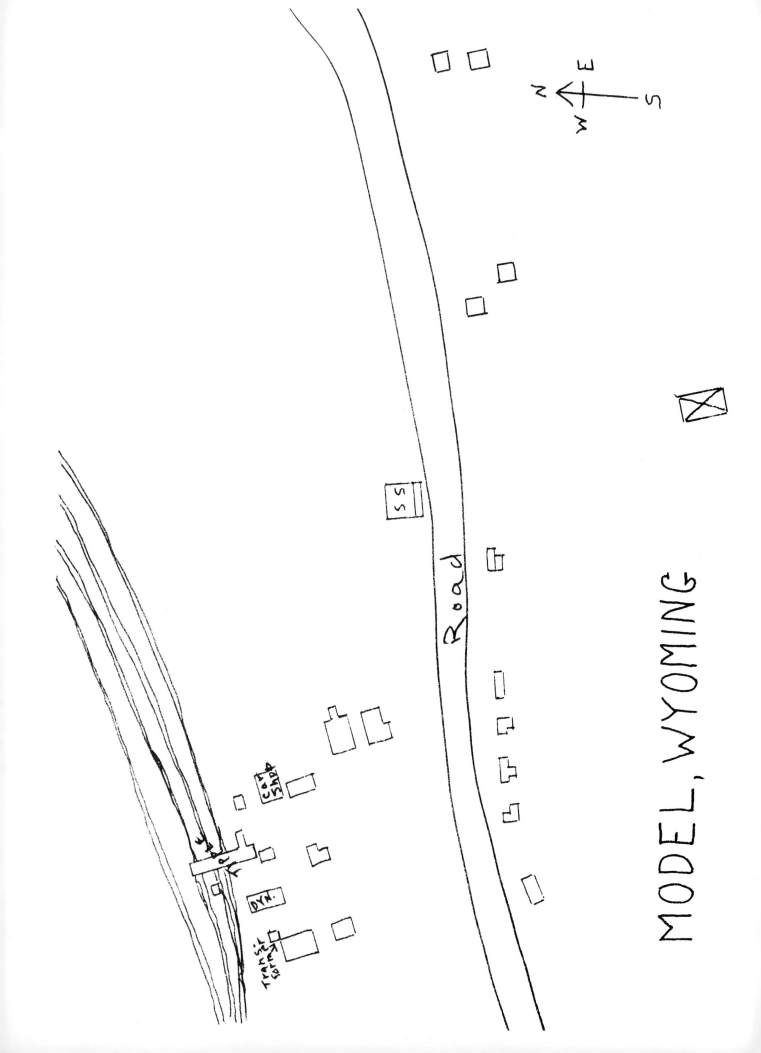

MODEL, WYOMING

Chapter 10

Model 1911-1921

5/16/11—"Notice of Incorporation."

Notice is hereby given that a corporation under the name of the "Model Coal Company" was incorporated, by filing its certificate of incorporation in the office of the Secretary of State of Wyoming, on the 6th day of May, 1911. Its term of existence is 50 years from the time of said filing. It is managed by a board of five directors, and those managing said corporation for the first year are John Peters, D. A. Fessler, J. W. Rilery, Frank W. Smith and Stewart Kennedy. It has a capital stock of $75,000.00, divided into 750 shares of the par value of $100.00 each,—". "Its principal office, shall be on the John Birchby property, adjoining the village of Carneyville, Sheridan County, Wyoming, and the name of the agent in charge of said principal office is Stewart Kennedy." "MODEL COAL COMPANY."

(The Stewart Kennedy named above is the same Stewart Kennedy who was superintendent of the early Dietz mine, later superintendent at the Monarch Mine, as indicated in another chapter, organizer of a coal mine at Coalmont, Colorado, and now again one of the organizers of the Model Coal mine. This information was given to me by Porter Kennedy in a recent taped interview. Ed.)

4/2/12—David Kendrick advertised Model coal in a display ad in the *Sheridan Enterprise* as follows: "Model Coal $2.75 a ton—Office, Scott & Grinnell, Ph. 376." "There will be no raise from this price on this coal for one year from date."

11/9/12—"Body of Miner Sent to Illinois." "Body of John Sherry who died of injuries received in an accident at the Model mine Wednesday sent to Kewanee, Ill. Man was working at bottom of shaft when cage came down without warning, crushing him."

12/6/12—"SUES COAL COMPANY FOR 27,000 DAMAGES. Administrator for Scherry

Estate Wants That Indemnity from Model Coal Company."

"Alleging criminal negligence against the Model Coal Company in compelling John Sherry to operate a mine car with defective brakes said to be responsible for his death November 6, James Mullen, appointed as administrator of the Sherry estate brought action in the district court in his own name for $27,000.00 damages."—"According to the petition, Scherry realized the impending danger ahead and tried to set the brakes, but they were defective, as alleged, and resisted his efforts to stay the speed of the car. It collided with the descending cage and Scherry was caught in the impact, resulting in his almost instantaneous death.

Scherry is survived by a wife, 22 years of age and a baby girl, 18 months old, both of whom are now living with relatives in Kewanee, Ill."

11/14/13—"POST REPRESENTATIVE VISIT THE SHERIDAN COUNTY MINES. MODEL MINE IS MODEL IN ALL PARTICULARS. REACHED BY SHAFT. And Workings at Bottom Unique as Compared With Those of Other Mines—Prices and Rates."

"The Model mine, owned by the Model Coal company, is the youngest and smallest of the Sheridan group of coal mines. Development of this property has been under way for less than two years, but is in a good stage of advancement—"

"But few of the men employed at the Model live at the mine. Those who do not live in Sheridan are provided with houses at Carneyville, which is only a half mile distant—Stewart Kennedy, manager of the company, is a great friend of Sheridan and encourages living here as much as possible, the men traveling back and forth on the interurban. For that reason, it has built no houses at Model. For the same reason, it has built no store, and Mr. Kennedy says that it will not, leaving the men free to trade where they will, preferably in Sheridan.

The Model company holds 120 acres of land

at the mine, most of it underlaid with two veins of coal. Where the mine is located, however, there is but one vein, the Carney. Along the Tongue River valley, the Monarch vein, the one above the Carney, has been burned away at some prehistoric time, leaving the hills on either side red and yellow, in reality burned clay. The Carney vein where the mine is now working is sixteen feet in thickness. It is really two veins close together, divided by a streak of clay varying from hardly noticeable thickness to about two inches. The lower part of this vein, ten feet four inches, is being taken out now. The upper part will be taken out later.

from the surface. He has been connected in one way or another with opening up and development of every mine in the district.

Author of Articles

Mr. Kennedy has studied the Sheridan field for years and is one of the best informed men on the subject to be found. He has made many borings at different places, has given much information to the government, and has written several articles upon Sheridan coal for scientific journals. He says that while in the immediate vicinity of the Tongue River mines there are but two veins, there are really eleven veins in the

Model, Wyoming—Note interurban posts on line of Sheridan Street Railway, the CB&Q Railroad, and Acme in distance.

Kennedy Opens Mine

Manager Kennedy of the Model mine has been connected with the development of Sheridan county mines almost from the time the first, the Dietz No. 1, was opened. A short time after the launching of that enterprise he was put in charge and conducted the mine from 1898 until 1903. Severing his connection with the Dietz mine, he went to Monarch and opened that mine

field beneath Sheridan. All of these veins are found totaling in thickness 120 feet. All but fifteen feet of that thickness is workable coal. The veins dip from northwest to southeast and north of here have been eroded away. They extend as far as Ulm and Clearmont in the other direction—"

1/28/19—"NEW HOME FOR THE MANAGER AT MODEL COAL CAMP." "Fred Harder, who has been connected with the building work which has been going on at the Model Coal camp during the past year advised The Post that the new five-room home which was built for General Manager B. B. McGee is now completed and occupied. The house is modern in every respect, with a large fire place, and solid concrete floors in both the kitchen and bathrooms.

A dozen new houses have been completed at that camp within the past year. The new brick car shop is also completed and proves a great relief in the car repair work, much of which has been necessary to handle in the open."

2/4/19—"HOW BLACK DIAMONDS ARE MARKETED AT MODEL." "Extensive Improvements That Are Being Made at One Sheridan County Mine." "Monster Screen That Cost $50,000 to Install—Enormous Tipple and How It Is Operated—How the Coal Is Loaded."

The above article reveals some of the observations of the Post representative. For example, there was a modern office, a bathhouse for employes with individual lockers. There were the stables for the horses, a power plant and boiler rooms. The tipple was said to be one of the most modern "west of the Mississippi."

attractive, on an appointed day, I walked from "Kuzaraville" all the way to Model, a distance of about 4 miles, paid Gilbert the $5.00 and proudly rode the "wreck" home. The unit had wheel rims of wood which had dried up from age. It wasn't too much later when, while riding my younger brother, Henry, on the handle bars coming down the Dietz hill, the front wheel collapsed causing us passengers to go flying through the air landing several feet ahead on the hard packed surface of the dirt road. Although no serious injury resulted, I ended up with a severe road burn on my left hip leaving a good sized scar.

Another recollection, that I have of Model occurred sometime in the early 20's. My father and I were returning from delivering groceries. As we approached Model, my father had mentioned that someone had run off the very narrow road, going over a rather steep bank on the left side the night before. Dad was then going to show me the spot where the accident occurred. It was just getting dusk, and that coupled with the fact that the headlights of the old Ford, the electricity for which was generated by a magneto, made visibility very limited. He had just

Model mine location as it looks today. Present Big Horn Coal tipple at left. In distance is the water tower of Acme, Wyoming and the Montana-Dakota utilities power plant recently closed down.

One recollection which I have of the Model Camp occurred when I was about a Freshman in high school. In traveling on the interurban, to school, I became acquainted with one of my classmates, Gilbert Gebo. A casual conversation revealed that Gilbert had an old bicycle which he would sell for $5.00. As the price was very

come to the spot and had practically stopped to point out the spot and with his and my attention directed to the spot, neither of us saw another vehicle parked there. The result was, we hit into the rear of the parked car. The little Ford we were driving had no body—it was simply an open seat with a small truck bed. It did however, have a windshield, a two piece affair, both sections extended out for air and better vision. As we hit, I went flying right through the open windshield, landing on the road ahead of our truck. Fortunately, neither of us was injured, but the front axle of the Ford was bent sufficiently where we could not proceed by car. We ended up walking the approximately four miles in quite pitch darkness.

Perhaps additional research would reveal that there might have been some sort of a school at Model; however, no mention was noted in the newspaper items scanned. Not until a few days ago, November 20th, 1976, did any such information come to light when I accidentally met a Mrs. Augusta Tryon (maiden name) White who states that her father worked at the Model Mine in 1919 after working the previous year at Carneyville. It was in that year of 1919 when she recalls attending her first grade in Model in what she vaguely recalls was a one-room affair over a store or some similar building.

Old hoist of Model mine still to be seen left undisturbed.

Model site today—Note windless in foreground which was used to pull cage. Powder house on right.

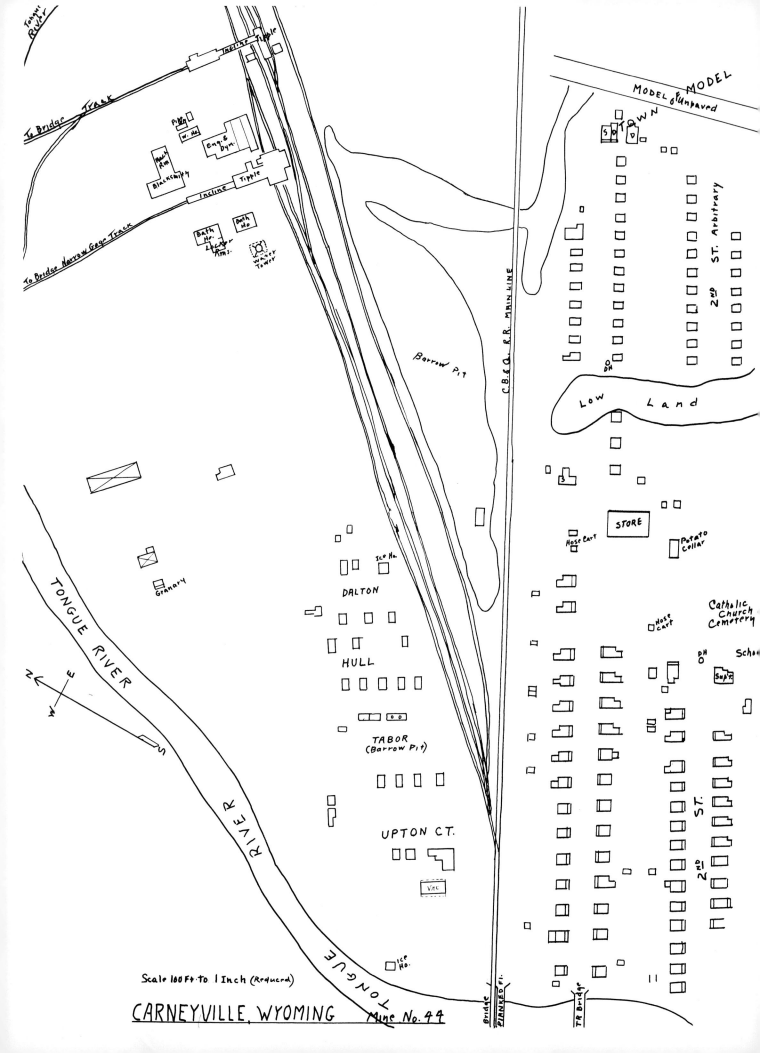

Tongue River

To Bridge Track

Incline Tipple

Pump Ho.

W. Ho.

Eng. & Dyn.

Mach Rm.

Blacksmith

Incline Tipple

To Bridge Narrow Gage Track

Bath Ho. Locker Rms.

Bath Ho.

Water Tower

MODEL

MODEL (Unpaved)

S O

D

TOWN

2ND ST. Arbitrary

Barrow Pit

Low Land

C.B.&Q. R.R. MAIN LINE

TONGUE RIVER

RIVER

Granary

DALTON

Ice Ho.

HULL

STORE

Hose Cart

Potato Cellar

Hose Cart

Catholic Church Cemetery

DH

Supt.

School

3

TABOR
(Barrow Pit)

UPTON CT.

VAC

2ND ST.

11

Ice Ho.

Ice Ho.

N
E
S
W

Scale 100 Ft. to 1 Inch (Reduced)

CARNEYVILLE, WYOMING   Mine No. 44

Bridge
PLANKED FI.

TR Bridge

TONGUE

Chapter 11

Carneyville (Kleenburn) 1904 - Feb. 1924

2/26/04—In one of the first articles appearing about Carneyville, the *Sheridan Post* states, "Carney Coal Co. Birchby Deal Made. Iowa coal mine behind operators. Capital, $100,000. Mine to begin soon as machinery and supplies available. Bought Birchby ranch and adjacent coal filing consumated. Wm. J. Carney, Joseph Rogers of Chicago, D. W. Carpenter, Judge David Ryan and R. E. Stout of Des Moines and R. E. Sears of Marshalltown, Iowa and joined by B. H. Carney of Grinnell, Iowa, L. S. Harper of Osceola, Iowa and L. C. Martin of Big Horn. Negotiatons completed for 2,000 acres of land covering coal. On Tongue River. Burlington R. R. running through land. Articles of Incorporation filed with Wm. J. Carney, Pres., Carney Coal Company."

4/1/04—"John Birchby and wife in town and now employed by the Carney Coal Company as its operator. In a few days expect to contract for houses 24 x 26 to be built."

5/24/04—Side tracks for Carney Coal Company being installed by the B. & M. Railroad. T. W. Carpenter, Manager Carney Coal Company of Iowa visiting."

8/9/04—There appeared quite a long article in the *Sheridan Post* describing Carneyville operation, and a few days later, in another article, it states that "modern equipment being installed in Carney which will be in operation next month."

1/29/07—*Sheridan Post.* "Carneyville. Fred Halden, a driver in the coal mines of Carneyville was instantly killed when he failed to properly adjust a switch. The car took the wrong track and crushed him between the car and the wall of the entry. Burial in Sheridan under the direction of O. J. Smyth."

2/1/07—"Citizens of Monarch criticize the *Post* for apparently accusing the fault of the deceased."

4/16/07—*Post.* "Carneyville. 3 Americans wounded by Dago On Streets on Sunday p.m. Coal mining camp of Carneyville was the scene of a desperate fight Sunday afternoon between several Italians and 3 Americans in which the latter got the worst of it. The row started over a dog fight. The Americans exposing the cause of one of the animals while the Dagos took up the defense of the other. All of the fighters had been drinking, and the Italians used knives on their adversaries with some serious results. The 3 Americans were Fuller, Hugh and Dan Reynolds. The former was cut in the back and his lower parts are paralyzed. The second cut across his abdomen so that his intestines came out. 19 stitches required. The third was cut twice in the neck but not seriously injured. The first two hospitalized and reported in a dangerous condition. Sheriff Benefield went down and captured 4 Italians and all jailed. Two still at large. (Names deleted by author)

4/17/07—*Post.* "James Huey, victim of the fight in Carneyville, died."

6/4/07—"Earl Spanogole, owner of amusement hall in Carneyville was visiting in Dietz."

5/1/08—In this issue of the *Sheridan Enterprise*, Mrs. D. H. Warner wrote an article about the Mines and of Carneyville as follows: "The Carney Coal Company is located at Carneyville, about half a mile from Monarch, and it is a model camp. No expense has been spared in putting in new equipment. Their tonnage averages about 1,800 tons daily. The Carney Company claim that they can double their output at the resumption of next seasons business."

Further referenced by the Sheridan newspapers continue:

3/9/10—"MINER IS INSTANTLY KILLED BY CAVE IN AT CARNEY." "John Wallace Crushed to Death by Falling Rock—Companion Workmen Narrowly Escape."

Carneyville Camp—Looking from northeast. Large building in center, office and company store. Butcher shop across street.

Carneyville today—From about same location as picture above (note powderhouse in foreground).

Carneyville, Wyoming looking north from hill.

"John Wallace, a miner in the employ of the Carney Coal company, was instantly killed at 9 o'clock this morning by falling rock in one of the lower levels of the company's mine.

Several other miners were working a few feet from Wallace when a section of the roof came in, but narrowly escaped uninjured. The body was covered with a couple feet of debris."—"Wallace was unmarried and had been in the employ of the company four years. He has a brother in Hartshorn, Oklahoma. He was a member of the Carney branch of the United Mine Workers of America."

3/11/10—"CARNEYVILLE MINERS WILL ATTEND FUNERAL."

A special train will be run from Carneyville to Sheridan and return, Sunday to accommodate the miners who will attend the funeral of Jack Wallace who was killed in the Carneyville mine Wednesday by a fall of rock.—"

5/12/10—(Carneyville Items)—Carneyville, May 11.

The mines at this place are now running full time and everyone hoping a continuance.

C. B. Seymour, general manager of the Carney Coal Company, received on Saturday a $6,000 forty horsepower Peerless automobile which if all reports are true can cover the distance between Carneyville and Sheridan in fifteen minutes.

Mrs. Chas. Tauver of Monarch, was calling on Carneyville friends Wednesday p.m.

Mr. and Mrs. Warren Wheeler were business callers in Sheridan Tuesday.

Thad Stephens and wife and Ruth Stephens and mother, of Sheridan, were visitors at the Upton home Sunday afternoon.

Mrs. Mary Harrison and sister, Mrs. Maggie Turner, and children were Carneyville callers Sunday afternoon enroute from Acme.

The ball game at Carneyville Sunday between the home team and Fort Mackenzie was not a very exciting game. There was a large crowd in attendance, quite a number of people from Sheridan and surrounding camps.

In speaking of the home team, will say that they have played under difficulties and never yet this season played two games with their full team some having left the camp, but have the honor of winning the first two games of the season. Sunday, May the 15th, they will cross bats with Dayton at that place.

There will be a big ball given in Carneyville Saturday evening May 14, by the Carneyville baseball team. It is hoped there will be a big attendance. Good music has been secured. Everybody is cordially invited.

An auto party consisting of Mr. and Mrs. Robbins of Sheridan and Mr. and Mrs. C. B. Seymour and Mr. and Mrs. H. N. Newton and daughter, Imogene, made a trip to Big Horn Monday evening.

Mrs. Clint Head of Monarch, was visiting her parents at Carneyville Tuesday and Wednesday.

Captain and Mrs. Johnson and Captain and Mrs. Hegeman and children were dinner guests at the Seymour home on Sunday evening."

6/6/10—"CARNEYVILLE BEAT ROYAL HIGHLANDERS"

The Royal Highlander baseball team went down to defeat yesterday at Carneyville to the tune of 10 to 2. The game was close up to the sixth inning, when Griffith, the heavy hitting catcher of Carneyville, hit the ball for a home run with the bases full. This brought in four runs and put the Highlanders out of the running.

Griffith was the star for Carneyville, playing first-class ball all through the game. Olsed did the best work for the Highlanders."

6/17/10—"MESSICK'S CUBS TO MEET CARNEYVILLE." "NEXT SUNDAY AFTERNOON IN BALL GAME ON THE LOCAL DIAMOND." "CONTEST WILL BE FAST ONE." "Local Manager Is Endeavoring to Secure Keenan, the Fast Pitcher of Fort Mackenzie."

Dick Keenan and R. Mills, the infield battery of Fort Mackenzie, worked for Ranchester and Stanley and Griffith were the Carneyville's battery in the game played last Sunday which lasted 13 innings.

July, 1911—(CARNEYVILLE ITEMS)

William Treat and Billy Moses spent Sunday fishing on Wolfe Creek and report a very good catch.

The ball game held at this place Sunday afternoon between the Sheridan Highlanders and the U.M.W. of A. resulted in a victory of 10 to 3 in favor of the union whizzers. The Highlanders brought a bunch of boosters along with them well equipped with paper horns but upon the arrival of the Carney boosters the Sheridan girls were seized with heart failure, their horns refused to respond to the many little sighs breathed through them. Oh, girls, we feel sorry for you but you must insist on the boys learning the game.

Miss Bessie Bateman visited her parents over Sunday.

The two tipples of Carneyville. Carneyville had two tipples and two mines, both of the latter across Tongue River.

Close-up of Carneyville tipple.

Miss Nettie Wright and Mr. Clarence Wiltsie were united in marriage at the Methodist pastorage in Sheridan on June 2, 1910 at 10 a.m. by the Rev. W. D. Traut. Those present were Mr. and Mrs. Wilmer Wright, parents of the bride and Mrs. Frank Johnson, a cousin of the bride. After the ceremony they took the west bound train for Billings and from there to Cody where they will spend a few weeks visiting the parents of Mr. Wiltsie. The bride is one of Carneyville's most accomplished young ladies and the groom is one of the highest respected young men. May they enjoy a happy and prosperous life is the best wishes of a host of their friends.

D. W. Jones, Peter Kooi and Thad Stephens attended the ball game here Sunday.

Dr. and Mrs. Levers and daughter, Ernestine and Mrs. Long visited at the Dennison home over Sunday.

Mrs. W. P. Bross of Monarch visited friends in Carney Monday afternoon.

Those who attended the dance at Monarch on Saturday evening were Messers. E. Madrus, Upton, Treat, Newton, Girous, Young, Hunter and Gilroy. They all report a very fine time and declare the Pythian sisters royal entertainers.

D. W. Jones of Kooi was calling on friends in Carney Monday evening.

Quite a number of people attended the wrestling match at Monarch on Sunday.

School closed on Friday and all youngsters are happy. The teachers Mrs. Newton and Miss Glenn planned a very pleasant time for their pupils by taking them for a picnic at the George Masters ranch.—"

2/26/12—"SHUTDOWN AT CARNEYVILLE DISPUTE OVER CONTRACT."

The Carneyville coal mine is idle today due to some misunderstanding between the operators and the mine workers. The shut down was authorized without the sanction of Thomas Gibson, president of District No. 22. Three hundred miners are affected, and until some satisfactory agreement is made, it is reported they refuse to work. The trouble is not in the nature of a strike but merely a shut down.

The officials of the Carneyville union claim a violation of a contract between them and the coal mining company. From authoritative sources, it is said that the misunderstanding has arisen through a misinterpretation of the contract.

The president, vice president and secretary-treasurer of District No. 22, U.M.W. of A., are already in Sheridan, and if the additional board members arrive in Sheridan this afternoon an executive board meeting will be held in Sheridan this evening to settle the dispute."

2/28/12—"Value of Life is Placed at $30,000." "James Mosley, Administrator of J. F. Wallace estate, Holds Carney Coal Company Responsible for Death of His Intestate." Died March 9, 1910.

Petition alleged part of roof of mine fell in a place some forty feet to seventy feet from mouth of entry. While deceased was removing fallen rock, huge stone fell on deceased from the roof of said entry above a crib of timbers some 25 feet to the bottom of the entry, killing deceased."

2/29/12—"Carney Coal Company Sues Local Union." "Mine Workers are Held Responsible for Shut Down at Mine."—"Claim is Made That Contract Disregarded—Named defendants are: Mike Broshears, Pres.; Hugh Bates, Financial Secretary; J. H. Gireaux, Treas.; Rees Davis, Robert McClusky, Trustees, of Union No. 2742, United Mine Workers of America."

The old Powder house (located some distance away from the camp as was the custom—powder houses of several of the camps still standing).

8/29/13—"Teachers Assigned for New School Year." Mrs. H. W. Newton, Prin.; Eunice Wilson, primary. 10/7/12—"16 and 53 pupils in attendance."

11/7/13—"Carneyville Has Holdup." "Bad Men Wearing Masks Rob Pasterski's Roost—Is What He Says—Claims Three Men Took $145 from His Residence—Had Ugly Looking Automatic Pistols."

11/11/13—"Boy Killed at the Mines."—Bad Accident Happens at the Carneyville Tipple. Nineteen Year Old Lad Crushed So that He Dies Before Reaching Hospital."

Frank Szturcek, while stooping over to pull out a pin to do some coupling, a loaded mine car weighing 6,000 pounds came down on him, striking him in the back. Dr. Dennison, the Carneyville physician unable to keep him alive until reaching hospital."

11/18/13—"POST REPRESENTATIVE VISIT THE SHERIDAN COUNTY MINES." "THREE THOUSAND TONS DAILY AT CARNEY MINE." "TYPICAL COAL TOWN ' "Undoubtedly Largest Works of the Sheridan Group—Over Four Hundred Men Employed."

"A double coal mine" is one way to describe the workings of the Carney Coal Company, located nine miles northwest of Sheridan, on the lines of the Burlington railroad and the Sheridan Railway interurban line. At this mine coal is taken from two main tunnels, sorted and loaded from two large tipples. The Carney mine is undoubtedly the biggest mine of the Sheridan group, and is producing about 3,000 tons of coal daily in one eight-hour shift, without Sunday work.

Carneyville is a typical coal town. It has a large number of cottages for the men and their families, all neat and in excellent repair, but little attempt has been made to beautify the town, and the interest of everyone is centered in getting out the coal. At that, however, the town has many improvements, including a plentiful water supply, fire protection and public baths for the men, with hot and cold water in abundance. Four or five hundred men employed by the Carney company live in the town, and in addition most of the men employed at the Model mine live there. There is a large general store, meat market and other business undertakings. The town is well policed, has good schools and has never had a case of typhoid fever originating there.

State Receives Royalty

The Carney Coal Company is part of a large corporation with headquarters in Chicago and owning a large number of mines at different places. It controls and owns a large acreage in this county, much of it underlaid with two veins of coal—the Monarch and Carney. Where the mine is located, however, there is but one vein, the Carney, and coal has been taken from it for nine years. The supply still in sight is sufficient for hundreds of years to come. A large part of the mine is located on state land and Wyoming receives a royalty on every ton taken from the pits.

The Carney plant is probably the most complete in itself to be found in the county. The company has its own power plant, its own shops for wood and iron works, its own water works, supply houses and commissary department. Cut off from the rest of the world, Carney would be able to exist and produce coal for weeks.

The repair shops are more complete than will be found in many good-sized cities. In the wood-working department, timber is cut for all purposes, from car-repairing to mine propping. There is a full complement of machinery of all kinds. In the iron foundry there are electric punching machines, electric hammer, drills, lathes, emery wheels, bolt machines and complete equipment for dismantling cars and motors, including a traveling crane for handling the heavier parts.

Big Store Houses

Nearby are located the warehouses, where repair stock valued at $20,000 is stored awaiting use. The oil house contains oil supply for several weeks despite the fact that the use of lubricant is by hundreds of gallons.

The storage tank for water is situated near the tipples. It has a capacity of 80,000 gallons, and is supplied by three large pumps. Water for use in the town is taken from a large spring, that for use at the works comes from the river.

All this work is done electrically with current supplied by a plant consisting of two Erie City engines coupled to Goodwin generators and driven by a battery of four boilers 72 inches by 18 feet in size and developing 150 horsepower each. Coal is carried to the boilers directly from the tipple by a screw conveyor and is deposited in front of the boilers as needed.

Tipple No. 1 of the Carney mine is interesting in that it differs from the other tipples seen in the group. It is a large structure built of heavy timbers and is driven by steam. No. 2 is electrically driven and is of steel and corrugated iron, a newer addition. But No. 1 is used most and most of the Carney coal comes from it.

Driving the Tipple

The steam plant driving the tipple is located directly under it and drives the heavy machinery by means of shafts and belts. At the foot of the incline, the loaded mine cars are seized by one of two endless cables and drawn to the top.

There the cars are dumped automatically, each car as it comes to the dump releasing the car ahead of it, just emptied. The empty runs by gravity to a Y track, turns back, is caught by a short cable which regulates their speed and transferred to the second of the long cables, which takes it back to the ground. The capacity of this tipple is about 2,200 tons in eight hours. The highest output this fall from the two tipples has been 3,200 tons in eight hours. Both have been in operation since October 1st.

Dumped from the mine cars, the coal at No. 1 goes into a large hopper and thence on to an immense double shaker screen where it is graded to any size desired. The sizes being loaded pass directly into the cars while the smaller coal falls to an elevator, is carried to the top of the tipple and passes through another screen of the steel cylinder variety. From there it goes into bins for the different sizes and is loaded into cars from the bins. Lump, egg, nut, pea, slack and combinations of two or more of the sizes are the classes of coal produced and marketed from Carney.

Method of Loading

The method of loading cars at Tipple No. 1 is also novel and interesting. Instead of loading box cars by hand, the cars are "spotted" upon a movable table, or rocker, operated by hydraulic power. The cars are tipped from end to end so that the coal rolls gradually and easily from the middle to the ends. In that way a car can be filled easily in a few minutes, and without much breakage of coal. An auxiliary loader is situated by the tipple for use in emergency or accident to the tipple loaders. The problem of profitable disposal of the slack has been solved by the Carney campany, and while ten percent of the coal taken from the mine is slack, not a car has been dumped in the past six months.

The two haulage entries of the Carney mine are located across the river, opposite the two tipples, and have several tracks leading to them from the tipples. Cars are hauled to and fro by means of electric motors, six of them being in operation. Four motors take coal from the mines and they made about forty trips per day, hauling out from sixteen to thirty cars at a trip. Each car carries a little more than three tons of coal. The large fans used in keeping fresh air in the mine are located near the entrances and the one at Entrance No. 1 handles 110,000 cubic feet of air per minute. The mine is excellently ventilated, being divided into three currents, reaching every part of the workings. The smoke from "shooting" is cleared from the mine in less than an hour after the shots have been fired.

Penetrates the Hillside

Entrance No. 1 of the mine goes into the hillside for a distance of 4,500 feet almost on a level. The grades everywhere in the mine are very slight, greatly facilitating the work of handling the cars. It has been possible to open nearly all of the working rooms and cross entries so as to give a down grade for loaded cars.

Coal is not encountered in No. 1 until 300 feet from the mouth but from there on coal is everywhere. In No. 2 entrance, the coal starts at the grass roots. While the two tunnels are operated separately, they are united underground and the men pass freely from one to the other.

All of the main tunnels of the Carney mine are being timbered. That is done not so much for safety, as the walls and roofs are perfectly secure, but to prevent air slacking of the exposed coal. The mine is electrically lighted throughout, is dry everywhere, and it is very easy to walk from place to place. The entire mine is provided with car tracks and there are many sidings. It is estimated that the mine contains fifteen miles of track.

Well Formulated Plan

Coal is mined from Carney mine upon a well formulated and strictly carried out plan. From the main entries, cross entries are driven into the coal. From these again, working rooms are opened, and it is so planned that a certain area of coal is cut off by itself by the tunnels. Into that mass of coal so isolated, the working rooms are driven, each panel, as it is called, containing twenty-eight or thirty rooms. A wall of coal fifty feet thick is left standing all around the panel with the exception of two entrances.

Work is pushed in a "panel" until all of the coal has been taken out. When the supply has been exhausted, only the walls remaining about the immense room, the two entrances are closed and sealed with concrete walls. The part is in that way cut off entirely from the rest of the mine. Fire could rage within that room for hours without endangering the rest of the mine, but sealed as they are, there is little danger of fire in them. It is a precaution taken for safety, but keeps the mine in an orderly state as well.

Awe-inspiring Sight

These rooms, when the last props are being taken out and the roof coal is falling, are imposing and awe-inspiring places. They appear of immense size, black as pockets, with roofs far above. Especially at shooting time are they fearsome. The shots in other parts of the mine reverberate through these large spaces, the air shakes and quivers, until the impression is given that the whole mine is falling about one's ears. The miners think nothing of it, however, and calmly load the coal as it falls from the ceiling, staying in a panel until every pound of coal is out.

The Carney vein at the Carney mine is about seventeen feet in thickness. A little more than ten feet is taken out on the way in, the overhead coal comes when the other supply is exhausted. At the Model, the vein is divided by a tiny streak of clay, being really two veins.

The Carney Company is now working about 450 men in one eight-hour shift. The payroll amounts to something over $2,000 per day, or between $50,000 and $60,000 per month. The mine has been working steadily since early in the fall and will probably continue all winter."

1/4/14—"MINER KILLED BY DELAYED SHOT IN MINE. Bernardo Nannarone Dies In State Hospital After Accident Friday Evening. HIS SKULL WAS CRUSHED. Returned to See Why Shot Failed But Found Fuse Still Burning.

—partner, Ruciano Fusko. The victim is survived by a wife and four children, one girl of about fourteen, and three younger sons. All live in Italy—"

1/23/16—"AWARDED EIGHT THOUSAND AS DAMAGES."

"Eight thousand dollars were awarded to Anton Maryanowsky by the jury at 12 o'clock Friday night at the conclusion of the trial of a suit against the Carney Coal company in which he asked that he be given $30,000 for injuries received when he was crushed between two coal cars December 8, 1912, while he was employed in pushing mine cars on to the scales at the mine at Carneyville.—"

2/14/16—"PAY CLAIMS UNDER COMPENSATION ACT."

"Checks amounting to more than $3,000 were received today from the state treasurer's office by George Nottingham, clerk of the district court, in payment of claims filed under the workmen's compensation act and passed upon by the district court here. Andrew Cieslar, who lost a leg in an accident at Carneyville, received $339. Mrs. Armenia Menigas, a widow whose husband was killed in the mine at Carneyville, received $1,000 and each of her two minor children received $500. M. R. Peters, who lost a finger at the sugar factory, received $122, James McNally who had his arm broken in three places while in the employ of the Carney Coal company, received $54.85. There were several other smaller claims allowed."

4/30/18—"CARNEYVILLE SCHOOL."

"The Carneyville school gave a free Liberty loan entertainment at Carney movie hall on Friday, April 13th. The program consisted of a five minute talk by Rev. Theo. J. Schultz; tableau by Carney Red Cross ladies: 'A World Wide Peace,' by intermediate grades; 'Allies' by primary and intermediate rooms. The junior high school engaged in a contest as their part of the program. Six students wrote and delivered speeches on 'How to Win the War.' A prize of three dollars was given the winner, Ellen Goode, who came to school the next Monday and bought a war savings stamp.

Mrs. Horatio Burns and Mrs. Fisher of Sheridan were visitors. Mrs. Burns presented the prize given by the Carney school.

Teachers: Helen Krajicek, intermediate, Mrs. Abbott, primary; Miss Gertrude Condran, assistant primary."

Carneyville cemetery as seen today from U.S. Highway 90. Names appearing on headstones at Carneyville Cemetery as noted Sept. 27, 1976—Mrs. Jozef Leja, 1882-1924, Carl & Barol 1940; Michael Belish born Sept. 22, 1918, died April 21, 1924; John Sus 1852-1927, Ludmila Sue 1849-4/18/24; Maria Assunta Silla 1888-1923; Stefania Zowada UR 24 LIP 1915, UM 17 MAR 1916; Joseph Gazur Apr. 7, 1902, Sept. 24, 1918; Anton Kuzma Oct. 28, 1892, Oct. 22, 1918; Francesca Ubaldi; Joseph Niemietz 1878-1918; John Bury May 22, 1904, Feb. 13, 1918; Mary Ruszin 1875-1911; Baby Silla, B & D July 8, 1939; Stanley Czarny 1909-1917, Joseph 1911-1923; Jan Czepczor Dec. 1, 19, Nov. 29, 1916; Ierzy Legerski born in Isterbns, Austria, died April 16, 1910, age 33 years; It Nykukszik Sabo Miholne, Szuletet Nagy Rosalia 1881, Meghalt 1918 Nov. 5; John Barbula 1900-1919; Mother Agnes Luke 1873-1917; Darling Daughter Sophie Luke 1908-1919; Angelo Menegas died Dec. 15, 1909. In addition to the above, there are a number of graves which sunken and unmarked or markers have deteriorated.

Crucifix in Carneyville cemetery.

In Carneyville cemetery there are a number of delapidated graves such as this one.

The Carneyville Bloomer Girls baseball team. L to R: Ellen Goode, George Dozah (batboy), Maude Hoffman Barbula, Nellie King Allen, Frances Hunter, Pearl Baron, Pearl Girous, Mrs. Frank Day, Mrs. Coast, Agnes Giroux. Mrs. Henry Barbula (Maude Hoffman), who submitted this photo, relates that when this game was played, a keg of beer was placed at third base, and when any of the men of the opposing team hit the ball, they would run to third base for his beer rather than to first. (No wonder the women won the game!)

Striking miners at Carneyville being rounded up by militia. *(Photo courtesy Elmer Reisch)* 11-16-19

Striking miners at Carneyville being herded by militia.

Striking miners at Carneyville about to be loaded on interurban to be taken to Fort Makenzie stockade.

1/13/21—"KLEENBURN" IS NEW TRADE NAME.

"Kleenburn," what does it convey to your mind? Clean coal that is really clean and coal that really burns? If so, then the guess of a stenographer in the Chicago office of the Peabody Coal Co., was not amiss. Not long ago a contest was conducted among the employes of the company to secure a new trade name for the coal mined by the Peabody company in Dietz, Model, Acme, Carneybille, Monarch and the Kooi mines near Sheridan. With the suggestion of this name because it represented two of the outstanding qualities of the Wyoming coal, the stenographer won the contest.

The camp at Carneyville and the name of the postoffice at that place was put under a ruling from the postmaster general and the company will copyright the name and all coal mined in the six camps will be known as "Kleenburn," it has been announced."

8/3/21—"Injuries Received Result Fatally." Terry ((sp) should be "Teddy") Wujcik died at Kleenburn after several weeks illness resulting from mine accident. Parents, Mr. and Mrs. Parrat, four brothers and four sisters survive."

8/18/21—"KLEENBURN WINS THE MESSICK CUP." "Largest Crowd of the Season Witness the Final Game of the Twilight League Series— Jones of the Mines Has the Elks at His Mercy."

Before the largest crowd of the season, the Elks went down to defeat at the hands of the Miners. The game started off in big league style and was a real ball game until big Bill Sopris lost control—." Ropes, Kirkland, W. King, Bateman, Barber, and Hans a few of the players for the mines; Bateman, Wright, and Thirwell and Sopris, for the Elks; Reynolds, Umpire.

9/20/21—Rocco Romeo, native of Italy injured when chunk of coal fell, cracking two ribs.

9/24/22—"Boy Slain in a Mellon Patch Row—Officers arrest (name deleted), a Kleenburn miner, for shooting Fred Hoffman, 15—Fred Hoffman, 15 year old youth of Kleenburn is dead from gunshot wound through the lungs—Assailant later sentenced to 40 years in the Wyoming State Penitentiary.

3/7/23—"Kleenburn Mine Closes Due to Lack of Orders—295 Men Thrown Out of Work When Mine Shuts Down"

"Shortage of coal orders was given today as the reason for closing the Kleenburn mine, which is working its final shift today. The mine will close this evening, throwing 295 men out of employment.

Kleenburn is the third mine operated by the Sheridan-Wyoming Coal company to close down this year, the mines at Kooi and Dietz having closed last November.

This leaves only Monarch and Acme in operation. Some 300 men are employed at each of those mines.

The mines have been operating on an average of from two to three days throughout the winter."

3/31/23—"EASTER SERVICES AT ST. THOMAS CHURCH."

"Easter will be observed in St. Thomas church, Kleenburn, with two Masses. The first Mass will begin at 9:15, and the following music will be rendered:

Introit: "Christ the Lord Is Risen Today," by Master Thomas Jones and Kooi choir.

Offertory: "By the First Bright Easter Morn"—Bariton solo by W. E. Jones.

Consecration: "Today He's Risen," by Master Thomas Jones and Kooi choir.

Communion: "To Jesus' Heart All Burning," Kooi choir.

Recessional: "What Happiness Can Equal Mine?" Mrs. Kovacic at the organ.

Father Schultz will preach on "He Is Risen."

The second Mass will be at eleven o'clock. The choir composed of Mrs. Kovacic, Mr. Motyka and Misses Diener, Kuzara, and Baker will render the following music:

Vidi Aquam: St. Basil's Hymnal, Kyrie, Gloria, Credo, Sanctus.

Benedictus, Agnus Dei: Wuerther.

Offertory: "He Is Risen," Congregation.

Between Mass and Bendiction: Regina Coeli Aetare: Duet, Mrs. Kovacic and Mr. Motyka.

Benediction: "O Salutaris Hostia," Choir; "Tantum Ergo," Choir.

Recessional: "Today He's Risen," choir.

The Sermon: "On the Third Day He Shall Rise Again."

St. Thomas Roman Catholic Church, Carneyville, Wyo., located on knoll near cemetery.

5/27/23—"MYSTERY BLAZE LEVELS CHURCH AT MINES CAMP."—"Catholic Edifice at Kleenburn Entire Loss; Sheriff Investigates at Scene."

"St. Thomas Catholic church at Kleenburn was burned to the ground early Saturday morning. The fire was first seen at 1:15 a.m. by E. J. Bottomley, Jr., who gave the alarm. A bucket brigade was formed, but the wooden building was doomed. Its original cost was about $6,000. Only the chimney and foundation were left.

The loss was partly covered by insurance. There had been no fire in the furnace for three weeks, it is said, and no candles were left burning after Friday services, according to Father Theodore Schultz pastor of the burned church.

People who watched the fire from the time it was first discovered say it appeared to burn in a peculiar manner, and it is thought the origin may have been incendiary. Sheriff Frank R. Toy went to investigate Saturday afternoon."

6/6/23—"WILL BUILD BRICK CHURCH TO REPLACE KLEENBURN EDIFICE"

St. Thomas church at Kleenburn, which mysteriously burned to the ground the morning of May 26, will be replaced by a modern brick structure with a seating capacity of 300, according to word received Tuesday from Father Theodore Schultz, pastor of the burned church.

In the meantime, the stone church at old Dietz will be utilized for services, but it is entirely too small to accommodate the people who want to attend Sunday service.

As soon as altars can be erected, Father Schultz will say Mass in the halls at Monarch and Kooi. Services in Dietz will be at the same hour as in the burned church, 9:30 a.m.''

6/12/23—"WORK ON KLEENBURN CHURCH IS STARTED" To be built opposite the rectory in down town. Entertainment held in Monarch July 2 to help fund its construction. Men donating labor, and by June 23rd, "Excavation Finished for Kleenburn Church" Mass is said at 9:30 o'clock every morning in the Dietz church. The Kooi chapel is furnished and services are held at 7:30 a.m. on Sundays.

Kleenburn Meat Co. lard pail (market owned and operated by George Stanko).

10/9/23—"Kleenburn Church, St. Thomas, Cornerstone To Be Laid By McGovern—will say Mass at Kooi chapel and administer confirmation at St. Hedwig in Dietz."

10/15/23—"Two Hundred Attend Ceremony. 42 confirmed at St. Hedwig in Dietz."

1/6/24—"2 Masses Are Held at New Kleenburn Church on Sundays."

Since the completion of the new St. Thomas Catholic church at Kleenburn, Catholic services have been discontinued in the old Dietz church, according to Father Theodore Schultz. Two Masses are said every Sunday and holy day at the St. Thomas church. The first mass, at 9:15 o'clock, is in English; and the second mass, at 11:00 o'clock, in Polish." 1/19/24—"Debt Small on New Kleenburn Church."

6/29/24—"FATHER THEODORE SCHULTZ LEAVING MINING CAMPS FOR NEW PASTORATE IN PITTSBURGH, PA."—"announcement has brought sorrow"—Father Schultz, in his six and one-half years as Catholic rector of the Kleenburn pasturate, has been more than a priest to his people—he has built them a new church, he has aided them in their troubles, he has guarded their ranches and property from unscrupulous persons, and he has been a leader in civic enterprises.

Knows Many Languages

His has been practical religion. Sent to Kleenburn from the cathedral at Salt Lake at the

Ad in Sheridan Enterprise 10/28/23.

request of Bishop Patrick A. McGovern, who had been unable to find anyone to handle the situation at the mining camps, Father Schultz immediately won the miners' confidence. He became one of them, because their pleasures were his pleasures and because he could converse with any of them in English, Polish, French, German or Italian." Many prominent people of all denominations gave elaborate testimonials to the outgoing prelate, with many more actually mourning his anticipated departure.

7/16/24—"CHURCH BURNED IN KLEENBURN IN MIDNIGHT BLAZE." "Is Second Catholic Edifice to Be Destroyed at Mine Town Within Year."

Destruction of the Catholic Church at Kleenburn resulted from a fire of mysterious origin early Wednesday morning.

The fire was discovered by Mr. and Mrs. Ed Bottomley, who live across the street from the building, about 1:30 o'clock in the morning. The whole building was then a mass of flames and burning rapidly. Immediate steps were taken to extinguish the conflagration, but the blaze had too much of a head start, and the church burned quickly to the ground, everything in it, all furniture, and fixtures being consumed.

The church was a new building, the first services in it having been conducted last Christmas morning. The older Kleenburn church was burned in much the same manner about a year ago. The two fires occurred at exactly the same time of night, residents of Kleenburn report, and from unknown causes. Although incendiarism is suspected by some, the sheriff's office thus far has taken no action.

8/12/24—"Kleenburn 'Miners' Will Face Soldiers in Game Here Sunday."

"The oldtime Fort-Mines baseball feud which waxed rampant during the early days of the current ball season will be renewed Sunday, when the Kleenburn champions face the Mackenzians at the government grounds at 3:30 o'clock."

Lineup as follows:

Fort	Mines
Basch, lf	Upton, 2b
Dowell, 3b	Mentock, 3b
Brammel, cf	T. Kine, lf
Morrow, lb	Carmichael, rf
Sopris, ss	McLean, cf
Houser, 2b	W. King, ss
Henshaw, rf	Hunter, lb
Slater, c	Berry, c
Bantle, p	Wondra, p.

8/24/24—"Pythian Parley Opens Monday at Kleenburn."

About 70 grand lodge members from 16 lodges expected at KP Hall, Kleenburn.

8/26/24—"Mine Boxer Has to Prove Ruggedness—Woodhead yet to Face Real Blow—Parker Boosted by Demeriti—Billy Woodhead, Kleenburn featherweight boder, Labor Day at Acme—Main Event.

10/17/24—"Sheridan Baby Is Drowned in Buried Ice Water Barrel Thursday When She Tries to Visit Her Father at Work—While playing in the yard of the Kleenburn Meat Market, Martha Wand Washut, 22 months old baby girl of Mr. and Mrs. Paul Washut fell into ice barrel and drowned before she could be rescued—Buried in Monarch cemetery.

7/7/25—"Cupid Knocks Out Mines Ring Pride."

"Cupid scored a decision Monday over William ("Billy")Woodhead of Kleenburn, for several years pride of the mining camps in the boxing ring.

"Billy" was married at the courthourse Monday to Nellie Mae Bennett of Acme by C. L. Carter, court commissioner.—"

1925—"MINER TEAM DOWNS SOLDIERS IN FAST GAME PLAYED SUNDAY ON KLEENBURN GROUNDS, 3 TO 1." "Wondra and Bantle Stage Pitchers' Battle—Play Is Replete with Strong Defensive Play—Large Crowd Gathers"—etc.

6/10/26—"J. Arthur Bottomley, son of Mr. and Mrs. Edward Bottomley of Kleenburn, arrived Tuesday from Champaign, Ill., where he has finished his first year at the University of Illinois. His brother, Edward Bottomley, Jr., who has also been a student of the university, will attend the Custer military training camp at Custer, Mich., early this summer, and return home the first of August."

1/23/27—Theater at Kleenburn owned by Sheridan-Wyoming Coal company and managed by Troy Wade burned Thursday. Equipment owned by Wade also destroyed—$1,000 loss.

5/6/27—"Bruno Belmont caught between coal car and a moving motor at Kleenburn—crushing his hip quite badly, breaking hip."

7/12/28—"Charles Catteral of Kleenburn critically injured when he was crushed between car and mine wall at Monarch mine."

7/24/29—"Coal Miner Is Wounded in Affray at Kleenburn—Mat Farley May Lose Sight of One Eye After Row at Mines—Witnesses Claim He Fired First Shots with Pistol—An alleged argument over a little white dog climaxed at Kleenburn: Occurred at home of Ben Daniels who retaliated with a shot gun—"

11/14/32—"Kleenburn Team Beats Wildcats"

The Kleenburn high school grid team defeated the Sheridan Wildcats Sunday by a score of 6-0. The game was played at Kleenburn on a muddy field. Members of the Kleenburn team were: Labay, Stanko, Stopka, Madia, Sulla, Byrtus, Patz, Trocche, Vine and Slovak. The Wildcats were: F. Harris, Martini, Logan, Booras, W. Harris, Shell, James, Dicesare, A. Martini and Aulerich.

3/10/33—"Kleenburn, Coal Mining Camp, Will Gradually Be Abandoned." "Residents Will Be Moved to Acme and Monarch Where Sheridan-Wyoming Mines Are Still In Operation—Offices May Move."

"The eventual abandonment of the town of Kleenburn has been announced by Harry L. Gandy, president of the Sheridan-Wyoming Coal company which owns the town.

It was stated that this will not be done peremptorily and that the convenience of the present residents at Kleenburn will be given every possible consideration. Some of the residents at Kleenburn work at the Acme mine and some at Monarch, while others are employed in the general office of the company or have outside employment. There are sufficient available vacant houses at Acme to take care of Acme employes living at Kleenburn. This is not the case, however, with respect to Monarch employes living at Kleenburn. Mr. Gandy expressed the opinion that Monarch employes living at Kleenburn would move to Monarch to the capacity of available vacant houses. It will then be undertaken to group the remaining residents of Kleenburn in one part of the town to better facilitate care of streets, water and electric light systems.

This year a two-year high school course has been offered at Kleenburn to students from both Kleenburn and Monarch. It is understood the school board of district No. 31 propose to continue this course another year. Third and fourth year high school students will attend the Sheridan high school as at present. It is further stated to be the intention of the local school board to offer the first, second and third grades with one teacher at Kleenburn, and grades one to eight inclusive will be taken care of at the Monarch school with four teachers as at present. This will make provision for the smaller children at Kleenburn and the others there in the fourth to the eighth grades inclusive will attend the Monarch school, the two towns being less than a mile apart.

Officials of the Tongue River Trading company stated that the policy of the Sheridan-Wyoming Coal company is eventually closing the camp at Kleenburn will result in the closing of the store and the division of the stock between the Acme and Monarch stores. Doubtless, in time the postoffice at Kleenburn will be abandoned and thus will pass what was once a prosperous mining camp on the Tongue river, 10 miles from Sheridan.

Mr. Gandy, was asked about the general offices of the Sheridan-Wyoming Coal company which are now located at Kleenburn and he stated that while definite plans therefore had not as yet been concluded, the office would undoubtedly be moved to either Monarch or Acme as the time comes for the complete closing of the Kleenburn town site." (Soon after, the general offices were in fact moved to Monarch.)

(Author's comments)—Of all of the quite detailed and rather complete references made by the Sheridan News media, very little reference was made to the cemetery located at Carneyville (Kleenburn). This cemetery was located behind the original Catholic church which burned in May, 1923 and which was located on the brow of a hill southeast of the Camp. With the camp of Kleenburn having been abandoned, the two churches burned and the Monarch church also abandoned, this cemetery soon began to deteriorate, and except for a few graves maintained by relatives still living in the area, many of the graves have sunk, and many of the markers obliterated.

In September of 1976, I visited this cemetery, took some snaps and listed those names still legible.

For several years, Troy Wade owned the theater in Monarch. He also operated the theater in Kleenburn. James Barello, later the postmaster at Acme, stated that for a time, it was his job to run from Monarch to Kleenburn carrying the movie reel following the showing at Monarch to be followed immediately with a showing at Kleenburn. I recall seeing Charlie Chaplin in one of his pictures at the Kleenburn theatre.

Another one of my several contacts with Kleenburn in addition to he fact that I assisted my father in delivering groceries to many of his Kleenburn customers, occurred while I was in high school.

As mentioned earlier in another chapter, I had been given violin lessons by John Antonkiewitz (who incidentally could make a violin "sing and cry"), and later by Joe Wiesniewski, so that as a Freshman in high school, I played second violin in the high school orchestra. One day, during a conversation with Joe Rulli of Kleenburn on the interurban while commuting to school, (Joe was an accomplished violinist), he suggested that he would also like to learn to play a trumpet. I informed him that my brother, Walter, had a cornet. If I would make arrangements for him to borrow that beat up cornet, he would give me violin lessons. As a result, Joe gave me several lessons. Self-taught, he became very adept in the wind instruments while I never did learn to play a violin to any appreciable degree.

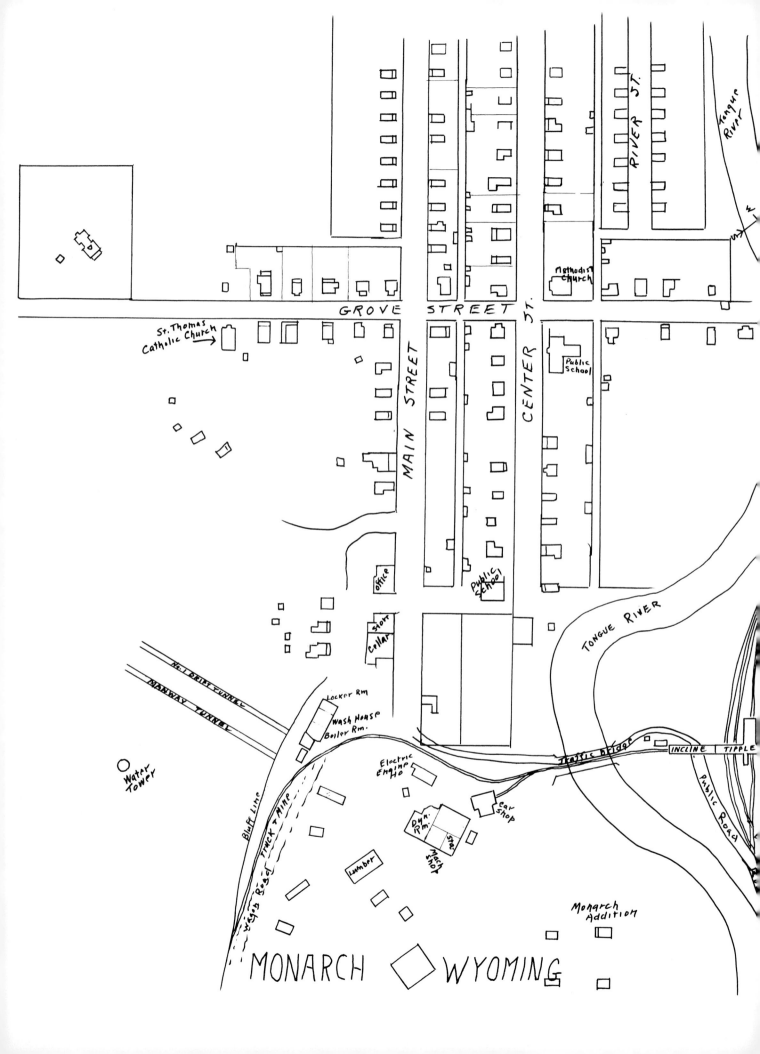

RIVER ST.

Tongue River

Methodist Church

GROVE STREET

St. Thomas Catholic Church

MAIN STREET

CENTER ST.

Public School

Public School

Tongue River

office

store

collar

No.1 DRIFT TUNNEL

MARWAY TUNNEL

Locker Rm

Wash House
Boiler Rm.

Water Tower

Bluff Line

Wagon Road

TRACK + MINE

Electric Engine Ho

Dyn. Rm.

store

Mach Shop

Car Shop

Traffic Bridge

INCLINE   TIPPLE

Public Road

Lumber

Monarch Addition

MONARCH ⬦ WYOMING

Chapter 12

Monarch 1903-1953

Issues of the *Sheridan Post* and the *Sheridan Enterprise* both contain articles describing the progress of the development of the various coal mines and camps of the Sherian area. In the issue of 9/24/03, there appeared an ad announcing as follows: "Stotts and Edleman opening Monarch Mines—delivered at $2.00 per ton and $1.75 in large quantities."

10/15/03—"Monarch-Sheridan Stage line leaving Sheridan 7:00 a.m. at Cottage Hotel. T. E. Roberts, Proprietor."

10/22/03—Stewart Kennedy building new camp, Monarch. 36 dwellings being built, store 22 x 60. Blacksmith Shop. Some coal already being shipped. School house also being built.

1/23/04—Monarch coal loaded 500 tons of coal on Monday.

1/30/04—First issue of Monarch News. School now running with 30 students.

4/12/04—William Patterson and bride have gone to housekeeping after having married Miss Ida Schubert of Sheridan. "Pats" friends welcome him and in the evening the Monarch band composed of 30 pieces serenaded him at the new cottage he had prepared.

5/15/04—Monarch now quite a town with 50 or 60 houses, electric lights and water service.

In a recent interview with Mrs. Tom King of Sheridan, she related as follows: "you see old Dietz 7 was Higby and my folks lived there—my folks' name was Wondra—Frank Wondra, and they knew this family that had Monarch—Monarch was their farm. My Mother helped make the deal to sell this land out at Monarch—it wasn't classed as Monarch then—just Dombrowski's farm, and she used to bring cream, butter and milk to my Mother at Dietz, and she couldn't speak very good English and of course, my Mother, through the Superintendent—my sister worked—she did house work for them, and it was through them that they bought this property at Monarch, and she said "you ask these Dombrowskis' what they want." So they wanted $300.00 and so he well agreed—he was a smart man—he knew there was coal there and said, "I would have given her 10 times that much had I known it," after they signed the papers. The Superintendent of the mine at Dietz—it seemed to me it was Kennedy—it was Mr. Kennedy." Then Tom King spoke up saying, "It was the second mine the land where the mine went into the red shale—that was the mine there—all that land along that river and all this Dombrowski (about 1905—Mrs. King was just a little kid, born in Gebo, Montana.)"

1/15/07 *(Post)*—"New Coal Company Incorporated. To be known as Monarch Coal Mining Co. Capital $100,000. Practically all local Wyoming men. Articles filed in Secretary of State at Cheyenne, Jan. 5, 1907. Life, 50 years. Officers elected Monday p.m. at meeting. J. R. Kendrick, Pres., L. H. Brooks, V. P.; Wm. C. Ervine, Sec.-Treas.; and Stewart Kennedy, Superintendent. Object: To own, develop and operate coal production. Located on the Backman ranch adjoining the present town of Monarch. Operations to begin as soon as possible. Mr. Stewart Kennedy, Mgr. who came to the area in 1898 and during five years as Manager at Dietz successfully developed that operation. In 1903, he was instrumental in organizing the Wyoming Coal Company as Superintendent assisted in opening the present extensive mines at Monarch. In 1905 he went to Douglas where he opened and developed the Big Muddy Mine. His knowledge is very valuable."

3/1/07 *(Post)*—"Crushed Between Cars. Accident in Monarch resulted in death to August Haine. Wednesday morning while moving empty cars and crushed to death between two cars. How the accident occurred no one could quite understand as the area was level. Head crushed until brains oozed out of skull. Burial O. J. Smith. Large funeral in Sheridan.

Very early view of Monarch, Wyoming, also mine tipple and power house.

Monarch No. 1 tipple.

In the May 1, 1908 issue of the *Enterprise*, Mrs. D. H. Warner, in an article about the Mines, writes of Monarch as follows: "The Camps of Monarch and Carneyville lie about nine and one-half miles from Sheridan, and each has a population of about 1,000 people. The Monarch mines were opened about five years ago, and for a single opening has been the best producer in the district. As high as 2,250 tons of coal have been put over one tipple in one day.

The Monarch mines employ in normal times about 450 men, and the monthly payroll amounts to about $30,000. During the past six months the Wyoming Coal Mining Company has

Early Monarch.

expended close on to $20,000 in putting in new equipment, such as a 3,000 ton steel tipple, new power plant, additional dwellings, etc. With this new equipment the company expects to double its present output for the next season's business."

1/19/09—(MONARCH)—"J. E. Stout is expected from Cheyenne, Tuesday.

A special train bearing a large crowd of enthusiastic lovers of the pugilistic game came out from Sheridan and Dietz Saturday evening to attend the Berry-Griffo sparring match. The hall was filled to its utmost capacity. After a preliminary between local men, the main event of the evening, a fifteen-round contest between Chas. Berry of Monarch and young Griffo of Dietz was pulled off and resulted in a draw.

The social given at the hall Friday evening by the Junior Ladies' Aid was a very pleasant affair. The young people also gave a dance at the close of the evening's entertainment which was well attended.

The regular band practices are on Tuesday, Wednesday and Friday evenings at the gymnasium. It is requested that each member be present at each and every practice.

A contribution to the Italian earthquake fund from this school that came in too late to be

sent in with last Thursday's remittance was 25 cents from little Luella Birkhaeuser. This makes $7.76 from the Monarch school to the Italian relief fund.

Wm. Seers and Chas. Roberts from Banner were visiting relatives in this city. Among the visitors to Sheridan from this city Monday were Misses Gladys Birkhaeuser, Hazel Leonard and Mr. and Mrs. Harry Harris.

Mr. and Mrs. M. C. Bowman drove to Sheridan Saturday."

3/16/09—"A GOOD POWER PLANT." "IS IN OPERATION AT THE COAL MINING TOWN OF MONARCH—Is in Charge of Charles Wilkin and a Force Carefully Selected, Experienced Men—Coal Mining Company Has Also a Good Lighting Plant."

"The power and lighting plant of the Wyoming Coal Mining Company is one of the best arranged and equipped of its kind. The efficiency and excellent working condition of this magnificent plant is in the main due to Master Mechanic Charles Wilkin and his force of carefully selected and experienced men.

Mr. Wilkin has been at the head of this plant since coming here nearly four years ago. He superintended the erection of the present commodious brick power house and has ever been on the lookout for any improvement that would further the efficiency of this very important factor in the successful mining of coal. Mr. Wilkin, before coming here, was chief engineer of the Deadwood electric lighting plant at Deadwood, S.D., and Mr. Birkhaeuser has proven himself to be a person of excellent judgment in selecting as superintendent of the motive power of his mine a man of Mr. Wilkin's calibre.

The present engineers of the plant are Leroy Lynn, who came here from Cambria, having occupied a similar position in that mine. He has held his present position two years. M. L. McColgan, a young man who had held a position in the Burlington train service as engineer for several years before coming here nearly three years ago, and Harry Harris, who received his training as an engineman on the Missouri & Pacific railroad at Pueblo, Colo., and is now entering on his second year's service for the Wyoming Coal Mining Company. The firemen are Louis Murtz, Charles Weigand, Samuel Young and James Quigley, who are all sober and industrious young men and have had careful training in their particular work. The building contains boiler, engine, machine and store room. In the boiler room there are three Kenny upright water tube boilers of 250 horsepower each, and having each a steam pressure of 140 feet per square inch; one fifteen horsepower Kenney open heater; two duplex boiler feed pumps, and one waterworks pump of the capacity of 35,000 gallons of water per hour and fitted up so that a direct pressure of 180 pounds per square inch can be put on city mains in case of fire.

The large engine room contains one 500-horsepower twin haulage engine. These engines will haul a load of 75 tons from the mine at eighteen miles per hour on a 6 per cent grade. Air is furnished to ten puncher-cutter machines and four pumps in the mine by two Norwalk compressors, one of 200 horsepower and another of 80 horsepower. These machines furnish 1800 cubic feet of air per minute and have a pressure of 80 pounds to the square inch.

In the electric room there is one 175-horsepower Westinghouse engine, and a 60 kw. alternate furnishing light for the mines, office, store, tipples and the town.

All steam, air and water pipes are hung overhead. The power for running the machinery at the tipples is located across the river near the tipples and consists of two tubular boilers of 100 horsepower each, open heaters, a Duplex boiler feed pump and two engines of 75 horsepower each.

The shaft is equipped with Twin 14x16 geared hoisting engine with a lifting capacity of 9000 pounds, and the steam for these engines is furnished from the main power plant. Steam from the main power plant is also driven through steam pipes to the fan house in which there is a fan 4x16 feet.

The machine shop contains one large drill, one sharpener, one power saw, and a number of power pipe machines.

The store room located in the southeast corner of the building is 30x30 feet, and contains a ten thousand dollar stock of supplies needed for coal mining purposes. This store room is in charge of Charles Parker. The plant employs only union labor, and the men work in three shifts of eight hours each. The machinery of power plant of the Wyoming Coal Mining Company is in first class condition and reflects credit to Manager Birkhaeuser, Master Mechanic Wilkin, and his excellent corps of men."

6/4/09—"The section house, which stood at Alger, a mile east of Carneyville, has been moved to Monarch and now stands near the scale house east of the tipple.

The foundation for the depot which is being moved from Carneyville, is also completed and soon Monarch people will no longer be compelled to walk a mile over a dangerous road to catch a train. The large storage yards at this place necessitated the removal of the depot to Monarch."

12/25/09—"ROYAL DAY FOR MONARCH'S "KIDS"—"EVERY CHILD IN CAMP GIVEN A CHRISTMAS GIFT BY THE COMPANY—PROGRAM IS ALSO HELD—Little Ones Render Songs and Recital for Entertainment of Camp's Residents."

"Children at Monarch mining camp had a royal Christmas day. Every juvenile in the town gloried in a gift presented by the Wyoming Coal Mining Company, including dolls, skates, sleds and toys of practically every description.

The presentation of the gifts was made at a gathering Christmas eve, in the school house. Nearly every employe of the company was present. The auditorium had been tastefully decorated by C. H. Wilken, master mechanic of the company. Electric lights of various colors were placed around the room and the Christmas tree was likewise decorated with lights.

Santa Claus was impersonated by Walter Trenkamp and the children and adults were kept in a continual uproar by his antics. An appropriate speech was made by Mr. Trenkamp, thanking Mr. and Mrs. E. M. Holbrook for the remembrances and Christmas greetings were sent both of them and to Mr. and Mrs. W. G. Birkhaeuser.

An excellent program of recitations and songs in keeping with the season was given by the children. The program was prepared by Mrs. Harry Valleau."

3/11/10—"TESTIMONY OF POLE PUTS CRIMP IN MACHINERY OF DISTRICT COURT—Court Reporter is Prostrated by Gutteral Expressions and Jarzyk Goes Free on Liquor Charge."

The case against Joseph Jarzyk of Monarch, charged with selling liquor contrary to law, was dismissed by County Attorney Kutcher today. The defendant is a Pole and the prosecuting witness was of the same nationality. No interpreter was available.

The witness could not understand the lawyer's questions and the jury could not understand the witness. Court Reporter Kelly made a heroic effort to reduce the testimony to writing but even the outlandish pot hooks used by short hand reporters would not represent the language the witness used.

Most of the words sounded like a cross between a sneeze and a yell. Failing to make the jury understand, the witness began making signs with his hands and body, and Kelly quit in disgust.

County Attorney dismissed the case."

4/9/10—"TERSE TAKES FROM MONARCH (By W. E. Jones)

Mr. Arthur Morgan, district vice president of the miners, attended the local union meeting here Monday evening on business.

A representative of the *Miner and Minerals*, a monthly magazine published in connection with the Scranton correspondence schools, gathered in a number of subscribers here this week.

Mr. and Mrs. Henman were Sheridan visitors Tuesday.

The local lodge of Woodmen gave an elaborate and most enjoyable banquet and dance Wednesday evening to the members and their chosen friends.

Dick and Jack Magoon left this week for the Buffalo district where they will do ranch work during the summer.

The following Sheridan ladies were the pleasant guests of Mr. J. E. Stout on Thursday: Mesdames Arnold Tschirgi, A. E. Church, L. E. Martin and O. P. Benefiel.

Sheriff Benefiel was also here the same day, but on a different mission. He took to Sheridan as his guests the following "club" keepers gathered from the country surrounding Monarch. They were Mike Jakisch, Crooked Town; Jno. Stanko, near Monarch; Jno. Bury, near Carneyville; Dave Henderson, Acme; and Joe Kominski, near Kooi. How many more were gathered enroute to Sheridan the writer does not know but it is rumored that others were awaiting the automobile train. It might be remarked here that Charlie Berry's establishment, formerly termed "Company Saloon," because the building is owned by the Wyoming Coal Mining Co., is the only one actually closed. Mr. Berry left last Saturday for Milwaukee and his host of friends here wish him well.

Mr. Denis Kriskoll and daughter, Mrs. Gillen, visited Sheridan Saturday.

Mr. Charles Hayes and Miss Nellie Taylor, both of Monarch, were married at Sheridan on Tuesday. They returned the same evening and were treated to the usual rattle of tin cans by the younger folks. The happy young couple will make their home at the home of the groom's parents, Mr. and Mrs. Robert Hayes, where Charles is in charge of the ranch. Their numerous friends here, where both are well and favorably known, wish them a most prosperous and happy journey through life together.

Mr. Birkhaeuser is improving Holbrook street by moving some of the three-room houses to a side street and replacing them with substantial buildings.

Berkey avenue is taking on an entirely new appearance, the residents voluntarily planting trees in front and along the side of their respective homes, which beautifies the street and insures comfortable shade for the hot summer.

Wm. Broadwater and Jno. Evans drove over to Dietz Friday to visit the Johnsons, who it is said are expecting to leave this country in a few days.

Tom Allen, the company's mine engineer, had a hair raising experience with a hammerless shot gun Wednesday evening. He had been considerably annoyed by hobo cats and concluded to have peace even at the expense of war. So accordingly, he borrowed a neighbor's gun and after being shown its mechanism he proceeded to picket against the enemy. Almost instantly Mr. Cat posted himself on a fence post as if to dare the attacking party to open fire. Military-like Mr. Allen drew himself up into an English Square and bombarded. Tom Cat fell before the onslaught and Tom Allen proceeded to the house for more supplies. In breeching the gun, however, the remaining load discharged, tearing away a portion of the floor in the house. The government (Mrs. Allen) ordered the warrior to surrender arms at once and return the same to its owners. Of much preparation and thunderous threats there remains a wounded black cat and a wiser man.

Miss Hazel Leonard and Mrs. Jno. Goode, also Mr. and Mrs. Joe Pollard drove over to Sheridan Friday. Mr. and Mrs. Goode have just returned from Cody, where they have made their home for about two years. Mrs. Goode, we understand, will remain here with near relatives until her husband finds a new location.

Mrs. W. F. Long of Sheridan was calling on her many friends here Friday."

4/18/10—"MINER KILLED AT MONARCH BY HIS OWN CARELESSNESS—Unfortunate Man was Riding on Front End of Mine Car Contrary to Rules of the Company."

Geo. Ligerski, a driver, was instantly killed in the mine here Saturday evening at 6 o'clock. While hauling a loaded car from the main entry he somehow fell in front of it and was instantly crushed to death—" John Yalovitch discovered body. Horses still hitched to car. Deceased was about thirty-five years of age, a native of Austria Poland, and leaves a wife and three children to mourn his death in the old country. A sister, Mrs. Joe Golek, resides here. Burial will be in the Catholic cemetery in Carneyville.

6/21/10—"THE WYOMING COAL CO. MANAGERS MAKE CHILDREN OF CAMP HAPPY"

Two wagon loads of Monarch juvenile population were driven to Sheridan this morning. One wagon load contained twenty boys while the other had twenty girls.

They represented the Monarch Coal Mining Company who had furnished them with spending money, tickets to the circus this afternoon and had decorated the conveyances with pretty bunting.

This last feat of the Monarch Coal Company further evinces the interest they have in the welfare and pleasure of their young people.

Last Christmas the company held a Christmas tree and provided presents for every boy and girl in the camp. They also furnished a large flag which was placed on the school house flag pole, and further than this the company has endeavored to place the camp in as sanitary condition as possible.

Reciprocity has been resorted to by the younger people and they in turn have endeavored to keep the camp clean by their individual efforts and show their appreciation of the company's attitude toward them."

(The author, in his review of the Sheridan news media, must have missed any publicity which might have appeared about the mine explosion at the Monarch mine in January of 1911. It was presumed that the explosion was the result of an unusual accumulation of gas. Fortunately it occurred just before the miners entered the mine resulting in no loss of lives or injuries. The force of the explosion, however, was of such terrific proportions as to send some heavy steel mine rails flying through the air imbedding them endwise in the ground several hundred yards distant, and causing many openings to the surface, much of which is still in evidence in the form of cave holes.)

3/17/11—"MINING AT MONARCH"—WILL BEGIN DELIVERING COAL NEXT WEEK— ARE TO USE HORSES—And Gravity for the Present—Motor to Be in Operation Within a Week—Fire Shut Off"

"For the first time since the explosion which occurred during the last days of January, the Monarch mine will begin Monday, pulling coal, and within a short time will be ready to supply its many patrons with their favorite black diamonds. For a few days, horse power will be used to draw the coal from the mine, and the haulage from the slope to the tipple will be made by gravity, but before the end of the week an electric motor will be in operation and most of the horses will be shoved into the discard.

The haulage slope will be in what is known as "No. 70," which before the explosion was an airshaft and manway. The grade of this slope is not heavy and the loaded cars can be easily drawn out by horses. From the opening of the slope to the flat just above the tipple there is a continuous grade, down which the cars will be sent by gravity, while the empties will be taken back to the slope with horses.

Heavy walls will be constructed in the seventh and eighth west, forming effectual barriers between the old fire zone and the new workings. Back of the first walls, a distance of twenty or more feet, other walls have been built and the space between these walls has been filled with dirt, so that all danger either from fire or explosion from this source is eliminated.

About 75 miners will be employed, and by doubling the shift the output will be equal to that of 150 loaders, and from the start will probably run to 800 tons per day.

Saturday evening, after the day shift comes out, an exploring party will enter the mine and attempt to push its way down the ninth west toward the old slope. It is not the intention to again attempt to use this old slope, but much valuable machinery remains in the mine and a determined effort will be made to salvage it. If the conditions permit, it is also the intention to build other walls which will completely isolate the fire zone and put an end to all danger from that source for all time to come.

No exploring will be done while miners are at work and the management believes that the exploring party will be in but little if any danger.

The use of horses for hauling coal was made necessary by the delay in receiving wire to be used in electrifying the railway track. This wire is expected by the middle of next week, and it will require only a short time to string the wire, when the motor can at once be put in commission."

5/2/11—"LAST MOTOR RECOVERED." "EXPLORING PARTY ENTERS MONARCH MINE—MACHINERY SAVED." "All Property in Mine Will Be Saved—Coal Mined as Economically as Before Explosion."

"A party of twenty miners, led by foreman Thomas Allen and accompanied by State Mine Inspector W. E. Jones, entered the Monarch mine, Sunday night, salvaged a large amount of valuable wire and brought out the last of the four big electric motors that were in the mine at the time of the big explosion during the last days of January. The exploring party also fixed wooden brattices at the various room-nicks and cross-cuts along the main entry, until it is now deemed safe for workmen to push their way within a little more than 2,000 feet from the main entrance, permitting the removal of all machinery and material, and the greater part of the track.

The party entered at entry No. 70, from

which the mine is now being worked, the fan being located at 71, where it exhausts the air. The men pushed their way through cross-cuts to entry No. 11 west. From there they went down the 11th west to the main entry.

Progress was now very slow, as it was necessary to close all the side openings in order that the air might follow the men. The copper wire was in the 10th entry. This wire was 1,800 feet long and about an inch in diameter, and it had to be removed before the 10th could be cut off. A half day was spent in removing this wire.—" (There was more description of the recovery of materials but in such detail as to be deleted at this time. There was one observation described in this article, however, relating to the merits of the acetylene lamp which evidently was beginning to replace the old oil burning lamp and which follows: "I made one discovery (reporter's observations), or rather, I had the opportunity to practically demonstrate a theory, that may prove of considerable benefit in the exploration of mines in the future. I discovered that an acetylene lamp is a reasonably safe guide when black damp is encountered).

In a recent number of a miner's journal I notice that the chief mine inspector of Ohio has condemned the acetylene lamp, probably for the reason that he believed it not a safe guide as to black damp—that it would burn in the air where a man would not live, the same as an electric light.

I found that this contention does not hold good in Wyoming mines. I had an oil lamp and some of the miners had acetylene. When we encountered black damp, my light went out, though the acetylene lamps continued to burn. Presently the damp became so thick that the acetylene lamp expired, but still we had not the slightest difficulty in breathing. I am therefore convinced that the acetylene lamp is a perfectly safe guide when working in black damp, for it will go out long before the gas becomes dangerous to a human being."

7/25/11—"The Wyoming Coal Mining Company is gradually getting its operations in better and more convenient shape." Damages caused by explosion now essentially repaired with "output running at about a thousand tons a day, brought to the tipple by motors from the new opening on the hill below the Birkhaeuser residence.—"

2/21/12—"MINER IS ALMOST FROZEN TO DEATH—George Sikora, Walking Between

Monarch and Dietz, Falls by Wayside With Temperature Six Below Zero."

Miner rode on interurban from Sheridan as far as Dietz, then began to walk to Monarch from there—recovered altho nearly frozen. Lost his toes.

9/10/12—"YOUNG SCHOOLMA'M AROUSES THE COUNTRY.—Gets Lost on Way to Commence Her Term But Finally Gets to the Right Place."

While trying to reach her school assignment on Ash Creek, seven miles northwest of Monarch, Miss Nancy McClelland, a 16 year old school mistress of Sheridan, became lost Sunday night, and in company with her driver, Stanley Patz of the coal mining camp, wandered over unrecognizable roads in the darkness and rain, until they reached Smith Creek, north of Dayton and fifteen miles from their desired destination. They were given shelter at a farm house for the remaining few hours of the night and were then directed on the right road back to Alger—."

10/11/12—"W. G. Birkhaeuser, President of Coal Company—Succeeds the late E. M. Holbrook as the Head of the Monarch Corporation—"

4/7/13—"POST REPRESENTATIVES VISIT THE SHERIDAN COUNTY MINES." "MONARCH MINES OBJECT OF INSPECTION WEDNESDAY—TONS BY THE THOUSAND—Great Importance to Sheridan of Vast Coal Mines Situated North of the City."

"Appreciating the importance to Sheridan of the coal camps situated to the north of the city, two representatives of the Post, on the day after election, started out on a junketing trip over the interurban line, their intention being to visit several of the camps, and learn something of the work going on and the way it is done. Their calculations missed fire in one important particular. The were able to visit but one camp and were reluctant to leave that one when the time at their disposal was more than consumed.

Leaving Sheridan at noon, the seekers after knowledge went straight to Monarch, the home of the Wyoming Coal Mining company. Monarch is reached by the Sheridan Railway company's lines, and, in fact, the terminus of the line at present. Monarch is not, however, the last camp on the line, as Kooi lies still farther out, being reached by wagon road from the sister camp. It is a large and important place and The Post junketeers plan to visit it at another time. One

thing they learned on the first trip is that but one camp can be "done" at a time, and that they are all worth the time devoted to them.

Reaching Monarch

Reaching Monarch by the interurban, after riding 30 cents worth, one steps out at a neat little station and takes a footpath from there to the town. The footpath leads first to the store of the Monarch Trading company, and to the office of the Wyoming Coal Mining company. Going to either of those places, the visitor is directed to the home of W. G. Birkhaeuser, president of the company.

Mr. Birkhaeuser has fitted up a delightful home in the outskirts of of Monarch, where he lives with his brother in "bachelor hall." He enjoys a reputation as a host which could be well understood by the Post men after partaking of his delightful hospitality. Although they walked in almost unannounced, had never intimated that they were going to visit him, Mr. Birkhaeuser met them at the door and placed his time and his home at their disposal. After freely answering their scores of questions, he gave them the treat of their lives, taking them through the mine and over the tipple, carefully and fully explaining every process of coal mining.

Sharing Big Business

The Wyoming Coal Mining company is sharing in the big business of the northern Wyoming camps to the fullest extent. The company is now 400 cars behind with its orders and is falling farther behind rather than catching up with them. This in spite of the large daily yield of the mine and the feverish activities of all connected with it.

Nearly four hundred men are now employed in the mine at Monarch and the number is to be increased, according to President Birkhaeuser. These men are divided into two shifts, each working eight hours out of every twenty-four. They are bringing out from the mine between 2,500 and 3,000 tons of coal per day. Were the mine working at full capacity this yield could be increased to 4,000 tons daily.

The Monarch mine, in common with the others of the Sheridan group, was handicapped by the sudden rush of business which came this fall. This rush was due to three things: The warm summer followed by severe fall weather, the agitation of coal rate questions, and the strike in Colorado. The latter is the least important to the Sheridan county mines. The warm summer made dealers dilatory in ordering coal. They also held off in hopes of lower rates on coal. So the cool weather found them with no coal in stock but eager to get it.

Effect of Strike

The strike in Colorado has increased business here but slightly over what it would have been. The only coal being shipped from Sheridan county to make up the shortage from Colorado is to the Burlington road. No commercial business whatever in the district usually supplied by the Colorado mines is being taken by the mines here. Business would have been practically the same had there been no strike in Colorado this fall.

The coal being taken out at Monarch is loaded directly into cars at the Burlington main line and shipped out each day. Mr. Birkhaeuser speaks very highly of the manner in which the Burlington has handled the situation. His company has been supplied with cars at all times, there have been no delays in handling them and everything has gone along smoothly despite the fact that a bigger business was never known on this division.

The miners employed at Monarch are paid every two weeks and the gross payroll last month amounted to more than $38,000. This month it will be larger, reaching at least $41,000, and probably a higher figure, practically all of it is paid the men in cash, the exception being small reservations for union dues, hospital fund, and other incidentals.

The men employed at Monarch all live there, the majority of them in homes furnished by the company. The houses are warm and comfortable and are lighted and heated by the company. No limits are put upon either electricity or coal used. The town has its own water system. There is a good school in the town employing three teachers and the men are discouraged from sending their boys into the mine until they have finished school.

Description of Work

It is quite likely that coal mining is more familiar to many of the Post's readers than to the writer, even after he has visited the Monarch mine. But a brief description of the work may prove interesting.

The mine at Monarch is fully a mile from the tipple, the latter being at the railroad. The two are connected by an electric trolley line over which the mine cars are hauled by motors. The mine cars have a capacity of three or four tons each and from twenty to forty of them are brought in at one time. One pair of motor engines operates between the mine and the tipple, another pair brings the cars out of the mine.

The mine enters the coal vein almost at the surface and follows the bottom line of the vein as it dips into the earth. The vein itself is from thirty-two to thirty-four feet in thickness and covers the entire property of the coal company. Another vein equally thick is a few feet below the first. The second vein has not been touched; the first has been barely opened up.

In the working chambers of the mine, the coal is undercut by a large machine, then brought down by two or three shots put in near the top. It is loaded on the cars by hand, the miners being paid by the number of tons loaded. As soon as a car is loaded, a team is attached and the car jerked out of the way. Eight or nine of them are coupled together, then the motor takes them to the surface.

Veins Dip Sharply

The vein where the miners are now working dips sharply and the grade is, consequently, very heavy. That makes the work of both teams and motors very hard and a cable system which will relieve them is an improvement contemplated for the near future.

No props are used in the Monarch mine, the coal being so solid that roof and sides are like stone walls. This makes the mine much less expensive, and leaves the coal more accessible. Not half the thickness of the vein is being taken out now, but when the lower half has been exhausted, the dividing walls will be knocked out and the overhead coal will fall and can be easily taken out. The mine is lighted electrically, well ventilated and dry.

When the loaded cars reach the surface they are seized by the motors waiting there and rushed to the tipple. There, each car is weighed and credited to the miner whose tag is attached. The coal is dumped automatically upon an endless elevator and carried to the top of the tipple. There it is dropped into the bins and sorted. The different classes of coal, lump, egg, nut, slack, and mine run are separated and issue from different tipples, falling directly into the cars. Seven or eight cars can be loaded at one time and it takes but a few minutes to fill a forty or fifty-ton car. The coal is then ready to be transported over the railroad hundreds of miles to turn the wheels of industry in hundreds of towns and warm the homes of thousands of people in all parts of the Trans-Mississippi territory.

A visit to a coal mine is much more interesting than it sounds when written down. None of the romance, nothing of the rush and hurry, the seeming confusion, which is really orderly haste, can be gotten into the confines of a newspaper article. The technical part of the business must necessarily be passed over. Our advice to Sheridan people is to visit one of the mines themselves and see with their own eyes what is going on.

The visit to Monarch is the first of several which The Post men hope to make within the next few weeks. Before this series is ended we expect to tell you something of the work at each of the half dozen coal camps within a dozen miles of Sheridan."

6/8/14 "THOSE BANDS WERE GOOD—MUSIC DID MUCH TO MAKE STAMPEDE SUCCESS—Monarch Aggregation Comes in For Large Share of General Praise."

"Nothing added more to the festivity and joy of Stampede days in Sheridan last week than the music of the two excellent bands which were always on the job, working practically night and day for the—amusement of the crowds."

"—A local man who has been closely connected with bands, and a player in several for twenty years, remarked that he had never, in all his life, seen a band play on a continuous march as long as the Monarch band did. Commencing to play at the bridge on North Main, the band marched up Main and around the Great Western hotel. By the Congregational church it stopped for the first time but only long enough to change music. Then, still playing, the band marched down Main to Grinnell, down Grinnell to Broadway to the Sheridan Inn. There the band halted but the music continued until the long parade had marched entirely by.

—The Monarch band has been in existence only about eleven months. A number of Polish boys at the Monarch camp had some cheap instruments which they had bought from a mail order house and were wont to play a little around the camp, although most of them could not read a note of music. At the request of a few friends, Prof. John Sanderson Joyce, advised the boys to form a band and get better instruments. Thru the assistance of Decker-Cummings Music Company the boys did secure first-class instruments. After they got so they could play a little, they decided to secure uniforms.

Mr. Pollock, manager of the Wyoming Coal Mining Company, told them it was the best

Monarch and Kooi bands.

thing they could do, and made a donation of $100 toward the cost of the uniforms. He also fitted up a band room in which to practice and has encouraged the boys in every possible way. Mr. Kooi, of Kooi, was also interested in the Monarch band and gave them several donations, the last being $40 for the uniforms. Decker Cummings donated $20.

Several of the band members cannot speak a word of English and Prof. Joyce frequently, in explaining and teaching, has to make use of an interpreter. Mr. Joyce is very proud of his band, as he has a right to be, and the Monarch camp is in turn proud of both Mr. Joyce and the band.

Several Sheridan people remarked upon the presence of George W. Messick with the band, acting as drummer during the three Stampede Days. When the band arrived in Sheridan, it was without a drummer and Mr. Messick volunteered his services, leaving his business for three days, and donated his work to help out on the celebration."

8/29/14—"Teachers Assigned For New School Year. Mrs. Amy G. Hendy, Prin.; Mrs. Blanch A. Rice, Inter.; Elsie Schoubel, Primary; 3 schools. 10/7/13—Attendance, 31, 17 and 15."

8/10/15—"Many Improvements To Be Made by the Monarch Coal Company During the Month.

Improvements to Tipple With Improved Screening System—Name of Company changed from Wyoming Coal Mining Company to Monarch Coal Company. Company had been in receivership for several months, presumed due to 1911 explosion, but now refinanced. M. F. Pettier of Chicago, President; Granger Farwell, Chicago, Chairman of the Board and Treasurer; and A. G. Lester, Chicago, Secretary. Resident officers, A. W. Pollock, Vice-President and General Manager and E. L. Waddell, Cashier."

3/12/18—(Post)—"License Revoked."

"John Hezko, a baker at Monarch, has the unsought distinction of being the first in the state to have his license revoked. Action to this effect was taken yesterday and his place of business ordered closed, Wednesday, March 13. The Home Bakery of Laramie was closed because it was doing business without proper license, but the Monarch baker is the first in the state to have his license revoked.

The charge against Hezko is that he was not using sufficient flour substitutes in his bread. The regulations require not less than 20 percent of substitutes which may consist either of corn meal, rye, rice flour, potato flour or potatoes."

7/25/19—(CAMP GLEANINGS—Mrs. George Kovacic). Monarch, Wyo.—Oct. 14, 1919.

"Mr. and Mrs. Oris Bassett and children of Parkman spent the weekend at the home of the former's sister, Mrs. A. Marshall of Carneyville.

Mr. and Mrs. Walter Upton of Carneyville entertained at luncheon Sunday in honor of their house guest, Mr. and Mrs. J. G. Stevens of Salina, Kansas. The following guests were present:—Mr. and Mrs. S. Stevens, Mrs. Phil Morgan and daughter, Selina of Acme, and Miss Mazie Joyce of Kooi.

Mrs. Joe Littler, Jr. of Monarch was a Sheridan visitor Monday, on a shopping expedition.

Mrs. May Brown of Sheridan journied to Model via Interurban Monday evening where she will take charge of little Patricia McGee, during her mothers absence as she is leaving for Thermopolis in search of better health at the springs for a few weeks.

Mrs. Fred Garrett and little daughter of Acme were pleasant visitors in Sheridan Monday.

Mr. and Mrs. Frank Mazie of Monarch were business callers in Sheridan Monday.

Mrs. J. Novicki of Dietz was a Sheridan caller Monday on a shopping tour.

Troy Wade the popular entertainer of Monarch will have roller skating every Sunday afternoon from 1:30 to 4:30 at the Monarch Amusement hall. Special music will be rendered during the afternoon.

Mr. and Mrs. Oric Bassett and children in company with Mrs. E. Turner and Mrs. Marshall of Carneyville journeyed to Sheridan Monday via auto to attend to a few errands.

Mr. and Mrs. Frank Welch of Monarch entertained at luncheon Sunday, Rev. T. J. Schultz of Dietz being the guest of honor.

E. F. Alexander and daughter, Miss Dora, of Monarch, attended morning services at the Christian Church in Sheridan, Mrs. R. P. Fitch and son, Junior, also attended services there.

Mrs. N. Scullen and daughter, Miss Margaret, with B. H. McCarty of Sheridan, were visitors Sunday at the home of Mr. and Mrs. Frank Welch of Monarch.

Misses Julia and Annie Mentock and Rosie Kuzara of Dietz were luncheon guests Sunday of Miss Marie Patricia Kovacic of Monarch."

Miss Mary Baker of Dietz No. 8, was a

pleasant visitor Sunday at the home of Mr. and Mrs. George Kovacic on Grove St.

Miss Anna Sieczkowski of Kooi, returned to Sheridan Sunday evening after spending the weekend with her parents. Miss Anna is attending the high school in Sheridan.

C. B. Seymour of the Carney Coal company states his company in receipt of many requests. Prices of available coal now $6.50 to $7.00 per ton."

As a result of this strike, the shortage of coal became so acute that the then Governor of

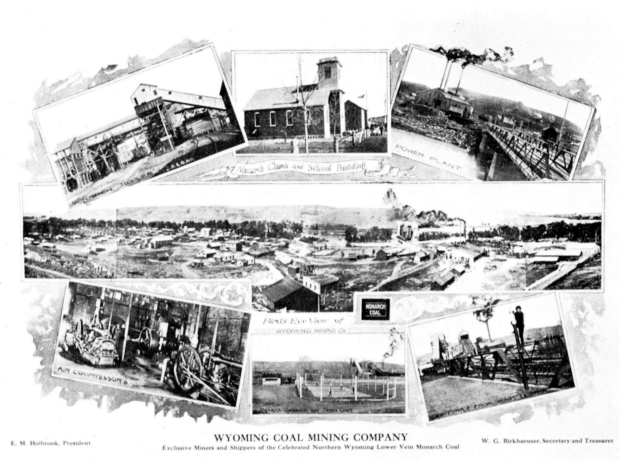

E. M. Holbrook, President   **WYOMING COAL MINING COMPANY**   W. G. Birkhaeuser, Secretary and Treasurer
Exclusive Miners and Shippers of the Celebrated Northern Wyoming Lower Vein Monarch Coal

Scenes at Monarch, Wyoming taken about 1910. (Boy on pole in lower right picture was Johnny Barbula who passed away in 1919 and was buried in the Carneyville Cemetery).

11/1/19—"Coal Strike In Effect Nationally and Locally. People warned for several weeks to stock up on coal in anticipation—no trouble locally, according to James Rennie, Pres. of the Sheridan County Trades and Labor Council— stated, however, that coal would be furnished to the electric light plant. Farmers of the Parkman area dig their own coal from a vein opened on Six Mile."

11/6/19—"Appeal For Coal Is Being Heard. Cry Comes From Other Cities. Many Families With Empty Coal Bins.

Wyoming, Governor Carey, called out the National Guard at Sheridan in an attempt to end the strike. The publicity of the events which followed are described in detail in another chapter of this book, "The Mines," inasmuch as it affected the three camps, Carneyville, Monarch and Kooi. However, what happened at the Monarch camp is described by one of the miners of Monarch who resided in that camp. His story follows: "Yes, it was during the World War I—in 1919. They came to the house (the national guardsmen)—got us all out—herded us down the street like cattle, with bayonets ready like soldiers—scooped us all up into the pool hall—like to suffocate with the smoke and so on. If you had to go outside to the "John," why, of course, you had to have a soldier take you out there and bring you back in as if you was a criminal. They had cannon setting down in front of the Monarch store—had the nurses—Red Cross nurses or what the hell they was supposed to be. I never will forget that. I can remember the officers of the Union fled to the hills or something, but anyway they got my Dad to be the spokesman for the outfit and he put it to a vote if they wanted to go to work, or if they didn't want to go to work, and they voted that they would go back to work—nothing, just go back to work—I don't know all the details—it was kind'a confusing but at the same time, we was jibing at the soldiers, but I remember that plain. There was some of the guys was herded around like cattle—put in box cars and took them to Sheridan to the fort—that was mostly the foreign element. Yeah, there were soldiers at that time—Ft. Mackenzie was."

Another miner who worked at Dietz stated, "I was on strike too at Dietz. You know, they loaded a bunch of fellows and locked 'em up at the fort—a bunch of coal miners—Monarch and Carney. You see, Carney and Monarch are just about a half mile apart—practically the same camp only a different name. I know they loaded a bunch of them from Carney and Monarch in box cars and brought them to near the old elevator then shipped them on up to the fort. I said, "They're not going to lock me up there." I went up in the hills, I had my gun hunting rabbits until it was all over with."

11/25/19—"CAMP BREEZES—Mrs. George Kovacic, Monarch, Nov. 24, 1919.

To celebrate Thanksgiving Day "services are being held at all places of worship, and in the St. Thomas Catholic church at Carneyville services will be held at 11 o'clock a.m. There will be special music for the occasion and people of any denomination may attend as a hearty welcome is extended to all.

Mr. and Mrs. W. C. Calhoun of Model were pleasant callers Sunday afternoon at the home of the latter's cousin, Mrs. J. E. Aminerman. Mrs. Calhoun came up to bid them goodbye as she is going on an extended visit to her parents who reside at Raritan, Ill.

Mrs. H. McLeod in company with her children, Ella and Jack, of Acme journeyed to Sheridan Saturday to attend to shopping errands.

Mesdames D. L. Glen and Walter Upton of Carneyville journeyed to Sheridan Saturday to attend to a few shopping wants.

Mr. and Mrs. E. G. Montgomery of Monarch were in Sheridan Saturday.

Miss Lena Lampert of Sheridan spent the week-end at the home of her parents.

J. K. Birkhaeuser of Monarch journeyed to Sheridan where he spent the week-end at the home of his mother.

John Davis of Monarch was in Sheridan Saturday on business errands.

Mr. and Mrs. Billy Wondra and daughter, Miss Gladys, of Monarch, were Sheridan visitors Saturday on a shopping tour.

Mrs. E. J. Keniston of Dietz mingled with Sheridan shoppers Saturday afternoon.

Mrs. G. W. Street and daughter, Miss Wilma, were Sheridan callers on Saturday at the home of her mother, Mrs. Rogers.

Troy Wade of Monarch is giving his patrons a treat this week by showing the photoplay of the "End of a Game" Tuesday night, also a Harold Lloyd comedy, Roller skating on Thursday, another episode of the "Lightning Raider," and a dance.

8/27/20—"Clem Benedict died as result of injuries sustained when he fell from a boiler and landed on his head."

1/21/22—Post—(CAMP BREEZES—Mrs. May Kovacic. Monarch, Jan. 19.—A very pretty ceremony occurred at the Christian Church parsonage of Sheridan Wednesday afternoon, when Rev. Clark joined Miss Rose Claribel Wondra, and Thomas Harvey King, both of this place, in the holy bonds of matrimony. The bride was charmingly gowned in a beautiful creation of pink georgette and carried a shower bouquet of roses and ferns. She was attended by her sister, Miss Mary, and Mr. and Mrs. John King were the witnesses. After the ceremony they all boarded the six o'clock interurban to escape their friends, who had plentifully supplied themselves with rice. They must have forgotten that the interurban stops at Dietz to throw the switch. So while the car was at a standstill in came a shower of rice for a minute it looked like a miniature hail storm. Word was sent to Monarch that the bride and groom were coming on the interurban. There they were met by a charivari party who escorted them to the home of Mr. and Mrs. Frank Wondra, Sr., where a most tempting dinner was served. The centerpiece was the bride's bouquet. The bride is the youngest daughter of Mr. and Mrs. Wondra. They are residents of this place of a good many years standing. Mrs. King is a very charming and accomplished young lady. Thomas Harvey King is the youngest son of Mr. and Mrs. John King. He has quite a reputation for being a splendid baseball player. Both young folks are well known and quite popular. They will make Monarch their home for a while. The best of wishes is extended them by their numerous friends as well as from ye scribe.

Mrs. J. L. Decker of Montana who had been spending the Xmas vacation with her parents, Mr. and Mrs. G. Orth of Acme, received a visit from his "storkship" who presented her with a bouncing baby girl on January the eighth. All concerned doing nicely.

Mrs. J. Allen and daughter Miss Ells, Mr. and Mrs. Ridley of Sheridan attended the home talent play given at Acme last Saturday."

2/19/22—"AMERICANIZATION CLASS AT MONARCH."

"The first meeting of the newly organized Americanization class for foreign-born men and women of Kleenburn, Monarch and Model will be held Tuesday evening at 6:30 at the Monarch school house, under the direction of Mrs. Bertha T. Peterson, principal at Monarch and Mrs. Alice Whitmire, principal at Kleenburn. The class has been organized under the direction of James R. Coxen of Cheyenne, state director of vocational education, through the agency of the county superintendent of the school boards.

Four meetings of the Americanization class for Sheridan foreign-born men and women have been held at the John S. Taylor school. This class which is conducted the direction of J. J. Marshall, principal of the high school, and Mrs. Hazel Barnes, first grade teacher at the Central school, meets Tuesday and Thursday evenings of each week. Of the 43 students enrolled, the following nationalities are represented: Hungarian, Sherbian, Germany, Bulgarian, Scotch, Swede, Bohemian, Greek, Finlander, Italians, Russians, Slaviks and Polish."

3/19/22—"MONARCH MAN AND YOUNG DAUGHTER TO BE REUNITED."

"Through the efforts of E. Gillette of Sheri-

dan, now on an extended visit in the east, Joseph Kulcsar of Monarch and his thirteen year-old-daughter, Vilma Kulscar, who arrived last week at New York City from Hungary, tagged for Monarch, New York, will be reunited next week—and a joyful reunion it will be.

An announcement appeared in the New York Sun, March 12 that the little girl had arrived in New York from Hungary, after a three months journey alone only to find that her tag was for Monarch, New York, and as there was no such place, she had been sent to the Travellers Aid Society. Mr. Gillette promptly phoned the society suggesting that Monarch, Wyoming be tried, and the result is given in the following clipping from the March 13th issue of the *New York Sun* under the caption "Wrongly Tagged Hungarian Girl Belongs to Wyoming."

Vilma Kulcsar, the thirteen-year-old child who arrived recently from Hungary after traveling for nearly three months alone, only to find that she was tagged for a place which did not exist, today is waiting the letter with the ticket which will carry her on the last lap of the journey to Monarch, Wyoming.

After the story of Vilma's plight came out in *The Sun* Friday, some person telephoned the Travellers' Aid Society, where the child is being cared for, that there was known to be quite a settlement of Hungarians in Monarch, Wyoming. Vilma's tag bore the name Monarch, N.Y. A telegram to the Western town brought an immediate reply from the child's father, Joseph Kulcsar, with the information that he was sending a ticket for her."

7/2/24—"Mike Bujok, Miner of Monarch, Dead After Coal Falls—Bujok, loading coal into pit car when loose chunk fell and rolled on leg—leg amputated, but died from shock. Survived by wife Susie, two daughters, Mary and Mrs. Eva Drobish, and two sons, Paul and John."

12/3/24—"Monarch Miner Died Here After Cave-in at Mine. Paul Herman, President of District 16 Years, Crushed to Death. Wife and 5 children in Bohemia."

7/19/25—"Coal Miner at Monarch Breaks Two Ribs When Crushed Against Wall of Tunnel—Bob McClain, a loader, was letting one empty car down into the mine when the brake of the second one slipped and caught him—etc."

Monument in Monarch cemetery placed there in 1923 designating it as a Lutheran cemetery. Inscription reads: "The Evangelical Lutheran Cemetery of Monarch 1923 'I am the resurrection and the Life.' "

Monarch, Wyoming cemetery 10/26/74, Company store, "Tongue River Trading Company," Mine office, water tank and powder house in distance, south across valley. Monarch, Wyoming cemetery burials identified by markers, as follows: JOHN DRONIC June 5-July 17, 1912; MARY DRONIC Aug. 13-Sept. 6, 1918; SUSIEN DRONIC Oct. 4, 1913-Oct. 31, 1918; SUSIE, wife of JOHN SAMETZ FROM MONARCH born March 26, 1905, died Aug. 21, 1921; MIKE BUYOK (2 burials names not legible); ANDREW SHASSETZ 1883-1925; JOHN NIEMCZYK 1873-1933; Julia P. Sturtz June 9, 1926, May 18, 1928; Hilma S. 1886-1923, KASVI H.S. 1914-1921 LATI; ROSIE WANTULOK, Mary 7, 1923-Jan. 26, 1926; TU ODPOCZYWA DZIECIE SUSIE KAWULOK June 11, 1917-Sept. 23, 1917; MARTHA WANDA WASHUT born Mar. 1920, died July 1920; ANNA CIESLAR, born June 2, 1919, died Oct. 20, 1921. In another spot about 50 feet from the above-enclosed area is a single grave overlooking the valley: GEORGE GILROY July 4, 1893-Oct. 2, 1909. Several graves have deteriorated, have sunken and have no markers.

10/5/25—"Monarch Miner is Victim of Fatal Accident Sunday on Hiway North of Sheridan. Andrew Shassetz, Father of Eight Children is Dead. Woman Thrown From Car."

10/8/25—"One of the first funerals to be held in the Monarch Church was that of George Mehalek. Father Szymanski officiated."

(It was reported that William F. Barbula and his partner, John Yorio, sometime about in the year 1926, together loaded 26 cars (52 tons) of coal in one eight hour shift, thereby setting a record which, as far as they knew, had never been broken at the Monarch mine. They were, at that time, paid 88½ cents per ton).

2/16/26—"Monarch Athletic Club Stages Fast Tourney Monday."

"The Monarch Athletic Club's first boxing and wrestling tourney, staged at the Merriburg pavilion, Monday night, gave the fans plenty of action, with five fast wrestling matches and five fast boxing matches on the card.

All of the events, with the exception of one wrestling bout, went the limit to a draw, although there was some furious milling in the boxing matches and some good exhibitions in the wrestling matches.

Joe Bachlet pinned Johnny Goddard to the mat after three minutes of fast wrestling in the 133-pound class. Eddie Kammerzall of Ranchester and Mike Bocek of Monarch wrestled ten minutes to a draw.

Fred Bell is manager of the Monarch A. C."

4/13/26—"Arndt and Bocek To Meet Saturday—Old Feud to be Settled in Monarch Bout.— The George Arndt-Mike Bocek feud will be settled at the Monarch hall on Saturday night, Apr. 17,—"

10/6/27—"Monarch Home Is Robbed—Two Men Get Large Sum At Point of Guns—$1,900 in Cash and Papers Taken—Two men take $300 in bills, $500 in Polish War Bonds and $1,100 in P. O. Certificates from Mrs. Joe Zowada while husband (not at home.)"

10/13/27—"At Monarch Theater Sunday—"Forlorn River," Zane Grey's Story. Added, the Eight Wade children in song and dance. Special music—20¢ and 40¢."

1/3/28—"Fire Destroys Monarch Hall—Fixtures of Shop are Saved, Rest is Ruined"

Pool hall and barber shop. Believe fire started around chimney. Large frame building owned by Sheridan-Wyoming Coal company. Pool Hall owned by Harry Mavrakis and the barber shop by Troy Wade. Fire noted about 5:00 a.m. by man sleeping in building.

3/7/28—"Monarch Man Gets Back His Stolen Bonds—All But $300 in Cash Recovered Now, Belief" Some of the Polish Bonds owned by Paul Gazur left with Zowada for safe keeping found on road by woman from Dietz on way to visit friend in Monarch.

7/12/28—"Charles Catterl of Kleenburn Critically Injured When He Was Crushed Between Car and Mine Wall at Monarch Mine."

1/29/29—"Miner's Skull Fractured By Piece of Coal—Victim Improves After Accident at Monarch—Andrew Mehalek injured when a large piece of coal fell on head."

Later view of Monarch, Wyo., taken in the 1920's. (Rear of Catholic church on left. Two story house formerly occupied by Ralph and Nell Carmichael and later by the Art Perry family. Art was inside foreman. House later moved to Kleenburn and still there).

2/8/29—"$10,000 Blaze to Close Monarch Mine for Week—Firemen Make Run to Camps in Bitter Cold—Scores of Men Out of Work Through Disaster—Top of tipple destroyed—Accident Handicaps Company Already Rushed.

"Between 150 and 160 men out of work temporarily."

6/14/29—"Monarch theater has installed a large Electric Player with dynamic speaker. Hear it Sunday with Wallace Berry and Raymond Hatton in, "Now We're In The Air—Adv.""

1/15/30—"Monarch School Burns in Early Morning Blaze—$7,000 Building and All Equipment."

Two Pianos Lost in Fire at Mining Camp. Believe caused by defective flu. Teachers, Wm. Seig, Principal and 7th and 8th; Helen Solberg, 5th and 6th; Dorothy Ketcham, 3rd and 4th and Emily Thomas, 1st and 2nd. Mrs. Andrew Mentock living next door, states her home scorched by blaze. School bungalow saved."

4/21/30—"Man Is Badly Hurt In Accident at Mine."

"Paul Sturtz of Monarch, an employe of the mines, suffered severe, but not critical injuries when he lost control of a horse-drawn coal car."

5/2/30—"Monarch Will Erect School—Contract Let for $10,000 Structure at Mining Camp." To replace one burned in January."

11/11/30—"Chris Shott Is Injured—Superintendent of Monarch mine sustained fracture of left leg while working in machine shop."

2/9/31—"Monarch Dramatic Club Will Give Play."

"Members of the Monarch Dramatic club will present their annual winter play, "An Arizona Cowboy," in the lobby of the Acme hotel Friday evening, February 20.

The Monarch club has appeared in a number of dramatic productions in the past several years, each of which has been well accepted.

"An Arizona Cowboy" is a four-act comedy drama of the old west and will be given by the following case:

Farley Gantt, the cowboy sheriff, Elmer Day.

Paul Qillian, his partner, Russell Beny.

Hezekiah Bugg, a glorious liar, Kenneth MacDonald.

Grizzley Grimm, a cattle thief, Joe Holiday.

Duke Blackshear, a crook, William Berry.

Yow Kee, a heathen Chinese, James Catterall.

Big Elk, a Navajo chief, Cliff Allen.

Marguerite Moore, owner of the ZZ ranch, Adelle Berry.

Mrs. Petunia Bugg, from "Indianny," Greta Schotzhauer.

Coralie Blackshear, an adventuress, Nellie Holiday.

Fawn Afraid, an Indian Maid, Lillian Henderson

Youngun, a poorhouse waif, Margaret Day.

The hotel lobby was chosen for the play due to the fact that the Monarch theater has been abandoned."

2/16/31—"Bocek Hall Near Monarch will be the scene of a carnival dance Tuesday evening, it was announced by Paul Bocek, proprietor. A short athletic show featuring boxing and wrestling will be staged during intermission, he said."

Dance Hall in "Crookedtown" (a section across river from Monarch, Wyoming). Men in picture, unknown.
(Courtesy William F. Welch)

4/3/32—"Harry Daniels of Monarch is Winner of Annual Marble Tournament Here Saturday—Another Mines Pupil Captures Second in Meet.—Will be presented with a handsome silver loving cup donated by Peter Kooi. Walter Zowada, teammate of Harry Daniels, second."

11/16/32—"Miner at Monarch Is Accident Victim—Frank Sobotka, 30, Monarch miner sustained a fractured pelvis in an accident at the Monarch Mine Tuesday afternoon. "George Sikora, 55, also injured when horse fell on him fracturing his leg."

11/22/32—"Monarch Drama Club Planning New Play—Members of the Monarch Dramatic Club are preparing to begin preliminary rehearsals of their annual stage play to be presented here in near future, it was announced today. Members of the club met for the first time this fall on Sunday with 14 present. A "pot luck" supper was held late in the evening.

Those present included: Mr. and Mrs. Joe Holliday, Elmer and Margaret Day, Sally and Sonny Joyce, Lillian Henderson, Bonnie Mae Spurlock, Billy Wondra, Cliff Allen and Mr. and Mrs. Charles Schlotzhauer. The name of the play has not been announced."

2/1/33—"Woman Hurt But Theater Act Goes On—Actress With Monarch Players Injured At Acme—Mrs. Joe Holliday who plays a leading role in the dramatic production of the Monarch players, "Sweetheart Trail," was painfully injured before curtain time in falling through a trap door leading to the dressing room, spraining both ankles—with scarcely a delay, Mrs. Greta Schlotzhauer, director of the play, donned Miss Holliday's costume and played the role—"

2/12/33—"Monarch Players Set Date in City"—"Feb. 22 in Orpheum Theater. Proceeds for unemployed relief."

2/23/33—"Monarch Players Please Large Audience In Presenting 'Sweetheart Trail' Here—Miss Sally Joyce and Elmer Day, in the leading dramatic parts, were well-supported by the rest of the cast—Features enjoyed between the acts were selections by a quartette—Frank Wakefield, Norman Cook, Reece Achenbach and Carl Bentzen, with Charles Putney at the piano; a tap dance by Miss Elaine Day; violin and piano duets by the Hewit sisters; and harmonica solos by Harold Amend with piano accompaniment by Miss Pearl Johnson."

(On July 9, 1934, Sheridan's first radio station began broadcasting. It was shortly thereafter that Mr. Joe Suska, a Polish miner from Monarch, began airing a program of Polish recorded music every Sunday morning with all the announcements in the Polish language.

I do not recall just how long Mr. Suska continued as the announcer; however, Mr. Joe Skatula, also a former miner from Monarch and at that time, an employee of the Sheridan Brewing company, took over as the announcer. The latter continued to conduct the program for fourteen years for that station until, for some reason, unknown to me, the program was discontinued, but was quickly taken over by radio station KROE with Mr. Skatula announcing. According to Mr. Skatula, that was some sixteen years ago. Recently, the station conducted a poll and found the Polish program so intensely popular that the station decided to double the length from the one former hour. Now, the program is heard each Sunday morning over station KROE from 10:30 a.m. to 12:30 p.m.)

3/14/35—"The condition of Albert Atkinson, 20, who was injured in the Monarch mine yesterday when caught between two loaded cars as they went around a curve in the mine, was still serious, his attending physician announced this afternoon although no internal injuries have developed as yet, his spine and head were seriously hurt. At the best, he will be confined at the hospital for a number of weeks."

4/12/36—"Monarch School Wins Kooi Loving Cup in Marble Tournament Finals For Third Time—Dick Catterall Garners Award For His School—Leland Geogen Is Second, With Ed Kukuchka Third"—"The trophy was won by a Monarch lad both last year and in 1932. Walter Zowada was the 1935 winner."

8/5/36—"Barbula, Former S.H.S. Grid Star, Is Hurt in Mine—Alec Barbula, former Sheridan High School football star suffered a severe pelvic injury at the Monarch mine when struck by a losed coal car."

10/11/40—"Joseph Motyka Dies Suddenly"— Monarch Resident Stricken on Friday At His Home."

Joseph F. Motyka, resident of Monarch since 1907, died suddenly today at his home, at the age of 55. He had worked in the mines yesterday. Born on Jan. 1, 1885 in Istebne, Poland, he had lived in Monarch 33 years.

Survived by wife, Anna and one daughter, Mrs. Joe Skatula."

(Joe Motyka, was an organist and usually played the organ at various Catholic church services. After the Catholic church was built in Monarch, Mr. Motyka and Mrs. George Kovacic were organists at that church.

8/28/41—"Dr. Clegg."

"This is the story of a man who was a practicing attorney . . . and a county prosecutor at that . . . but who changed his mind about his

life work . . . and went back to school to study medicine and became a doctor.

He is Dr. E. G. Clegg of Monarch . . . physician and surgeon for the UMWA at Monarch for the past 22 years.

The faith of the miners in Dr. Clegg was again demonstrated Thursday night . . . when he was overwhelmingly elected for his 12th two-year term as mine doctor.

Dr. Clegg first came to Monarch on April 1, 1919 . . . and every two years since then, just as regularly as new union contracts were signed, the miners have again chosen him as their doctor.

There are many lawyers and many doctors . . . but there are very few men who hold both law and medical degrees . . . and Dr. Clegg is one of them.

He graduated from the law school at Valparaiso, Ind., University, in 1904 . . . and went to Gettysburg, S.D. to hang out his shingle.

Two years later he was elected county attorney . . . but while serving in that office he decided he'd rather be a doctor . . . and so he gave up the job and went back to school.

He attended the medical school of the University of Illinois at Chicago . . . and emerged with his M. D. Degree in 1910.

First, he set up shop as a general practitioner at Harrisburg, S. D. . . . and later went to Sioux City, Iowa, as assistant surgeon to Dr. Van Buren Knot.

From Sioux City, he came to Monarch . . . where he has remained ever since, employed by the United Mine Workers of America."

In the *Sheridan Press of Aug. 31, 1941*, there appears an article entitled, "Jack Carey."

"John P. Carey, veteran station agent at the mine camp of Kleenburn, is going to retire on Monday. (The Kleenburn depot of the C. B. & Q. was located nearer the camp of Monarch than Kleenburn).

"Mr. Carey's philosophy . . . what's the use? I had to come back to this country to go fishing anyway."

"Mr. Carey, who is 71 years old and who has been at Kleenburn for 31 years, is going to stay in this country.

He has built himself a home at nearby Dayton . . . and right now, he has laid the foundation for an office. He isn't going to work . . . but he says that it will feel great to get a good desk under his feet again.

Mr. Carey came out here in the good old days . . . There were six independent mines . . . and his railroad station had seven employes.

And this widely-known Kleenburn station was not always in its present location.

It was first at Model, then at Carney, and finally at Kleenburn—which in reality is in Monarch. The miners couldn't agree where the station should be located, and there was too much professional jealousy to give it any of the names of the mining towns.

It was first called "Alger" after a pioneer Sheridan banker . . . then the Peabody company came into control and held a contest to find a new name for its coal . . . The person who submitted the name of "Kleenburn" received $50 in cash—and the Alger station changed its name to Kleenburn.—"

Kleenburn Depot at Monarch, Wyoming.

(Monarch tipple just before closing, note modern diesel engines).

7/6/45—"Sheridan-Wyoming Coal Retires All of Its Bonded Indebtedness."

"A release from the Wall Street Journal announced that the Sheridan-Wyoming Coal Company, Inc., retired all of its outstanding bonds as of July 2, 1945, in the amount of $579,500." In 1937, indebtedness was $1,438,000.—

"Government records indicate that the Monarch mine is one of the largest producing coal mines in the United States—"

A memorandum dated November 15, 1945, from the office of the Sheridan-Wyoming Coal Company, stated that "the Monarch Boarding House to be operated by the Sheridan-Wyoming Coal Company, Inc., at our Acme Camp will be ready for occupancy on Friday, November 16th. The cost of board and room to our employes will be $60.00 per month.—"The preparation of food and housekeeping details will be under the supervision of Mr. and Mrs. Andrew Slovak—"

4/27/46—"TWO WEEKS FROM DREAM TO ACTUAL RECREATION PROGRAM IS RECORD OF LADIES CLUB AT MONARCH MINE"

Members of the Monarch Ladies club have given every community something to shoot at when it comes to real action in providing community recreation.

Two weeks ago, a few women of the coal mining camp ten miles north of Sheridan felt that something should be done to provide activities for boys and girls who had "no place to go and nothing to do."

And today, thanks to whole-hearted cooperation of men, women and children in the camp, and the Sheridan-Wyoming Coal company, a double tennis court is already installed by the school auditorium and a baseball diamond is being hewn out of the bottom land between the school and Tongue River."—

—"Everyone has been wonderful about helping," says Mrs. Ethel Yorio, president of the Monarch Ladies club, and we want to express our appreciation to all the people in the community and to the company." Mrs. Martha Sobotka is secretary-treasurer of the club, and Mrs. Emma Barbula is vice-president. Special members of the project committee were Mrs. Mary Mentock and Mrs. Bernice Ketcham. The club has only about 20 active members—"

Following all of those incidents described to this point—those incidents which made life so interesting for those earlier years of the Monarch camp, life continued, but in a more modern trend.

Finally, with the increased conversion to the use of natural gas for home cooking and heating, both in the home and in industry, and particularly as the railroads converted to the use of diesel as their main source of energy, the demand for coal began to diminish. Each of the coal mines, one by one, closed its operations, Monarch being the only one of the larger mines still in operation, but it, too, could not resist the trend and on July 15, 1953, an announcement appeared in the Sheridan papers as follows:

"Coal Company Is Closing Monarch Camp"—"The Sheridan-Wyoming Coal Company is vacating its Monarch camp "effective the earliest possible date."

"In letters signed by Walter J. Johnson, president, and dated this week, Monarch residents are "requested to vacate as soon as you can possibly do."

"The Monarch store was closed today.

On May 8, a joint announcement was made of consolidations by the Sheridan-Wyoming Coal Co., Inc., and the Big Horn Coal Co. Production will be handled by the Big Horn Coal Company

St. Thomas Catholic Church in Monarch, Wyoming. (Third church, built of rock, after two previous ones mysteriously burned in Carneyville. Church is abandoned but still remains.)

Recent Monarch, Wyoming general office of Sheridan-Wyoming Coal Company at right. Tongue River Trading Company (company store) on left. (Office more recently mysteriously burned).

Monarch abandoned—Office building remained until burned in 1976.

and sales by the Sheridan-Wyoming Coal company, the announcement said.

At that time, employment severance notices were given to miners employed in the Monarch mine. Before the spring layoff, 118 men were employed—76 underground and the remainder in outside work and office work. Some of the families have since moved from Monarch.

The Acme camp and store have been sold to Gothard Bylund, who will resign from the Sheridan-Wyoming Coal company and devote his full time to the Acme camp and store, according to the letter.

A limited amount of housing accommodations will be available at Acme, according to Johnson's letter, which stated "we regret deeply that conditions are such as to require this action" (closing of the Monarch camp)."

Following this announcement, it only followed that the residents of Monarch, lacking employment, quickly vacated the camp. Most of them moved their families to Sheridan, and just as quickly became assimilated in other employment.

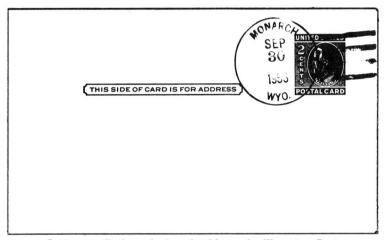

Last cancellation closing the Monarch, Wyoming Post-office, Sept. 30, 1953. *Courtesy Nell Carmichael.*

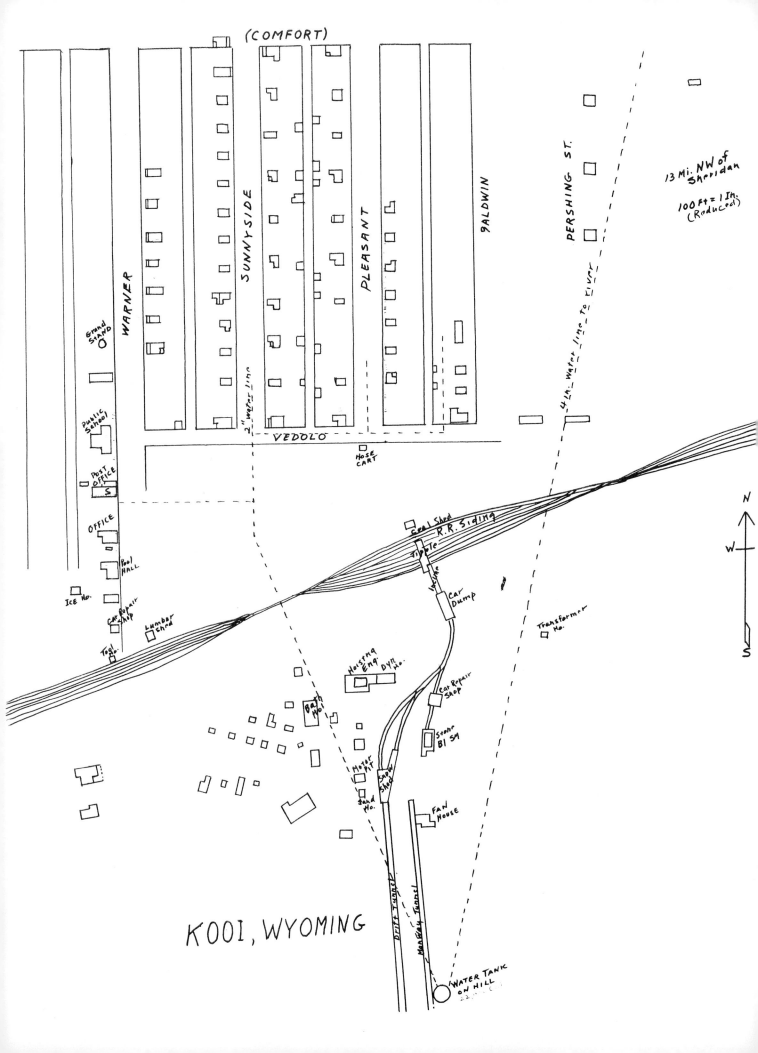

KOOI, WYOMING

5/1/08—*Sheridan Enterprise.* "THE SHERIDAN COAL FIELDS," by Mrs. D. H. Warner. "—Two and one-half miles west of Monarch we have a new mining camp called Kooi. This mine has only been in operation a few months. The first shipment of material and machinery did not arrive on the ground until the latter part of July, 1907, but since that time over $150,000 has been expended for development work, building a town, putting in a modern 2,500 ton tipple, etc., which is all properly installed, and has been in working order for the last 60 days. The present output is between 500 and 600 tons daily. This camp, while still in its infancy, will soon be in the market with from 1,000 to 1,200 tons of coal daily.—"

Kooi, Wyoming (Albert Bull, carpenter, erecting smoke stack at Kooi Mine).

She further writes, "One mile north of Kooi is located the Riverside Mining company. This company is still in its development stages, but we need not be surprised to see this place equipped with modern machinery, and doing a thriving business by fall."

"The above are all (Dietz, Carneyville, Monarch and Kooi) on the line of the C.B. & Q. railroad. There are also a number of other small coal mines in the vicinity of Sheridan which carry on a thriving retail business, hauling their coal from the mines to the consumer by wagon, not to mention thousands of acres of undeveloped coal lands, which in the near future will make the state of Wyoming a second Pennsylvania. The veins of the Sheridan district are from eight to 30 feet in thickness.

In view of he above facts and the importance of this industry to the people of Sheridan, it stands them in hand to do everything possible to promote the interests of the aforesaid camps."

News releases in the Sheridan news media reveal more of the history of Kooi as follows:

1/7/09—"Kooi coal advertised at $3.50 per ton."

6/16/11—"In a news column entitled, 'Kooi,' appears—

"The Misses Bella and Hariet Green arrived recently from Consett, England to make their home in Kooi with their father, Jack Green.

A number of people from Kooi attended the Indian-Ranchester ball game at Ranchester last Sunday.

The people of surrounding country are cordially invited to spend the Fourth of July at Kooi and enjoy themselves. We are to have games and sports, a ball game, dancing and excellent fireworks in the evening. The band is practicing and we will be assured of some good music to fill in the intervals of the program of sports.

Ben Joyce and Jack Green (latter returned to England) in one of the first tents in Kooi, Wyoming 1907. Father of Maisie, Malcolm*, Fred*, Ben, Margaret, Sally, Sonny. * Worked in mines.

Dr. J. E. E. Nelles was a professional caller in Sheridan, Wednesday.

Mrs. A. F. Hufford was in Sheridan, visiting relatives, from Wednesday to Saturday last week.

The houses in Kooi have been much improved by all receiving a coat of fresh paint, which adds greatly to the appearance of our camp. Several porches and additions have been built also, and the well kept gardens of many people in Kooi show their desire to do their part in making the camp as attractive instead of an unsightly place.

D. W. Jones was a welcome visitor at Kooi, Wednesday."

7/27/13—"Sheridan Coal Mining Coal Tonnage . . . Year 1912." "Tons Produced as Per Official Records of Five Principal Mines in Sheridan County."
Wyoming Coal Mining Company—
Monarch Coal . . . . 328,271 tons
Sheridan Coal Co. . . . . 195,665 tons
Carney Coal Co. . . . . 175,148 tons
Acme Coal Co. . . . . 167,231 tons
Kooi Coal Co. . . . . 161,700 tons
$3.00 per Ton
Delivered by the Model Coal Yard, Ph. 84."

8/29/13—"Teachers Assigned for New School Year; Mrs. W. W. Anderson, Old Acme; Mrs. Jennie R. Ayles, Slater Creek; Inez Quigly,

Coal mine camp of Kooi, Wyoming.

Kooi, Wyoming as it looks today.

Monarch. 10/7/13—Attendance, Monarch, 41; Old Acme, 18; Ash Creek, 8."

11/25/13—"SEVEN DAYS TWO LICENSES." AUSTRIAN GIRL NEWLY ARRIVED FIGURES IN ROMANCE." "First Wooer Did Not Suit Her So She Takes The Second—Is Married."

"Two licenses to wed, dated within the limits of one week, and both containing the same name as the prospective bride, do not come to many girls even in this land of the free thinker, and equal rights for all who can take them, irrespective of sex of race. Insofar as to get two marriage licenses is a distinction, Mary Czepzar, now Mrs. Jacob Malyjurek of Kooi, is distinguished. For Mary was a prospective bride twice within the narrow limits of seven days. This is how it happened.

About two weeks ago the young lady came to America from her native land of Austria. The object of the trip was to wed the man of her parents' choice, a young miner. Mary came, saw and acquiesced. The license was obtained. Then Mary chose to assert her feminine prerogative of changing her mind. She refused to use that license. A dozen new suitors at once offered themselves. From among the number, Mary chose one. The first license was returned, another secured and the belated but none the less joyous nuptials celebrated in a fitting manner."

11/25/13—"POST REPRESENTATIVES VISIT THE SHERIDAN COUNTY MINES." "SIX COAL CAMPS HAVE BEEN ROUNDED UP." "KOOI IS THE LAST." "Owner Has Good Mine Surrounded by Pretty and Comfortable Mining Village."

Kooi, the last of the six coal camps near Sheridan to be visited by The Post representatives, and the one farthest from Sheridan, is situated about three miles beyond Monarch on a small plateau above Tongue River. Kooi is not reached by the interurban, as that line stops at Monarch. The Kooi railroad point is at Alger, some miles distant, so the camp is comparatively isolated. It is none the less important, however, among the camps, and is entitled to be regarded among the big ones.

Kooi was opened in July, 1906, by Peter Kooi, sole owner and operator of the mine. Mr. Kooi has never incorporated but has remained the individual owner of his large property, holding several hundred acres of land underlaid with at least two veins of coal, the Monarch and Carney. He is now operating in the Monarch vein.

The town which Mr. Kooi has built up about his mine consists of about forty dwelling houses for families, bunkhouses, an office building, a store building, a pool hall and other structures, bringing the total of buildings outside the mine buildings up to seventy or more. The town is neatly laid out, the streets are wide and kept clean, trees are being planted and lawns encouraged. The town is lighted by electricity and in every house are electric lights. In most of them there is running water. The houses themselves are modern and a large percentage include bathrooms than in most cities. They contain from three to five rooms each, are well finished and entirely comfortable.

No Labor Trouble

During the years Mr. Kooi has been operating at Kooi he has had no labor trouble, very little trouble of any kind, in fact. The men have been contented and many of them, especially the family men, are permanent residents. A record of but one man leaving the camp during the slack summer season is held by Kooi.

The Kooi mine has been running steadily since October 6th, and has now orders ahead sufficient to keep running for several weeks without receiving any more. Eighteen hundred tons, between forty and fifty carloads of coal, are being produced daily. The mine itself is opened to a capacity of 3,000 tons and the out-put can be increased to that amount at any time by merely adding to the force at work.

Kooi coal is marketed all over the northwest, there being well organized sales offices in practically every important section. Mr. Kooi is a firm believer in publicity backed by "the goods," and "Kooi, the Quality Coal," is known from the river to the coast. Mr. Kooi says that "repeat" orders are the rule rather than the exception.

Entered Two Ways

The mine itself has two entrances but a few feet apart, the "main haul" and the "manway."

the normal, healthy condition, however. It is explained by the expansion of the air in the mine by increased temperature. The air as it enters is several degrees lower in temperature than that outside. As it passes through the mine, rubbing against the rough walls, friction raises the temperature and the air expands.

The length of the "main haul" is 1,500 feet and coal is brought out by means of the "tail rope" system. The first 170 feet of the entry

Kooi, Wyoming—Mr. Kooi preferred Polish miners, so states his daughter, Doris (Kooi) Reynolds, because, she says, "if they should fight they do so with their fists."

The coal is brought out through the main haul, while the men and horses enter by the manway. The same openings are used for ventilation, air being forced through the mine by an immense fan situated near the mouth of the manway. The air enters through the main haul, and actual measurements Saturday showed that 85,085 cubic feet per minute were going in. At the manway, where the air comes out, it measures 102,600 cubic feet per minute. There is a phenomenon which puzzles the novice at first, why more air should be coming out than enters. It is

descends at a five percent grade. It is up this grade that the coal is brought by motors which pick up the cars as they are brought from the working rooms by horses.

Mine Equipment

The first 170 feet, which is the distance through earth to the coal vein, is heavily timbered with 8 x 12-inch timbers lagged with 2x8 planks. It presents a very neat appearance and all danger of a cave-in is obviated. The mine is timbered for a short distance after it enters the coal, heavy roof timbers being needed to prevent cave-ins. The coal is hard and firm, but the difference in temperature of the air entering this way expands and contracts the wall and ceiling coal, causing it to crumble. When greater depth is reached, where the temperature is more even, no timbers are needed or used.

The parting also plays an important part in marketing Kooi coal. It is declared to be much easier to get out coal there than where the vein is thicker, the lumps coming down larger in size and not breaking each other to pieces as they fall. That fact, coupled with the method of handling, is making Kooi a "lump coal mine" and lump coal commands the highest market price.

Panel System Used

The main entry of the Kooi mine runs directly south from the entrance. The panel system of mining is used, entries opening from the main haul and four panels being opened from each entry. The rooms are opened in those panels, each room being 22 feet wide and forty feet between centers, leaving a pillar of coal 18 feet thick between two rooms. After a panel has been worked out, it is sealed up with concrete stoppings to prevent fire in abandoned workings. It has been demonstrated that bituminous coal if left to the action of the air will invariably fire sooner or later. Sealed up, there is no danger of that in the rooms, as no fresh air gets into them and fire is impossible. There has never been a fire of consequences in the Kooi mine.

The coal is mined by means of electric chain machines and air-driven punchers. The punchers are being replaced by electric machines as fast as possible, however, as the machines take the coal out in better shape and less broken up. The coal, broken down by the machines and blasting, is loaded into pit cars, hauled to the entry by horses and to the tail rope by motors.

For ventilating purposes the mine is divided into sections so arranged that each section has its own air and not more than fifty men are ever working in a section. That insures pure air at all times and the mine is considered the best aired in northern Wyoming by experts who have visited it. The roads in the mine are kept free and clean and dust is regularly laid by means of sprinkling. The mine is very dry and hardly enough water accumulates in twenty-four hours to keep the pumps busy one hour. Three air-

Kooi Trading Co.

driven pumps are installed to handle what water there is.

At every entry are signs pointing the way out of the mine and at each crossing the electric wires are protected by board troughs. Each crossing and parting is electrically lighted and where the horses work the wires are again found protected.

All Precautions Taken

Every precaution is taken at Kooi to prevent accidents and at the entrance of the manway are posted rules for the conduct of each set of

Kooi First Aid Team (Roy Russell in center).

Miners with horses.

workmen in the mine. These rules are strictly enforced. They cover all manner of actions, carelessness, unnecessary risks, neglecting precautions, and so on. One of the most emphatic is that against men entering the mine while under the influence of liquor. Drunkenness is frowned upon at Kooi, and offenders are frequently given short shift.

The tipple at Kooi differs markedly from those found at other mines of the district. For one thing it is much lower than any other, the coal being elevated barely high enough to drop into the cars. After being dumped, it passes over a set of shaker screens and from them directly into the cars. The system is designed to avoid breakage of the lumps as much as possible. All grades of coal are produced, lump, nut, egg, slack, mine run and combinations of these classes. The lump passes over seven-inch holes, egg over two and a half inch holes, nut over inch and a quarter holes. All smaller than that is slack. The trackage is so arranged that five cars can be loaded from the tipple at the same time.

Engine and Boilers

Just outside the mine is the engine and boiler house. This is equipped with two 150-horsepower boilers, a 150-horsepower air compressor, a double drum for tail and rear ropes which pull out loaded cars and send back empties. An electrical substation is also located here and contains one Westinghouse direct current generator. Current is received from the Sheridan County Electric Company power station at Acme for running the generator, the pumping plant for the town and mine, and for lighting the town. Water from Tongue river is pumped through 1,600 feet of four-inch pipe to a tank 170 feet above the river which supplies mine and town.

Two hundred and sixty men are employed at Kooi at the present time and they are divided into two shifts. The main shift works during the day, quitting at 4 o'clock. The second shift then goes in and mines for four hours and loads and dumps coal for four hours. The men are receiving about $30,000 per month, all but a small portion of which they get in cash. Store bills, rents and union dues are deducted but even after that many of the men draw over $100 in cash for two weeks' work.

Much of the business of the Kooi miners comes to Sheridan. The Kooi Trading company maintains a store at the camp with about $18,000 in stock but mostly necessary articles of food and wearing apparel and supplies for

Kooi Band 1915—Top row: John Pilch, John Baxter, Mike Wawrzacz, Paul Kawulok (Kempka), Mike Viska, Frank Kawulok, Joe Kawulok. Middle: George McDonald, Joe Legerski (Wonterek), Mike Kawulok, John Legerski (Kepus), John Legerski (Domovy Debol), Joe Siegoski, George Baxter, Mike Zowada, Jack Michalek, Ory Williams. *Photo courtesy Frank Kawulok, Jr.*

Kooi, Wyoming Fourth of July parade (school house in background).

Kooi, Wyoming Fourth of July parade (note woman cranking auto).

mining. All the rest of the trade of Kooi reaches this city and adds to Sheridan's prosperity.

1/16/14—"RUMORS WERE EXAGGER-ATED." "SITUATION AT MONARCH LESS SERIOUS THAN REPORTED." "Had Pretty Lively Time, But No Dead Have Yet Been Observed."

"That the rumors of trouble in some of the coal camps, so persistent in Sheridan the first

part of the week, were founded in fact although distorted and exaggerated, is the report of Undersheriff Veach, who was sent to Monarch to investigate after the rumors had been taken to county officials by a *Post* reporter. Mr. Veach spent nearly the entire day at Monarch, Tuesday, and inquired into all phases of the trouble.

The story he brought back is that on Sunday evening a wedding occurred at the ranch home of Leon Checofski, between Monarch and Kooi,

Kooi, Wyoming baseball team. Standing, L to R: Mike Jurosek, Mike Zowada, A. A. Wilcox, Geo. Hotchkiss, Jake Malyurek, Mike Viska. Squatting: John J. Legerski, Henry Scott, Joe Sieckowski, Henry (stable boss), John Capus.

which was attended by large numbers of persons from both of those camps. After the ceremony had been performed, the usual refreshments, consisting of good things to eat and strong things to drink, were brought out in great abundance and the multitude partook thereof quite freely, especially of the drink.

Not Enough Women

Unfortunately, there were many more men than women present at the celebration and when dancing started a number of the boys were left without partners. They felt themselves agrieved thereat, and grievance and beer combined to create a feeling of intense jealousy. Fights were started and individual trouble developed into a "camp" fight, in which the forces of Kooi were arraigned against those of Monarch.

Knives, clubs and fists were freely used by both sides, according to the story, and the melee was a brisk and interesting one. Kooi proved to

have the advantage, however, of superior force or more valiant warriors, and soon vanquished the legion from Monarch. Monarch drew off from the charge, leaving the stricken field until some later time when forces would be more evenly matched. No serious wounds were suffered on either side, but the house of Checofski was a wreck.

Saloon Is Attacked

Losing interest in the wedding and the celebration, the Monarch representatives set out for home. Their feelings were hurt more than their bodies, and they brooded over their wrongs. Inspired by no one knows what motives, they went to the place of business of one Charles Berry, who is listed in the county directory as the proprietor of a saloon, and proceeded to roughhouse the establishment. Berry naturally resented the effort and resisted with might and main, using only his fists, but to such good end that at least one invader was carried from the second field of combat, laid out cold. A companion of Berry's is said to have seized a hammer with intent to use it if need be, but did not find such extreme measures necessary. From that fact, doubtless, grew the story that a man had been hit on the head so hard that his eyes popped out.

Defeated a second time, the war-like revelers withdrew, the injured one going under the care of a physician and the others to their homes. No arrests were made by Mr. Veach, nor is legal action of any kind anticipated. The injured is said to be getting along nicely and the whole affray is attributed to over-exuberance of spirits."

3/13/14—"CAME TO AMERICA UNDER FALSE NAME." "Austrian Girl Then Tried to Get Kooi Man to Marry Her and Got Money From Him." (From Monday's Daily).

"Attorney _____ has given to the *Enterprise* the story of Mary _____ , the young Austrian girl who was arrested here Thursday by Agent Evans, of the federal labor department and who will be deported on account of immorality. Mr. (attorney) said that he protested against the statement made by Mr. Evans that the girl's downfall was due to the miners at Kooi. The girl was immoral before coming to this country, the local attorney stated, and in no way did the people at Kooi bring about her downfall, Mr. (attorney), in recounting the history of the girl, added:

"Last December one of the miners at Kooi sent two tickets to Austria for the purpose of having his two daughters come to this country and to Kooi. One of his daughters was unable to come, so this Mary _____ impersonated her and gained admittance to the United States in this way.

"Shortly after arriving here this girl sent another woman to a man at Kooi and had this go-between tell him that she had heard of him in Europe and that she had conceived a great love for him and desired to marry him. The Kooi man at first declined to consider the matter but upon her assurances that she was in earnest he finally consented. He first gave her money to buy clothes with and later paid the father who had sent the tickets to Austria to get his daughters here, the sum of $96.50, the cost of her passage. As soon as the girl got the money she immediately made flippant remarks about the

man and declined to have anything to do with him. This was the cause of her trouble which will result in her deportation. He preferred charges against her under the law that provides that all immoral people who come to this country shall be deported within two years after emigrating from their mother country. She confessed to Mr. Evans her immorality. If she had treated the Kooi man square she would not have gotten into trouble."

10/8/20—"(CAMP BREEZES) Monarch, Oct. 7—Sunday morning at 11 o'clock first Holy Communion service will be celebrated at the St. Thomas Catholic church of Carneyville for the children of Kooi, of which there will be about 18 who will receive. Father Schultz will deliver a sermon befitting the occasion. Music will be rendered during services and appropriate hymns will be sung during high mass. A cordial invitation is extended to all who wish to attend.

Mr. and Mrs. Ben Barnhart and baby, of Cambria, Wyo. accompanied by the former's sister Miss Lilian have moved to Monarch, to make their future home.

Mr. F. P. Barrier of Monarch was a Sheridan Visitor Wednesday to consult a dentist.

The post office from Dietz has been moved to Dietz No. 8.

Mr. and Mrs. J. R. Buchanan and little daughter Dorothy, were attending to shopping errands in Sheridan Wednesday afternoon.

Mesdames John Juroszek, Paul Wiska, Andrew Kajcer and M. Maleyurek of Kooi were passengers on the interurban Wednesday forenoon enroute to Sheridan.

The new pool hall at Dietz No. 8 is nearing completion, and will soon be opened with the most modern equipment."

Kooi, Wyoming (patriotism at Kooi).

Kooi tipple remains (foundations today).

Although the Kooi mine succumbed to the increased consumer conversion to other fuels, closing its mine in 1922, a few of the inhabitants continued to live in the camp. Some buying surface land in the vicinity and turning to farming, others taking farm and other employment in the area. The company store continued to operate for several years (no doubt under different management). On August 16, 1925, the store was robbed. No further details of this incident have been made available to me.

The school at Kooi continued to operate but in about 1940, the original building burned. A new smaller building was built, however it was closed completely in a year or two. Mrs. Naomi Malyurek who taught school in Kooi as Naomi Ellis, in 1933 and 1934, states that by that time nearly all of the houses had been removed.

In 1933, my brother, Joe, bought a house in Kooi, tore it down, section by section, and rebuilt the house at "Kuzaraville" where he lived for a short while.

Years later, about 1954, he moved this same house to 1329 N. Spaulding Street in Sheridan. He completely remodeled it to become the home of our widowed mother. She occupied this house then until she passed away in 1964. The property now belongs to my sister, Anna Eccli who lives next door.

Chapter 14
Mines-General

In previous chapters, I have tried to cover the histories of the individual mining camps, albeit no doubt very sketchy as compared to all the events which actually occurred.

There was, in addition, much that happened which did not pertain to any specific camp, but perhaps covered the whole area or the entire industry, therefore, it is in this chapter that I will attempt to relate those events.

Again, I'm sure much will be missed, but these few references will, I hope, give the reader a general idea of the industry and its problems, the people as a whole, the mining camp life in general, the labor union, and the complexities of those events which preceded our present generation, but which contributed so much to the composition of our current society, particularly that of Sheridan.

Some of the little things which were never told in the newspapers, for example included itinerant salesmen coming not only from Sheridan but even from out of state peddling their goods at the mines.

There was, for example, Mr. Hull who during the "teens was labeled "The Tea Man." He, I recall, sold various herbs and teas.

Then there was Mr. Tony Pelesky who used to haul vegetables delivering in his spring wagon; and others, while Mr. John Zucca particularly patronized the tastes of the mines element with his rare foods such as those pertaining to certain nationalities shipped from the east or even overseas. In addition, he would buy carbide in 100 pound lots, transfer them to 10 pound cans, and sell them at profits of over 100 percent.

Then there was the story told of Albert Wondra, the great pitcher on the mines baseball team, and how he would drink soda pop, purposely getting some on his pitching hand for a better grip on the ball.

Gypsies, too, would frequent the camps quite periodically causing the residents of those camps to either lock their homes which they did not ordinarily do, or keep a very close watch on them.

Or how about this interesting little vignette, as told to me by James Barello (who later married my sister, Helen)? When he was a small boy, he used to run the movie film from Monarch to Carneyville. It seems that Troy Wade, owner of the movie houses at both Monarch and Carneyville, would show a reel of film at the Monarch show house, immediately after which he would send the reel by runner to Carneyville where the audience was impatiently waiting.

Also, I was told by Mary Kumor about herself when she was first married. Her maiden name, by the way, was Mary Nekos (changed to Nickless). She married Andrew Banas (whose original name was Banish) in Dietz in 1918. At that time, she was employed at the Dietz Trading company store which, incidentally, was managed by Archie Wilson.

Well, there happened to be a large group of itinerant gypsies which had stopped and pitched camp nearby to ply their trade of reading fortunes. In the evenings, they would gather around their campfire for singing and dancing. Inasmuch as there were several musicians amongst them, the young couple hired them to play for their wedding celebration which, she tells, was attended by over 500 hundred merrymakers.

It is very particularly interesting to note that many of the medical doctors, most of whom later moved their offices to Sheridan, had their early practice at the mines. From somewhat scant information, it appears that the following doctors were among those who had got their start in this fashion:

Dr. _____ Pratt
Dr. _____ Kirtland
Dr. _____ Dawson
Dr. Thompson, Acme, 1924
Dr. J. E. Carr
Dr. E. G. Clegg, Union Doctor at Monarch for many, many years
Dr. H. S. Holmes, Acme, 1928
Dr. L. C. Booth, named to succeed Dr. L. C. Meridith at Acme in 1933

Dr. Dennison, Carneyville, 1913
Dr. Burkheieser, Dentist
Dr. Schunk, Dietz, 1913
Dr. R. E. Crane, Acme
Dr. W. M. Hoel, Kleenburn, 1921

In this and other parts of this book, I related many of my own experiences as they might pertain to the subject matter of those particular chapters.

To this, I now add such information taken from research which does not pertain to any specific camp or mine; but being of a more general nature is being included in a chapter of its own.

In this respect, I would like to refer to a Government Bulletin which provides a very brief but factual summary of the early history of coal in general in the Sheridan area as well as a description of the strata. This Bulletin No. 341-R of the Department of the Interior—U. S. Geological Survey was entitled, "Investigations of the Coal Fields of Wyoming in 1907, under

U.S. government bulletin, 1907 mines general.

the heading, "Development," Page 148, wherein we find the following:

"Coal mining in the Sheridan district, except for local domestic fuel, is restricted to the coal beds of the Tongue River group on Goose Creek and Tongue River. The thriving mining communities of Dietz, Carneyville, Monarch and Kooi are an index to the rapid growth of the coal-mining industry. The following information in regard to the development of the field is obtained from an article by Stewart Kennedy in his "Mines and Minerals, vol. 27, 1907, pp. 294-297" and from field work in 1907.

Quoting from Mr. Kennedy's dissertation, "As early as 1880 coal of a workable thickness was known and mined for domestic use by ranchmen at the present location of Dietz. From this time on to 1893, when the first commercial mining began, coal from several prospects on what are now known as the Dietz coal beds Nos. 1 and 2 was mined and hauled to Sheridan. A drift was run on the Dietz No. 1 coal near the east side of Sec. 34, T. 57 N., R. 84 W., in the winter of 1892-93 and the first shipment of coal was made in the following May. Operations continued until 1899, the coal being mined by pick and hoisted by mule power. A modern steam plant was erected in 1899 for the development of mine No. 1 and the output was greatly increased. A shaft was put down in 1900 in sec. 35, T. 57 N., R. 84 W., to the Dietz No. 2 coal bed and the development of mine No. 2 began with the erection of a complete hoisting plant and shops. Later a large electric plant was built and machine mining and electric haulage were established in the Dietz mines. In 1903 a shaft was sunk on the Dietz No. 2 coal bed in Sec. 3, T. 56 N., R. 84 W., and a modern hoisting plant established as mine No. 3. Also a slope was driven on coal bed No. 2 in Dietz and a drift on the same bed 1½ miles north of Dietz, with adequate equipments, as mines Nos. 4 and 5, respectively. These mines at and near Dietz, operated by the Sheridan Coal Company, employ at the present time about 800 men and support a population of about 2,000 persons.

A slope mine was opened in 1904 by the Wyoming Coal Company on the Monarch bed at the west side of Sec. 19, T. 57 N., R. 84 W., and a complete modern equipment for extensive mining, including electric power, was installed. This plant employs about 325 men and the town of Monarch, established here, has a population of nearly 700. Recently a shaft has been sunk at the Monarch mine 86 feet to the Carney coal bed. Both the Monarch and Carney beds, with an aggregate of at least 34 feet of clear coal, will be exploited at this plant.

The Carney Coal Company opened mines on the Carney coal bed on the north side of Tongue River, near the southeast corner of Sec. 17, T. 57 N., R. 84 W., in the latter half of 1904. A modern equipment for mining, hauling, hoisting, and loading coal, including an electric plant, was erected on the south side of the river. The mine is driven north of west on the rise of the coal bed. Later a second mine was opened adjoining the first on the same bed, in the SW ¼ Sec. 16, and recently a second tipple was erected to accommodate the increased output. The mining town of Carneyville has a population of approximately 1,400, and the company employs about 500 men.

The mining town of Kooi was established in the N. ½ Sec. 23, T. 57 N., R. 85 W., during 1907, and a slope mine was driven on the Monarch coal southward from the outcrop. The village is reported to contain 100 inhabitants, with about 75 men employed in mining operations. A spur connects the mine with the Chicago, Burlington and Quincy Railroad on the north side of Tongue River.

Late in the season of 1907 the Riverside Coal Company began operations on the Upper Masters coal bed in Sec. 14, T. 57 N., R. 85 W., but the extent of the development is not reported. A mining plant was in process of construction at Kendrick station, in Sec. 25, T. 55 N., R. 78 W., by the Wyoming Smokeless Coal Company, for exploitation of a 12-foot coal bed.

Prior to 1900 the Sheridan coals were used principally for domestic fuel. They were not regarded as successful for steaming purposes, especially where strong drafts and small fire spaces were used. The difficulties with the use of this coal for steaming, especially in locomotives, seemed to be due to the decrepitation of the fuel when suddenly heated. The small particles of coal that are thrown off by the sudden application of strong heat are in large part either blown out of the stack or fall between the grate bars used in the ordinary fire box of locomotives and other engines.

The Burlington Railroad began a series of tests of the Sheridan coals in its locomotives in 1900. By the use of specially constructed grates of large area, with modified fire boxes and stacks, the Sheridan coal is said to produce very satisfactory results. Coal from all the beds now mined is used extensively in locomotives and stationary engines.

A large part of the production of coal in the Sheridan district is used by the Burlington Railroad. It is marketed in Wyoming and Nebraska as far east as Omaha; in the Black Hills region; at Billings, Butte, and other points in Montana, and as far west as Idaho and Washington."

* * * *

The following dated references have been taken from the Sheridan newspapers previously named which will cover events as they occurred and which contain much additional information about the mines and miners in general:

2/12/09—"NEW OFFICE." "Sheridan Coal Will Be Weighted on City Scales."

"Charles Long has secured about the best location in the city for his coal office and will be located in the future at No. 1 Main Street, in the Pioneer Electric Supply Company's office. He is after the business and you will hear and read much about Sheridan coal in the future. Mr. Long is making another innovation in connection with his business. He has a good scale at the old yard, but this will be abandoned, as he is determined to let a customer know that he is getting exactly what his weigh ticket calls for when he gets a load of Sheridan coal. From now on all Sheridan coal will be weighed over the city scales. Mr. Hart is under bonds to give absolutely correct weights and is subject to a fine of $100 if he fails to give correct weights. The scales are owned by the city and controlled by city ordinance."

1/6/09—"Sheridan County"

"—There has been considerable advancement made in the schools of this county during the past two years. By the school census—in Dietz, a wing was built to the one-room building last year and a new schoolhouse erected at Mine No. 5 this year, making five schoolrooms in District No. 28. In District No. 30, a comfortable building has taken the place of an old log one rented by the district. In Monarch, a two-story building has been built with schoolrooms below, and a large hall above for entertainments. The old building, owned by the Monarch Coal company has been turned into a gymnasium for the miners.

In Carneyville, the one-room building proved inadequate and it was sold and a new two-room building is now rapidly nearing completion—"

1/28/10—"NORTHERN PACIFIC WILL CONTRACT WITH SHERIDAN MINES FOR A COAL SUPPLY." "Representative of Railroad in This City to Arrange for Shipment of 1,000 Tons Daily to Huntley."

The Northern Pacific road will within a few weeks let a large contract to the mines in the vicinity of Sheridan for the delivery of Sheridan coal to the amount of over one thousand tons per day.

A representative of the railroad company arrived in the city last night and will inspect all the mines within a few days and take away samples of the product to the laboratory of the railroad company for a test.

In years past the Northern Pacific used the Sheridan coal almost exclusively on one or two of its divisions, but for the last year the supply has been received from a Montana mine under a contract, which it is understood will expire within a short time.

That the coal mined here is of an extra good grade for locomotive use is evidenced by the volume of orders received from the Chicago, Milwaukee and Puget Sound Railroad Company. The latter company has a contract for the supply used on four of its sub-divisions with the mining companies tributary to Sheridan.

The ability of the local industries to deliver a uniform product and the railroad facilities in connection therewith form a valuable asset and one which is highly favorable to the making of contracts with the mines at Monarch, Acme, Carneyville, Dietz and Kooi,

The value of the coal as a fuel for locomotives is unsurpassed from a heat producing and cleanliness standpoint. The small amount of ash and the entire absence of clinkers make it such that it is better than the bituminous coal.

The equipment of the mines mentioned is such that they can deliver the goods every day in the year and there is nothing to prevent their part of the contract."

6/17/10—"HYDRAULIC CARTRIDGES REVOLUTIONIZE MINING." "Demonstration of the New Method Before Operators of Northern Wyoming Yesterday."

All mine operators in the northern part of the state congregated at Dietz Mine No. 4 yesterday to witness demonstrations of hydraulic mining cartridge, which is a wonderful invention and its general adoption all over the country would revolutionize the mining industry.

Dr. Henry M. Payne has charge of the demonstration here. He is accompanied by William Taylor, who was formerly in charge of a coal mine in England and used the hydraulic mining cartridge. C. B. Delamater is the western representative and has headquarters at Denver.

Dr. Payne has lately come from Rock Springs, Wyo., where he successfully demonstrated the hydraulic mining cartridge, which has been adopted by the Superior Coal Company in all their mines near that city.

Two shots were fired yesterday morning and another in the afternoon, which was a crucial test of the efficiency of this new form of mining. A pint of water is the only substance used, and this is placed under one hundred and fifty tons pressure, by hydraulic machinery, which is operated by one man. With the usage of this hydraulic cartridge all explosives are entirely eliminated, and the danger is materially lessened. It is also estimated that the amount of slack will be reduced from 40 to 10 per cent.

The northern Wyoming coal mining operators interested in the movement are W. G. Birkhaueser, of the Wyoming Coal Mining Company, C. B. Seymour of the Carney Coal Company; Peter Kooi of the Kooi Coal Company; A. K. Craig of the Acme Coal Company; Edward Gildroy, superintendent of the Carney Coal Company; W. D. McCormich, vice-president of the Sheridan Coal Company, and J. U. Gridley, general manager of the Sheridan Coal Company.

Dr. Payne was formerly professor of mining at the University of West Virginia. A few years ago he was commissioned by the governor of that state to proceed to England and investigate the mining conditions there and discover if possible the great difference in the casualties of Great Britain and the United States in the coal mining industry. Dr. Payne found these hydraulic mining cartridges in use at Hulton, England, and they were perfectly satisfactory and had been used for some time.

The hydraulic machinery costs in the neighborhood of $450 and if the operators of the Northern Wyoming decide to adopt it they will be unanimous in placing machines in their respective mines.

Dietz, Wyo. June 17—The demonstration of the new hydraulic mining cartridge which was made at the Sheridan Coal Company's Mine Number Four at Dietz yesterday proved a success. As D. Henry M. Payne, the expert in charge of the demonstration has claimed, the cartridge showed most wonderful power to push down the coal when undercut and there is no question but what it will be used very largely in future mining operations in this part of the country.

The cartridge which was used in the demonstration at Dietz yesterday was capable of one hundred and ten tons pressure. The cartridge proper is a forged steel cylinder about thirty inches long with eight duplex rams, or pistons arranged in a row along one side. The diameter of the cylinder is three inches, and the expansion of the duplex pistons is two and one quarter inches. For different coals where the vein is lower than in the Sheridan field, a cylinder with six pistons is used. The action of these pistons is simultaneous, the pressure being applied through a pipe about six feet long and about a pint and a half of water being forced into them by a pump at the outside end of the pipe. This water is absolutely the only thing used in connection with the cartridge and the same water can be used over and over. The cartridge is practically undestructible and sells for around five hundred dollars. The cartridge has been in use in England for several years, being the invention of one James Tonge, a mining engineer of Hulton, England, and was brought to this country by (here there appeared errors in type-setting) . . . Dr. Payne discovered this new cartridge and later when the North American rights were sold to a New York syndicate was offered the general management and accepted same.

The use of the new cartridge, it is believed will revolutionize the mining industry, doing away as it does with the powder smoke which is now such a drawback in the proper ventilation of mines, and the absolute danger by explosions as no explosion is now necessary and the cartridge being practically "fool proof" there is no danger of any accident, however slight, ever occurring.

The operators who witnessed the demonstration, representing, as they did, every coal company in this field are jubilant ever the success of the invention and there is no doubt but what a new scale will be arranged for at the coming convention of operators and miners to be held next month, to cover the scale to be paid for mining under these new improved conditions . . ."

3/14/11—"Filing for citizenship: Al Forsberg-Sweden; Theodore Kleinberg-Russia; John Minagez-Italian; Domenico Carbone-Italian; Wm. Scott-English; Samuel Hall-English; W. J. Tubbs-English; Andrew Andregg-Swiss; John Toblier, Austrian; Les Oulette—Canadian; James M. Sampson-Scot; Louis Alexander-Horovitz-Russian; Gregory Kumor-Pole and Joseph Sassin-German."

6/23/11—"The Election of Mine Workers . . . Held throughout District 22 on Tuesday. . . . Overwhelmingly Reelected Wm. Gilroy, brother of R. E. Gilroy of Carneyville; International Executive Committee-Thos. Fakey; Mine Inspector, Northern District-W. E. Jones (Altho Mr. J. J. Lytle, Sr. had the endorsement of the local group)."

3/18/12—Citizen Applications: "John Kuzma, Austria, Carneyville; Joe Anton Karch, Austria, Carneyville; Frank Richardson, England, Sheridan; Sam Pilch, Austria, Dietz; Michael Slovizczef, Austria, Carneyville." Second papers were issued to: Mrs. Theresa Bartello, Italy, Sheridan; John Bartello, Italy, Sheridan; Michael Pasterski, Austria, Sheridan."

5/15/12—"Pay Day for the Miners at the Camps."

"Estimated That About 1,350 Men Will Draw About $25,000 for Two Weeks Work." Men are not working full time, but are doing more than usual at this time." Mines at Dietz, New Acme, Carneyville, Monarch and Kooi have been operating from two to four days a week; at Kooi, 200 men find similar employment. At Dietz, 300 men work from two to three days" . . . "In wintertime . . . the miners reap a good harvest and oftimes each man will earn as high as $10 in a shift of eight hours."

8/30/12—"Miners and Operators in Agreement—Work of Joint Committee is Completed and All Harmonious—Increase in Wages—Same Raise Granted Here As in the Southern Field Where Increases Are." The following changes, "Men getting $3.40 raised to $3.45; Firemen raised from $3.00 to $3.15. Outside labor raised from $2.50 to $2.60. Twenty cents a yard increase for cross cuts and room turning. Pick miners, shooting and loading increase of 2 cents. Increase in loading, timbering and track laying rate 34¢ to 41 cents a ton. All disagreements here-after to go to executive committee of miners and operators. No individual strikes contenanced." (All of this after some three weeks of negotiations.)

9/5/12—*(Sheridan Enterprise)*—"SAVE MONEY ON COAL THIS YEAR." "Sheridan Schools to Use 800 Tons, Which Will Cost Them Less Than Year Ago."

By letting a contract for the season's supply of coal at $2.00 a ton, the directors of School District No. 7, embracing the city of Sheridan, this year will save about $400 over last year's figures when they were forced to pay $2.70 a ton. This year the contract was let to the Carney coal agent at the above figures while last year Dietz coal was used. It is estimated that fully 800 tons will be used by the ten school buildings in the city for heating purposes during the school year, costing the district $1,760, against $2,160 for last year. Three other local agents of the Sheridan County Coal, Monarch, Acme, and Kooi, submitted prices but were underbid by the Carney coal agent."

9/19/13—"Miners' Union Building Hall—New Structure at Coal Camp to Cost Over $10,000 . . . Hall will be Magnificent Modern Building to Be Used for Social and Commercial Purposes." To be located on Union property between Monarch and Carneyville on interurban line. Will also house store, 2 stories high . . . Central meeting place for miners families.

1/27/14—"GILDROY IS STATE LABOR BODY'S HEAD." "Sheridan Man Succeeds James Buckley in Wyoming State Federation of Labor."

W. W. Gilroy of Sheridan has succeeded James Buckley as president of the Wyoming State Federation of Labor, the headquarters of which is in the Mine Workers' building. James Morgan continues as secretary-treasurer of the organization.

Mr. Gilroy was elected president of the Federation at an annual convention held several months ago, with the understanding that he would not assume office until Saturday. James Buckley, whom he succeeds has served as president of the Federation for several years.

President Gilroy, has addressed to the union men of Wyoming a statement which in part is as follows: "There is imperative need of more organization work, and in this our state has its quota to look after. With the active cooperation of the union men of Wyoming, let us hope that the coming year may see the inauguration of many new local unions, as well as an increased interest on the part of those already formed."

2/17/14—"COAL MINING BUSINESS."

"Stewart Kennedy, one of the leading spirits in the management of the Model coal mines and business, has submitted to this office some interesting figures—a summary gleaned from the state coal mine inspector's report as to tonnage in connection with coal mining business. They will be examined with interest:

Tons produced per employe per day	Tons produced per keg of powder
8.7	61.4
5.6	90.7
5.1	56.4
8.0	67.8
3.5	56.0
5.4	67.8
3.9	72.2
2.5	79.7
3.3	73.5
5.7	31.8

Percentage of whole purchased by railroad	Percentage of whole lump shipped
62	11.2
43	30.
59	13.6
None	48.2
45	14.6
453	26.6
90	None
17	31.0
12	36.4
48	10.9

Name of Mine	Tons produced per employee per year
Sheridan Coal Co.	1,110
Kooi	865
Wyo. Coal Mining Co.	1,076
Model	1,176
Acme	640
Carney	921
Cambria	793
Owl Creek	570
Big Horn Coal Co.	833
Poposia	1,165

	Total Tonnage Produced, 1913
Sheridan Coal Co.	163,299
Kooi	176,401
Wyo. Coal Mining Co.	281,948
Model	25,876
Acme	190,079
Carney	264,525
Cambria	337,994
Owl Creek	143,480
Big Horn Coal Co.	133,360
Poposia	143,310
	1,860,272

2/27/14—"A German Scientist claims that by means of electricity he can turn coal into fluid. Never mind about ours, old man. Joe says it gets out of the coal bin and into the furnace fast enough."

4/1/14—"MINERS CELEBRATE THE EIGHT-HOUR-DAY."

All the mines are shut down today, and the camps are celebrating the anniversary of the eight-hour day in the United States. All of the camps are in gala attire and this evening a dance is to be held at Union Hall at Carneyville. This noon, the Monarch band came into Sheridan and played a number of selections on Main street advertising the day. This afternoon a large number of miners were in town."

4/30/14—"CAP SNIVELY LEASES LAND." "MINNEAPOLIS MAN SECURES VALUABLE COAL CONCESSION." "TO BUILD RAIL-ROAD" "It Will Connect Mine With Burlington—"

An agreement has just been signed by which Captain Scott K. Snively, of Sheridan, leases for fifty years, with option to buy, a valuable tract of coal land to A. L. Cornman, of Minneapolis, an experienced coal operator and a thorough business man.

Mr. Cornman, who has been in Sheridan recently, expects to return just as soon as he has closed some other business matters, and will begin work at once to open and operate the property—." "It lies in Sections 12 and 13, Township 57, Range 85—."

10/30/14—"AKEN GETS THE JOB."

"George Aken of Dietz has been appointed by Governor Carey to be State Mine inspector for District No. 2, the Northern Wyoming District to fill the vacancy caused by the resignation of Wm. E. Jones."

12/30/15—"GILDROY ELECTED PRESIDENT MINERS."

"According to the unofficial returns of the election held December 14 by the United Mine Workers of America in District 22 which includes all the miners in Wyoming, W. Gildroy of Carneyville was elected president of the district to succeed A. G. Morgan who was not a candidate for re-election. Paul J. Paulson of Rock Springs was elected international board member; George Young of Rock Springs, vice-president; James Morgan of Cheyenne, secretary-treasurer; and George Bateman of Dietz and John White of Rock Springs, auditors. Since the election was held, White had his back broken by a fall of rock and will remain a helpless invalid the rest of his life.

Mr. Morgan, the retiring president, left last night for Cheyenne where he will remain for a few days and then go to Indianapolis to attend the international convention which convenes there in January. He will return to Sheridan some time during the month.

Mr. Morgan will retire as president April 1, and will devote his time to ranching."

6/13/16—"FOUR NEW CITIZENS BY NATUR-ALIZATION."

"Those granted citizenship yesterday were Abraham Abrahams, Walter Ross Harrison, Bartolomeo Barello, and Mike Krezelok." Judge C. H. Parmelee presided and the examination was conducted by D. L. Sullivan, naturalization examiner for this district.

4/2/18—"LABOR CELEBRATES." "The Twentieth Anniversary of the Establishment of the Eight Hour Day." "BIG PARADE IN SNOW STORM." "Addresses in Afternoon at Orpheum Theater Attended by Large Audience—Dances and Entertainments in Evening in Which All Participate—It Was a Great Day for Labor."

"Never in the history of Sheridan has the importance of organized labor to the city's welfare been made more evident than in the parade and attending ceremonies of yesterday, when the twentieth anniversary of inauguration of the eight-hour day was celebrated. Weather conditions could not well have been more unfavorable, but in spite of the tempest that howled,

DEPARTMENT OF THE INTERIOR
WASHINGTON

September 1, 1917.

My dear Sir:

    Will you see that this appeal made by
the President to the miners of America is posted
in the place where most of the miners will see
it. And you may have more of these posters by
addressing the Director of the Bureau of Mines,
Department of the Interior, Washington, D. C.

                Cordially yours,

Letter from Secretary of the Interior.

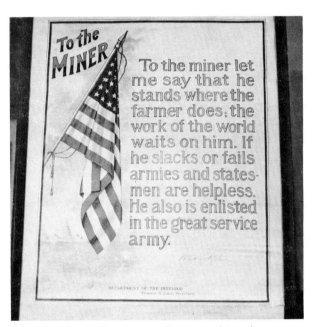

President Wilson's war effort appeal to miners.

in spite of the blizzard that prevailed, the people were on the streets by the hundreds, the gala spirit was not dampened and the program was carried out almost in its entirety as primarily arranged.

At an early hour a snow squall struck the city, and with scarcely a moment's intermission the storm fiend raged throughout the entire day. At times so dense were the flying particles of snow that it was impossible to see across the street. On this account however, no one remained at home, or if they did, their absence could not be noted.

At 11 o'clock, new time the special on the Burlington, carrying the delegations from the various mining camps of the valley arrived, and the parade was formed on Fifth Street, the right resting on Main. Scarcely had the formation begun when the interurban began arriving, bringing miners and their families by the score to augment the rapidly growing crowd. It was indeed an inspiring sight to see the visitors, with flags flying and banners streaming, braving the elements determined to take part in a demonstration that was to be an evidence of the patriotism as well as to commemorate the winning of organized labor's greatest victory.

The most conservative estimate places the number of the parade at one thousand and this did not include the ladies on the floats. These floats alone made an imposing spectacle, and although the moisture in the air dimmed the brightness of the bunting and made it impossible to work out some of the effects intended, they all made a brave and beautiful showing. Every float showed evidences of ingenuity in conception and every idea was well worked out.

The floats that received the most marked attention were those of the Red Cross auxiliaries, but the Kooi float which exemplified the principle of the eight-hour day also came in for its full share of applause. Each mine was also represented by a float upon which was stored a goodly supply of the product of the industry, and this coal was later sold to the highest bidder at public auction and the proceeds donated to the Red Cross.

At 1:30 the speaking at the Orpheum started in place of immediately after the arrival of the parade as first announced. Mayor Camplin delivered the address of welcome and he was followed by Judge Burgess and H. W. Reckard, president of the Commercial club. T. W. Taylor, president of the Trades and Labor council was scheduled for an address but on account of lack of time did not appear.

Then came the real event of the program—the address of John H. Walker, president of the federation of labor of the state of Illinois. Mr. Walker is a fluent speaker, forceful and eloquent and unaffected by the weather, yesterday he was at his best. The Orpheum was jammed to the doors but he held the crowd from start to finish and the inspiration that he gave will make not only Mr. Walker, but organized labor, which he represents, live long in the memory of the people of Sheridan county.

Later came the announcement of the awarding of parade prizes, made by Reece Davis, the veteran, to whose efforts perhaps more than to those of any other man—mayhap to every other man—were due the success of the celebration. There was some friction, as was to be expected, with every local and every man on his metal and striving to do his very best, but all realized that the committee made a most earnest effort to settle the matter equitably, and the decision was gracefully accepted. Carneyville was awarded the first prize of $80 for having in the parade, the best appearing delegation. The boys from the mines made a splendid appearance, the band did itself proud, but it is an open secret whispered about only among some thousands, that it was the ladies' auxiliary that really brought home the bacon. It was the float manned (?) by Carneyville femininity that was the deciding factor and threw the determining weight upon the balance that was so periously wavering. For every delegation made a splendid appearance and the judgment of a Soloman was needed to determine which looked the best. The U.M.W. of A. who formed the majority of the awarding committee, did not deem it "unfair" to take into consideration the fact that practically every woman on the Carneyville float had a son, a sweetheart, or a relative, either "over there" or on the road, perhaps dying at the same hour their duty-doing women were facing the storm to inspire the stay-at-homes.

The brewery workers pulled down the prize, for which only Sheridan locals were privileged to compete for the largest percent of membership in line. The boys from the brewery were there 100 per cent strong, and although they had close competition they were awarded the prize.

With James Scrivner as auctioneer, later the consignments of coal donated by the various mines, were sold to the highest bidder, and the proceeds turned over to the treasurer of the Red Cross.

The piece de resistance of the entire program was the banquet held last night at the Western hotel. Unique it was, but enjoyable. An inovation it was only in that it was perhaps the first

time that organized labor in Sheridan was ever the host of employes and business men. It was a get-together meeting in every sense of the word and no opportunity that might have been presented for labor, capital and middle men to arrive at a better understanding, was neglected. It must be admitted that there was some inconsistencies, for while the able speakers expanded upon the necessity of food conservation, the waiters served a six-course supper in which squab on toast, halibut and practically every other delicacy for which the George Brown hostelry is famous formed only part of the menu.

James Scrivner presided as toastmaster, and not only did himself proud but reflected credit upon the organization which he represents. Attorney Marshall led the array of after dinner speakers and acquitted himself in the manner for which he is famous. John H. Walker came next. To a large extent his remarks were supplementary to those he had made earlier in the day, but every phase rang with true Americanism. Mr. Walker touched lightly upon questions affecting labor specifically but in concrete his whole talk was upon labor and its importance and responsibilities at this crisis.

"This is the crucible," he said, "in which men's souls are being tried, and time will tell who are the true Americans. Some will subordinate public welfare to private desires; some will permit old emnities to rule and will be unable to get away from the inbred feeling that we should give the employers a _____ good licking, but most will prove themselves pure gold and when the show down comes they will measure up as Americans should.

And for those who fail when the test comes I have sympathy rather than sorrow. They don't know. Before the war, I myself opposed it. We could not bring ourselves to the point of realizing that it was necessary. But it has come and the fate of humanity is in the balance."

Mr. Walker elaborated upon the big order that the United States has undertaken but expressed his emphatic opinion that it would be carried out even to the last man and the last dollar. He told of the treachery of the Central powers and dwelt at length upon the causes leading up to the war. For more than an hour he spoke and there were patriotism and solid sense in every word he uttered.

"There is no chance to lose," he said in conclusion. "German domination means reducing the people of this country to the condition of slaves, and this cannot be done with Americans."

Other speakers followed Mr. Walker, among them being Rev. I. W. Kingsley, W. W. Gilroy, president of the district 22, United Mine Workers; James Bludson, Judge Metz, Mike Lovata, Joe Bosone, G. E. Haywood and others."

5/31/18—"PATRIOTISM AT CAMPS." "HOW MINERS CAME THROUGH FOR RED CROSS." "DONATORS' NAMES." "At Kooi, Acme and the Model, All Do Their Complete and Full Duty."

In the Red Cross drive Kooi and Acme both did their part nobly and came through with almost two thousand dollars each. Kooi leading by a small margin. The Model the smallest and youngest mine in the valley gave one-third as much which is exceptional under the circumstances. A list of the donators at the various mines are as follows:

Kooi

(Many of the following names are misspelled or otherwise inaccurate).

$1,000 contributions: Kooi Coal Company
$100 contributions: W. W. Anderson, Mrs. Peter Kooi, Doris E. Kooi, Vera M. Kooi, George B. Masters
$20 contributions: Fred Baines
$15 contributions: Benefit dance
Contributors of $10 and less: Ralph Arrison, John Antonkiewitz, Joe Adam, Mrs. J. Baxter, Jr., Joe Baxter, Sr., Mrs. Joe Baxter, Sr., Albert Bull, John Bestivana, George Baxter, John Baxter, Jr., Frank Boyka, John Byrtus, Mike Byrtus, Mike Bocek, Adam Byrtus, Bart Bondi, Joe Boyko, John Chiscina, Thos. Czys, Adam Czepsor, W. L. Driskill, Fred Deines, Paul Geryl, Paul Green, John Golik, Bella Green, Paul Gazurm, R. F. Hotchkiss, Mike Haratyk, Wm. Hergert, George Huss, John Hararyk, George Hararyk, C. L. Jones, Ben Joyce, George Kawulok, John Kawulok, Mike Kohut, Joe Krenzelok, Paul Krenzelok, George Kukuchka, John Kuzma, Joe Kiepus, George Krenzelok, George Kawulok, Jake Kawulok, Jake Kawlok, John Kohut, George Krenzelok, John Kawulik, Joe Kobielusz, John Kawlok, Mike Kawulok, Andy Kawulok, Harry Kukuchka, K. Katano, H. Kodani, Mike Kohut, Joe Kubit, Paul Krenzelok, Paul

Kobielusz, John Legerski Kiepus, Paul Kawulok, Joe Lestominok, Mike Legerski, John Legerski, Paul Legerski, Paul Legotski, Paul Lotzek, Henry Legerski, John Legotski, Joe Legerski, Mike Lupizovitz, Mike Legerski, John Legerski, Frank Loboy, Carl Lehman, Mike Mehalok, John Mates, Anton Maluryk, Mike Maluryek, Joe Mukina, Jesse McPhllamy, George MacDonald, A. V. Nye, Paul Pindor, Paul Polok, Dr. H. R. Rankin, James C. Reynolds, Tom Ross, Stanley Rozdowski, John Slifki, Tom Sikora, Jacob Schwartz, Jr., Jacob Schwartz, Sr., Frank Suday, Mike Sikora, John Sieczkowski, Frank Sabotka, Paul Secora, Tom Skurok, Henry D. Scott, Walter Sevier, Joe Sieczkowski, John Stanko, Jos. Scotkowski, John Schlauer, Mike Szkawran, Tom Sikora, George Urbatchka, Paul Urbatchka, George Visca, Mike Vevratch, Gregor Vovratch, Paul Washut, A. N. Waymach, Paul Wallach, John Wollney, John Washut, Anton Winski, George Washut, Tom Yuraszek, John Yuraszek, Mike Zowada.

Acme

$500 contributions: Acme Coal Company
$100 contributions: A. K. Craig, Ora Darnell
$30 contributions: J. T. Kessinger
$25 contributions: Mrs. E. P. Fitzgerald, Sheridan County Electric
$15 contributions: Frank H. Fraser, Ed Fitzgerald
Contributions $10 and less: S. Amasaki, G. Akagi, Frank Allen, John Acton, Steve Allen, John Andi, Charles Allen, Jaces Armstrong, Levy Aspass, Acme Meat Co., Kelle Aho, Roy M. Brown, John Blackburn, Bart Barello, E. J. Berry, E. R. Bateman, J. E. Baker, Frank Bellis, Mary Bocek, John Benegalia, Frank Benegalia, Frank Bonardi, George Bateman, Jos. Buerch, Ernest Bartlott, Adam Brimm, Frank Bartot, John Bonardi, Wm. Bennett, Adam Boyko, Paul Brytus, Gene Benedict, John Benegalia, Archie Bennett, William Baker, C. Benedict, R. E. Crance, W. C. Craig, Paul Calatis, L. T. Cox, Joe Cherni, J. N. Cooper, Lora Larke, Charles Crouch, Leo Chamber, E. P. Chambers, Dan Christ, Herman Core, A. T. Covington, George M. Cool, Chas. Carter, Paul Ceislar, Jas. Delatcher, John Davidson, L. T. Dazey, Yovan Dantich, C. M. Elich, Fred Eccli, Gus Ebner, George Evanoff, Louis Ertl, S. O. Fox, John Fraser, Mike Feider, John Feider, Chas. Grimm, George Goodever, George J. Gouthers, Mike

Gromshok, John Goyrl, Louis Gyurchek, Sam Goddard, George Gaidrica, Paul Groska, B. J. Grinnell, Krist Georgoff, E. H. Hunt, Lewis Hoskins, Victor Hokkenen, Karl Holman, John Hydic, A. H. Hughes, Matt Hemmila, Hans Holen, George Hooper, W. L. Heinz, J. R. Holliday, T. O. Holland, Wm. Hair, Paul Holnek, Wm. Hunter, George Houston, John Inetski, J. Itoya, Mary Juresak, Gust Johnson, Henry Jacobs, Victor James, Philip Jam, Frank Jurasek, J. A. Johnson, Chas. Konzcius, Charles Kolander, Aug. Konciditz, George King, George Kelse, John Kynaziur, Joe Koeblitz, Paul Kuenari, Paul Koska, P. Kohlruss, Pete Krovokopich, Joe T. Krimada, Eli Krivokopich, Ernest Kendrick, George Kvenchlal, George Kiecko, J. W. Knight, Matt Kostenbauer, Tony Kuzma, Earl Kelsey, Mike Kubitska, Steve Kigotenchek, John Ligocki, John Lund, J. Larson, Mary Long, George Legerski, Joe Lupizovitz, Pete Loss, Howell Lewis, Paul Logocki, Oscar Larson, Isaac Lahti, John Ligerski, Andy Long, A. S. Little, John Legerski, Ted Lull, Frank Mathews,

Joe Maxima, Ed Miles, Mike Matches, Mike Martinek, Herman Meyer, R. L. Michael, Pete Migratti, Wendel Maruski, Mike Mahaleg, Pete Mantino, George Mahalek, Caesar Migretti, Phil Morgan, A. S. Misiuk, Matt Maki, Frank Marionocky, George Manly, K. Mijacaki, John Martin, W. S. McClanahan, James McQuenn, Frank Newsbacker, Babtista Nova, John Nemet, John Neslanick, C. A. Nagar, Mrs. John Nelson, John Nelson, Charles Owens, Louis Olayos, K. Oyama, Joe Plott, C. H. Patterson, J. G. Pavuk, Percy E. Putney, Alex Ponak, Joe Plazcek, Sam C. Parsons, Ora Pudkey, Tony Podobnik, George Peck, Charles G. Palmer, Paul Padornosky, A. K. Perry, G. M. Pointer, Arther Pine, Pete Pavlico, A. C. Parkinson, George Pilch, John Posner, Paul Plazcek, John Ruby, George Roski, Dick Ryan, Santa Rosa, W. M. Richardson, Alex Romyn, John Reuche, George Romahak, Wasley Romyn, C. V. Reed, Martin Rogi, Stanley Roskoski, Joe Serentha, John Simas, Mike Saarnen, Herman Steiner, George Satkowski, Joe Stuskie, Christ Shott, Mike Stetz, Felix Samson, Sam Sturgeon, O. T. Solbert, Frank Seigel, Dave Savage, F. L. Sharp, Paul Stanko, Sam Shott, Simon Stevens, E. M. Seymour, Tony Sefercek, J. J. Sampson, George Statz, John Secora, Frank Sciler, Frank Smith, Chas. F. Shott, Joe Sikora, W. L. Selser, Ernest Shott, Harry A. Thayer, Bart Tavora, Lawrence Thomas, David Taylor, John Toblier, Tim Taira, Aug. Theistouck, Joe Trzcinski,

Sylvester Tinsky, Wallace Treat, Andrew Traar, Con. Uzenski, John Vesulka, F. L. Vanlangham, Archie Watson, Steve Wojdyla, John Wornly, William Waker, George Washbaugh, H. D. Woodard, H. C. Williams, Dick Wilson, Ora Williams, Geo. Wantulak, Joe Weisnoski, George Yoshi, Louis Yamer, F. Yama, Joe Zule, John Ziebert, Dan Zackovich, Robert Zeigler.

Model Mine

$250 contributions: Amalgamated Development Corp.

$50 contributions: Belmont B. Magee

$40 contributions: Paul G. Selway

$25 contributions: H. C. Edwards, Hugo J. Setzke.

Contributions of $10 and less: James J. Bledsoe, Joe Birchby, Harry Bailey, Mike Baldwin, Lyle Corey, Joe Colosimo, J. A. Cody, Geo. Cipcor, J. P. Cecchini, D. A. Carr, Alex Dubich, S. Forbert, Jas. A. Greenwood, Geo. Gebo, Wm. Hunter, Sr., Wm. Hunter, Jr., Hazel Lee Helvey, Hugo Haack, Jesse Kemper, F. H. Little, Herman Lahti, Frank Laky, Sam B. Musser, Wm. Murray, Mrs. Wm. Murray, Nick Miller, Eli Manovich, Elrens Marks, Eds. Newcomb, Dr. D. R. Nelson, Charles Patvaros, Bruno Romeo, Perry Robb, J. A. Snyder, Romeo, Robb Perry, J. A. Snyder, Eula Snow, Carl Sicoli, John Seikkula, Gerald Slater, Anna Slater, Ed Payala, Joe Vian, Clay Wardlaw, Louis Zinge.

11/1/19—Coal strike in effect nationally and locally. People warned for several weeks to stock up on coal in anticipation—no trouble locally, according to James Rennie, Pres. of the Sheridan County Trades Council . . ."

11/26/19—"NATION'S COAL BINS NEARLY EMPTY. DRAG NET THROWN OUT AND SIX ARE JAILED. Miners Fail to Heed Warning of Military Commandant. SITUATION HAS IMPROVED. Though Two Mines Are Still Idle—Other Mines Working, But in Most Instances with Diminished Crews.

Six members of the miners unions in the Sheridan coal fields were gathered in by the drag net Sheriff Thomas spread over the camps yesterday, in an effort to bring about a resumption of work to full capacity at the different mines. Two of the Offenders were arrested at Kooi, one at Monarch, and at Carneyville and two at Acme.

Following a report that the miners were not working at Monarch and Carneyville and only a small force at Kooi, despite the warning given them the day before, Sheriff Thomas chartered a special car and left for the mines at 10 o'clock. Accompanying him were undersheriff Kirby, Deputy United States Marshal Sevey and three deputy sheriffs.

Officers Arrive

Arriving at Monarch the party was divided, Sheriff Thomas and Marshall Sevey going to Kooi and the others, in charge of Undersheriff Kirby taking care of Monarch and Carneyville. The men for whom the officers were looking were hard to find and it took a thorough search of all the most likely places to locate those who were arrested. They were all foreigners and their compatriots were very dense when questioned as to the whereabouts of the much wanted men.

Men Arrested

Sheriff Thomas and Marshall Sevey arrested Joe Kawulok and Jake Mahalek at Kooi, and brought them to Monarch where they were put on the special and placed under guard. In the meantime Undersheriff Kirby picked up W. L. McClain at his home in Monarch and then went to Carneyville where after a search of more than two hours located and arrested Frank Nania.

The special was then taken to Acme, and Undersheriff Kirby dropped off and the car was switched back to Monarch, Sheriff Thomas got off at Carneyville, hoping to pick up two other miners who were wanted, believing that the men might put in an appearance, thinking the special had pulled out for Sheridan, but he was unable to locate anyone.

Chairman of Meeting

McClain who was arrested at Monarch was the chairman of the meeting at Carneyville Sunday afternoon at which it was decided to strike. The two men taken in custody at Kooi were accused of interfering with the men at work and trying to get them to quit. At this mine only the Americans in the camp are working. Frank Nania, arrested at Carneyville, was one of the active workers at the Sunday meeting. Mike Lupezovich, the man arrested at Acme nearly caused a fight at that place yesterday morning when he tried to induce four Polish miners to take off their work clothes and stay away from the mine.

Situation Improves

The situation at the mines in production, showed considerable improvement yesterday over Monday. At Acme the largest force since the strike was first inaugurated over two weeks ago was at work. The Model Mine was working at nearly capacity. While at Dietz the miners who showed up for work were nearly double in number of those of the day before. At Monarch and Carneyville it was stated that a few men were in the mines digging out the coal, none of which, however, was hoisted. In these two camps the Americans are willing and anxious to go to work, but there are not enough of them to take care of the work properly. Several of them expressed a determination to go to work tomorrow and fell some coal, even if it could not be hauled out."

(Several of the miners working at Monarch gave me various versions and some side lights which did not get to the news media). For example, one miner stated, "the national guard went from house to house, and with fixed bayonets, forced the men as they found them, whether completely dressed, and herded them like cattle to the pool hall. Two machine guns were placed on the hillside overlooking the camp. After trying to force the men to go back to work without success, the men were loaded on railroad cars and hauled to Ft. Mackenzie. One individual who worked in the office told of an incident which occurred there. It seems that one of the guardsmen came into the office, and as he poked a miner who happened to be there, with the point of his bayonet, one of the girls in the office said, "Goody, goody, stick him again." When this incident was later reported to her superiors, she was quickly fired from her job.)

11/27/19—"WAGE ADVANCE OF 14 PER CENT FOR MINERS." "DISCORDANT SPIRITS MADE TO FEEL HEAVY HAND OF THE LAW." "Half Hundred Disturbers Are Arrested." "Sheriff Raids Camp." "Backed by Regular Soldiers Armed With Rifles and Machine Guns."

"Fifty-one miners from Carneyville; all of them foreigners are prisoners at Fort Mackenzie, as the result of arrests made at that camp yesterday by Sheriff U.A.C. Thomas and his deputies, backed up, by his request by a detachment of the Fifteenth cavalry, under Major

Warren Dean. The arrests were made without disturbance, only an occasional miner affording a diversement by not obeying orders promptly or offering excuses why he could not go to the appointed detention place.

While the residents of the camp had learned that the soldiers and civil officers were coming, they evidently did not realize just what this meant until the soldiers put in an appearance. There was considerable scurrying around and uneasiness was evidenced on the faces of a good many of the people, especially among the women and children.

The people of Sheridan realized that something unusual was going to happen when the fire whistle blew early in the morning, as it was generally known that this was the signal for the mobilization of the local national guard. The presence on the streets of several big motor trucks from the fort and the hurrying of the guards to their headquarters where they were loaded into the trucks increased the interest. It was thought they were taken to the fort and held in reserve for emergencies.

At 1 o'clock two special cars pulled out for the camps. On board the last car were Major Dean and Captain Mandell of the Fifteenth cavalry, Sheriff Thomas and deputies and U. S. Deputy Marshal Sevey.

Arriving at the crossing of the street car tracks and the railroad at the elevator on North Main street, the regular troops from the fort were taken aboard. They consisted of one machine gun platoon, one automatic rifle platoon, and a rifle platoon. Undersheriff Kirby joined the party at Acme.

Arriving at Carneyville the specials were stopped at the east end of the camp, close to the two pool halls. The troops alighted, formed in line and were ordered to fix bayonets. Then at double quick they went to the pool halls which were surrounded and the inmates placed under guard. Thirty or forty men were found in the two places. Then the round-up of the camp began.

Searching Houses

The sheriff and his deputies entered every house, the soldiers receiving and guarding the men turned over to them by the sheriff's men, sending them to the pool hall to keep company with those already there.

The soldiers were in charge of Captain Man-

dell who formed a line up the middle of the street. When a miner was turned over to the troopers he was told to keep in the middle of the street and the soldier boys saw to it that he did so. Once in a while some one would start down the side of the street, but was promptly told to "hit the middle of the road and stay there," and always obeyed.

It took considerable time to ransack the camp but after a thorough search the men were all gathered in the lower pool hall, where they were segregated into nationalities. The Italians and Montenegrins were held in the lowerhall and the others sent to the upper place. All the men at the upper hall, after a short talk by Major Dean agreed to go to work Friday morning, today being a legal holiday.

Those at the lower hall fifty-three in number were not so amiable, so they were escorted to the cars where they were placed under guard. Two of those men were later released proving to the satisfaction of the authorities that they were all right.

Officers at Monarch

The specials were then taken to Monarch, where the same tactics were pursued. The pool hall was quickly surrounded by one detachment of the troops while another picked up quite a number of miners who were waiting at the station to take the regular car into town. Sheriff Thomas and his men went to the upper part of the town, the soldiers following, taking care of the men as fast as they were turned over to them. This time, however, they were not sent along to the pool hall by themselves but were kept together and taken in a body to the meeting place.

After the miners were all gathered in and as Major Dean was about to classify them, union officials asked the Major if he would grant them a few minutes before any further action was taken and allow them to hold a meeting. The request was granted and in just about the time it took to call the meeting to order, state the nature of the business and take a vote, the trouble at Monarch was over, as the miners voted to return to work Friday morning.

At 3 o'clock the special cars left Monarch and at the crossing four big trucks were awaiting. The prisoners were loaded into these and taken to Fort Mackenzie, where they are being held in the guard house, but not as federal prisoners. They are held there at the request of the sheriff as there is no room in the county jail to accommodate them.

Individual warrants will be sworn out against them, under section 76 of the Wyoming session laws of 1919. They will be charged with inciting to riot. It is also probable that some of the men will also have to answer to the federal authorities.

Sheriff Thomas, all through the trouble at the mines, has been acting under instructions from Governor Carey, and has been backed up, at his request by Major Dean, representing the federal authorities.

Breaks Up Poker Game

When Sheriff Thomas tried to enter one house at Carneyville, he found the door locked. After considerable pounding the door was unlocked and the sheriff just caught a glimpse of three men pulling money off a table and putting it in their pockets. The sheriff says he secured the deck of cards, but would rather have got his hands on the money. The players are among those now resting at the fort guard house.

Sneaks Into Brush

While Undersheriff Kirby was searching one part of Monarch he saw a man sneaking off into the brush in a part of the camp not yet visited. Mr. Kirby noted the spot where the man appeared and when he reached that vicinity in the roundup, promptly grabbed his man.

Some Good Excuses

Some of the excuses offered by the miners why they should not be taken into custody were amusing. One of the men told Major Dean that he had a sack of corn on the station platform and it was imperative that he should go after it at once. The Major asked the man if he would go to work. He said, "If the rest of the men do." "That is not what I asked you," replied the Major "will you go to work individually?" The man promised faithfully to report for duty Friday and he was dismissed from detention, much to his satisfaction.

Undersheriff Kirby ran up against one man who had a good excuse for not going to the rendezvous. Asking the lady of the house if her husband was in she pointed to the next room. The sheriff entered and saw a man lying on the bed. He told him to get up, put his coat on and come on. The man threw a light covering off his legs and pointed. Mr. Kirby excused him. His leg was broken.

One of the deputies seeing a miner easing off in a direction that did not lead to the pool hall, stopped the man and asked him where he was going. He said his wife was waiting dinner for him and that he was late already. He stated he was in for a good curtain lecture right then and if compelled to go with the crowd he would sure catch hell.

Two Men Released

Two men taken into custody by the sheriff Tuesday were released by him after he was more than satisfied that an injustice had been done both of them, W. L. McLain who was arrested on the charge of being the chairman of the meeting Sunday afternoon was discharged and given a clean bill of health when it was found upon examination that he was not the McClain who presided and had always born an excellent reputation at the camp.

Mike Upezovich, apprehended at Acme by Undersheriff Kirby, was given his liberty and a clean score when it was ascertained that the reason he was not working at Acme was because when it was thought the strike was going to come off he went to a small wagon mine and worked for a day not wishing to remain idle, not returning to Acme in time to go on shift."

11/27/19—In this same issue of the preceding release, it was revealed that the fourteen percent increase offered to the miners evidently would not be acceptable to the United Mine Workers of America, headed by John L. Lewis. The Fuel Administrator, Garfield made this offer which was approved by Secretary Wilson and President Wilson.

11/28/19—"WEEDING OUT THE AGITATORS AND RELEASING THE HONEST WORKERS."

"Two of the men arrested when Sheriff Thomas and his men, backed by the Fifteenth cavalry, raided the town of Carneyville, were ordered released last evening, it having been made clear to the officers that they were not radicals and had been taking no part in the strike agitation. A rigid investigation is now in process and the individual cases of each of the fifty men now under guard at the fort will receive attention and if it develops that any of the men have been injustly accused and they are ready to return to work, they will be released and permitted to resume their duties as miners.

In a drag net haul such as took place Wednesday it is obvious that some men, not agitators, should be caught, and it is equally as obvious that some of the guilty escaped. It is the intention of the officers to take up each case and decide it upon its merits without regard to the nationality of the man, and if it is found that he is willing to go to work and has not been guilty of trying to prevent others from going to work, in all probability he will be released without trial. The radicals, however, so it is stated will be prosecuted under the state statute and if that is found inadequate, it is possible that the federal authorities may take the matter in hand.

Quiet at Mines

Reports from the mines indicate that there will be a general resumption of work today—"

11/29/19—"WILL TOLERATE NO INTERFERENCE WITH MINES." "PRISONERS RELEASED AND WORK IS RESUMED." "All of the 52 Men at the Fort Released." "MINES ARE ALL WORKING." "Production of Coal Is Approaching Normal—Coal Strike Crises Apparently Passed."

12/3/19—"MINES AT WORK OUTPUT NORMAL." "Everything Peaceful at the Mines in Sheridan County—Wage Increase."

The output of coal from the mines of the Sheridan district has about returned to normal, and a heavy tonnage is going out into the states where there has been a shortage for sometime past—Notices were posted Monday at all the mines advising that an increase of 14 per cent in wages will be allowed from the time they returned to work about November 15, which is in accordance with the instructions given out by Fuel Administrator Garfield."

12/13/19—"THIRTY-FIVE STRIKING MINERS IN STOCKADE AT FT. MacKENZIE." "Charged With Violating the Proclamation of Governor Carey." SHERIFF THOMAS MAKES THE ARRESTS." "Hold Meeting at Kooi and Vote to Quit Work—Sheriff and Deputies are Supported by Detachment of Regular Army Soldiers."

"Thirty-five Polish miners were arrested yesterday evening at Kooi, charged with violating the governor's proclamation of December 6. Sheriff Thomas and four deputies made the arrests. The sheriff was accompanied by Major Dean and a small detachment of soldiers of the 21st Infantry, to guard the prisoners, and to be on hand in case of serious resistance. No resistence was encountered, the miners being taken completely by surprise.

Sheriff Thomas and his party left here about four o'clock, and were taken to Kooi by a special train. They arrived at the mine about five, and by six had completed rounded up their prisoners. The men arrested were detained temporarily at Ft. McKenzie, as there was not room for them in the county jail.

Yesterday afternoon these miners held a meeting, and decided to quit work. They walked out of the meeting in a body, and in a body went to the mine office and asked for their time. By this action they threw themselves liable to arrest, as the governor's proclamation orders and directs that "no assemblages shall be held within twenty-five miles of any coal mine within the State of Wyoming" and that "civil and military authorities shall take prompt and effective action to surpress and disperse any such assemblages as may come within the prohibition above."

The action of the miners arrested was taken in direct violation of that proclamation. It was also in open disregard to the orders from the miners' officials ordering the miners back to work after the settlement of the strike. Mine officials say that the governor's proclamation had been read to all the miners, and had been posted on the company's bulletin board, where all might see it. Only by permission of the governor of the state or the commanding officer in charge of the forces at or near the mines may any kind of a meeting be held, and Major Dean is emphatic in stating that he would not have granted permission for such a meeting had the application been made. What makes the case of the miners worse is the apparent flagrancy with which they not only violated the governor's orders, but flouted the military and local authority in so doing.

It is expected that these men will be prosecuted to the limit, as the authorities are determined that no further restriction shall be placed on the production of coal by such concerted action on the part of irresponsible persons. So far as the *Post* can learn no reason was given by the Kooi miners for quitting. They simply walked out.

When the sheriff's party reached the mine, they found the mine officials ready for the round up. The names of all the men participating in the walkout were in readiness, and lists were supplied the sheriff. The latter divided his force into five groups and directed them to cover different portions of the camp where the miners live. For the most part the arrests were made at the shacks of the miners, although a number took to the brush when they learned what was happening. These were pursued and routed out of their hiding places. As the prisoners were taken they were herded to the Burlington special train.

In an hour the raid was accomplished. At the train a poll was taken, and it was found that all but a very few of the offenders had been taken into custody. These were loaded into one box car, under guard of four soldiers, while the rest of the soldiers occupied another box car. The prisoners were unloaded at the elevator west of town and taken in trucks to Ft. McKenzie."

12/14/19—"TWENTY-SEVEN STRIKERS RELEASED FROM ARREST." "—Eight are being held and will be tried—" "—It appeared that the men released were not to be classed as agitators—" Probably couldn't understand the bulletin, but were simply loyal to the group. The release was based upon the promise that they would return to work.

12/20/19—"STRIKING MINERS ARRESTED BY THE FEDERAL OFFICERS."

George Mahallik, John Lagerski, George Kawalok and John Yaroszek, four of the miners arrested last week at Kooi, and the only ones held out of the bunch arrested, were brought to town today from Ft. MacKenzie, where they have been detained, and turned over by the county officials to the United States marshal, who took them under a federal warrant. They will be held in the county jail for a hearing before the United States commissioner."

12/21/19—"ARRESTED MINERS ARE ALL RELEASED." "Will Not Be Prosecuted—A Record Production Is promised at Mines—Question of Cars."

—"George Morgan, secretary of the miners' union for Wyoming district who has been here for several days, says he thinks the situation is in excellent shape now." All miners now released.

12/25/19—(CAMP BREEZES—Mrs. George Kovacic) "Monarch—The Christmas program held at the Dietz Hall Tuesday night was a decided success. The communities of both Dietz and Dietz No. 8 wish to express their thanks to Rev. Theo. J. Shultz for giving them such a pleasant and entertaining evening. They also wish to thank the children who participated and the local union for their treat to the kiddies. Teddy Parrat in the role of Santa Claus was the star of the evening. The Dancing snowflakes under the supervision of Father Shultz was a beautiful sight, and the singing and playing was splendid, especially the violin solo by Masters Kuzara, Aiken, and Gibbons, boys under fourteen, who have been taking lessons only about 6 months, under Father Shultz supervision.

Mrs. Geo. Aiken of Dietz No. 8 spent a very enjoyable afternoon at the home of her mother, Mrs. H. Scullen of Sheridan.

Mrs. W. H. Hoel and daughter Miss Lucia of Carneyville were Sheridan visitors Tuesday on a Christmas shopping tour.

Mrs. J. L. Landes of Acme was a passenger on the interurban Tuesday morning—.

Miss Elsie Thompson of Monarch was a Sheridan caller Tuesday morning on errands pertaining to the Christmas tree program. The teachers have certainly worked hard with the children in helping them with their various parts, and deserve much credit. Mr. and Mrs. L. A. Norman of Dietz departed for El Paso, Texas on the sad mission of attending the funeral of the former's sister, Christine.

Mrs. A. Schaal of Monarch spent a very enjoyable afternoon Tuesday in Sheridan."

Others shopping in Sheridan during the week included the following: Mesdames Joe Cammock, M. E. Sevier of Dietz; Miss Lila Wade of Monarch; Mrs. Joe Wentzell of Monarch; Mrs. J. T. Carey of Alger; Mesdames Billie Wondra, John Sobotka, R. Stephenson and son Raymond, Miss Mary Wondra and brother Albert; Mr. and Mrs. Joe Cecchini with Mr. and Mrs. A. Schaal of Monarch; Mrs. George Bateman of Acme; Mrs. Leon Siezkowski and daughter, Miss Katharine of Monarch; Mrs. J. T. Carey, accompanied by her daughter, Mrs. M. Huffington and son, Junior of Alger.

5/20/20—"INDUSTRIAL GIANTS VISIT WYOMING." FINANCIERS TO INSPECT COAL MINES; FIRST VISIT." "Billions of Capital Represented by Distinguished Visitors" "WILL ERECT BUILDINGS." "Combine Business and Pleasure in Three-Day Stay; Will Be Guests at Big Horn Ranch."

Captains of industry representing more than $3,000,000,000 of resources are visitors in Sheridan today, and will remain here for the next three days. The group of distinguished gentlemen represent the owners and operators of the Sheridan-Wyoming Coal Company—" Arrived by special car.

"The purpose of the visit is to make a comprehensive survey of the mines, to erect new buildings and make improvements, to increase production and to make a general inspection of the properties. Heading the group of visitors is F. S. Peabody, president of the Peabody Coal Company of Chicago.

Presidents of four of New York's largest financial institutions in the party include: H. W. Ward, Irving National Bank; Harvey Gibson, Liberty National bank; Eugene Thayer, Chase National bank and Charles Townsend, Townsend Bond company. Others in the group are: Moses M. Peltier, operating vice-president of sales, Sheridan-Wyoming Coal Company; G. M. Shaffer, secretary to F. S. Peabody; Herman Hetler, president of the Hetler Lumber Company of Chicago; George Getz, president of the United States Distributing Company and A. P. Farrand—." "—Tomorrow the party will be the guests of the Sheridan Commercial club and will be entertained at the Willis Spear Ranch at Big Horn.—"

6/6/20—"Northern Miners and Operators To Confer—Will Meet to Ratify Wage Agreement and to Adjust Local Matters—Union Offiçials to be Present—No Matters of Serious Import—Miners Already Receiving Scale as Fixed by the National Commission."

8/8/20—"Gas Company Installations—New Installation and Equipment Installed in Past Few Weeks—" 89 installations of heater or ranges or both—effects coal consumption.

8/25/20—"Commissioner Berkhaeuser Retires Sept. 1—Leaving for Denver."

"Mr. Berkhaeuser became associated with the Wyoming Coal Company, which was later absorbed by the Peabody Coal Co. in 1903, and from 1903 until 1906 he was in charge of the sales department of this company with offices in Milwaukee, Wisc. In 1906 he came to Monarch and accepted the managerial position with the same company here, which he held until 1913. In 1913, he moved to Sheridan where he engaged in private business and became Sheridan City Commissioner."

3/9/21—"(CAMP BREEZES—Mrs. George Kovacic). Monarch, March 8—"

Those shopping in Sheridan this week included the following: Mrs. J. Lee; Mrs. D. L. Glen of Kleenburn; Mrs. LeRoy Lynn of Acme, accompanied by her sons, Howard and Kenneth: Mrs. James Bledsoe of Model, and daughter Mina and grandson, Archibald; Mrs. Robert Gault of Dietz; Mrs. J. G. Hobbs and Mrs. J. R. Rann of Acme; Mrs. Ralph Pack of Dietz; Mrs. Phil Morgan of Acme and daughter, Selina; Mr. and Mrs. Joh Sinkler of Monarch; Dr. W. M. Hoel of Kleenburn; Mrs. M. Groska of Dietz No. 8; Misses Mora Johnson and Theresa Scullen of Kooi; Mr. and Mrs. Joh Mentock of Dietz No. 8; Miss Lila Wade of Monarch attended church in Sheridan.

"The Misses Theresa Scullen and Mora Johnson of Kooi, Mary Baker of Dietz No. 8 and Rosie Kuzara of Dietz suburb spent Sunday afternoon at the home of "ye scribe."

Members of the U.M.W. of the Sheridan Valley local, held a meeting Sunday forenoon at the union hall near Kleenburn, in order to decide about their First of April celebration, which will be at Acme this year. The following committees have been appointed: Arrangements, Messrs. James Bateman of Monarch, John Conley and J. T. Parsons of Acme; sessions, Messrs, John Tomasi of Monarch, Stewart McDowell of No. 8, H. W. Goss and Frank Pelch of Kooi; music, Messrs, John Tomasi and James Bateman of Monarch; finance, Messrs. Bert Capps of Hotchkiss Heights, Pete Komich of Dietz, and James Conley of Acme. There will be a game of baseball played, sports of all sorts with prizes, also dancing in the famous Acme pavilion. Refreshments of all kinds will be obtainable at the various booths. Messrs. James Cox of Kleenburn and Stewart McDowell of Dietz No. 8 are elected as floor managers during dancing and will see that every one present has a good time. They will also see that there'll be no wall flowers and provide dancing partners for those that will not have any. The principal speaker of the day will be Neal James Terry of Hazelton, Pa., international board member U.M.W., District No. 7. The officers of this local are Harry Taylor of Dietz No. 8, president; and Henry Caudron of Kleenburn, secretary-treasurer. Each above named member will strive his utmost to assure everyone present a good time, weather permitting. A cordial invitation is extended to the public at large to help celebrate the eight-hour day of the miners. Arrangements are being made with Mr. Jones of Sheridan, for excursion rates on the interurban, also extra cars, if available, to accommodate all who wish to attend. An open air concert during the forenoon is under discussion, and the famous "Lucas orchestra" will delight all who trip the light fantastic.

Troy Wade of Monarch was a business caller in Sheridan Monday."

5/7/21—"COAL AGENCIES CONSOLIDATED—5 Retailers to Close Doors" Peabody Coal Co. selects Merchants Transfer Co. of Sheridan to handle "all of its retail selling business"—"to be named "The Kleenburn Coal Agency."

10/30/21—(CAMP BREEZES—Mrs. May Kovacic) Monarch, Oct. 29—"Mr. and Mrs. T. McCoy of Kooi entertained at a birthday party last Saturday afternoon in honor of their little daughter, Miss Eleanor, who was seven years old. The following guests were present: Misses Doris Ross, Sally and Margaret Joyce, Florence and Edith Ruth Bull of Sheridan, Norma Barrier, Helen and Doris Yurosek, Maud Gross and Masters Billie Ross, Vaud Nye, Walter Siegoski and Albert Joyce. Mrs. Ross assisted Mrs. McCoy with the serving and entertaining the little folks. The day being ideal, the kiddies played wonderful out-door games and when serving time arrived they all had splendid appetites and did full justice to the delicious refreshments provided for them by the ladies. When going home time arrived the little folk were all loath to leave, as the time slipped by so rapidly they could scarcely believe they'd been there all afternoon. They wished their playmate many more happy birthdays.

New lights have been installed at Hotchkiss Heights, and at night it gives one the impression of being a very busy place.

Mr. and Mrs. Motyka of Monarch entertained at dinner Wednesday evening in honor of their daughter's, Miss Mary's fifteenth birthday. Covers were laid for the Misses Mary Wolney, Katie Luke, Mary Novarra, and Mary and Annie Bareno. The evening was pleasantly spent in playing various games."—.

1/8/22—"A number of young men from the various coal mining villages are all leaving for other parts, due to the mines being shut down indefinitely."

1/8/22—"WHY THE MINES WERE SHUT DOWN" "Statement Made by Official of the Company—

"Understanding that the recent closing of certain coal mines owned by the Sheridan-Wyoming Coal Company and operated by the Peabody Coal Company in this vicinity has been a topic of some general interest of late and that a number of rumors have been circulating in Sheridan—the companies wish to make the following statement to a Post representative:

"The companies have operated throughout the year 1921 five and for a portion of the time all six of the mines controlled by them—on an average of about one day per week per mine. The reason for this very small percentage of operating time has of course, been the great depression existing throughout the United States—Unusually mild winter—hoping business would pick up—operating at a great loss. The closing down of certain of the mines at this time is of course, solely for the purpose of concentrating the operations and giving some employes a reasonable amount of work and also in order to reduce the very heavy overhead expense—removal of all of the offices to Kleenburn will complete the concentration and will eliminate all avoidable expense—."

1/19/22—"Big Decrease in The Production of Bituminous Coal During Last Year—Highest Point in Production Reached in 1918—Coke Production Also Decreased During Last Year by Nearly 74 Percent—Anthercite Production slightly Lower."

2/19/22—(Camp Breezes—Mrs. May Kovacic) Monarch, Feb. 18—

"Joe Giroux of Sheridan was a passenger on the interurban on Thursday enroute the Union Hall near Kleenburn where a class of young men were taking the work of the Knights of Pythias of the Tongue River Lodge No. 25, "Ye scribe" was enabled to get the following names: Messrs. Fred Bell, Jr., Wade Radcliffe, Harry Marcus, Paul Mavrakis, Gus Thomas, Tom King, Luther Rice, James Neese, Anton Motosa, Geo. E. Masters, George Johnson, Robert Flockhart, Frank Ruziska, Joseph Rusich, Frank Colson, John Stanko, Joe Wondra, Dr. R. E. Crane, John Drobish, John and Frank Sabotka and Bert Capps. These young men belong to various mining villages in the valley. This makes quite an increase in their membership. Anything of this kind is a great help in a mining community. They have several plans on foot for recreation, one of them being a baseball team to contest for the cup offered by Geo. H. Messick of Sheridan, who is an enthusiastic baseball fan. A community reading room will be established shortly and good reading literature will be available. A club has also been formed by them to give home talent plays in the near future, which will be a source of enjoyment as well as education, for the spectators as well as the actors. The anniversary of the K. of P.'s will be celebrated by holding a dance at the Union Hall near Kleenburn on Feb. 21. Invitations have all been sent out to the friends of the members. A royal good time is being anticipated, as they never do things by halves. There will be good music to dance by, and later a lap luncheon, the goodies being brought by the ladies who are certainly cullinary experts, when it comes to making cakes and salads."

8/22/22—"Mines Will Start Work Today—Wyoming Coal Strike Comes to an End Monday Evening—8,000 Men will be employed—Superintendent of operations at Kleenburn Advises That as Many Mines in Sheridan District Will Resume Operations for Which Men Are Available—when the whistles blow, the miners will be cutting coal for the first time since nation wide mine strike called April 1st" from word received by Edward Bottomly, Superintendent of the six Sheridan-Wyoming properties and Peter Kooi, President of the Kooi Coal Co.

8/23/22—"Three Mines Start Work Tuesday—Number of Men to Be Increased to 1,000 Today—The Kooi, Monarch and Carney Mine No. 2 got underway yesterday."

8/29/22—"Peabody—Big Coal Man Dies—Peter Kooi Receives Word of Death of Chairman of the Board of Directors of the Peabody Coal Company, and holding the same position with—"

10/22/23—"KLEENBURN MINE TO BE RE-OPENED."

"Receipt of instructions from the Chicago office of the Peabody Coal Company for the immediate opening of the Kleenburn Mine was announced Monday morning by Edward Bottomly, superintendent of the company's mines in the Sheridan district.

Preference in applications for work will be given former employes, Mr. Bottomly stated. Three mines are now running steadily, the mines at Acme and Monarch being the other two.

About 150 men can be used in the Kleenburn Mine, it is stated. Six hundred are at work, and as soon as the three mines get into full operation about 200 men in all can be used."

5/2/23—"BURLINGTON STORES WINTER COAL STOCK 500,000 TONS NOW." "Coal mined at Sheridan is used almost exclusively on the Burlington between Billings and Ravenna and McCook, Neb., it was said by the local officials Tuesday."

2/22/23—"SHERIDAN-WYOMING COAL COMPANY ELECTS HARRY N. TAYLOR OF NEW YORK SUCCESSOR TO PETER KOOI."

"Harry N. Taylor, new President of the United States Distributing corporation of New York City, and formerly vice president of the Central Coal and Coke Company of Kansas City, was elected president of the Sheridan-Wyoming Coal Company at the annual meeting of stockholders of the company here Tuesday. He succeeds Peter Kooi, resigned.

The resignation of Mr. Kooi which was announced some time ago, was accepted at the meeting with regret.

Mr. Taylor is a coal operator of long experience and national reputation and the local company is fortunate in obtaining his services as chief executive. He will probably retain his headquarters in New York.

Mr. Taylor was a recent visitor here."

5/1/24—"30 to Seek Papers as U. S. Citizens in Court Hearing Here."

"Thirty foreign-born men and women and two American-born persons who lost their citizenship by becoming citizens of Canada will be naturalized at the hearings at the beginning of the June term of court, if they are able to pass the examinations at that time. The date set for the hearings is June 9.

The following petitions for naturalization have been filed:

Austrians—Joseph Ligocki, Jacog Schmontz, John Wolney, Joseph Meich, Alex Chomyn, Sam Banich, Jacob Malyjurek, Thomas Skorak.

Poles—Joseph Zogotta, Stanley Bohenko, Mike Vawrach, Andreas Bujok, Paul Gormak, Paul Martinek, Jan Saniec (John Sametz), Wasyl Chomyn, Mike Niznik, Andrew Sokolowski, Mike Joe Sikora and George Urbacka.

Sweden—Alma Maria Lundquist Johnson.

Russia—Mallie Kraft Kerbel

Italy—Antonio Capillupo

England—Elizabeth Rees
Germany—Otto Franc Blakenburg
Scotland—Mary Jane Davidson
Montenegro—Mike Boxkovich and Andrew Sovich
Greece—Thomas George
United States—Joseph J. Connolly and Anna Louise Connolly."

6/8/24—"Walter Upton, Spanish War Veteran, Finds He's Not Citizen, After Voting Many Years."

"Although he had lived in the United States since he was 14 years old, had voted since he became of age, served with the United States army in the Spanish-American war, and held positions open only to citizens, Walter Upton, resident of Sheridan county for 22 years and superintendent of the mine at Dietz No. 8, discovered Saturday morning that he is not a citizen of the United States but still owes allegiance to John Bull.

The case came to light when Upton appeared before M. F. Lence, naturalization examiner, as a witness for Louis Horvath, Hungarian, who resides at Dietz. Upton states a citizen, but it later developed that he was born in England and had never been naturalized.

The mine superintendent came to the United States when 14 from a town named St. Helen, located in Lancashire, England. He was adopted by an uncle and aunt who live in town, and believed that through his adoption he became a citizen. He was informed Saturday that adoption does not change nationality. For 19 years he has been superintendent of the mine at Kleenburn and for three years has been superintendent of No. 41 at Dietz No. 8. He is a member of the school board at Dietz.

Mr. Upton immediately filed his application for citizenship and will have his hearing in November. He will be naturalized under the provision of the law which permits honorably discharged soldiers who served in the United States army prior to Jan. 1, 1900, to become American citizens.

Other applications for citizenship filed before the naturalization examiner since noon Thursday were as follows:

Peter Ghirighello, Italian, Monarch; Paul Cieslar, Pole, Monarch; John Kuchera, Austrian, Monarch; Mike Peter Kavulok, Pole, Kooi; Mike Liegocki, Pole, Dietz; Pavie Lozar Stevovich, Jugo-Slav, Monarch; Andrew Cieslar, Pole, Mon-

arch; Louis Horvath, Hungarian, Dietz and Milan Navkovich, Jogo-Slav, Kleenburn."

8/15/24—"TWO CARS OF COAL TO DAKOTA DAILY FROM MINES HERE."

The contract awarded Thursday to the Peabody Coal Company to furnish coal for the South Dakota cement plant at Rapid City will mean that approximately 800 cars a year or more than two cars a day will leave the company's mines near Sheidan for Rapid City beginning next month, officials declared Friday.

The contract calls for 40,000 tons each year.

The large contract will also allow the Peabody Company to dispose of its screenings in the winter. The contract will run until Sept. 30, 1926.

The cement plant, which is being built at a cost of $2,000,000, is said to be the largest state cement plant in the United States."

9/17/24—"THIRTY-NINE TO APPLY FOR PAPERS HERE." "Naturalization Examiner to Come From Denver."

Thirty-nine applications for naturalization will come up at the hearings to be conducted in district court here this winer by a naturalization examiner from Denver, it was announced Friday morning. The date for the hearings have not been decided.

Austria heads the list with 12 applicants and Poland comes second with seven people who want to become Americans. The list of petitioners posted in the office of the clerk of court follows:—

Joseph Ligocki, Austria, Sheridan; Stanley Bohenke, Poland, Sheridan; Otto F. Blankenburg, Germany, Sheridan; Jan Samiec (John Sametz), Poland, Monarch; Mike Boskowich, Montenegro, Monarch; Wasyl Chomyn, Poland, Acme; Mike Niznik, Poland, Monarch; Theodore Begenisich, Austria, Kleenburn; John Brug, Russia, Ranchester; Joseph Golab, Poland, Dietz; Jacob Wesner, Russia, Sheridan; Joannis Vacilakopoulos, Greece, Sheridan; Albert Leonard Bull, England, Sheridan; Aususta Marie Eisenman, Germany, Sheridan; Frank Kowalowski, Austria, Kleenburn; George Krenzelak, Austria, Sherian; James Wondra, Czecho-Slovakia, Sheridan; Mike Peter Kavulok, Austria, Kooi; Mike Ligocki, Poland, Dietz; Peter Gheringhello, Italy, Monarch; Paul Cieslar, Austria, Monarch; Joseph Bury, Austria, Monarch; Joseph Byrtus, Austria, Monarch; Joseph Motyka, Austria, Monarch; John Kuzhera, Austria, Monarch; Pavie Stevovich, Monarch; Andrew Cieslar, Poland, Monarch; Louie Duranto, Italy, Kleenburn; Louis Harvath, Hungary, Dietz; Walter Upton, England, Dietz; Milan Novakovich, Montenegro, Kleenburn; Stanley Stravinski, Russia, Acme; Mrs. Alice Stevens Upton, England, Dietz; Charles James White, Texas, Sheridan; George Gligorea, Rumania, Big Horn; Joseph William Solosky, Austria, Sheridan."

11/9/24—"NEW CITIZENS ACCEPTED BY COMMISSIONER." "Thirty-seven Admitted by Denver Examiner Friday."

Since applicants were previously named, these will not be repeated; however, "Those entering petitions for citizenship are Jacob Michalek, George Washut, Kosto Melovich, Paul Kobelinsz, Sam John Carr, Rado Medenica, Charles Kazo Koren, Richard Ernest Ralph, Mary Lucretia Ralph, Stefania Verhovnik Schmontz, George Legerski, Tony Chepchor, Frank Laboy, George Cienciala, George Bouchard, Paul Wallach, Joseph Bazzier, Anna Begenisich, Agnes Novakovich, and Anna Pilch."

11/14/24—"THIRD MINE MAY BE RE-OPENED NEAR SHERIDAN, OFFICIAL SAYS." "New Operations by Sheridan-Wyoming Coal Company Would Give Employment to 200 Men."

A possibility that a third mine in the Sheridan-Wyoming Coal Company district will be opened within the next few weeks, giving employment to about two hundred more men, was expressed by Edward Bottomley, general superintendent of the company Friday.

Between six and seven hundred men are now employed in the Monarch and Acme coal mines which are operating every day, Mr. Bottomley announced.

"The two mines that are working every day are proving a boon to the miners, and the company hopes that the demand for coal will be sufficient to justify the opening of a third mine in the near future," the general superintendent said. "The weather is of course the big factor in regulating demand for coal. If it stays cold and stormy, we can undoubtedly open the third mine, but if the weather turns temperature and it is a mild winter, we may not be able to do it."

Mr. Bottomley, who is president of the Northern Wyoming Coal Operators association, left Friday noon for Denver, where he will attend a special meeting of Wyoming coal operators called for Saturday at the Brown Palace Hotel. The northern Wyoming district is made up of the mines in Sheridan County, the Basin country, Hudson and Cambria. All of the large coal operators of the state are expected to be at the meeting."

6/4/25—"SHERIDAN MEN ASK TO BECOME CITIZENS OF THE U.S." "Kenneth M. Stuart, Beckton Sheepman, Files Papers."

Kenneth M. Stuart, prominent Beckton sheepman and his wife, Bessie Glidden Stuart, were among the eighteen persons who appeared before M. F. Lence, United States naturalization examiner, Monday with petitions for citizenship. Mr. Stuart is a native of Scotland, while Mrs. Stuart became a British subject.

Another person appearing before Mr. Lence was Zarif Khan, well known in Sheridan as 'Hot Tomale Louis' who operates a restaurant on Grinnell Avenue. In presenting his petition for citizenship, "Louie" renounces his allegiance to Amanullah Khan, Emir of Afghanistan. He was born in Afghanistan 35 years ago and emigrated from Bombay, India to Seattle in 1907.

Other persons appearing Monday were Joseph Pawlus, George Kabielusz, George Karones, Mike Lupiezowiec, Paul Brantz, Joseph Leja, Anton Janoszek, Joe Krazelok, John Drobish, Adam Bojko, George Kurz, Paul Madzia, John Wolny, John Zowada, and Joseph Haratyk.

Mr. Lence will remain here the entire week accepting petitions for citizenship preparatory to the naturalization hearing to be held at 10:30 o'clock Monday morning June 8."

10/9/25—"COAL PRODUCTION INCREASING HERE." "Sheridan-Wyoming Company Ahead of Last Year's Mark."

"Promise of increased coal mining activity this season is borne out by the fact that already the October production of the Sheridan-Wyoming Coal Company mines is 5,000 tons ahead of production the same period last year.

Daily production is 5,500 tons, and much coal is being shipped to Montana, South Dakota and North Dakota. Some is also going to Washington.

An improved coal market and increased demand for local coal is the reason for the increased production, Edward Bottomley of Kleenburn, general superintendent of the Sheridan-Wyoming Coal Company said Friday.

The Acme Mine is working every day and the Monarch Mine three and four days a week. About 500 men are employed. Monarch was open all summer and Acme was closed for only a week for the installation of machinery.

It has not yet been decided whether any more mines in the field will be opened."

9/3/25—"NEW LOADING DEVICE HERE." "Sheridan Coal Company Installs Machines."

"The mines of the Sheridan-Wyoming Coal Company, operating at Kleenburn and Acme" (no doubt it is Monarch and Acme) "have installed mechanical loading machines which have greatly facilitated the work of production.

Four machines of the type known as the Joy No. 5 B.U. are working nicely, these being used exclusively for all narrow work in the mines such as entries, cross-cuts, room necks, etc.

In addition to the No. Fives, the company has in operation eight Goodman power shovels for loading all room coal. By reason of the great proportions of these shovels they are suitable only for wide work in the mines. The Goodman device has a capacity in excess of 200 tons per day for each machine, while the No. 5 will handle 150 tons.

New Coal Mining Features

These are comparatively new features in coal mining operations, having been in use only a few years. The Sheridan-Wyoming Company is the first west of the Mississippi to install these modern labor-saving devices, it is stated. It was not until after a thorough investigation of the merits of these mechanical loaders by Edward Bottomley, superintendent of the company, had been made that the machines were placed in use in the Sheridan County mines. Results of the work in Indiana, Illinois, Pennsylvania, and West Virginia were investigated by Mr. Bottomley about the first of the present year, and upon his recommendation the company decided to give the machines a try-out. While they are yet more or less in the experimental stage in Sheridan County mines, Mr. Bottomley is already convinced of the practicality and success of the machines.

While new machines may not revolutionize the mining of coal, it is the opinion of many that ultimately all mines will employ mechanical loaders. The smaller mines, of course, may not use the large machines but the manufacturers are now said to be working on devices suitable for the smaller mines.

Increases in Business

It is the contention of companies using the mechanical loaders that business is thereby increased to an extent that warrants the ultimate employment of more men in mining operations.

One of the great advantages of the larger machines is that it makes possible the production of a larger amount of lump coal as the machine is constructed to pick up a thousand-pound chunk at a load. Another splendid feature of the new machine is that it reduces the number of mine accidents as there is not nearly the danger in loading with the machines.

Another innovation in the company's mines is the installation of six locomotives to facilitate the work of hauling, thus displacing a large number of horses and increasing the efficiency of the mines. The new machines entail an expenditure by the company of approximately $200,000.

Hotchkiss Will Install Loaders

R. A. Keenan, president of the Hotchkiss Coal Company advises the Journal that his company expects to install three of these loading machines and that the first has been received and is now being installed.

That modern improvements are being installed in the Sheridan coal mines, to compare with any in the country shows the enterprise evident in our coal industry."

3/12/26—"FIFTEEN ALIENS ASK FOR PAPERS." "Eight Applicants Are From Poland, Report."

Fifteen aliens filed petitions for their second papers before M. F. Lence, U. S. naturalization examiner, Tuesday and Wednesday, in district court. Of that number, eight of them were natives of Poland.

Final citizenship hearing will be held in Sheridan on July 3, it was announced. The petitioners were: John Tancheff, Bulgaria; Paul Heczko, Czechoslovak republic; Efstalthias Kallias, Greece; John Haratyk, Poland; John Kobieluwz, Poland; Robert Moss, England; Paul Kaurilok, Poland; John Ivan Besich, Jugo-slvakia; John Frank Chepchor, Poland; Joseph Judoszek, Poland; Mike Haratyk, Poland; Paul Matzura, Czechoslovak republic; and Canakis Rilsakis, Greece."

4/18/26—"COAL PRODUCTION IS INCREASED HERE." "Sheridan-Wyoming Co. Issued Figures for Year."

"Production of the Sheridan-Wyoming Coal Company coal mines this year has been about

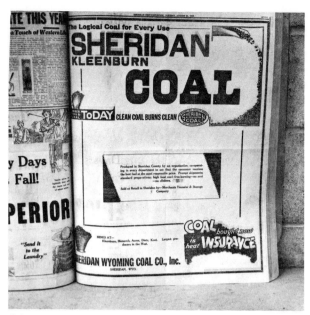

Advertising urging use of coal for fuel, *Sheridan Enterprise* 8-21-26.

75,000 tons greater than last year, according to an announcement made Saturday by Edward Bottomley, general superintendent of the company.

Exactly 11,000 more tons of coal were mined the first fifteen days of April this year than were mined during the corresponding period of last year, he said.

Monarch is working two to three days a week, and Acme from four to five days. It is expected that work will be good for the rest of April. May and June are always slack months."

6/15/26—"FORTY TO APPLY FOR CITIZEN-SHIP."

Forty applicants will appear for the final naturalization hearings to be held in district court on July 3, it was announced, Tuesday, by Mrs. Anna B. Smith, clerk of the district court. The time for the hearing has been set for 10 o'clock.

The applicants are Rado Medenica, Joseph Haratyk, Martha Cichonski, Paul Krenzolek, Otto Ranio, Frank Madia, Martin Benegalia, Jr., Tony Fonti, Joseph Boyda, Yeropoli Rocco Domenico, Alendro Argin, John Kohut, Peter Londos, Mike Patz, George Schneider, Joseph Alois Urbaczka, Paul Washut, Mihal Kawulok, George Pilch, Peter Kohlruss, George J. Urbaczka, Frank Sperl, Jr., Mike Ligocki, Frank Bojko, John Tancheff, Paul Heczko, Efstathias Kallias, John Haratyk, Joseph Kobielusz, Robert Moss, Paul Kawulok, John Ivan Besiah, John

Frank Chepchor, Joseph Juroszek, Michial Haratyk, Andrew Wantulok, Paul Padzorski, Paul Matzura and Kanakis Ratzakis."

12/27/26—"More Coal Sold Here Than in Other Mining Regions of Wyoming." "Sheridan's Output Valued At Nearly Two Million." "—The Sheridan mines employed a total number of 682 men. Of those, 445 were employed as miners, loaders and shot-firers, while 115 worked on the surface—."

11/28/26—"OUTPUT OF COAL TO ECLIPSE 1925 AT MINES HERE." "Sheridan-Wyoming Plants Are Working Every Day."

Monarch and Acme mines in the Sheridan-Wyoming Coal Company string are working every day, furnishing employment to 420 men, and promising to eclipse last year's production record.

The production of the company mines up to October 31 showed an increase of 28,896 tons over the same period last year, while the outlook for the remainder of the winter is encouraging, according to officials of the company.—" "The Hotchkiss Coal Company mine is also offering steady employment to its men."

10/5/27—"FINAL HEARINGS FOR ALIENS ARE SET FOR OCT. 28." "Man from Denver Office to Conduct Session Here."

Final hearings on the petitions for citizenship of 17 aliens of Sheridan County will be held on October 28 in the district courtroom in Sheridan. A representative of the Denver naturalization office will conduct the examinations. Eleven aliens will appear for their first final naturalization hearings, while six aliens, who have been continued from former examinations, will appear this month to make another attempt to pass the tests.

The petitioning aliens who have become ready for the final hearings since spring are James Morton Bloomfield, Sheridan (Scotland); Janet Bloomfield, Sheridan (Scotland); Mike John Sikora, Wyarno, (Poland); Carmelo Gnnaro, Arvada (Italy); Eva Shazzets Bujok, Monarch (Austria, now Poland); Mary Durdrink, Mandich, Sheridan, (Poland); Andreas, Slowiak (Slovok), Monarch (Poland); John Wiselka, Sheridan (Austria, now Poland); Joseph Frank Washut, Monarch, (Austria, now Poland); Frank Sperl, Ranchester (Austria); and John Cieluszak, Monarch, (Poland).

The aliens whose petitions have been continued are Tony Fonti, Monarch, (Italy); George

Schneider, Home Ranch, Sheridan (Russia); Paul Podzorski, Acme (Poland); Tony Mike Sikora, Sheridan (Poland); Albert Wenzel, Kleenburn (Poland); and Marion C. Dillon, Sheridan (Great Britain)."

11/4/27—"Sheridan Miners Average High In Coal Production." "County's Output Third in State—10.48 tons per man—"

12/7/27—"Bus Delayed So "Kids" Run to School Classes—They Make Distance From Monarch Almost on Time." Boys were Tony Rulli and Lyle Parker of Kleenburn, Raymond Garrett and Rudolph Loss of Acme and Mike Kuzara of Dietz.

6/25/28—"KLEENBURN SCHOOL WINS TRACK MEET STAGED AT MINES."

The Kleenburn school is now exhibiting a silver trophy cup, which was won by its pupils in the triangular track and field meet held Wednesday afternoon at the Kleenburn field between the Kleenburn, Monarch and Acme grade schools.

Kleenburn and Monarch divided first place honors in the meet. Kleenburn won the cup for placing first in the first 16 events of the meet with a total of 76 points. Monarch placed second with 43 points, and Acme was third with 25 points. The second part of the meet consisted of nine "free-for-all" events and a boys' and girls' relay race. The Monarch school triumphed in the "free-for-all" events, scoring a total of 41 1/3 points. Kleenburn placed second with 25 1/3 points, and Acme was third with 24 1/3 points.

Acme won the boys' relay race and Monarch won the girls' relay race. Each winner received a pennant.

The meet was conducted and judged by Coaches Rathburn and Erickson of Sheridan high school. They were assisted by James Rennie, Sr., Clifford Irwin and the Rev. Cheney as judges. The Mines band furnished music during the meet. The men of the mines treated the children to Eskimo pies after the meet.

The outstanding contestants of the meet were Annie Martinek of Acme with 14 points. Antonina Cieluszak of Monarch with 15¾ points, Tommy Schurok of Kleenburn with 14 points and Norman Novakovich of Monarch proved to be a valuable contestant to his team by scoring a total of 27 points."

6/1/28—"Natural Gas for Sheridan Near Realiza-

tion, Report—Pipes May Be Laid to Billy Creek Field."

10/12/28—"Wyoming Miners Get Wage Increase of $6.72—Highest Scale Yet Adopted Over Country—Formal Ratification Only Step to Be Taken."

1/17/30—"Sheridan-Wyoming Coal Concern Passes to Van Swerengen Group—Pittsburg Company Announces Purchase of United States Corporation in Large Eastern Deal—The Pittston Company, organized by the Van Swerengin interests to take over the Erie Railroad coal properties, had purchased control of the United States Distributing Corporation, it was announced today."

2/23/30—COAL COMPANY ELECTS ALL OF OLD OFFICIALS." "No Change Is Made In Sheridan-Wyoming Firm."

All of the officers and directors of the Sheridan-Wyoming coal company have been re-elected, it was announced Tuesday through the company offices at Kleenburn.

The elections substantiate the announcement of Harry N. Taylor of New York city, President, that the recent transfer of the control of the United States Distributing company, to the Van Swearingen interests would have no effect upon the Sheridan-Wyoming company.

The officers, elected at New York City on February 19, are as follows: Harry N. Taylor, chairman of the board and president; H. D. Gibson, vice-president; E. P. Fitzgerald of Acme, vice-president; J. E. Friel, treasurer; J. E. Lee of Sheridan, secretary; Guy E. Stewart, assistant secretary; J. T. Kessinger of Sheridan, assistant secretary.

The directors, who were elected on February 18, are Harry N. Taylor, J. R. Edwards, J. E. Friel, George F. Getz, H. D. Gibson, Gardner Pattison, H. T. Peters, D. L. Reardon, E. M. Reardon and Frank C. Wright."

2/27/30—"Many Students Come In From Mines Daily." "Four Trips Daily Are Made by Sheridan-Mines Bus."

Seventy students attending S.H.S. come in from the mines every morning.

Twenty-three, or about one-third, of the mine students are from Kleenburn, while Monarch and Acme each have 18 and Dietz 11. At 7 o'clock the Sheridan-Mines bus leaves Monarch and brings the students from Kleenburn and Monarch to Sheridan to school. After leaving this first group, the bus makes a second trip to the mines for those living in Acme and Dietz.

After school the bus makes two trips to the mines, at 3:30 it goes to high school to take the students home, and then makes a later trip to the mines at 5:30 for those who do not go on the first bus. Some of the students come in cars, but the majority depend upon the bus. The following are those who come to S.H.S. from the mines:—

Nine B—Edith Kawamoto, Dietz

Nine A: Dietz—Julia Matches and George Williams

Acme—Rose Bondi, John Coassin, Mark McManus, Shirley Perry and John Cheslar.

Kleenburn—Ida Daniels, Mary Floretta, Don Madia, Rosie Montegna, Helen Stanko and Wilfred Catterall.

Monarch—Dorothy and Harold Bell, Helen Michalek, Mary Novara, Lance Novakovich, Earl Rice, Andrew Slovak, Agnes Urbatchka, and George Wondra.

Ten A: Dietz—Anna Karpi, Viola Woods, Josephine Mentock

Acme—Katherine Banich, Nina Bechtold, Gene Bondi, Mary Burden, Edward Long, John McManus, Anna Placheck and Orville Shott.

Kleenburn—Joe Arnieri, Joe Bury, Robert McIntyre, Katherine Madra, Betty Montegna, Angeline Musso, George Nick.

Monarch—Marie Durante, Helen Kuchera, Stanley Novara, George Urbatchka, Luella Wade.

Eleven A: Dietz—Enid Marsh and Ada Williams.

Acme—Robert Burden.

Kleenburn—Stanley Baker, Mike Byrtus, Mary Daniels, Joe Gilroy, and Harry Trocche.

Monarch—Mae McIntosh, Daniel Novakovich, John Novara.

Twelve B: Kleenburn—Anna Gilroy.

Twelve A: Dietz—Dorothy Weaver, Walter Marasok.

Acme—Calda Dazey, Agnes Hair, Jennie Loss, Selena Morgan.

Kleenburn—Allard Caudron, Eli Daniels.

Post Graduates: Kleenburn—Bernice McIntyre, Willard Catteral.

4/29/30—"Mines to Show Large Drop in Census Report—The mines towns near Sheridan showed a decrease of 58 percent on the basis of returns filed to date from enumeration in that district. Acme's population is 264 compared to 550 in 1920; Dietz is 222 as compared with 676 in 1920; Kleenburn has 290 residents where it had 915 in 1920; and Monarch's population is 543 as compared to 1,288 10 years ago."

11/20/30—"Natural Gas Comes to Sheridan" (Press Supplement gives complete story).

It is noted that announcements of the introduction of natural gas to home and industry users are becoming more and more frequent and while many potential users are resisting its installation due to their faithfulness to the coal industry even though they may no longer be dependent upon their income from that source as they have gone to other employment, nevertheless some installations were gradually being installed, replacing the traditional coal fired ranges and heaters.

2/1/31—In this issue of the press, it is reflected that interest in the Mines apparently began to diminish. Under the heading, "News From Surrounding Communities" columns did appear from Arvada, Gillette, Moorcroft, Clearmont, Osage, Birney, Wyola, Ashland, Parkman, Dayton, Buffalo, Big Horn, Banner, Story and Big Goose, but none from any of the mining camps. Perhaps this was simply due to the fact that no one was available to write the news for the papers. This does not mean, however, that there was no longer any activity as evidenced by some following releases.

2/17/31—"Taylor Will Retire As Coal Firm's Head." Harry N. Taylor, President of the United States Distributing Company including the Sheridan-Wyoming Coal company will retire effective March 1, 1931.

8/23/31—"New President of Coal Firm May Speak Here—Michael Gallagher, President of the Sheridan-Wyoming Coal company, now in Sheridan may speak at the Labor Day celebration planned."

9/29/31—"Three Mines Will Run at Top Capacity." "Monarch, Hotchkiss and Acme to Employ 400."

"All three mines of the Sheridan-Wyoming Coal company will be operating at full capacity for the winter months beginning Thursday, according to an announcement Tuesday by Edward Bottomley, General superintendent.

Mr. Bottomley said approximately 400 men would be offered steady employment for several months as a result of the increased mining activity.

The mines are located at Monarch, Acme and Hotchkiss, in the valley north of Sheridan. Monarch and Acme have been operating intermittently during the summer, but the Hotchkiss mine has been completely shut down for several months, he said.

Work was resumed at Hotchkiss early this week with a full force of men, while Acme will commence winter operations on Thursday.

Mr. Bottomley did not say how long the demand for coal would continue but that all three mines would be operated for several months at least."

10/14/31—"Miners Here Oppose Any Wage Reduction"—Locals at Acme, Monarch, Hotchkiss in valley north of Sheridan—voted unanimously to oppose any wage reduction.

12/27/31—"Rapid City Man Will Become Sheridan-Wyoming Coal Head." "Harry L. Gandy, President of Pittston Coal, Inc., of New York, Will Take Over New Duties First of Year."

Effective January 1, Harry L. Gandy of Rapid City, S. D., will become president of the Sheridan-Wyoming Coal company, according to word received here Saturday.

Mr. Gandy, who is also president of Pittston Coal Inc., will succeed Michael Gallagher, who will continue as chairman of the board of directors. Announcement of the change in the presidency was made by Mr. Gallagher.

The Sheridan-Wyoming Coal Company, with general offices at Kleenburn, is the largest coal producer in northern Wyoming. It operates mines at Acme and Monarch.

Edward Bottomley, general superintendent, said he too had received word of the election, but he said he knew of no changes contemplated in the operation or management of the mines. Mr. Gandy visited the mines north of here several weeks ago but made no announcement at that time, it was learned.

Prior to his connection with Pittston Coal, Inc., Mr. Gandy was for seven years executive secretary of the National Coal association, nation-wide organization of bituminous coal operators.

Mr. Gallagher's announcement also carried with it word of the election of C. R. Nash of New York as an additional vice president of the Sheridan-Wyoming Coal Company. Mr. Nash also is vice president and comptroller of the Pittston firm. Both companies have offices at 17 Batter Place, New York."

5/10/32—"Gandy, Sheridan Mining Head Holds Out Hope of Agreement But Warns In Address That Problems of Competition Must Be Met If Coal Industry Is To Survive."

"Harry Gandy president of the Sheridan-Wyoming Coal Company and former congressman from South Dakota spoke at a meeting at the Labor Temple and pointed to the need for greater efficiency in competing with other fuels. Also hoped an agreement could be reached between labor and management to avert impending coal strike. By June 1st at a meeting of Miners and Operators a strike seemed averted when miners agreed to a 20% cut in wages, however a referendum was yet to be voted by the miners with first voting on June 22 showing early results opposed to cut.

6/30/32—"Mines Beat Sheridan in Sparkling Baseball Game by 2 to 0. On Mines team were Barker, Daniels, Mentock, T. King, W. King, Carmichael, Flockhart, Upton, Matches and Marosok."

7/3/32—"Mines Idle Over North Coal Area—Gebo Trouble Halting Agreement For District—includes mines in Sheridan Area."

8/4/32—"Sheridan Mines to Open Again—Hudson and Sheridan Fields Accept Cut of 20 percent in Wage Scale, But Gebo and Crosby Will Stay Closed."

"The new wage scale in the Hudson and Sheridan Fields will be $5.42 a day, the same as in southern Wyoming."

8/21/32—"Large Mine at Acme to Reopen Soon—Monarch Mine Probably to Begin in September."

10/27/32—"Coal Output Proves Good During Fall—Sheridan, Wyoming Field Ships Trainload Per Day. Coal Production at the mines of the Sheridan-Wyoming Coal company and the Hotchkiss Coal Company, near Sheridan, is moving this fall at a rate which shows that the Sheridan field coal has not lost hold on the market in the Missouri valley and the northwest—coal to Burlington slightly under a year ago. This week the Hotchkiss Coal Co. was put into production, according to R. A. Keenan, President, who also announced that R. R. Goodman and W. M. Burkhotter of Spokane, Washington have been engaged to represent Hotchkiss in the Spokane area, replacing C. L. Jones, deceased."

11/10/32—"Two Eastern Men Prominent in Sheridan Development Die. Edwin N. Sanderson, President of Light Company and Harry N. Taylor, Coal Company Magnate, Succumb.

Harry N. Taylor, former President of the Sheridan-Wyoming Coal Company, preceeding H. L. Gandy passed away Thursday in Chicago, it was reported by A. K. Craig, President of the Sheridan Trust and Savings bank . . ."

12/19/32—"Forest Richardson of Omaha passed through Sheridan Sunday enroute to Roundup, Montana, for an inspection of the properties of the Roundup Coal Mining Company. Mr. Richardson has for many years been vice-president of sales of the Sheridan Coal Company of Omaha, which company formerly owned and operated the Dietz properties in this field, and is well known to many Sheridan citizens. He was recently made president of the Sheridan Coal Company, succeeding H. S. Hopka, resigned."

7/2/33—"J. E. Lee, treasurer, to be in charge of the affairs of the Sheridan-Wyoming Coal Company during July and August while Harry L. Gandy, President, goes east on a business trip.

9/19/33—"J. E. Lee, New General Manager of Sheridan-Wyoming Coal Firm." "Three Promotions Announced by Company President, Harry L. Gandy. N. A. Gallager and P. L. Shields Given Higher Posts." Gallagher becomes Assistant to General Manager and Sheilds becomes sales manager.

11/1/33—"Wagon Miners May Join Union." "Effort Being Made Here to Enroll All Coal Mines" George Lambert, Vice-president of the United Mine Workers of America has been successful in forming a new local at the Storm King and the Black Diamond Mines west of Sheridan. Attempts also being made to organize the Star Coal Co. and the Custer Coal Co. north of Sheridan. The National Recovery Act is making possible the enforcement of organized labor with its minimum union wage scale as required by NRA."

11/2/33—A display advertisement in the *Sheridan Press* announced to the public that wages have been raised and the number of hours reduced to conform with NRA requirements. That ad was signed by Victor Eccli, Bob Fanto and R. F. Hotchkiss as representatives of the

employees. (This ad reflects the successful organization of the workers in the wagon mines as well as those already previously unionized).

1/29/34—"Martin J. Cahill Heads State Federation of Labor—Local Resident Defeats Young in Run Off Vote—Former Mine Workers Chief Leads by 127½ Votes."

2/24/35—"Coal Deposits Abound." "Under normal conditions the mines are capable of producing more than 10,000 tons of coal daily. The mines are completely modern, being entirely mechanized and electrified.

The coal is mined entirely by mechanical means, being first undercut by cutting machines, the holes for blasting being drilled with automatic drills, and after shot down the coal is loaded into pit cars by machinery and transported to the tipple for loading into railroad cars by heavy haulage motors, all operated by electric power.

The machines which load the coal into pit cars are of two types; one of the Goodman power shovel, resembling a miniature steam shovel. It weighs 18,000 pounds and is capable of lifting 1,200 pounds of coal at a time. The other, known as the Joy loading machine, in its operation resembles somewhat the movements of a crawfish, clawing the loose coal onto a belt conveyor which conveys it into pit cars—after the pit cars are loaded with coal, they are taken to the main haulways by small gathering locomotives (which perform the service usually performed by horses or mules)—"

9/23/35—"Sheridan Coal Mine Situation Uncertain As Strike Spreads Approximately 300 Miners in the Valley May Not Work Tuesday—Officials of Company Hope Mines Will Operate." George Bateman of Acme, a member of the union said that the miners had received word to quit working at midnight"-."

9/24/35—"—300 Miners Join Coal Strike Here—."

9/27/35—"Soft Coal Strike Ends As Miners Win." "Pay Increases Are Provided In Agreement"—50¢ per ton of coal loaded—."

2/2/36—"Mines Here At Peak Production As Fuel in Cold Belt Dwindles—Coal Officials Encouraged As Large Orders Pour In." "Fuel shortages throughout cold belt area. Acme and Monarch operating at peak production turning out black diamonds in near prosperity era quantities."

"Work tomorrow" orders continued to be posted at the mines, and workers, for years barely able to eke out an existence on their meager pay checks, looked forward to the fattest pay envelopes in many months." "J. Ed Lee, general manager of the concern, said Saturday, the two mines in January shipped approximately 67,000 tons, an increase of about 2,000 tons over production in January, 1935—."

2/26/36—"J. E. Lee Killed in Auto Mishap on Icy Curve Near Wheatland." Man Prominent Here and Over the State Is Victim."

"General Manager of Sheridan Wyoming Coal Co., Age 47; Also President of the Wyoming Taxpayers League On Business Trip For His Company—" (Andrew Kuzara of the Star Coal Mine of Sheridan also a member of the Coal Commission Committee along with Lee was to have accompanied Lee to the Denver meeting but was unable to make the trip. The two had previously traveled together on several occasions attending coal commission meetings).

Paul Shields, sales manager for the Sheridan-Wyoming Coal Company left immediately to attend the meeting of coal officials which was to have been attended by Lee."

4/30/36—"Kessinger Is Named To Position of Coal Firm General Manager"—"Other Promotions Within Sheridan-Wyoming Coal Company Announced Here—Bylund, Strayer and Schott Advance—J. T. Kessinger today was named general manager—according to an announcement made at the general offices in Monarch by Harry C. Gandy, President, filling vacancy caused by the death of J. E. Lee. Other promotions are: Gothard Bylund, Treasurer; William H. Strayer, resident auditor; and C. M. Shott, general superintendent of operations."

5/20/36—"Arthur K. Perry Wins Promotion From Coal Firm—Acme Inside Repairman To Become Assistant to Shott." Perry, inside repairman at Acme to become supervisor of tipple, shop and bath house at Monarch."

9/27/36—"Gandy Gives Up Duties In East To Devote All Time to Coal Firm."

"Harry L. Gandy, president of the Sheridan-Wyoming Coal Company, who has for the past several years spent a portion of this time in the east in connection with his duties as officer of several associated retail coal companies, has resigned from his eastern duties and is returning to Sheridan to devote his entire time to the management and sales of the Sheridan Wyoming Coal Company and its affiliates, the Hotchkiss Coal Company and the Tongue River Trading Company."

11/16/36—"Coal Firm Adds Improvements As Mining Outlook Brightens." "Production for Year to Hit Half-Million Tons, Gandy Says In Announcing Improvement Program Launched by Sheridan-Wyoming Coal Company."

"Production reached more than 100,000 tons ahead of last year. New machinery being installed. The last of five Joy loaders—mechanical devises capable of loading between 275 to 300 tons of coal a day—three at Monarch mine and two at Acme. Total of 13 Joy loaders and one Goodman loader. Improvements also being made to houses while some of the older buildings are being torn down including an old Acme landmark, the old frame hotel building."

8/15/37—"Ogenite Will Succeed Gandy In Coal Firm—Delbert H. Pape Is Named To Head Hotchkiss, Sheridan Mines."

11/15/37—A display ad in the Sheridan paper advertising as follows: "For Sale—Houses in Good Condition—Priced for Quick Sale."

Dietz:—46 three and four room houses.

Acme:—One 1-room house and two 2-room houses.

Monarch:—Eight 2-room houses.

See these bargains soon—they're going fast!—Sheridan-Wyoming Coal Co.—Monarch."

11/16/37—"Dietz Abandoned After Boom Glory"—(See page 85)

12/15/37—"15 Coal Producers In County Taxed by U. S. Gov't. Under the Bituminous Coal Commission Act. One percent per ton fee assessed on all coal sold."

2/9/38—"Coal Mining Boom Here May Follow Ruling by Bituminous Commission—Burlington Business May Be Switched To Local Field."

"Fixed prices of coal set by Commission at $2.57 for lump and $2.20 for egg may force the closing of the Rocky Mountain Fuel Company of Colorado and coal supplied by them to the Burlington would cease, diverting the business to local firms, according to C. M. Shott, general superintendent. Delbert Pate leaves for Washington, D. C. to confer."

2/22/38—"More than 1,000 persons attend the Polish community dance held Sunday nite at Lakeside. The dance was one of the largest ever to be held in this region. Music was furnished by a Polish seven piece band." Dance chairmen were Joe Skatula and Mrs. Ed Kumor."

2/23/38—"Minimum Coal Scale Is Cut by Commission—Court Orders Responsible for Suspension—New Rates Planned—The bituminous Coal Commission decided today to revoke government fixed minimum soft coal prices."

6/2/38—"Dietz Makes Plans to Renovate Old Sheridan Inn Here—Genial Gould Dietz who will be remembered by long time Sheridan residents as the Secretary and Treasurer of the Dietz Mining Company here more than 40 years ago is a visitor in Sheridan this week.

Dietz, now president of the Dietz Investment Trust of Omaha is here with Mrs. Dietz to inspect the Sheridan Inn, widely known hotel which was purchased by the Dietz interests last winter.

12/12/38—"Monarch Gridsters Win Coal Bowl Championship Sunday." "Six Man Play Attracts Large Crowd—Acme Team Unable to Score Until Late in Third Period."

"The Coal Bowl six-man football classic which was played on the Acme grid-iron Sunday afternoon ended in a 33 to 12 triumph for the Monarch gridsters—.

Some 400 fans from Sheridan and the mines braved the cold wind that blew over the field all afternoon to witness the battle which was featured by flying fists and many arguments.

Members of the teams were:

Monarch—Leon Siegoski, line; Henry Washut, Line; Lester L. Novakovich, Line; Phil P. Novakovich, Back; John J. Kawamoto, Back; George G. Kawamoto, Back; Harry Daniels, Sub; Legerski Sub.

Acme—Henry Stanko, Frank Gruber, George Wantulok (deceased), Dick Merryhew, Harold Griffith, Maurice Plott, _____ Adams, Sub, _____ Frank Zowada Sub (deceased).

Officials—Danny Madia, John Novara, John Yorio.

1/18/39—"Man, Known Here Dies in New Mexico—R. P. Fitch, well-known mining engineer who was formerly an executive of the Sheridan-Wyoming Coal company, died this morning of pneumonia.

A mining engineer at the Monarch Mine before the purchase by the Sheridan-Wyoming Coal Company, Mr. Fitch remained with the new company for several years after the pur-

chase, first as assistant general superintendent of all the mines and then as superintendent of the Monarch Mine. He left here about 1924."

3/21/39—"New Uses for Coal" (Editorial) tells of discovery of new silk-like material* stronger than but resembling silk made of coal, air and water—all of which are in abundance in the Sheridan area, and invented by Dr. Wallace H. Carrothers of the E. I. DuPont de Nemour Co., and patented only 20 days before his death in 1937. *(Ed.-Nylon)

10/2/39—"Utilities Company Must Seek Gas Reserves—Wyoming PSC Orders Diligent Search" for new gas reserves and denies cutting of commercial users. Also, 10/2/39—"Prices of Coal to Be Advanced in City Tuesday—Six Operators in Sheridan County Field Take Action; Sheridan-Wyoming Coal Company, the larger operator in the field and five wagon mines, The Storm King, the Tongue River Coal Company, The Black Diamond, the Star Mine and the Custer Coal Company. Lump from $3.75 to $3.80; Egg, from $3.70 to $3.80; Nut, from $3.15 to $3.25; Pea, from $2.65 to $3.15 and Slack, from $2.05 to $2.75."

(Note: It was about this period of time when a rumor was being circulated about Sheridan area of a gas shortage began to frighten many gas users to reconvert to coal only to find several years later that additional gas sources were found).

1/3/40—A display ad in the Sheridan paper appeared in this issue as follows: "An Appreciation—We Wish to express our sincere appreciation to the public for their splendid support of the POLISH RELIEF BENEFIT DANCE. We assure you that all the money cleared will be used for the relief of Polish war victims." (Signed)—Charles B. Mazure, Committee Chairman." (Charles Mazur, we cannot overlook mentioning, was quite an unusual individual. A very well-read and self-educated person, a miner who had come to this country from his native Poland, developed the ability to speak the English language with very little trace of accent. He had no formal legal training, but became quite familiar with the law and court procedures, much of which was the result of his many appearances as an interpreter in court trials. He was quite often called the "Polish Lawyer" and his legal advice was much sought after by his compatriots).

2/29/40—Montana Dakota Utilities announces a new natural gas supply by constructing a pipe line from Billy Creek to Casper to bring in gas from Sand Draw and Muskrat fields in central Wyoming.

2/26/40—"D. H. Pape Explains Coal Mining Problems—Monarch Mine To Remain Open, President Says." "Only 50 Out of 350 Men Will Be Out of Work—." "—Problems forcing mines to mechanize to greater degree to maintain production. Substitute fuels also contribute to reduction of demand.

"Mines closed down thus far as follows:
Old Dietz No. 40 1921
Dietz Mine No. 41 1922
Kooi Mine No. 46 1922
Carney Mine No. 44 1924
Hotchkiss Mine ....1939"

10/15/40—"Charles Catterall Retires After Many Years at Mines—After more than 30 years of working in and around Sheridan county coal mines, Charles Catterall, 66 has recently retired and moved to Dayton, Wyo. to make his home.

Born in England in 1874, he came to the U. S. at the age of 32, and after spending a year in Kansas, came to old Dietz in 1907. He worked in the mine there until it closed in 1909 (probably Dietz No. 4), and he then went to Monarch.

He was appointed night foreman at Monarch in 1910, working in that capacity until the mine blast in 1911, when he was advanced to the position of assistant foreman.

In 1917, he became mine foreman of the new Monarch mine and kept that position until 1920, when he was again advanced to mine superintendent. He moved to Kleenburn in 1921, and served as superintendent there the four years until the mine closed in 1925.

The next three years he lived in Acme, where he was assistant mine foreman, and from there he moved to Monarch, where he remained until March, 1939. In October 1939, he was injured in the Hotchkiss mine the day it was closed."

* * * *

It's happy Holiday Time again! Soon stockings will be hopefully hung on countless chimneys everywhere . . . crystal clear carols will fill the air . . . and merrily ringing church bells will announce to the world: CHRISTMAS is here! I hope your Christmas will be a really memorable one . . . sparkling with good cheer and jollity. May it usher in a bright New Year abounding in Happiness and Good Fortune for you and your dear ones . . . that is the earnest wish of a firm which sincerely appreciates your friendship and good will.

Sincerely,
Sheridan Wyoming Coal Co., Inc.
J. F. Rulli
Sales Manager

December 1947

Greetings

5/8/53—"Coal Companies Join Operations. Sheridan-Wyoming and Big Horn Firms Announce Production Program.

The Sheridan-Wyoming Coal Company and the Big Horn Coal Company jointly announced today that effective immediately, all of the coal production of both companies in the Sheridan district will be sold through the Sheridan-Wyoming Coal Company, under the trade name of "Kleenburn" . . . "all of the production requirements will be produced by the Big Horn Coal Co., according to the announcement."

Severance notices to employees of Sheridan-Wyoming Coal Company were simultaneously being issued, thus ending the era of the underground coal industry while surrendering to strip-mining which was already in operation by the Big Horn Coal Company.

5/15/53—"Jobless Miner Problem Cited by Pritchard. A serious problem concerning the termination of employment for 116 miners at Monarch was brought to the attention of the Sheridan Council of Social Services this morning by J. I. Pritchard, manager of the Wyoming Employment Service . . ."

5/26/53—"87 Miners Enter Job Applications" (at local employment office).

6/13/53—"Another Big Polish Dance—Sponsored by the Sheridan Poachers Club at Fair Grounds. Monarch Polish Band . . . Tickets $1.00."

* * * *

And so, as time went by, many of those who had worked at the mines eventually found other employment in the area, moved their families to Sheridan and simply had to adjust to a new way of life, but regardless of whatever adjustments had to be made, they steadfastly clung to most of their old customs whose influence certainly evidenced its effect on the rest of the Sheridan community.

For example, there continued an occasional Polish wedding even though one of the members of the marriage couple might not be Polish. Here it was observed that the non-Polish were enjoying themselves and wholeheartedly accepting the new ritual.

Businessmen occasionally would have their advertising written in Polish, not only to appeal to that particular element, but simply for effect; however, again the influence was evident.

Periodically, some of the eating establishments would arrange for an all Polish meal consisting of various Polish dishes prepared by some of those ladies who still knew how to prepare the old recipes. These are always well-attended by those of all nationalities.

For many years, former residents of Monarch annually held a picnic at "Pine Island" in the nearby Big Horn Mountains. As the years went by and the attendance began to dwindle,

Polish Dinner and Dance

Featuring a Polish Band
Friday, March 8

POLISH DINNER MENU

Ogorki z Kisle Sznietanon i szedem innych salatow	Cucumbers in sour cream and seven other salads
Golontki	Pigs in Blankets
Kislon Kapusten ze Szwinskin Miesen	Sauerkraut with Pork
Kury Pieczone Kislom Sznietanon	Baked Chicken in sour cream
Pierogi	Filled envelopes
Poleszniki	Potato Pancakes
Szthchane Zennioki	Mashed Potatoes
Kolache	Coffee Cake
Potica	Walnut and Poppyseed Bread
Ryby	Fish

Serving 5:30 P.M. — 10:00 P.M.

Recent Polish menu at Sheridan Inn

the event became a "Miners' Picnic" including all those families who formerly lived at the mines. People would come for many miles to attend these "get-togethers" to renew old acquaintances and to talk over "the good old days."

About the year 1970, Harold "Cattle King" Griffith who inherited the title from his father, Dave "Cattle King," one of the miners who formerly lived in Monarch, coming all the way from California to attend the annual picnic, suggested that there should be some sort of a symbol to memorialize the miner, and offered to make the first contribution.

A committee was quickly formed which not only began to search for such a fitting memorial, but also a source for funds. At first, the project seemed somewhat remote and the committee in fact was looking outside of Sheridan for talent that could produce something fitting.

Suddenly, it was discovered that just such talent was available right here in our own com-

Annual Miners picnic 1976, Pine Island, Big Horn Mountains, Sheridan, Wyoming.

CONGRATULATIONS TO THE GUYS AT SHERIDAN AGRI-CENTER FOR A PRIZE-WINNING IDEA

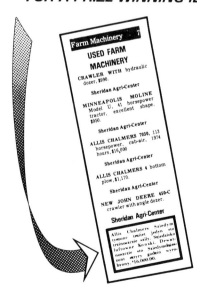

Lots of great ideas aren't born... they just sort of evolve slowly from casual conversation. Especially when the participants are the kind of people who prefer to be known as Brad (Cassidy) Waters, Dick (Big Horn Kid) Garber and Ken (Kid Curly) Heuermann. These three outlaw types got together with Linda DeTavernier, advertising salesperson for The Sheridan Press, and created a classified ad, printed in Polish, for a tractor. Linda, luckily, has a mother-in-law who writes and speaks Polish fluently. Then it was some trick to get our ad-setter to set it. He thought it was one big typographical error. But, all in all, the ad finally appeared and the tractor was sold on a lease-purchase agreement.

The ad was entered in a 7-state Mountain Ad Men Association competition and won first prize for the best classified ad. There it was recognized for what it was, by the top notch 'working-admen' who judged the contest... not a gimmick, but a genuine attempt to reach, in their own language, the many Polish ranchers in our area.

The Sheridan Press

Sheridan Agri-Center Ad in Polish, *Sheridan Press,* 1976 (tractor was actually sold to a Polish farmer as result of this Polish ad).

GRATULATIONS TO THE
GUYS AT SHERIDAN AGRI-CE
FOR A PRIZE-WINNING IDEA

Farm Machinery 7

USED FARM MACHINERY

CRAWLER WITH hydraulic dozer, $990.

Sheridan Agri-Center

MINNEAPOLIS MOLINE Model U, 41 horsepower tractor, excellent shape, $950.

Sheridan Agri-Center

ALLIS CHALMERS 7030, 113 horsepower, cab-air, 1974 hours, $16,000

Sheridan Agri-Center

ALLIS CHALMERS 4 bottom plow, $1,170.

Sheridan Agri-Center

NEW JOHN DEERE 450-C crawler with angle dozer.

Sheridan Agri-Center

Allis Chalmers Sziedym tyszonc trziiet jedyn sto trzinoszczie szily. Sziedzisko luftowne Konski. Dewatnoszczie sto Sziedymdzieszont sztyry godzin wyrobyony. '16,000.00.

Lots
of ev
ly wi
who p
Dick (b
Heuerma
with Lina
The Sher
printed in
a mother-ir
fluently. The

Blow-up of Polish ad appearing in previous picture.

munity. John Kuchera, a former miner, had in the last several years taken up sculpturing by welding and when approached, assured the committee that he thought he could produce a statue of a miner which might be acceptable. Immediately, the committee, consisting of Sylvia Silla, John Bury, Walt Pilch, Bill Laya and others, initiated a campaign for funds with Roman Skatula of the Bank of Commerce as the person to whom contributions could be deposited. The response was beyond expectations and on June 24, 1973, a somewhat larger than man-size statue of a miner was dedicated at the Tourist Information Center just off U.S. Highway I-90 at Sheridan, Wyoming with Walt Pilch, President of the Miners' Picnic, presiding, and a Polish band furnishing the music.

At this dedication, I was on the program and gave a brief history of the mines. This memorial is now on display at the Information Center, as a fitting tribute.

City Liquor Store ad (owned by Eddie and Kathy Brantz).

Chapter 15

Miscellaneous Mines

In addition to the so-called "railroad" mines (those which had railroad sidings and shipped coal to points away from the local area by rail) there were several "wagon mines" which served only local trade, as they had no railroad connections. These mines served only those truckers who were in the coal-hauling business, taking coal orders for delivery and serving most often regular customers, but they also served those who preferred to come after their coal themselves, coming in pickup trucks or pulling two and four-wheeled trailers with their automobiles; also those farmers coming with their wagons pulled by horses.

Very little information is available about these operations, their owners or operators having passed on and, being smaller operations, very little publicity was given them inasmuch as there were no camps as such and therefore no social activity.

Such mines included the Black Diamond, the Riverside Mine, the Old Acme Mine, the Hart Mine, the Storm King Coal Company, the Custer Coal Company, the Schreibies Mine and the Star Coal Company.

* * * * * * * * * *

The Black Diamond Mine

One of the earliest references to this mine appeared in the *Sheridan Post* issue of 9/30/04 in the form of an ad as follows: "We opened a new coal mine on Big Goose Creek formerly called the Owl Creek and Baker Coal Mines and ready to supply coal to its customers and will be known as the Black Diamond Coal Mine. Leave orders at the George Small's Drug Store at Union Lumber Company's office or at Jenkins and (Berry?) Grocery or call the mines phone number,——etc."

This mine was located about 6 miles west of Sheridan and about a half mile north of the present Big Goose Highway. The remains of the tipple still stand. This mine had a rather early history with brief references as early as the first part of this century.

Black Diamond Mine (as it looks today abandoned for some 20 years).

The July 6, 1911 issue of the *Enterprise* includes the following; "THE BLACK DIAMOND BURNING INTERNALLY. Coal Mine on Big Goose Creek Doomed by Smoldering Fire Which Breaks Into Entry.

The smoldering fire in the Black Diamond coal mine on Big Goose Creek, seven miles from Sheridan, has eaten its way through the old workings to the main entry and is now baffling all attempts by the mine owners to segregate it to a remote portion of the mine.

The Black Diamond coal mine was abandoned two years ago because of the underground fire and since that time it has slowly been burning and eating its way along the course of the main vein of coal. Recent caveins along the top of the surface are supposed to have fanned the smoldering embers into leaping flames, which were quickly communicated to the other workings not yet touched. The mine is probably doomed to any further usefulness and after this more serious fire has died down it will probably be a total loss.

The principal damage which has resulted from the immense amount of smoke issuing from the different openings has resulted to the crops on Big Goose Creek in the immediate vicinity. It is claimed by the farmers that the smoke and soot and gases have injured their crops already and that if the opening is not sealed up within a short time or if the smoke does not subside of its own accord, the resultant damage to their crops will be great.

The OK coal mine is located one-quarter of a mile from the Black Diamond mine and is being worked every day."

This mine, which had an "on again, off again" experience evidently had its fire extinguished and in the late 1920's was reopened. George Aiken, who had been a foreman in the Dietz No. 8 mine, assumed the operation of the Black Diamond. It is not definitely known just how long he operated the mine, but I believe it existed for perhaps another eight or ten years until about in the late 1930's.

* * * * * * * * * *

Riverside Mine

This mine, referred to previously, was located about 13 or 14 miles north west of Sheridan, immediately north of the present I-90 Highway.

From an old issue of the *Sheridan Post*, dated Feb. 12, 1907, we find the following reference:

"A New Village"

"Quite a little village is being built on the Fred McPhillamey place, across Tongue River, west of the coal town of Monarch. Clinton Head, who was with the Monarch Trading Company for a number of years, and E. C. Moore, who recently sold his ranch at Parkman have formed a co-partnership and will open a store there. Their building, which will be 20 x 50 feet, is now in course of construction, and will be ready for occupancy in about a week. For the present Head & Moore will handle gents' furnishing goods, working clothing, etc. They are both substantial, reliable gentlemen, and will succeed.

At this new village the local miners' union of Monarch is erecting a hall of considerable size, the same being 28 x 70, one story. J. J. Rennie & Son handle meats and groceries, and are doing a nice business here. Carr and Wondra also conduct an establishment, where distilled and fermented wet goods are dispensed to such as insist that Tongue River water is not good enough for them to drink."

And on May 1, 1908, Mrs. D. D. Warner, in an article appearing in the *Enterprise*, refers to the mine of Riverside as one of the main mines in the area north of Sheridan.

Then, under (Kooi News) appearing in the Sheridan paper under date of Nov. 20, 1914, is the following:

"The miners got four days' work last week and bid fair for a good week this week.——We understand that Riverside has her strip pit opened up, and is putting out coal. It is said that in the near future a steam shovel will be at work there stripping coal to ship."

The article further reported that there was only nine feet of over-burden. Then it goes on to say, "Riverside had her dance, talked of so much, last week. It was attended by people from far and near—from Slater Creek, New Acme, Ranchester, Kooi, Sheridan and Big Horn. It is reported that all had a good time with song and dance until 4 o'clock in the morning."

(Tom McCoy, who was working at the Kooi mine during this period, just informed me that he and his wife, Edna, attended probably this very dance referred to above, stating that they wheeled their infant daughter, Eleanor, in a baby buggy, all the way from Kooi to Riverside, a distance of about a mile. It so happens that this "infant daughter, Eleanor" is now a grandmother; and it also just so happens that she is the grandmother of three of our grandchildren, as her son Gerald Kilpatrick, is married to our daughter, Janet! Tom McCoy further related that his father, Dan McCoy, owned and operated a saloon at Riverside.)

Other references to the Riverside Mine in the Sheridan papers appear as follows:

8/19/24—"Mine Owner Crushed to Death at Riverside." "John Adams, half-owner of the Riverside Mine, a private coal mine 15 miles north of Sheridan instantly killed"—by slate roof falling.

1/8/30—"Young Miners Badly Burned by Explosion—Injured Man Taken to Hospital in City—Three youths were seriously burned in an explosion at the Riverside Mine, located northwest of Monarch late Tuesday. Glen Clark, 19; Marvin Clark, 16; and Berdie Mooney, 25. Blast from premature explosion occurred in a quantity of blasting powder."

2/4/30—"Youth Dies of Injuries in Riverside Mine Blast—Marvin H. Clark, 16 Year Old Miner, Is Victim of Explosion of Jan. 7th—Two Others in Hospital."

An earlier reference was made to a strip-mining operation being employed at the Riverside mine. Recently, I was informed by Leslie C. Sharp who now lives in Sheridan, that in the early 1930's, he operated that mine and actually recovered coal by strip mining it. He states that he used a slip pulled by horses to remove the over-burden.

* * * * * * * * *

Old Acme

What scant information there is about this operation, I had previously included in the chapter on "Acme."

* * * * * * * * *

The Hart Mine

About the time that old Dietz No. 7 closed down in 1921, one of the Italian workers by the name of John Panagutti opened up a "wagon mine" about a half mile north of old Dietz No. 7. Inasmuch as his name was difficult to pronounce, he was often called "John Hart" and so named his mine the "Hart Mine." This operation was rather short-lived, being in existence only about three or four years before Mr. Panagutti and his family moved back east.

* * * * * * * * *

The Storm King Coal Co.

This mine, located on the Big Goose Highway about six miles west of Sheridan was owned and operated by William Patvaros. Mrs. Anna Patvaros who resides in Sheridan and the widow of "Bill," informs me that Bill opened up the mine in about 1919.

This mine, as were all the so-called wagon mines, was a slope mine and sold graded coal to the trade. It was especially active during the 1930's thru 1940's and into the early 1950's.

I recall that when, in January of 1950, I had purchased a home in Sheridan which had a coal-fired boiler heating plant. The temperature was about 30 degrees below zero and I discovered only about 50 pounds of coal in the bin. In desperation, I called for a coal delivery only to find that the coal miners were on strike and all outlets unwilling to make delivery except to their old customers. Very frantically, I called the

Storm King Mine and was informed that coal was available but I would have to come after it, so I hooked up my two-wheel trailer and hauled in two loads of coal. Frightened by that experience, I quickly made arrangements to convert to a gas-fired unit.

News releases in the Sheridan papers concerning the Storm King mine appear as follows:

3/30/32—"Mine Accident Fatal to William T. Jenkins, Employee at Storm King"—"Miner Crushed between horse drawn car and side of shaft "rib."—No Other Workers Saw Accident." Mine owned by William Patvaros who stated first fatal accident in ten years.

12/8/37—"County Coal Contract Awarded to Storm King—The Sheridan County Board of Commissioners today awarded the contract for supplying coal for the use of the courthouse during the next year to the Storm King Coal Company. The Storm King bid was $1.95 per ton. The contract specified that the coal must be union mined and hauled, commissioners said."

1/31/40—"Storm King Coal Co., announces the Purchase of the Retail Coal Business of the Sheridan Artificial Ice Co.—office located at 332 Broadway—Formerly Operated by Frank Robinson, Effective Feb. 1, 1940." Storm King also announces wax-treated stoker coal for cleaner handling.

Storm King Coal Company (as it looks today).

* * * * * * * * *

The Custer Coal Company

The Custer Coal Mine, opened up by James Armstrong about 1932 or 1933, was located just off the old, old county road between old Dietz and Carneyville in the hills just west of Kuzaraville.

An article about this mine appears in the Sept. 12, 1934 issue of the Sheridan newspapers stating: "Armstrong Mine Will Be Improved." "Extensive improvements are to be made in the coal mine of James Armstrong, located six miles north of Sheridan, it was learned today. The mine is at present operating on a small scale and it is announced that a stock company is being formed to enable operations to be carried on a larger scale.

One of the stockholders, S. G. Cook, of Grand Island, Neb. has gone through the mine and states that he is well pleased with conditions there. He is said to be highly pleased with Sheridan and the surrounding country, which he says is 'a wonderful section of the U.S.A.'

Temporary headquarters of the company are to be at Grand Island under the charge of Cook it was said."

It appears that this formal organization was never realized; however, a stock company was formally organized in January of 1940 under the name of the "Custer Coal Company, Inc." The officers of the Corporation were: James A. Armstrong, President; Nell Erwin, Secretary; and Edward Kumor, Vice-president. Capitalization, $50,000.00.

This mine continued to operate until 1952 when the land was sold to Howard Jorgenson.

* * * * * * * * *

The Schreibeis Mine

This mine, sometimes called the Tongue River Mine, was located about nine miles north of Sheridan about a half-mile west of the Tongue River road.

It was first opened up by Jacob Schreibeis, father of George Schreibeis who currently lives in the area, in 1919, and continuously supplied the local trade until the late 1930's. George informs me that many times he hauled coal from the mine to customers in Sheridan using a four-horse team.

From time to time, the mine was leased to others to operate. Apparently to Les Sharp at one time, and to Sam R. Thomas, father of Bernard Thomas, our prominent local artist and of Lloyd Thomas, a current real estate broker of Sheridan.

Although the coal was run over a screen while loading, it was also forked to eliminate some of the finer slack, so George informs me.

* * * * * * * * *

Star Coal Company

This "wagon mine" was located only about 2½ miles north of Sheridan just east of the Burlington railroad tracks off the old county road to Dietz.

Originally, this mine was named "Minersville" as evidenced by the following article in the Sheridan papers dated April 26, 1926: "A Contract for Minersville Mine Output Is Made by Plumbing-Heating Company."

"A contract for the entire output of the Minersville Coal Mine, located two miles north of Sheridan and operated by Eugene Groat and Steve Kutcher, has been made by the Sheridan Plumbing & Heating Company, it was announced, Saturday.

J. W. Belt and L. H. Ehrke, proprietors of the Sheridan Plumbing & Heating Company will retail the coal in Sheridan and vicinity. Mr. Groat and Mr. Kutcher will remain in charge of operations at the mine.

Mr. Groat is a veteran coal mine operator, having been in the business for forty-five years. He is also a pioneer in the Sheridan field, having opened the old Dietz Mine in 1900, the Black Diamond Mine in 1904, the Storm King Mine in 1907 and the Big Goose Mine in 1920.

He opened the Minersville Mine in March of 1925, slightly more than one year ago. Mr. Kutcher, who became associated with him in the development of the mine, also has long experience in coal mining.

'Minersville coal is entirely free from slack, fire clay, black jack and other foreign matters commonly found in Wyoming coal,' Mr. Groat said. Saturday, 'it runs unusually high in heat units and is practically free from sulphur, rendering it absolutely safe when stored in large quantities, even under the most adverse conditions.

To my certain knowledge Minersville coal is equal, if not actually better, than any coal mined in northern Wyoming for heating and other domestic purposes.' "

It was not long after, perhaps a year later, when this mine was bought by George Kuzara, my father who still had the grocery store at "Kuzaraville," where a couple families, plus several bachelors still lived on the place.

Being an old coal miner himself, and feeling that the plan of the Minersville Mine had not been very scientifically laid out, he immediately closed it down and began a new hole into the side of the hill a few hundred yards north of the old mine. He was assisted by my oldest brother, Walter, who happened to be at home at the time.

I shall never forget and only wish I had a picture of the horse going around and around a turn-table winding a cable which would pull a car of dirt at a time filled by one or two men inside the slope. Two hundred feet from the face and several weeks later, the vein of coal was finally reached. Of course, the entry had to be timbered as they went along. His meager output was at first almost given away on a first come, first served basis, and dumped into two-wheel trailers or trucks just as it came out of the mine, slack, pea, lumps, etc. without any screening.

The demand for the coal was there, so it was not long before, Dad acquired an old coal-fired boiler and a steam engine to pull the cars of coal. This was enhanced with a tipple and screens as his business flourished.

Before the year was over, Walter had left to work in the East and Andrew, my third to the oldest brother who had previously worked in several of the local and other mines, came to assist Dad.

By the end of 1927, several truckers were hauling coal from the Star Mine serving customers in Sheridan. Two particular truckers, who restricted their source of coal to the Star Mine, advertised in a Sheridan newspaper on Nov. 29,

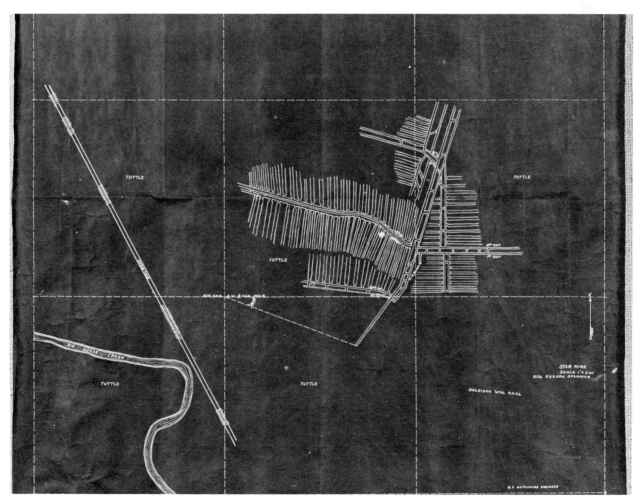

Star Coal Company underground Plat—engineer's survey.

1927 as follows: "Ellsworth & Grimshaw, @ $3.50 per ton."

By now, other improvements had been made and more machinery installed including a larger steam boiler, a motor-generator which generated electrical current, etc. At the same time, his business increased selling as many as 120 coal cars of coal daily in the winter months.

Most of the miners employed at the Star Mine lived in houses rented to them, two or three of which were located at the mine site and the rest at Kuzaraville. Over these families and men, Dad always maintained a certain control to see that they bought their groceries from his store. He even bought most of their working clothes, buying at discount in Sheridan and taking his commission. In addition, he also kept them supplied in their liquid requirements so that by payday, most of their earnings had already been obligated.

One could go on and on, describing in detail all of the facets of operating a mine even of this size, the hardships, the starting of his trucks in

below zero weather, the hauling of his men back and forth to the mine, etc.—enough perhaps to fill a book in itself.

I cannot, however, overlook relating this experience with the labor union in about 1933 when the miners were given so much prestige under the National Recovery Act with their minimum wage scales.

It must be understood that in an operation such as a wagon mine, one never knew when to expect customers even though it could be assumed that colder weather would bring in more trade. It was therefore quite necessary for my father to work a full crew to be in position to take care of whatever demands might be required. Opposed to this, the larger mines would work only those days of the week as required to fill orders already received, working sometimes as little as one day a week.

Under the National Recovery Act, the United States government more or less took control of the coal industry with the formation of the Bituminous Coal Commission. Among

Star Coal Company—(Note wagon about to be loaded—horse team unhitched to avoid being frightened as coal is dropped down chute).

Scene at Star Coal Mine, L to R: George Kuzara, owner; Helen Sawa of Chicago, visitor (obscured); George Kuzara, son of Andrew Kuzara; John Kuzara, also son of Andrew; Michael Kuzara, brother of Author; Charlotte (Kuzara) Adamy, sister.

other things, it recommended a minimum wage scale to be paid to coal miners of $5.42 per day. The labor unions, as I recall, seemed to adopt this base scale of pay, enforcing it at whatever facility they were organized. Under the NRA, the Unions, with the power given them under this Act carried on a concentrated program of union organization at all the mines.

Organizers contacted the miners of the Star Coal Mine attempting to form a union local of the miners, but upon vote of the men, they voted not to organize. It was their feeling that they were fortunate to even have a job, especially considering the very high degree of unemployment during that depression. Perhaps they also considered the fact that there were times when they were paid for periods of time they were actually not producing.

The union organizers threatened to boycott the mine. It was then that my father pleaded with them outlining his problem, but to no avail. He then suggested that the only way he could survive paying such high wages was to bring in commercial electricity thereby lay off all those men required to operate the boilers and generators; in other words, reduce his force. Again, as I happened to be within hearing distance at the time, I heard the organizer say, "We don't care how many men you employ or lay off. All we are interested in is that each man receive a decent wage." Again, the mines voted not to organize, and a boycott followed.

Union picketers were placed at all roads leading to the mine, threatening all union

truckers, and discouraging all others from going to the mine.

There was no alternative. Dad called his men together and after explaining his problem, requested that they form a local—the union succeeded.

As predicted, the mine was a losing proposition, but my father survived only because of his other sources of income as mentioned earlier, the rentals and sales from his store, etc. Later, however, there came an increase in the price of coal which, of course, brought relief.

The first serious accident at the Star Mine occurred in 1936 which was described in the Sheridan newspaper of Dec. 11th as follows, "George Legerski of Dietz suffered a badly fractured left leg in an accident yesterday at the Kuzara Mine. Legerski is said to be in satisfactory condition today at the Sheridan County Memorial Hospital. Details of the accident could not be learned."

The land on which the Star Mine was located belonged to two sisters who had inherited it and who lived somewhere in Texas. Dad had the use

Scene at Star Coal Mine after tour of mine. L to R: Charlotte (Kuzara) Adamy, visitor Helen Sawa, Michael Kuzara.

of the surface and paid a royalty of 10¢ per ton on all coal mined.

Over the several years, he grazed some cattle on the surface (raising cattle was his first love, but he could never afford to really go into the cattle business). Gradually over several years, he had acquired a herd of about seventy-five head. I believe it was in the summer of about 1935 when old A. K. Craig, the man who many, many years before had the Old Acme Mine and later developed the "New" Acme Mine, but who was now president of a bank in Sheridan and a very good friend of my father's, happened to be talking with my father at the mine when their conversation drifted to a point where my Dad stated he felt he should think about retiring and devoting his remainder years to the less-demanding cattle avocation. Mr. Craig then mentioned how he missed the coal mining business in which he had been engaged for so many years. One thing led to another, and before the conversation was concluded, an agreement was made—Mr. Craig would buy. He promptly pulled out his check book and wrote out a check to my Dad in the amount of $9,000.00 as a down-payment.

Within a few days, Mr. Craig had a crew of his own men at the mine who immediately began building forms for a foundation for a new tipple, and a few days later had actually poured the concrete when again Mr. Craig and Dad engaged in another conversation. Before long, Mr. Craig said, "You know, George, I should never got myself into this so late in my life." Whereupon, Dad replied, "I'm going to kind of miss this old mine and my men." Mr. Craig then mentioned how he supposed it was now too late to do anything about it but to proceed. Dad was quick to reply, "No, if you want to change you mind, you may," as he reached in his pocket and pulled out the check which Mr. Craig had given him over a week ago and held it out to him. Mr. Craig, upon seeing the check, without hesitation, reached over and took it—the deal was off! No papers of any kind had been signed and Dad had never deposited the check!

Shortly after that incident, Dad and my brother Andrew who had worked with him for several years and who seemed to have a very good understanding of the operation of the mine agreed that Andrew would buy the mine.

It was in that summer that I had been married, but unable to announce it as I did not have any work; however, after my brother took

Scene at Star Coal Mine—George Kuzara and daughter, Charlotte.

STAR COAL COMPANY

N⁰ 5841

Date _____

Customer's
Name _____

Address _____

_____ Lbs. Gross

_____ Lbs. Tare   Grade of Coal _____

_____ Lbs. Net $ _____ Per Ton _____

Sales Tax _____

Total _____

_____   _____
(Shipper's Name)   (Driver's Name)

_____   _____
(Weigher's Name)   (Customer's Signature)

THE MILLS COMPANY, SHERIDAN 56711

Customer's weight ticket, Star Coal Company.

over the mine, he hired me and it was very shortly after that when in October, Pauline and I announced our marriage. In December though, I received word of my appointment with the National Youth Administration beginning on Jan. 1, 1936.

Chunk of coal taken from the Star Mine, March 4, 1929. This large piece of coal was on display in front of the Log Cabin Tourist Court in Sheridan, and a contest was held offering this piece of coal to the person guessing its weight most closely. Have lost the record of the person winning; however, the weight of this piece of coal was 2,550 pounds!

Andrew continued to operate the mine but only a short while when he began to feel the absence of my father's help, and it was not too long before he returned the mine to him. In the meanwhile, Andrew then left the mine for a while during which time he tried unsuccessfully to operate a grocery store and work in a department store in Sheridan.

Again, he returned to work in the mine thinking he would like once more to buy it, and

again, Dad and he made the necessary arrangements. By this time, his two boys had grown some and could help with some chores around the outside, with his sister-in-law, Zona Egbert as office clerk and my brother Mike who had worked there off and on for some time, he took over, operating the mine until World War II began to show its effect. Men were going into the service and what men were left were hard to come by. This, due to the fact that the consuming public was more and more turning to the use of gas as their source of heat, he finally and permanently closed the mine in 1942, but not until after it had supplied the fuel needs of the area for some fifteen years and not until it had furnished employment especially during the winter months to as many as 35 persons of the community for some fifteen years.

An incident, one of many but one which might contain some human interest is told by my sister, Charlotte.

"Strategically located air shafts were required for clean air circulation. The Star mine's first air shaft was excavated in a vertical position, the spot chosen by a surveyor, to minimize the distance upward in regard to hills to be avoided. The shaft was lined with a ladder for exit or entry, and a locked structure surrounded the opening at the top.

As the mine grew and expanded, a new air shaft was required. The second shaft was planned and surveyed to be excavated in a slanting position, the slope quite steep. The fascination for me was the miracle of engineering knowledge—the digging to be done from both the inside and the outside, to coincide and meet. When it was completed according to plan, again a structure was built to surround the outside opening with a locked door. It was about ten feet square and about twenty feet high.

Papa spoke of the problems involved in digging out the shaft and the probability of an accurate joining until the eventual completion. This aroused my ten year old curiosity to see this new shaft. I begged until he consented to show it to me. He allowed me to go into the mine with him while he made a tour of inspection. He encountered so many problems, and became so preoccupied and harrassed that when we reached the point where the new air shaft started upward, he told me to go ahead and climb to the top. He would look in on a couple of rooms, then walk out the main entrance, cross over the hills on the outside and unlock the entrance door and meet me coming out.

I climbed happily away, marveling at the magnitude of the undertaking I witnessed. At the top, I removed my carbide lamp, extinguished the flame and sat to wait—and wait. I tried to relight my lamp, intending to re-enter the maize of the mine and try to find my way out. The lamps are rather tricky and it would not re-light. I shouted and cried in frustration, then terror.

Finally, I calmed down and began to examine the enclosure. I found a spot where a short length of 1 x 8 board had been nailed. I applied all my strength to kick, and claw and pry this board loose. Be removing my coat, I was able to squeeze myself through this opening. Then, sobbing and bewildered, I made my way over the hills back to the tipple.

Papa had encountered a rush of business and had forgotten all about me. When I stumbled into his line of vision, bedraggled, torn and tear-stained, he turned white, reached out his arms to comfort me and explained so apologetically. I instinctively knew that he suffered more at the sight of me than I had in my hours of confinement."

* * * * * * * * *

Cambria

I feel I should make a brief reference to the coal mine at Cambria, Wyoming inasmuch as so many of the miners at Cambria moved to the Sheridan coal fields when that operation finally closed down in 1928. Of importance also is the fact that the Cambria Mine opened up some years before coal was produced in commercial quantities in the Sheridan area.

Cambria, Wyoming was located only a few miles north of the present city of Newcastle, Wyoming. It consisted of a coal camp of some 1,500 persons whose workers were employed by the Cambria Fuel Company. Today, there is practically no visible evidence that such a camp ever existed at that location. To drive to the area today one needs a four-wheel drive vehicle and must pass thru privately owned land.

Some snapshots of the tipple and camp were given to me by Josephine (Mihalski) "Canary" Hodgson who was born in Cambria and now, a widow, lives in Sheridan, Wyoming. In addition, the Cambria operation is reflected in an article which appeared in the *Sheridan Post-Enterprise* of May 23, 1929 as follows:

"CAMBRIA MINES ARE CLOSED NOW." "Forty Years of Industry Is Now Ended, Report."

"Newcastle, March 23.—The last day of a great industry drew to a close last Thursday afternoon when the 4:30 o'clock whistle sounded the death knell to an industry that has prospered in this county since 1887.

Forty-one years ago, the coal deposits of what has been the Cambria mines, was prospected. In 1888 the development work started

Cambria, Wyoming—One of the sections of the Cambria coal camp.

Cambria, Wyoming mine (trestle leading across valley to tipple).

in earnest and in 1889 probably the first coal was produced for shipment.

Since that time approximately 12,500,000 tons of coal have been taken from the hills around Cambria and the market value of the product over the thirty-nine years has been in the neighborhood of $20,000,000.

As many as 500 men have been employed in the mines at the peak of their production and it is estimated that as many as 1,200 men, women and children have made their home in the coal town at one time. About 85 men were employed at the end.

The history of the Cambria Mine has been an unusual and at the same time a fortunate one. At no time has an accident occurred that has taken more than one life at a time and most of these accidents have been due to carelessness on the part of the employee. The mine has always been free of gas and any quantity of dust. Then ventilation has been perfect, thus insuring the best of air.

Last Thursday, when the whistle blew for the last time, it found a number of employees still on the job after spending more than a quarter century in the employment of the Cambria Fuel Company. Charles Six was probably the oldest employee in point of years' service, having been at Cambria and employed in the mines since practically the first year of their development."

* * * * * * * * *

I have carried the story of the mines in some detail through the year 1940, and although the Monarch Mine continued to operate until 1953, and the camp of Acme still contained many residents, and while many items of note must have occurred during this later period, it seems to me that here we approach an entirely different era when mining changed from the underground method to the strip-mining method—one

Big Horn Coal Company—Section of farm land before stripping for coal.

could write another book on this subject, but my main object in writing this book was to record the early history.

By the year 1940, it was becoming evident that natural gas had won out as a principal source of heat and other energy—the heyday of the underground mining industry was rapidly fading even though some demand for coal still remained.

In the early 1940's, the Big Horn Construction Company, a subsidiary of the Peter Keiwit & Sons Construction Company, established offices in Sheridan. This company had become a giant during the World War II years, building air strips and military installations all over the world. Following the war, they became active in earth-moving and road construction.

With such heavy equipment at their disposal, they conceived the idea that they could put much of their heavy equipment to use in the surface recovery of coal, and so, the Big Horn Coal Company was formed, and after some preliminary experimentation in the area, a tipple was built on the C.B. & Q. railroad near the Old

Acme location, shipping their first coal in 1943. At that time, there was little regard to reclamation nor had the public become aware of the potential destruction of the surface. The next few years revealed huge mounds of dirt with nearby ponds permiscuously scattered over the area. The course of Big Goose Creek was changed and a steel bridge under which the creek formerly passed was left sitting on now only a mound of ground high above the surrounding excavations until such time as the company with its influence was successful in changing the road and removed the bridge altogether. The recovery of coal in this manner evidently proved successful and in expanding their operation, they bought out the Sheridan-Wyoming Coal Company in 1952 and plunged into surface mining in earnest.

A new more modern and larger tipple was then built in the vicinity of the old Model location also on the C.B. & Q. Railroad, replacing the former tipple. The main source of supply of coal was then concentrated in an area between Acme and the Hotchkiss Mine Locations

Silo of Big Horn Coal Company located on former farm property shown in previous picture.

(where the bridge previously referred to was located). This area even extended over some of the old Dietz No. 8 workings, and is being worked today.

It is ironic that about sixty years ago, my father and my sister, Rose Barbula, were riding in the hills north of Sheridan and she related to me how he then predicted that some day this whole area would some day experience an industrial revolution. Some sixty years later, the Barbula-Turley Ranch located some fourteen miles north of Sheridan on the Decker, Montana road and consisting of over 2,000 acres of fee land and coal, just this December, 1976 sold their land and leased the coal for an amount that suddenly placed them in an opposite independent financial position.

Then, in the late 1960's and early 1970's, the world suddenly became acutely aware of air,

land and water pollution, and when it became known that the coal of this area contained less of these pollutants, and this coupled with an equally sudden realization that the supply of natural gas was becoming quite critical, the demand for Wyoming and Southern Montana coal became dominant. Surface mines began to spring up by the score in northern Wyoming and southern Montana, and whereas thousands of tons of coal had previously been mined, today millions of tons are taken out daily.

Simultaneously, came crys of IMPACT! CONSERVATION! RESISTANCE! RECLAMATION! ECOLOGY! Organizations were formed in resistance while others were formed to resist that resistance. The potential is frightening! What the future holds, time will tell, but what the past held has been, in some measure, recorded in this review.

1974 Big Horn Coal Company tipple (taken from across BN railroad where old Model mine located).

Big Horn Coal Company—(in stripping operation shovel caved into old Dietz No. 8 mine tunnel tipping shovel on its side, 12/16/71).

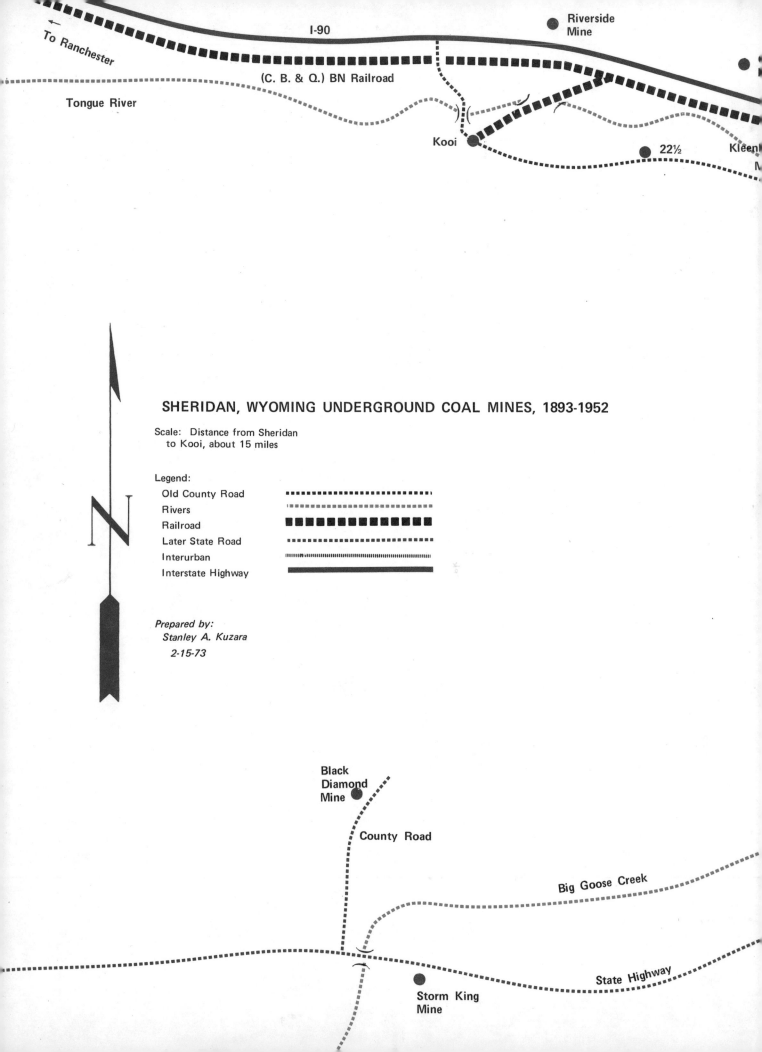

To Ranchester

I-90

Riverside
Mine

(C. B. & Q.) BN Railroad

Tongue River

Kooi

22½

Kleen
M

SHERIDAN, WYOMING UNDERGROUND COAL MINES, 1893-1952

Scale: Distance from Sheridan
to Kooi, about 15 miles

Legend:
Old County Road
Rivers
Railroad
Later State Road
Interurban
Interstate Highway

Prepared by:
Stanley A. Kuzara
2-15-73

Black
Diamond
Mine

County Road

Big Goose Creek

State Highway

Storm King
Mine